BASEBALL
from a
Different Angle

BASEBALL
from a
Different Angle

BOB BROEG
and
WILLIAM J. MILLER, JR.

Diamond Communications, Inc.
South Bend, Indiana
1988

BASEBALL FROM A DIFFERENT ANGLE
Copyright © 1988 by Diamond Communications, Inc.

Manufactured in the United States of America

DIAMOND COMMUNICATIONS, INC.
POST OFFICE BOX 88
SOUTH BEND, INDIANA 46624
(219) 287-5008

LIBRARY OF CONGRESS
Library of Congress Cataloging-in-Publication Data

Broeg, Bob, 1918–
    Baseball from a different angle / Bob Broeg and William J. Miller,
Jr.
        p. cm.
    Includes index.
    ISBN 0-912083-27-1 (pbk.) : $12.95
    1. Baseball—United States—History.   I. Miller, William J.,
1925– . II. Title.
GV863.A1B747   1988
796.357'0973—dc19   88-9556
                                                              CIP

*To the Baseball curious —
past, present, and future.*

Contents

Introduction

Once upon a time, when ballplayers left their gloves on the playing field, when the big leagues barred radio broadcasts and when darkness sent everybody home, a history of baseball was as novel as . . . well, as unusual as many events noted in this book.

Back there before President William Howard Taft squeezed his ample posterior into a ball park box seat — no, Mr. Taft really didn't begin the seventh-inning stretch tradition — a St. Louis newspaperman named Alfred H. Spink was asked about a history of the sport. Not even the aging press box pioneer, Henry Chadwick, the man who invented the box score, ever had heard of a published chronicle.

So in 1910, Spink, founder of *The Sporting News*, wrote the *National Game*, most interesting because it captured aspects of a game played professionally for 40 years and for an undetermined period previously. To show that every generation views its era and players through rose-colored glasses of nostalgia, Spink ranked the 1885–88 St. Louis Browns as better than the Philadelphia dynasty that began in '10.

As the Old Roman, the Chicago White Sox's Charley Comiskey, purred with contentment and pride, Spink noted that the Brownie ball club Comiskey managed — and for which Comiskey first strayed off the bag as first baseman — not only played better, but they also dressed better. Al remembered that Commy's fellas had neat, white uniforms. It's good that Spink didn't endure into the tattle-tale gray day of the grimy Gas House Gang!

Over the years since Spink wrote sentimentally and sartorially about the "good old days" more than three-quarters of a century ago, history books about baseball have been written abundantly and often quite capably as, for instance, those to which the authors are indebted in their research for this effort. Namely, by Lee Allen, Lowell Reidenbaugh, James Kahn, John Thorn, Peter Palmer, William Curran, and Bill James, to whom credit is accorded throughout these pages — credit whether in agreement or stubborn disagreement.

Most definitely credit must also go to two men, Dan Krueckeberg and Carl Schoen, who not only helped by contributing their own research generously, but who also clucked maternally over these pages. Schoen, a retired postal clerk, has researched and built miniatures of ball parks, many of them long gone with their last home run and first headache ball. Krueckeberg, a Ph.D., is a master of games, puzzles, trivia and historical research. Verily, a latter-day Lee Allen as a researcher with a sense of humor. And, as he demonstrated here, a cheerful, eagle-eyed helpful editor.

Why, then, if there have been so many books on baseball history, why another one? Because Bill Miller, the professor, and Bob Broeg, the sportswriter, believe that this one is *different*. Hence, the title: *Baseball from a Different Angle.*

Whether speculating how a thumbs-down from Judge Landis in the case of immortals Ty Cobb and Tris Speaker might have endangered birth of the Hall of Fame at Cooperstown, New York, and the grass-roots' grab of the game itself . . . whether questioning the harsh umpiring decision that made a career "goat" out of Fred Merkle . . . or questioning the legality of the highly questionable catcher's play in blocking a plate . . . or —

Whether sticking in their own opinionated noses, the authors like to feel they've touched all of the bases, seriously or occasionally humorously, trying to go from the ball-bat-glove-and-uniform basics through the dollars and sense of a truly captivating game.

What they've done, hopefully, is write a baseball textbook for Bill Miller's class at St. Louis University and other sports history classes elsewhere and, just as hopefully, strung together enough entertaining facts and viewpoints that Bob Broeg's first literary love, the *St. Louis Post-Dispatch,* and other reviewing publications might consider it to have trade-book quality.

You'll see, we know, and you will judge. Just one thing more. Although research material is acknowledged and any bibliography self-contained in the text, you'll find no footnotes straining the eyes or providing distraction, as noted best one time by John Barrymore, the great actor. In grumping about footnotes when studying Shakespeare, Barrymore beefed: "Going down the page to read a footnote is like going downstairs to answer the doorbell on the first night of your honeymoon."

Well said, Sweet Prince. Read on, MacDuff!

Bob Broeg   *William J. Miller, Jr.*

1
Edisons
of
The Game

Bernard Malamud said it best. Yes, Malamud, better known to many for having reunited Robert Redford and his first love — baseball — than for having written the novel that sat there waiting for the movie actor. Redford, a boyhood teammate of Hall of Famer Don Drysdale, brought his handsome phiz and physique to a colorful film adaptation of *The Natural*.

In a line that said a lot in a little, Malamud wrote, "The whole history of baseball has the quality of mythology."

So why shouldn't Redford do literally for the silver cinema what the first bleacherite — or "groundling," as they first called baseball's "cranks," i.e., fans — long since had implored: "Knock the cover off the ball."

Baseball's origins are indeed as mysterious as the dipsy-do of Christy Mathewson's fadeaway, ancient George Strickland's spitter, Bruce Sutter's split-fingered fastball, and, of course, Candy Cummings' first curveball, thrown even before alma mater Yale played Harvard in that rougher autumn phenomenon called "football."

As everyone has known for too long (yet surprisingly latter-day historians keep dredging it up as a deep, dark, skeleton-in-the-closet secret), there's considerable doubt that Abner Doubleday invented baseball. That, of course, still comes as a considerable shock to some,

1

including broadcasters, who like to suggest that, in a dramatic moment in a close game, when the bases are loaded, two out, a full count on the losing side's batter, "Abner Doubleday has done it again."

Heck, poor Abner probably didn't even do it the first time, if you put two and two together and don't get five. (At one time, you did get five strikes and seven balls as the wonder game evolved, regressed, and progressed.) After all, Doubleday was only a cadet at West Point in 1839. That was the year in which an old man named Abner Graves contended, in a letter written in 1905, he'd witnessed General Doubleday's incredible athletic gestation at Farmer Phinney's field, Cooperstown, New York.

Funny thing, though, if you want to add an O. Henry twist to the weary old plot, there *was* an Abner Doubleday with whom Graves could have played in Cooperstown in '39. Because no one knows for sure when baseball was invented—even the Baseball Hall of Fame's library director, Thomas R. Heitz, points out the "evolution vs. creationism" as a fascinating conflict—Graves and the older Abner Doubleday's kid cousin *could* have played the game. The kid cousin, 10 years younger, was only 10 in 1839.

So it's entirely possible that Mr. Graves, who left behind a scarred, blackened old ball as an attic-closet keepsake, could have played with his boyhood buddy a game divided into 11-man teams of four outfielders, five infielders, one backup catcher, and the "tosser" in the middle. Come to think of it, when your side is getting clobbered, the pitcher does look like a "tosser" and you wish you did have 11 men against the other side's nine.

Point is, whether the younger Doubleday was the one his aging friend had in mind with that 1905 letter and ball of misty origin, there's really no reason to buy *any* explanation of the game's actual origin. After all, the term "base ball" appeared in a British children's book as far back as 1744.

At Valley Forge, where George Washington and his men fought the enemy and frostbitten morale for the infant United States's survival, baseball was played in 1778. The United States Supreme Court's venerable dissenter, Oliver Wendell Holmes, insisted he played "base ball" at Harvard in 1829, the year the *second* Abner Doubleday was born.

As for General Doubleday, a blue-coated veteran of Fort Sumter and the battle of Gettysburg, historian Harold Peterson put it neatly: "Abner Doubleday didn't invent baseball. Baseball invented Abner Doubleday."

Branch Rickey, one of baseball's most quoted sages as imaginative front-office executive extraordinaire, aware that General Doubleday had fired the first shot in defense of the federal island installation off Charleston, South Carolina, said, "The only thing General Doubleday ever started was the Civil War."

Probably. For all its pride in the Baseball Hall of Fame and Museum, not even Cooperstown, New York, goes too far in establishing a fact out of likely fiction. Although the state itself pinpoints a cute baseball dollhouse—Doubleday Field—as the site of the game's "discovery" on Farmer Phinney's former field, the Hall of Fame retains its self-respect.

Abner Doubleday isn't in the Hall of Fame, but Alexander Cartwright is. Cartwright, the Johnny Appleseed of baseball, was an engineer credited with having "introduced" the game to the New York Knickerbockers in 1845. Cartwright, who would take the game westward in a search for gold, even teaching the Indians en route to California, carried the game as far away as Hawaii before he died as a merchant prince at the turn of the century.

Cartwright introduced the "baseball square," as today's diamond was called, and extended foul lines. (Why weren't they called "fair lines"?) He devised three outs to an inning, initiated three strikes and nine men on a side, and stalked off 42 paces to form the magical distance of the eternal race of man against ball, running speed against strength of arm—90 feet.

Cartwright wasn't quite so accurate with his early pitching distance, 45 feet with a squared throwing area, from which the ball was tossed underhanded to home plate, itself then a one-foot square. The "New York" game was perpetrated by Cartwright on the Elysian Fields of Hoboken, New Jersey, in 1845, but there's no reason to believe that it was first any more than the Doubleday fantasy of Cooperstown six years earlier.

No one probably ever will zero in on baseball's actual origin, because it seems likely that it's a spinoff of "Rounders," "Townball," "One Ol' Cat," and others. Most recently researchers indicate that two Midwest games called "Three Out, All Out" and "Run Around" also might have been precursors of the "New York" game. And other members of the Knickerbockers apparently contributed to the concept.

But evolution-over-creation probability gets its strongest boost from comparison with such early English games as "Club Ball," "Stool Ball," "Goal Ball," "Bittle and Battle," even cricket, and, of course, Rounders.

Eminent baseball historian Harold Seymour put it best when he observed in the mid-1950s, "Broadly speaking, no single person invented baseball. The game was the result of an evolutionary process over a long period of years. . . . To ascertain who invented baseball would be equivalent to trying to locate the discoverer of fire."

If, however, baseball had a stepfather, the distinction undoubtedly would have to go to Cartwright, if only because his rules eliminated one that undoubtedly cut into the sport's popularity—"plugging." That is, Cartwright threw out the previous practice of retiring a runner by hitting him with a ball rather than throwing to a baseman or stepping on a bag.

Most players, past and present, would heave a sigh of wincing relief that they don't have to *be* hit and probably not to have to hit the opposing player, too. For one, though, Pepper Martin, colorful St. Louis Cardinals' outfielder-infielder of the Depression 1930s, might have liked the pre-Cartwright plugging.

When Pepper moved in to play third base from the outfield, he was a strong-armed, wide-shouldered guy who would knock down hot smashes with his manly chest, but he was weak coming in to field bunts. The Wild Horse of the Osage didn't like it whenever anyone forced him to charge awkwardly for a tapped or topped ball. So if the score permitted (if St. Louis was far ahead or far behind), Pepper would throw the ball at the runner, not to first base.

Said a chuckling first baseman, James (Ripper) Collins, commenting some years later, "You'd be surprised how few times the other clubs bunted. They got Pepper's 'message.'"

Baseball could have used more like Pepper Martin, an all-out, crowd-pleasing player, in any era, but he was a physical mess for the famed Gas House Gang. He disdained sanitary inner stockings, wore no sweatshirt, and perspired profusely through dirty uniforms. A considerable contrast to the first baseball uniforms devised by Cartwright in 1849—neat white blouses, long blue trousers, and matching neckties.

From that cricket-style apparel to the form-fitting polyester of the present, baseball changed rapidly with the trains that clickety-clicked and the telegraph that clackety-clacked across the frontier. Baseball, like the United States, was growing up.

Sewing machines, in which Cooperstown's philanthropic and baseball-minded Clark family had an interest, began to change and/or standardize equipment, as will be noted later. But there were other "firsts" that quickly followed the first monkey-suited team of 1849, though, unfortunately, research does not identify the first ball club that ever climbed aboard a train, perhaps the first all-pro Cincinnati Reds of 1869, or the first newspaper baseball story.

However, the first box score appeared in 1853 in the *New York Clipper,* one for which credit went to British-born Henry Chadwick, a cricket player who fell in love with the new game and, obviously, became the granddaddy of baseball writers. Chadwick was an editorial force behind the game until his death early in the following century.

Trouble was, the pioneer press box critic never could accommodate himself to the cruder, broad-beamed players who now and then hit a silly thing called a "home run" rather than show the scientific touch by bunting the ball and place-hitting it.

The bunt is credited often to Wee Willie Keeler, the pint-sized "hit-'em-where-they-ain't" star of Baltimore's rough-and-ready champions of the Naughty Nineties. Fact is, Keeler, John McGraw, and others of Ned Hanlon's Orioles were clever as well as salty performers, refining the hit-and-run, the stolen base, and the "Baltimore Chop," pounding pitches into the dirt for high-bounding infield hits. But, by then, the bunt was old hat. Used before Keeler by Slidin' Billy Hamilton, the long-time, base-stealing champion, the bunt actually was invented in 1866 by one Dickey Pearce.

By then "firsts" were exploding over baseball like Redford's pennant-winning home run against the light towers in *The Natural*. The ordinary bat, though no Excalibur like "Wonder Boy," was perfected by Industrial Revolution machinery, a factor in baseball's progress. The bat was restricted in dimensions by the new National Association in 1858, yet the flat vs. circular controversy continued until 1893. The length was set at 42 inches by the National League in 1876.

The first called strike was recorded in 1858. To the shame of fielders then and forever, it also was decreed in 1864 that thereafter first-bounce was not out. You had to catch a fly ball in the air. In 1859, a chap named F. R. Boerum, who merits more attention than received here, first moved up as catcher to hunker down directly behind the batter, following an experimental ruling that year. He established a practice that became a rule with catcher's standard status in 1901.

By the time, barehanded and without mask, Boerum bravely set up shop behind the hitter, spectators had been requested to pay for the viewing privilege. Fifty cents was charged in 1858 for a New York-Brooklyn game at the Fashion Race Course.

The Boerums of the future were spared noses knocked galley west by foul tips in 1875 when Frederick Winthrop Thayer perfected the first catcher's mask from fencing equipment. Fred Tyng of Harvard University used it first. Years later, 1907, Roger Bresnahan is credited with having brought shinguards to the New York Giants. More recently, Los Angeles' Steve Yeager invented the Turkey Wattle to protect the throat, the catcher's and the plate umpire's.

Back there after the Civil War amalgamated the game, if not the country immediately, "firsts" were frequent. Eddie Guthbert became the first to steal a base by sliding in a game between the Brooklyn Atlantics and the Philadelphia Keystones.

Next year, 1866, shortly after Abraham Lincoln's tragic death brought

Andrew Johnson to the White House, Johnson became the first president to attend a game as he witnessed the Washington Nationals and the Brooklyn Excelsiors. Delayed by a cabinet meeting, the chief executive didn't arrive until the seventh inning. He watched from a carriage in deep right field.

Theoretically, at least, no one was paid then, but in 1869 the Cincinnati Redlegs formed the first professional team. By then, Yale University's little Arthur (Candy) Cummings had been credited with throwing the first curveball for the Excelsiors in 1867.

Emerging as an early-day hero like Chicago's Adrian (Cap) Anson, who played so long that he became "Pop," George Wright shortstopped the Red Stockings, commanding a $1400 salary, compared with $500 to $1000 for the rest of a team that breezed through the season unbeaten. But, proving that only times change, not situations, folks then complained that the guys were getting paid too much for playing a boys' game.

Wright is credited with having made the first double play when he trapped a ball against the Brooklyn Atlantics in 1870, but the first traditional, ground ball double play, with a second baseman pivoting gracefully or a shortstop covering second, has become the Lost Atlantis of baseball research. Who? When? Where?

The professional success of Cincy's Redlegs and the chance to make an honest buck playing ball spurred improvements. When the National Association of Professional Ball Players was formed in 1871, as a players' organization, the ball was standardized at approximately nine inches in circumference and five ounces, a size undisturbed over the years. Maybe that's why—with a straight face despite tongue in cheek—baseball manufacturers have attempted to insist that "the ball has never changed." Haw! Read the chapter on the ball, please.

Names that would become significant in the sporting goods industry surfaced after the Civil War. For instance, the Hall of Fame honors A. J. Reach as actually having been the first paid player—$25 a week— even before the Redlegs' avowed professionalism. Reach would become better known as a sporting goods manufacturer who for years produced the American League ball and an annual baseball guide. His rival, Al Spalding, a name with which to be reckoned as A. G. Spalding in the sporting goods game, went Reach one better.

Spalding, 47–13 with a .305 batting average as player-manager of the champion Chicago White Stockings (Cubs), acquired the right that first year of the National League (1876) to produce the baseball. For exactly 100 years, taking over Reach's company en route and leaving the former foe's name on the American League product, Spalding produced both leagues' ball. The baseball, made since 1977 by Harry

Figge's Rawlings Company of St. Louis, merits a longer, more penetrating look.

So does the game's equipment in general, but it's incredible, explaining in part so many early errors, that the game was played glove-less until 1875 when Charles Waite of New Haven, his sore catching hand stone-bruised, slipped on an ordinary street glove from which he had cut away the finger tips. Two years later, branching out of position and in business, too, Spalding wore a rudimentary mitt at first base. Another future Hall of Famer, William (Buck) Ewing, a hard-hitting, durable catcher, decided in 1885 to pad the mitt he used.

Baseball was spawned by America's era of "rugged individualism," the Industrial Revolution that featured J. P. Morgan, John D. Rockefeller, Andrew Carnegie, George Pullman and then the box office likes of Cap Anson, King Kelly, and Cy Young.

Denton True Young, the old Ohio sodbuster, won so many games that, years later, as a watery-eyed old man, when asked by a young reporter how many games he'd won, Cy said softly, "Son, I won more games than you'll ever see." He was credited with 511 and insisted he'd been shortchanged one.

Young *was* young, a kid of eight throwing stones in Tuscawaras County, when an unsung hero of the sport that became the national pastime, William Hulbert of Chicago, organized the National League in 1876. A St. Louis jurist, Judge Orrick C. Bishop, who would live to see his hometown win its first National League pennant a half-century later, joined Hulbert and wrote the constitution for the league. A reformed player, the judge also drew up the first player contracts.

Of the eight cities that answered the opening bell—and for years baseball had the equivalent of a boxing-ring bell in the dugout to signal time for the home team to trot onto the field—only one never left the National League. That was Chicago.

The White Stockings . . . er, Cubs . . . had St. Louis, Cincinnati, and Louisville in the West. Boston, Hartford, Brooklyn, and Philadelphia represented the East. Of these eight, only Chicago, St. Louis, Cincinnati, and Philadelphia survive.

The game has gone from regional to national, from trains to planes, from day to night and, as superstar Stan Musial noted in his autobiography, from cabbage leaves under the caps to air-conditioned clubhouses and even dugouts. Most dramatically, too, from natural grass to artificial turf that in some parks makes a rainout almost as obsolete as the old-fashioned getaway-game disclaimer when a waddling field announcer would intone through an oversized hand megaphone: "No inning of this game will begin after 6 P.M. so that both teams can catch a train. . . ."

Now, no doubt fans who sit up into the wee hours of the morning for extra-inning games would lynch ownership if they were flimflammed into a short-order contest. But, for a fact, blue laws prevented games on Sunday or forced second games of Sunday doubleheaders to be snipped. The American Association as a major league existed, 1882–1891, largely because the league charged only two-bits, not 50 cents, and, indicating times really *haven't* changed, the Association offered Sunday ball—and beer!

Crowds picked up, leading to "firsts" that must be acknowledged. Turnstiles first appeared in New York in 1878. By 1882 when Manhattan College played a crack semi-pro team, the New York Metropolitans, a Catholic cleric, Brother Jasper, serving as Manhattan's athletic director, wilted in a blazing sun. In the seventh inning, leaving the players' bench, he walked to the stands and beckoned to his college students to stretch and move about.

So the famed "seventh-inning stretch" was begun, unless you like better the story that George Wright told of how the Cincinnati Red Stockings' fans would rise spontaneously in the seventh to cheer on their team, probably for exercise if for no accountable reason. Maybe that's where William Howard Taft got the noble notion, though it's a well-known fact that the former Yale athlete, ample and affable, had an oversized presidential posterior that needed relief when he was cramped at ball games as a White House fan.

Myths do persist, as indicated at the outset. Jackie Robinson wasn't the first big league black in 1947. Moses Fleetwood Walker played with Toledo, then a big league franchise, in 1884. Fleetwood's brother, Welday Wilburforce Walker, also played. Night ball wasn't born when President Franklin D. Roosevelt flipped the switch in 1935 for Larry MacPhail's first floodlight game at Cincinnati. As far back as 1880, a night game was played in Nantasket Beach, Massachusetts. Fort Wayne, Indiana, laid claim to an experiment in 1883, too.

Cap Anson, a great player whose prejudice led to the bigotry that kept blacks out of the bigs, is credited by many with having inaugurated spring training for Chicago in 1885, taking the early-day Cubs to Hot Springs, Arkansas. Three years later a Washington ball club with a tall, skinny catcher named Connie Mack became the first team to train in Florida. But some sources insist that ball clubs went south before Anson did.

Baseball has come far from the ridiculous. By 1867, a hitter could call for the pitch he wanted, high or low; and in one year, 1887, they counted walks as hits, giving James (Tip) O'Neill of the old St. Louis Browns a tainted .492 major league record.

The pitching distance, though inching up, was increased a whopping 10-feet 6-inches total in 1893, though actually only five feet more than previously because the pitcher no longer could run up to throw. Back then, the pitcher delivered the ball from a square box rather than the pitching rubber. But even in the expansion, a myopic surveyor misread his own measurements and added that unnatural six inches to the long-time 60 feet.

A crazy game, all right. For instance, even the authorship of baseball's best known poem, "Casey at the Bat," long regarded as Ernest L. Thayer's personal property and contribution, is in dispute. "A Ballad of the Republic," as flailing Casey's failure at Mudville was subtitled, was claimed by another man, George d'Vys.

Umpires, too, figure in the obscurities. Truly, the old American Association deserved a bow for having hired the first full-time men in blue or, if you will, blue jackets and gray pants, the current compromise between the American and National leagues. The one-umpire system established as a profession in 1882 led eventually, of course, to adoption later of two-, three-, and, most recently, four-men crews. But, again, there's a point of dissension.

When 5–4, 148-pound Bill (Dummy) Hoy played the outfield for an assortment of major league clubs from 1888 to 1902, accommodations had to be made to communicate ball-and-strike counts to the deaf mute. But the regular right-hand strike signal apparently came later, a result of a gesture used first by Charles (Cy) Rigler at Evansville, Indiana, in 1904, a year before he went to the National League. (Rigler is a forgotten pioneer of modern umpiring.)

Yeah, things aren't always what they seem. Baseball's best known song, "Take Me Out to the Ball Game," credited generally since 1908 to Jack Norworth, a man who spent a stage lifetime taking a bow for the effort, was really a result of collaboration with Albert von Tilzer. Oddly, von Tilzer, who later wrote a lilting standard, "Shine on Harvest Moon," didn't see a ball game until 20 years after he had teamed with Norworth. The Dutchman merely had been inspired by watching and listening to enthusiastic fans taking a subway or streetcar trolley to the ball park. H'mm, you'd think Cracker Jack would put up a statue to both men for the everlasting lyric commercial.

Different angles exist, all right. At a time Reggie Jackson was the dimpled darling of New York Yankee fans, a candy bar came out bearing his name, "Reggie." Properly, Jackson was delighted, presumably the first player ever to have candy named for him. But, wait, some said, what about Baby Ruth?

That's what the Babe wondered early in the 1920s when he was offered part profits of a new candy to be called the "Babe Ruth Home Run" bar. (Candy bar, that is; the Babe already was quite familiar with other bars.) To Ruth's surprise—and annoyance—the Curtiss Candy Company sued over the similarity to its prominent Baby Ruth. Hell, wondered the Babe, they had a nerve when they'd been trodding the legal foul line for years, using a name so similar to his.

True and false, Curtiss maintained, noting that they not only had been there first with the product, but that Baby Ruth had been named after the first presidential child born in the White House, Grover Cleveland's daughter. The Babe lost the case. He never did like Baby Ruth thereafter. Or Grover Cleveland, either. Or Grover Cleveland Alexander.

The "firsts" in baseball were frequent. The raincheck was the brain-child of New Orleans' Abner Powell in 1889. Powell is credited with having invented Ladies' Day, too, but that one is in dispute. When Cincinnati had a handsome, Irish-born, ambidextrous pitcher named Tony (The Count) Mullane, elegantly subtitled "The Apollo of the Box," the Reds' management cleverly admitted the fair sex free whenever The Count pitched in 1889. Pretty good bucko, that Mullane. Won 285 games, lost 213.

Others insist that Chris von der Ahe, the German saloonkeeper who won four straight pennants under manager Charley Comiskey with the old St. Louis Browns in the 1880s, invited the ladies as box office guests first.

So, you see, there are many disputes over "firsts" in the grand old game. Others will be included, invariably, in rules' changes, traditions, and at the end of this tale, too. But we're just waiting now for someone to shoot down the tail . . . er, tale, of the hot dog.

Back in 1899 as the first organized sports' concessionaire, Harry Mozely Stevens, plied impressive wares at New York's old Polo Grounds—scorecards, cigars, beers, peanuts, soft drinks, and a new item offered first on a cold, rainy day. It was a steamy-hot, skin-clad, slender sausage. (Stevens boiled 'em, didn't grill 'em.) And a ball park vendor called out, "Get 'em hot, your red-hot dachshund sausages."

Watching was a popular New York sports cartoonist, Thomas A. Dorgan. "TAD," as he signed himself, was like most newspaper artists. He didn't spell well. "Dachshund?" Hell, the Irishman came up with "hot dog" as a more manageable term. And the hot dog, like Cooperstown, was here to stay.

If Cooperstown really isn't the birthplace of baseball, if only because neither Abner Doubleday the first nor the second likely invented the game whose origin is as much a myth as Bernard Malamud suggested, the scenic village in upstate New York is the kind of community in which the game should have been created or begun.

The constantly growing Main Street headquarters of the Baseball Hall of Fame and Museum is the kind of place where, if Robert Redford hadn't broken "Wonder Boy" in the game-winning homer of *The Natural,* they would have wanted to put the movie box office star's bat next to schoolboy teammate Don Drysdale's Hall of Fame glove.

2
Spheres of Influence

Even though baseball real estate, meaning the size and shape and dimensions of ball parks, has affected scoring and particularly power in baseball, nothing has had such an impact as the content and quality of the ball itself.

To repeat, the ball park size, shapes, and forms, worth examining further, have had their effect on batting averages, home run production, and overall scoring. And the bat itself, sophisticated, slenderized for a more forceful swing, has played a part, largely in lower averages, more strikeouts, and, where ball park dimensions permit, more homers hit by more players.

From the peewees through the preps and even college ball, the aluminum bat has affected the game, too. Setting aside the difference in sound between the dull ping of the ball off the aluminum and the musical crack of wood against leather, professional scouts suggest that aluminum extends the flight of the ball some 30 feet.

That's an unofficial estimate, the 10-yard distance, but just think of how much that can mean in the outcome of a fly ball, and particularly in pro baseball's estimate of a college prospect. If that ping-pounded pitch hits a fence or clears it when swung with aluminum, just think how disillusioning it is professionally when the batter's best with wood is merely a long, high lazy fly. Alarmed, the big leagues subsidized the purchase of wood bats in 1985 for a college summer league.

So, just as the difference between the amateur aluminum and professional bats creates an irreconcilable difference at times, the resilience, or lack of it, of the ball can make such a collective and individual difference.

Baseball has come a long way, indeed, from the time in 1871 when a New York ball manufacturing firm proudly proclaimed, "Our professional dead balls are made of all yarn without rubber and are the deadest balls made."

At the other extreme, the Goldsmith "97," a minor league standard for years, particularly in the South, quivered with long-eared joy. There couldn't have been a ball livelier through the Depression era of the Dirty Thirties than the good ol' jumping jack rabbit—"97."

The major leagues might have had to subtract from the potential of a graduate of a league that used the "97," but the majors have had their own problems, especially in 1929–30.

If you're like Bill Veeck, the late promotional baseball whiz who became a hair shirt to club-owning colleagues as an iconoclast, those were the best of times. Veeck, a teenager then, lived usually in the fire house across Waveland Avenue, the street behind the left-field fence at Chicago's Wrigley Field. (His father general-managed the Cubs then.) The Cubs symbolized the power that was in both leagues then, particularly when Hack Wilson hit a National League record 56 home runs and drove in an astonishing major league high of 190 runs in 1930.

That year, playing in dollhouse Baker Bowl, the midget park of the majors, the Philadelphia Phillies hit .315 and finished dead last, handicapped by poor defense and a pitching staff that was shellshocked from having had to face that close-up corrugated Philly fence in right field 77 times. The National League had 55 hitters at .300 or higher. The entire league averaged .303 and the pennant-winning St. Louis Cardinals averaged 6.5 runs a game.

Fun, all right, as Veeck suggested, but not as recalled one time by puckish former infielder Fresco Thompson, later general manager of the Los Angeles Dodgers: "When you're a .290 hitter, suddenly hit .320 and they want you to take a pay cut, it's not funny."

Thompson was really an amusing man who didn't mind it at all when a news item said, "Lafayette Fresco Thompson and all his names were released today." He could recall that when the Phillies were at their worst, a fan scribbled a postscript onto Philadelphia's outfield sign—"The Phillies Use Lifebuoy." The scrawled addendum read: "And They Still Stink."

But it wasn't funny to Fresco or the big league bosses when the stock market collapse plunged the nation into the depths of the Depression. Chuck Klein batted .386 and Babe Herman .393 and couldn't win the batting championship. Neither could defending champion Lefty (.398) O'Doul. O'Doul, the man in the green suit, batted .383 in 1930 and finished fourth to Bill Terry's .401.

So the clubowners demanded elimination not only of the sacrifice fly, a pimple on the inflation of batting production, but also a change in the ball. As noted by St. Louis researcher Dan Krueckeberg, a master of baseball trivia, batting averages skidded. Chick Hafey nosed out Terry and Jim Bottomley with .349 in 1931 and, more significantly, home runs in the majors were cut nearly in half, 1068 from 1565.

If you follow the history of the bouncing ball—and the bat, too— from research available, you'll find plenty to counter contentions by former manufacturers of the baseball, the Spalding Company, that the horsehide was not changed the last half-century of its production. The size, they must have meant.

By 1800, boys in the East, playing whatever 'n heck game it was, used discarded, flat-sided cricket bats and old worn-down, smaller cricket balls. By the time Alexander Cartwright's Knickerbockers went to bat in 1845–46, the ball was bigger and heavier than now, 10 to 10½ inches in circumference, 6 to 6½ ounces. The ball had an India rubber center and was wrapped in yarn, so it was a lively critter. Hence, it wasn't hard to score the 21 "aces" that decided the game.

By 1863, bats had to be round, no more than 2½ inches in diameter, appeasing pitchers working from the 40-foot box. Four years later the rule was refined, but not until 1876 was a 42-inch length limit set for the bat. Four years previously, the size of the ball was standardized virtually to today's size—9 to 9¼ inches in circumference, 5 to 5¼ ounces.

When the National League opened in '76, with Al Spalding pitching and setting up shop to manufacture baseballs, a rule required all official balls to be obtained from the National League secretary, and that the balls be "composed of woolen yarn and shall not contain more than one ounce of vulcanized rubber in mould form and shall be covered with leather. . . . "

More uniformity was achieved because good-hitting teams had been introducing livelier balls than poorer-batting ball clubs. But hanky-panky with the product, freezing a ball to deaden it, has persisted through the years; the cold moisture apparently takes the sting out of a ball before the plate umpire gets a supply for rubbing off the shiny gloss. Similarly, a heated ball gets more bounce to the ounce.

They haven't been able to do much to make a batter do what many of us have found impossible, i.e., hitting a round ball with a round bat. But there has been professional help ever since John Hillerich of Louisville shaped the first custom-made bat for hometown slugger Pete Browning in 1884. So "Louisville Slugger," a trademark of tradition and prestige, became 100 years old in 1984.

By then, other companies had been formed, going from hickory to ash in all shapes of legal form. Hillerich and Bradsby was first, of course, but Mr. Hillerich might have decided to make gloves, too, because Browning could have used one. Even though he hit .354 for 13 major league seasons, including one over .400, "The Gladiator" must have been a shoemaker defensively. He never has made the Hall of Fame.

Only a few years after Browning put down the first Louisville Slugger, A. G. Spalding branched out (1900) and bought out A. J. Reach, but for years on end the name of Reach was imprinted on the American League ball. For years, also, until the mid-1930s, the two major league baseballs were stitched differently. Before the current single red threading was used, the ball carrying the Spalding stamp and the signature of the National League president of the moment was stitched alternately red and black. The Reach-stamped American League ball, carrying through 1927 the signature of founder Ban Johnson, was stitched red and blue.

Before and after Johnson, a former Cincinnati newspaperman, stubbornly ramrodded the AL into existence in 1901, the ball usually was as dull and as drab as its color. Contents and composition weren't so hot, either, and the penny-pinching policy against using many in a game was a factor. So, by all means, was the beating and the battering the poor ball got from the defense, mainly the pitcher. Poulticed with tobacco-caked dust, it was dropped accidentally on purpose by infielders who then sprayed their cud onto it. The ball might get a talcum-powder shine from a pitcher on one side, or a stitch ripped or cover nicked by a sharp belt buckle or other rough object.

Not even the cork center, introduced secretly in the late weeks of the 1910 season, helped completely because of relaxed rules and owners' corner cutting. They traded free seats for any return of a ball batted foul into the stands or, occasionally, out of the park.

By 1863, a British cricket player had introduced a cork center into the cricket ball, but efforts to duplicate it in baseball were unsuccesful until a smaller center sphere was introduced late in '10. At first, research indicates, only a handful of men knew about the accomplishment—the league presidents, George Reach, Ben Shibe, and a man who became a baseball legend, Connie Mack.

The cork center perked up the offense immediately in 1911, increasing major league home runs from 359 to 509, a high until 1920. In the '10 World Series, as noted by Krueckeberg, Philadelphia's Athletics batted a robust .318 in beating the Chicago Cubs.

The next big bang came in '20, the year the spitball was barred and also all foreign substances. A most fortunate improvement because the base hit explosion, notably the emergence of Babe Ruth as a spectacular slugger, eased off disclosure with a week to go that eight members of the Chicago White Sox had been involved in an attempt to "throw" the 1919 World Series to the Cincinnati Reds. Ruth, who had raised brows when hitting 29 home runs at Boston as winning pitcher turned outfielder, had been sold to the New York Yankees and unloaded an awesome 54 homers.

The Babe's power was so devastating that gifted George Sisler of the St. Louis Browns, author in 1920 of a record 257 hits in 154 games, went to his grave many years later proud that he had been second in the American League to Ruth in homers—with 19!

Researching the batting upsurge of 1920, writer-historian Frederick G. Lieb suggested five years later that the ball had been "souped up," mainly by introduction of a new wool imported from New Zealand, and also by mechanization that permitted tighter winding of the yarn. Certainly 630 home runs, up from 446 in '19, was a springboard to the power production of the next several seasons—937, 1055, 979, 895 and 1167.

A different twist was provided several years ago by Edd Roush, a premier outfielder-hitter of the period, when sympathizing with another future Hall of Famer, Lou Brock, as the 3000-hit, base-stealing champion signed autographs for young and old at a game the St. Louis Cardinals played against Japan's touring Nankai Braves in Florida.

Roush, a whiz in center field, batted .315 for the Cincinnati Reds, New York Giants, and Cincinnati again, in a 19-year career through 1931. Crustily, at a time when ballplayers had only two chances to win a salary snit, little and none, Roush held out the entire 1930 season at New York. At 36, he not only lost a full year's pay, when asked to take a cut after matching his career average at New York, but he also missed a hitter's paradise year. In 1931, dealt back to the Reds, he fell back in hitting and quit.

To Brock, an interested audience, Roush told how it had been back there when the ball was jacked up in '20. In spring training he had played shallowly as before and grumbled when one ball after another seemed to elude his quick-breaking retreat. Finally Pat Moran, who a year earlier managed the Reds to their tainted Series triumph over the Black Sox, exploded.

"Damnit, Edd, don't you realize they've hyped the ball," snapped

Moran. Roush recalled that even Cleveland's Tris Speaker, the ne plus ultra of defensive centerfielders, had to give ground from his traditional close-up coverage.

Roush's point was more significant to the development of the game. He recalled that many times in the era of the doctored, anemic ball used for too many years, he had caught a line drive and literally reshaped the ball before returning it to the infield.

"Then," he said, "they not only took away trick pitches with the livelier ball, but they began to use more balls. So the ball stayed white and resilient. When Ruth began to hit more balls into the stands, fans didn't want to give them up for free seats. They wanted them as souvenirs. Soon, they began bringing balls around for the Babe to sign them. Other players, too."

Roush grinned, patted Brock on the back and said, "That's why you're signing so many now. Blame the Babe!"

The Ruth prevailed, indeed. More than once, including 1927 when he hit 60 homers for nearly 13 percent of the American League's total, the Babe outhomered every other *team*. More and more players began to copy his batting style.

Ruth wasn't the first hitter to go down to the batting knob with his grip. Frank (Wildfire) Schulte had done it when he uncorked 21 off the cork center for the Cubs in 1911, and rangy Fred (Cy) Williams did the same at Chicago and with the Philadelphia Nationals. But the Babe "unbuttoned his vest" more than any other hitter, swinging a bat that weighed an astonishing 48 ounces.

Bats had been largely unglamorous, even after Hillerich designed one for Browning 40 years earlier. Basically, hitters swung bats with little taper, thinner at the top than now and thicker at the handle, more like an ax handle. Ruth's bats, even the heavier ones, had a bigger barrel and thinner handle. Another slugger who followed shortly, Hack Wilson, personally as thick and even stockier physically than Ruth, yet much shorter, swung a thin-handled bat.

Over the years, hitters would lighten bats for greater velocity if not necessarily more consistency. One who dropped below 30 ounces and still hit with power was the Cardinals' Stan Musial, who asked for a model that would incorporate Jimmy Foxx's slender handle and Ruth's thick barrel. Stan the Man relied on a sharp eye to smudge the bat only at the big business end of the barrel.

Musial, like Ruth a converted pitcher if not nearly so great, summed up the Babe best when he said, "Just think, he struck out more than 1300 times and still averaged .342. When he made contact, he *had* to be a .400 hitter. He made big league baseball look like high school ball. He could pitch and bat fourth!"

Ruth's impact on the hitting spiral of the 1920s, replacing the place-hitting, scientific, base-stealing era of Ty Cobb, was evident in averages and home runs; but even gaffers like Cobb and Tris Speaker got their second wind offensively in the era, and, of course, Rogers Hornsby, second baseman of the Cardinals, averaged .400 over a five-season period, 1921 through 1925. His .424 in '24 became the highest of the so-called "modern" era.

Oddly, Hornsby's average dipped as a pennant-winning manager in 1926, the year Spalding introduced the cushion cork center in the ball, but home runs also fell off briefly that season from 1167 to 863, the lowest total from the lively white-ball explosion of 1920 until the balata ball fiasco of wartime 1943.

Maybe introduction of the resin bag in 1925, permitting pitchers to tighten the pitching grip, had helped. Maybe, too, pitchers had begun to adjust better from the shocking move by which the spitter and foreign substances were barred in 1920. It appears that when the spitball was barred except for 17 registered users — Burleigh Grimes threw the last *legal* spitter in '34 — pitchers who had relied on other chicanery were temporarily stripped naked.

Although the need for a "third" pitch to go with the fastball and curve probably had existed since Pop Anson was a kid, too often that "extra" pitch must have been one that became illegal. Apparently, too, not enough pitchers changed up or, at least, not well enough. When Wee Willie Sherdel, a slender little lefthander with St. Louis in the 1920s, craftily mixed up a letup time and again. They raved about Sherdel's "slow ball."

So the assumption is that few pitchers had a good change and, in addition, even though Ruth had brought a full swing into play, more batters still used a choked grip for better bat control and made better contact. Strikeouts were fewer, so solid contact with heavier bats against defensive players using gloves smaller and less sophisticated than later led to more hits.

A theory, if you please, though not necessarily a fact, of baseball that applied as Spalding advertised its new ball in 1926. The factory at Chicopee, Massachusetts, imported cork from Spain or Portugal, rubber from Malaya. They stretched "two layers of soft rubber (one red and one black) tightly over the cork and about one-fourth inch thick." Women wound the ball in three layers of wool yarn — blue-grey, white, and blue-grey again — covered with white cotton strips. The center, tightly wrapped with a quarter mile of yarn, was dipped in rubber cement and then covered with horsehide acquired in the States or from Canada. Two covers shaped like a figure "8" were attached with 108 hand stitches.

The result was a steady upsurge in home runs from 922 in 1927, the year of Babe Ruth's 60, to 1093, 1349, and 1565 when, as suggested, alarmed clubowners, faced with more punch, higher averages, and lower income, opted for a change in the ball.

Even John J. McGraw, hard-bitten martinet who had lorded over the National League for nearly 30 years as manager of the New York Giants, spoke up for a change. Said McGraw, "Every time I pick up the paper, I expect to read where a third baseman or a pitcher has been killed by a line drive."

To believe Spalding's wide-eyed insistence years later that the ball hadn't been changed or that the ball used by the two leagues was identical was an insult to intelligence as well as statistical evidence to the contrary.

One of baseball's most astute observers, Hall of Famer Al Lopez, a great defensive catcher and highly successful manager with Cleveland and the Chicago White Sox, offered an interesting commentary, explaining—in part, anyway—the rapid demise of Hack Wilson, who had homered 21, 30, 31, 39 and 56 times the previous five seasons, knocking in 159 and 190 runs in 1929 and '30.

"I know Hack didn't take care of himself," said Lopez in reference to Wilson's drinking problem, "but a reason he had such a rapid decline, I think, was that deader ball in '31. He was a right-handed hitter who hit hard to right-center at Wrigley Field and elsewhere, but that long shot of his then began to fall short."

Lopez had another commentary that coincided with the contention of Joe Cronin and Bill Terry, rival playing managers, that a different ball was used in the two leagues. Their clubs—Cronin's Washington Senators and Terry's New York Giants—played in the 1933 World Series. Both men insisted that the National League ball had higher seams than the American League ball, presumably helping breaking ball pitching.

Lopez thought the raised seams on the NL ball turned Carl Hubbell from good to great. Hubbell was a 16-season lefthander whose screwball—"reverse curve," Branch Rickey always called the seldom-seen pitch—became the famed "butterfly" and Terry's managerial meal ticket.

To throw the screwball, a left-handed pitcher twists his wrist clockwise, against the normal rotation. As Lopez said, "Because of the higher seams, Hub, long-wristed, could grip the ball longer in his release and, as a result, got a bigger, better dip in the screwball, down and away from right-handed hitters."

Hubbell was devastating in 1933 as the Giants went from a tie for sixth and seventh to a World Championship. He was 23–12 with a 1.66

earned-run average, beginning a string of five successive 20-game seasons, highlighted by 23 victories in a row over split seasons, 1936 and '37. In '33, the season of the wider seams, he went from no shutouts to 10.

After the season in which the winning Giants had 23 shutouts despite the chipshot foul line fences at the Polo Grounds—they called 'em "Chinese homers" there because of early-century cheap coolie-labor complaints against Oriental imports—National League President John Heydler told *The Sporting News*: "Maybe we deadened the ball too much. The fans are tired of seeing all those shutouts. They want more action and plenty of runners on the bases."

The ball was hyped up a bit in 1934 and presumably standardized at a time the alternate colored stitches became red on each league's ball. Home runs, which fell off 497 in 1931 and then increased 289 to 1357 in 1932, the year Jimmy Foxx hit 58 for the Philadelphia Athletics, spiraled again in 1934. The total went up from 1068 to 1344.

Years later, then motion picture director for the majors, Lew Fonseca, a standout hitter in both big leagues, was asked to identify the peak period of hitting. Fonseca, director of many films on hitting as well as of the annual World Series, picked the period from 1927 through 1936. The period would be from the introduction of the cushioned cork-centered ball to an era that ended, curiously, a year after its greatest batting exponent, Babe Ruth, hung up his number "3."

The American League best symbolized Fonseca's assessment. In 1936, 49 players in 10 or more games battled over .300, and the New York Yankees scored a record 1065 runs. The AL averaged .289, the National .285.

Even without Ruth, the long ball continued to prevail. Homers went up to 1365 in Fonseca's era-ending season, 1936, and then to 1430, 1475, 1446, and, finally, 1571, as the Frantic Forties replaced the Dirty Thirties. By then, baseball was on the threshold of its last .400 season, Ted Williams's .406 as a willowy, 23-year-old, third-season player in 1941, and Joe DiMaggio's amazing 56-game hitting streak the same season.

Oh, yes, the threshold of World War II, too.

Some held their breath that baseball would be asked to turn in its bats and turn off the lights, which had begun to flourish after Larry MacPhail succeeded not once, but twice. MacPhail, who introduced big league night ball in 1935 at Cincinnati, began his financial resurrection at Brooklyn with lights in '38. That did it. Floodlights began to flicker like fireflies, but what about the wartime blackout? Or brown-out? Or the nation's need for manpower?

In what became known as the "green light" letter, President Franklin D. Roosevelt, answering a request for guidance from the baseball commissioner, Judge Kenesaw Mountain Landis, put the Judge and baseball at ease. Although FDR believed that every able man should be called to service, as needed, he felt baseball would provide relief from wartime pressure.

Comic relief, many must have felt, when the 1943 season began with the fewest runs since the old Orioles of Baltimore outfoxed and outfought the foe in the Naughty Nineties of nifty baseball. Because the Far East and Southeast Asia were in the hands of a wartime enemy, rubber was as scarce as oil. So Spalding produced the "balata ball," named for a tree in the West Indies that produced a milky substance used in electrical insulation.

H'mm, the balata ball didn't electrify anyone, but many players and others in baseball wanted to electrocute the men who had assured them that the balata would be as delightful as the Balalaika. The ball was a capital "D" dud.

The St. Louis Cardinals, World Champions, lost their opening game at Cincinnati in 11 innings, 1–0. Next day Stan Musial tripled and didn't score. St. Louis lost again, 1–0. Third day Musial stole home for one run, scored another on a passed ball, and the Cardinals won, 2–1. Their fourth game they won, 1–0.

As Musial recalled, smiling, "Three runs in four games and we split even. When I hit that triple off Ray Starr, the ball sounded like a rock or a nickel rocket."

Eleven games were played in the majors before the Yankees' Joe Gordon hit the first home run. Representing irate clubowners, Cincinnati's Warren Giles, later National League president, raged in a letter to K. M. Landis, marking in L. E. Coleman, vice-president of Spalding, for a copy:

"I am beginning to lose faith in Spalding. . . . Why any baseball manufacturer would wait until a day before the opening game to discover that a material they were using is unsatisfactory is beyond me. The thing I am mostly interested in is getting a baseball equal in all respects, particularly resiliency, to that of the 1939 baseball. Until that time comes, I am going to be a stormy petrel, a thorn in the side of. . . ."

Un-huh, poor A. G. Spalding, which acknowledged that the fast-hardening substitute for reprocessed rubber had 25 percent less "oomph" than the normal baseball. Fortunately, the company had enough prewar baseballs to turn the balata ball into a memory rather than a blot on the record book.

To show what a difference a ball can make, only nine homers were hit in 72 American League games before the balata was buried without honors. The first day the leftover 1942 supply was used, Sunday, May 9, 1943, the AL hit six homers in just eight games.

Musial, en route to a .357 average and his first of seven batting championships, looked back fondly and with amusement. "I can remember (manager) Billy Southworth's frustration," Stan recalled. "Billy would say, 'You'll have to choke up as they did in the old days, fellas, and bunt more.'

"I did pretty well with the balata"—Musial was batting .327 with five doubles and three triples among 21 hits—"but I wouldn't have hit nearly what I did with the regular ball. At least, I learned what Wee Willie Keeler must have learned in his hit-'em-where-they-ain't days."

The 905 home runs in 1943 were the fewest since 1926 and the fewest since then—period.

By the end of World War II, with fresh materials, the home run total continued to climb. The 1947 New York Giants, though only fourth, hit a record-setting 221 home runs, which included 51 by Johnny Mize, 36 by Willard Marshall, 35 by Walker Cooper, 29 by Bobby Thomson, 17 by Bill Rigney, and 13 by Sid Gordon.

By 1950, the major league home run total had passed 2000 (2073), and the feeling was that tighter wrapping of the ball had helped the hitting output. Six years later, Cincinnati tied the Giants' home run record, hitting exactly 221, including 35 by Ted Kluszewski, 29 by Gus Bell, 38 by Frank Robinson, 36 by Wally Post, 28 by Ed Bailey, 15 by Ray Jablonski, 12 by Smokey Burgess, and 10 by George Crowe.

By 1956, with only the Braves' transfer from Boston to Milwaukee and the Browns from St. Louis to Baltimore having marred a half-century's status quo, there was no glaring reason for the home run output. But, to cap the Flourishing Fifties as the decade of the home runs, the average homer per game in '56 (2294) was 1.9. By decades, as Dan Krueckeberg indicated, the 1950s were the highest ever, 1.69 a game. By 1987, however, the American League averaged 2.3, the NL 1.9 homers.

Westward ho, the moving wagon would change ball parks as well as geography, and a rash of new ball parks, bigger and more symmetrical to accommodate football as dual-purpose stadiums, would affect home run hitting, too. But just as the schedule changed, creating more games and bringing in more minor league pitchers, the Yankees hit the jackpot.

Swinging like the Bronx Bombers of old, the Yanks walloped 240 in the 162-game schedule of 1961, including a record-breaking 61 by Roger Maris. Maris and teammate Mickey Mantle dueled all season for the individual title. Mantle hit 54. Others were Yogi Berra, 22; John Blanchard, 21; Elston Howard, 21; and Clete Boyer, 11.

This was a far cry from the early decades of the century, as Krueckeberg noted, from an average of one-third a home run a game until 1920, then from four-fifths a game until the 1930s. Thereafter, any game without a home run is an unusual one because it was 1.12, then 1.05 in the war-marred period, 1.69 in the 1950s, as mentioned, 1.64 in the '60s and 1.47 in the '70s.

By then—for the first time ever—the stolen base and the home run were living together as strange bedfellows.

Batters, meanwhile, were handicapped in ways and means to hit the ball better. For instance, Heinie Groh, a good New York-Cincinnati third baseman, used a wider-barreled, longer hitting surface, coupled with a normal batting handle. Heinie, a 16-year major leaguer (1912–27), also had a batting stance as unusual as his bat. He faced the pitcher, square on, bat held in a military present-arms position. He batted .292.

An even better hitter, Goose Goslin, a former American League batting champion, tried with the old St. Louis Browns to get by with a striped watermelon bat in 1932, but umpire Harry Geisel shot him down opening day. Ah, nobody has a sense of humor, now or then. You could Brown Betsy a bat, as Joe Medwick did or Harry Walker and others, but, nope, no stripes.

Can't tape it, either, or nail it or insert a cork hitting center, as batters tried to do. (Norm Cash hit .361 with a cork insert center for Detroit in 1961. The New York Mets' Howard Johnson was cleared of charges in 1987.) And as recalled in a celebrated case in 1983, it's a no-no to put pine tar too high on the bat, though American League president Lee MacPhail overruled umpires for having denied Kansas City's George Brett a game-winning homer. You could throw out the bat, you see, but not the result. What if, although officially not guilty, the berserk Brett had struck the ump? They'd have thrown out poor George, too.

The ball goes on its merry way, making noise almost as loud if not as melodic as animated or screeching scoreboards of the moment. Once a $1.50 treasure, the ball can't be bought for seven bucks now, but ball clubs that once used them so sparingly now figure on losing 25 or so in batting practice alone, and the home club provides the plate umpire with a half-dozen sealed boxes of baseballs before a game, aware he might need more.

For years, big league ball clubs were given many free baseballs as a subsidy from Spalding, but, later, a cash grant was made and baseballs were just sold cut-rate to the ball clubs. That's the way it has been, white ball or yellow or orange.

Larry MacPhail, the "roaring redhead," as described in a Diamond Communication book (1987), experimented with a yellow baseball in 1938, conscious that a color contrasting more with white shirts that were more fashionable at the ball park then might contribute to the game's offense. But his starting pitcher, fat Freddie Fitzsimmons, beefed that the dye came off the ball, which also seemed too slick.

They credit Oakland A's president Charley Finley, the man who did the most to change the baseball uniform since Nap Lajoie quit wearing a buttoned-down, turned-up collar early in the century, with having introduced an orange ball, too. For a fact, Finley did use an orange ball in spring training games in 1973, but, heck, like more than one promotional gimmick of the A's president at Kansas City and Oakland, this one came off Ray Dumont's drawing board.

Dumont, cigar-gnawing president of the National Baseball Congress at Wichita, Kansas, would have done anything to publicize his semi-pro baseball group. He even played sunrise games for wartime night-shift workers, serving free coffee and doughnuts. So, having found that a phosphorescent ball he tried to use at night without lights proved devastating to depth perception, he trotted out a day-ball gimmick, his orange Glo-bal. The Chicago White Sox and Cardinals pegged it around Wichita's Lawrence (Dumont) Stadium before a spring exhibition game in 1956. Liked it, too . . . Horsehide, that is, not cowhide. The ball became cowhide in 1974—due to the mechanization of Russian agriculture, a shortage of horsehides from Eastern Europe caused the new change.

Spalding yielded its cowhide business to Rawlings in 1977. Rawlings, best known previously for its vast improvements in gloves and baseball uniforms, put together the "pill" in Batesville, Mississippi, and then shipped the rubber-cork center to Port au Prince, Haiti. There, at 10 cents a ball, each finishing about three dozen a day, 650 Haitian seamstresses covered and stitched that red-center core or "golf" ball, as some call the nucleus of the present ball.

It's not *that* lively, even though the suspicion is that an X-5 experimental ball was adopted. Even before the offensive outcry in 1987, some longtime critics note that even foul balls go farther now, i.e., even breaking windows in cold weather at the Wrigley Field press box, far removed from home plate. Although George Foster hit 52 homers for Cincinnati in 1977 before moving into New York and semi-obscurity, not even Mike Schmidt had reached that figure. Henry Aaron got to his record 755 home runs by playing much longer than Babe Ruth and by hitting his favorite figure, his uniform number—"44"—four times.

Aaron, a wrist-flicking wonder, showed that for the gifted eye and quick-reflexing athlete, hitting that round ball with a round bat isn't so difficult after all, even if the swiftest pitcher hums it up to the plate between 90 and 100 miles an hour.

That's "only" four-tenths of a second, as noted by researcher Bill Sones, meaning the batter has exactly one-tenth of a second to decide and another one-tenth to pull the trigger. The collision of bat and ball, sugar sweet unless you're on the side getting beat, takes only .005 seconds.

Is Wyatt Earp in the house? Or Wild Bill Hickok?

3
Mitts
and
Monkey Suits

Although the baseball is white, shiny, a thing of hemstitched beauty, heck, it's been that way for six decades. The bat, though thinner-handled and lighter to meet individual hitter's efforts for swifter impact, still is the same well-grained hickory and ash of old. But the third basic piece of equipment, the glove, ah, now there IS the biggest difference between baseball past and present.

Only since the beginning of the 1960s has the glove become so sizable and so sophisticated that, with no reflection on the modern day fielder, if you don't catch the ball, it will catch itself. An overstatement, of course, and perhaps mistakenly interpreted as a putdown of the present day player.

Perish the thought. In fact, fielding now is better than ever, a tribute in part to the truer bounce of artificial turf, where the bad hop has become something associated only with a bad batch of brew. Largely, it's because the gloves themselves are larger and better, giving good defensive players a chance to become great and great ones to become superstars.

Years ago, along about the time crusty Zack Taylor was coaching a St. Louis Browns' team with a one-armed outfielder (1945) and managing one with a midget (1951), the durable, longtime catcher, a self-styled Florida cracker, made an observation that seems on the mark.

26

Said Taylor, "The biggest difference between the minors and majors is not the better control of big league pitchers, though that's significant, or the fact that the majors separate the men from the boys as hitters. It's day-in, day-out defense. The majors make the great fielding play of the minors merely good. And the good catch in the minors is merely average in the majors."

In Earl Weaver's autobiography, the feisty wizard of winners as a manager, put it succinctly, "Fielding is the most overlooked and maybe the least understood talent in baseball."

A far cry from the commentary of Rogers Hornsby, baseball's highest-average right-handed hitter, that it was possible to shake good fielders out of trees. Maybe then, but probably never. St. Louis shortstop Ozzie Smith, who probably would be viewed sneeringly by Hornsby as "a banjo hitter," Rog's cutting comment about offensive weak sisters, earned one of baseball's top salaries with his glove in 1986. The Wizard of Oz fielded his pivotal position probably more expertly than anyone in the past. He was paid a record $2,340,000 in 1988.

Although from time to time voters in Hall of Fame elections, modern writers and old-timer committee members have relented in their judgment or have been swayed by a player's other abilities, it's a fact that one of baseball's best early day hitters, Pete (The Gladiator) Browning, is _not_ in the Hall of Fame. His defensive deficiencies live 80 years after his death.

By marked contrast, giving defensive play probably its greatest boost since Rawlings Sporting Goods Company combined with _The Sporting News_ in 1957 to salute the first annual Gold Glove team, a player was elected his first time eligible for the Hall of Fame largely as a fielding phenom. That would be Brooks Robinson, Baltimore third baseman.

B. Robby, captain of the Orioles, was a slow runner with some power, but he batted only .267 for his 23-year career. Players elected previously to the Hall of Fame primarily for their defensive skill included Rabbit Maranville, a colorful character as a Peter Pan of shortstops, and Ray (Cracker) Schalk, a pintsized, pepperpot catcher with the Chicago White Sox before and after the 1919 scandal. But Maranville won election from the baseball writers only in his last year of eligibility, 30 years after retirement shortly after his death in 1954. And Schalk was tapped by Cooperstown's Veterans' Committee in '55, 36 years after he last hunkered behind a hitter.

Robinson, finishing his career in 1977, was elected overwhelmingly his first time eligible for induction, a tribute largely to defensive derring-do that was at its breathtaking best in spotlighted situations, specifically the 1970 World Series victory over Cincinnati.

Further, the significance of defensive play was given recognition when William Curran, a 65-year-old former New York boyhood bleacherite, turned out a book called *Mitts*. The book, published in 1985 by William Morrow and Company, New York, was a 239-page salute to the baseball glove and the skilled men who have worn it.

For years at the outset, when obviously the ball was softer, lighter, and not driven nearly so savagely, players fielded with their bare hands. Curran researched the "crabshell catch," suggesting it was New York-stamped, one in which players cupped hands closely together. As the old saying goes, "Two hands are better than one," but, h'mm, as he fielded barehanded, a defensive's player mobility certainly would be limited if he used both calloused paws to crabshell or muzzle the ball.

As suggested by Curran, it's hard to believe that *someone* wasn't a hand-wringing pussycat before the first professional team, the 1869 Cincinnati Red Stockings, had a player (catcher Doug Allison) who reportedly used a glove. Nat Hicks, a catcher for the New York Mutuals, was reported a pioneer in padding, too. Generally, the consensus is that outfielder Charles Waitt of St. Louis wore a flesh-colored glove in 1875.

As reported by Al Spalding, the great early day pitcher better known for the long association with the A.G. Spalding Sporting Goods Company he founded, Waitt was razzed by the fans in Boston as chicken even though the glove was merely a street-dress leather glove. Other indications are that Waitt wore a glove on each hand, logical with that crabshell-catch technique, cutting off the finger edges on his throwing hand's glove.

The legendary Spalding, revived in a biography written in 1985 by a Michigan State professor and baseball historian, Peter Levine, opened up his sporting goods house in '76, the year the National League was founded. Next year Al moved to first base, and, as noted in Spalding's own autobiography in 1911, he silenced the crowd boldly, wearing a black leather glove that was obvious.

Sure, Spalding was tired of swollen palms and jammed fingers, as Curran noted, and it wasn't bad business—sporting goods—to sell baseball gloves.

Early gloves cost a buck to $2.50 for premium "Indian tanned buck," as advertised. They included little padding and were listed as "catcher's gloves." Ads suggested that "no catcher or player subject to sore hands should be without a pair of these gloves."

The price now not only is $150, but by comparison in craft more like an artistic portrait verses a kid's crayon sketches. Now, too, in part because of the glove's refinements and a bad habit of slovenly fielding, many players one-hand catches that properly should be made with two. Not only is there a safety area in using two hands, though some will argue that the present glove design favors one-handed catches, players also get into the habit of catching the ball to the side, often the side of the gloved hand. As a result, there is a delay in bringing up the ball over to a throwing position.

Although many of the old managerial monarchs, a tyrannical John McGraw or more merciful Connie Mack, would do a double take at the size and shape of gloves now, they probably would do what manager Charlie Fulmer did back in 1882. When Red Stocking first baseman Henry Luff one-handed a ball, probably giving it a bit of razzmatazz or the early hot-dog treatment, Fulmer fined him a fin. Luff left in a huff.

As used by, endorsed by, and sold by Spalding, the glove became prevalent in the early 1880s. By '82, a talented shortstop named Arthur Irwin created what Curran described as "a serviceable padded fielder's glove," produced and promoted by the Draper-Maynard Company of Plymouth, New Hampshire. Later, one Joe Gunson, a catcher, testified he first jerry-built a catcher's mitt when playing in the Western League in 1888. Gunson's mitt, which he suggested mildly had been used as the design for Harry Decker's first thickly padded catcher's glove for Reach Company, was built of canvas, sheepskin, and buckskin, stiffened with the wire handle from a paint can.

Novel, indeed, but there were imaginative men in that era. A pitcher named Ted Kennedy was forced out of baseball with a sore arm in 1886 after two years in the big leagues. He not only became a glove designer and manufacturer, but he also was trying to produce an automatic scoreboard when he was electrocuted in St. Louis in 1907.

Although use of gloves was paramount by 1886, a few years before Decker patented his glove for Reach (1891), two standout second basemen of the first century never wore gloves—Fred Dunlap and Bid McPhee.

McPhee, whom archivist Paul MacFarlane of _The Sporting News_ has stamped for Hall of Fame recognition, played 18 years through 1899, several times leading in fewest errors. Dunlap, nicknamed "Sure Shot," finished in 1891 after 12 years, batting 17 points higher than McPhee. He had a fielding skill that would have made him, gloveless, most unusual. Ambidextrous, Dunlap could field a ground ball at second base and flip across the body with his left hand to the shortstop for a force out or to begin a double play without having to move his feet.

Back in the early 1930s when author Broeg was a smart-aleck kid, pontificating in a barber shop about the great second basemen of the moment, i.e., Frank Frisch, Charley Gehringer, Billy Herman, and an aging Rogers Hornsby, an old gentleman whipped a hot towel off his freshly shaved face and snarled, "What do you know, sonny? You never saw Fred Dunlap."

The old man was right. Dunlap, the gloveless wonder, hit .412 for St. Louis in the Union Association in 1884 and became so skilled when playing with six clubs from Cleveland to Washington that he reached handsome salary heights, $10,000. "Sure Shot" was a sure thing on a ground ball, but not with his money. Although he retired with $100,000, a handsome ransom, he died penniless in Philadelphia 11 years later.

By then, 1895, the rules committee had felt the need to install a rule, limiting players to gloves of 10 ounces or lighter, no more than 14 inches in circumference, as measured around the palm. No dimensions were established then for catchers' mitts or first basemens' gloves, but over the years the language had to be toughened and more precise. Commissioner Bowie Kuhn, a lawyer himself, finally persuaded rules' makers to come up in 1972 with a reworded Rule 1.14 that would hold up. Fielder's gloves now are limited to 12 inches long, 7¾ inches wide.

The baseball glove got its greatest influence from a pitcher, Bill Doak, and a Rawlings' employee with a curious interest in designing gloves—Harry (Bud) Latina, later called "Doc."

Near the end of World War I, Doak, then a rangy right-handed St. Louis pitcher with a pretty good spitball, walked into Rawlings' office in St. Louis and asked a good question. Why did baseball gloves have to be two pieces of leather sewn together? Couldn't the heel be built up, like a cushion of a cupped hand, to form a natural pocket to catch the ball? And why not spread the thumb and fingers with a webbing?

The Doak model, built in 1919, was a sensational step forward in the development of baseball gloves. The preformed, natural pocket with an inner greased palm and reinforced, multithong webbing laced into the first finger and thumb, created a standard and a standby. The Doak glove stayed in use and paid royalties until shortly before Doak's death in 1954. He was 63.

Doak's conspirator then was William P. Whitley, Rawlings' production chief, but lurking around the company corner was a young man who had ideas, good ones that—for a time—enabled the company to sell by far the largest percentage of professional gloves.

Latina, sitting at St. Louis's Sportsman's Park in 1926, watched the Browns' Ken Williams, tagging up on a fly ball, try to score after a catch. Obviously going to be out at the plate, Williams kicked the glove off catcher Ralph (Cy) Perkins and was safe. Perkins, embarrassed, was hurt physically when Williams' spikes cut into his instep.

That night, Latina, accompanying Philly first baseman Joe Hauser with whom he had played semi-pro ball in Wisconsin, visited an unhappy Perkins in the catcher's hotel room. Why, Latina wanted to know, didn't catchers wear leather loops inside their catching mitts to keep the hand from sliding loosely inside the mitt? Good idea, Harry, but, hey, why didn't the Rawlings factory superintendent do something that would help protect catchers' insteps beneath the shinguards?

So Latina became the glove doctor, 15 patents later, nicknamed "Doc" by Joe DiMaggio after DiMag had watched Latina oil and repack a glove for Yankee outfielder Charley Keller. The year was 1947 when son Rollie Latina joined his father. Joe Dee was delighted when Harry said, sure, he'd help reservice an ancient and honorable glove.

When heel spurs slowed DiMaggio a few years later, the great Yankee outfielder called Latina. Bud or "Doc" said he's show DiMag how to regain that half-step lost in the outfield. He urged a newer-model, larger glove to help make up for the inches difference in the fly ball caught or missed.

Before Harry Latina died in 1980 at 84, a member of the Hall of Fame of the Athletic Goods Manufacturing Association, he credited Cincinnati's former steady, sure-fingered shortstop, Eddie Miller, with having given him the idea for the U-shaped pocket and webbing of later gloves.

When Curran was preparing *Mitts,* he interviewed Harry's son, Rollie Latina, who fingered as the greatest glove invention of this century the Edge-U-Cated Heel patent, 1959.

"Before then," the younger Latina observed, "all gloves had a big, wide-open heel and there was never any actual snugging action of the glove on the hand. In other words, it was more or less loose. The Edge-U-Cated Heel brought the sides of the glove into the contours of the hand and the wrist and the glove actually stayed on your hand better that way."

As a stepping stone toward today's Star Wars' defensive contraptions, Detroit's Hank Greenberg created a rhubarb in the 1930s when he introduced a first baseman's mitt. It was a bit larger with a "fish net" webbing. The "superheated logomachy," as Bill Curran phrased it with his Fulbright erudition, reached the commissioner. Judge Landis gave Greenberg's gimmick the back of his autonomous hand.

Recognizing a hint on high, the baseball rules committee ruled in 1939 that first baseman's mitts could not measure more than 12 inches from top to bottom, not more than 8 inches at the palm. Significantly, the fish-net flap was concluded by a ruling that limited webbing to 4 inches from thumb to palm.

Curiously, a year later, at the same time Latina devised his deep-welled fielder's glove, he brought out a trapper-style first baseman's glove, which had an extra "finger" between thumb and palm, creating, in effect, what Greenberg had in mind. The design lasted nine years before the rulesmakers issued a nyet ukase.

Over the years catchers had begun to use smaller mitts with almost as much flexibility as a first baseman's glove, permitting them to one-hand a wide pitch or clutch it more quickly than the toilet-seat rigidity of catcher's mitts that couldn't hold many throws.

The tendency toward smaller catching mitts was shattered when owl-eyed and wise, Paul Richards, managing Baltimore, urged Wilson Sporting Goods Company of Chicago to help him solve a problem: that is, how to handle the dipsy-doodle effect of Hoyt Wilhelm's knuckler.

Wilson's result was an ingenious aid, a floppy thing that looked like a tanned version of an uncooked pizza. Bespectacled catcher Clint Courtney and Gus Triandos used the hinged, widely-webbed glove, "only slightly smaller than a trash-can lid," as Curran put it. The flap over the flapper caused fewer passed balls, all right, but also a rules change, one that limited catchers' mitts to 38 inches in circumference, 15½ inches from botton to top.

As mentioned, with the size of gloves virtually making players lopsided, Commissioner Kuhn's efforts for better use of simplified, specific King's English in 1972 reduced size and standardized gloves, but nothing was done to limit the exposed finger of the gloved hand, a result of an accident. The Yankees' Yogi Berra had a tender finger he withdrew from his glove, in the 1950s, to ease the strain and pain. An awkward master, Yogi did so much better with his finger behind the glove, not in it, that other catchers began to use the style. So now, too, do players at other positions, indicating not only a monkey-sees-monkey-does imitation, but also a feeling that the back-of-the-glove finger offers easel-effect support. After all, with the hand no longer stuffed up into the glove as of old, it's the glove that seems to close automatically around the ball, not the hand.

It appears that fewer base hits are banged off gloves now than in the too-hot-to-handle heyday before the glove's manufacturers reached the present pinnacle of near perfection in mitt-making. Couldn't this have cut into batting averages?

If official scoring was done more generously in the past, the inadequacy of gloves could have been a factor in scorers' judgment then. Maybe not. For one, Edd Roush, a brilliant fielding centerfielder at Cincinnati and with the New York Giants, insisted testily that scorers were excessively liberal with Rogers Hornsby in St. Louis.

"Maybe that's why George Sisler also hit .400 there," beefed Roush, the outspoken Hoosier who was the oldest living Hall of Famer in 1988 at the age of 95.

Roush was a colorful character in his own wonderful way. Back in 1920, just after winning his second batting title, he wearied of an argument prolonged by manager Pat Moran and several players with umpires at the Polo Grounds. So in the vast outfield of New York's famed horse-shoe shaped stadium, Edd put his glove to good use. He propped it on the lush outfield grass, used it as a pillow, and fell asleep. When play finally was resumed, teammates' shouts could not raise him. Third baseman Heine Groh finally had to trot out and awaken him. Thereupon, an umpire thumbed Roush toward the center-field clubhouse, ejected for having delayed the game.

If Roush wore any man's color, it probably was the shirt-style neck of uniforms seen often for ball clubs after the early long-pants era in which ballplayers dressed almost formally like cricket players or old-fashioned croquet putters. We have been unable to find who first decided on the beknickered bloomers that have prevailed, from the biscuit-bottomed early days of heavy flannels to the trim, two-way stretches of today's form-fitting polyester.

Early uniforms included a collar that could be buttoned at the throat and turned up to cut down the wind on a chilly early season day. Now, in cold weather, some players wear neck chokers.

At one time players wore high-button shoes, probably without spikes or cleats. Neither is there evidence of when the whiter woolen stockings were stirruped for use of sanitary socks. Undoubtedly, health was a factor with imperfect dye creating a hazard for perspiring players or with a foot sore or spike wound. Colored stockings or socks reportedly led to the fatal poisoning of John Coolidge, President Calvin Coolidge's son, a tennis player.

As recalled by Oscar Roettger, a former big leaguer who tailored uniforms for Rawlings into his mid-80s, athletes were at one time required to provide their own understockings, sweatshirts, and shoes. As a result, many players wore shoes too long and gray or white undershirts that were shabby, and prowled 5 & 10 stores for inexpensive women's cotton hose. The sanitary-hose substitutes often were worn until team trainers shamed players into buying a new pair.

As far back as 1912, Rawlings tried to build sliding pants into uniforms. The archaic sliding pad, a quilted wraparound for the upper thigh, was designed to eliminate or, more accurately, reduce sliding abrasions, best described in the vernacular as "strawberries." The painful wounds, composed by summer heat, sweat, and frequently infection, were a deterrent to 100 percent effort.

The sliding pad was tightened around the waist with string and, like a cowboy's gun holster, with another loop at the lower part of the thigh. The pad not only was warm and uncomfortable, but it tended to roll and, therefore, exposed the fleshy part of the thigh to the rough ground, creating the kind of annoying abrasion the pads were designed to stop.

A great improvement was provided by an imaginative trainer, Harrison J. (Doc) Weaver, who ministered to the muscles and morale of the St. Louis Cardinals from 1927 until his death in 1955. Weaver wore a summer-length version of old-fashioned woolen underwear. He urged players to buy the lighter, leg-snugging underpants and to put the clothing under their athletic supporters, which minimized friction. Fewer strawberries were gathered.

Although ball clubs formerly provided one uniform each for players, traditionally white-based at home and gray on the road, athletes cut into uniform shirts as well as ripped sleeves off their own undershirts in hot weather. (At one time later, the Cubs "invented" vest-style tops.) More recently, teams provide two home and two road uniforms each and as many as four for heavier-perspiring players, such as catchers.

As far back as 1883, Cincinnati, the cradle of professional baseball, put numbers on players' uniforms, but the policy was shortlived. Players apparently thought they looked like "prisoners," and some fans thought the numbers reflected management's ranking of the athletes' ability.

An eagle-eyed observer, Cliff Kachline, a longtime member of *The Sporting News* and also former historian at the Baseball Hall of Fame in Cooperstown, New York, noted a photo taken by the *St. Louis Post–Dispatch* in 1923, showing the Cardinals' first baseman, Jim Bottomley, standing on the bag as a baserunner next to the man he had replaced, Brooklyn's Jacques Fournier. Bottomley had a small number "5" on his left sleeve.

The modern method of numbering, however, was established in 1929 by the New York Yankees, who earlier had pinstriped in blue their white home uniforms to slenderize their bulging power man, Babe Ruth. Typical of the era, the Yanks first used the batting order for numbers. Over the years, they have retired the numbers of Hall of Fame players—Ruth "3," Lou Gehrig "4," Joe DiMaggio "5," Mickey Mantle "7," Bill Dickey and Yogi Berra "8," and also Roger Maris "9," and Phil Rizzuto "10."

The last to give up the you-can't-tell-'em-without-a-scorecard tradition was Connie Mack with his Philadelphia Athletics in the early '30s. Until then, trying to discourage bootlegged scorecards bought outside parks, usually two for the nickel price of a card inside the place, club

managements varied numbers almost daily on the scorecard and scoreboard, but, to repeat, did not identify players with uniform numbers.

By 1960, when maverick Bill Veeck ran the Chicago White Sox, the
iconoclast put the players' names on their uniform backs. Immediately, Bing Devine of the St. Louis Cardinals brought the policy into
practice in the National League.

By then, too, an aggressive dissenter named Charles O. Finley, a
Chicago insurance whiz, had taken advantage of the musical chairs
played with franchises. First, he bought the Kansas City A's after the
ball club had been sold by the Philadelphia Macks to Arnold Johnson
and moved to Kansas City. Next, spending heavily to line up draft
choices after baseball established a copy of football's reverse-order selection, Finley moved to Oakland with a ball club that was ready to
take off.

When the Oakland A's ripped through both leagues in the early
1970s, before Finley wearied of the sport and balked at increasing
costs, he tinkered with the color and traditions of the game. Now and
then, a ball club had switched colors, the way John McGraw did with
his all-black uniform for the 1905 World Series. The Chicago White
Sox briefly wore blue uniforms with completely white stockings on the
road in the late '20s and early '30s. Additionally, Rawlings turned out
a raglan-style sleeve for Rogers Hornsby, managing at Beaumont, Texas,
using a different color for the sleeve.

"Trouble was," recalled Roettger, smiling, "it looked too much like
a softball uniform, but that didn't stop Finley."

Beginning with white, green, and gold, the outspoken eccentric
went all the way. He turned baseball shoes from black to white, inner
stockings from white to gold, and varied pants and shirt fronts, switching to pullover jerseys in contrast to previous buttoned and/or zip-
pered jerseys.

Before they became disenchanted with Finley at contract time over
the years, the champion A's got into the act with the high spirits of
Charley O.'s mascot, a high-kicking Missouri mule. They broke out
mustaches and beards, a throwback to the very o-l-d days. Nobody
had dared darken his upper lip with hair since devilish Stanley (Frenchy)
Bordagaray drew down manager Casey Stengel's wrath at Brooklyn by
showing up in spring training with a mustache in 1936.

Although Rollie Fingers, with the splendiferous, bewaxed 'stache,
and his merry mates made it look as if Cap Anson, Mike Kelly, and
the heroes of the early diamond days were back, new material and
styles plus a different race showed a vast difference to the uniform,
too. Different and better.

With snug-like polyester, uniforms were better tailored, better looking and better fitting, too, except on pot-bellied managers or coaches or an occasional overweight player. As Roettger noted, uniforms that once weighed eight or nine ounces had been reduced to half the amount.

One thing that annoyed the old baseball tailor and former player, though, was additional tightness that, he felt, might restrict movement and, also, the combination of wearing pants longer and stretching sox stirrups so high that virtually all that was left visible of colorful hose was the white understockings. Better looking, yes; more colorful, no.

At one time Carl Hubbell, Al Simmons, and Ted Williams, three superstars, were unique in wearing pants long, but their uniform stockings still showed. Players long since had discarded the pinched roll just below the knee, flaring out the pants to a gentle roll just above the calf. The influence of the newer, longer look and hiked-up stirrups, as evidenced by Frank Robinson, George Hendrick, and others, appeared to be an impact made by black big leaguers.

The "high five," an overhead hand-slapping that replaced the handshake, especially after a home run, seemed also to be a result of athletic integration. But black players, underprivileged so long and barred unfairly from the "bigs," had reason to be cheerful.

So, too, did white players on whom caps with a built-up crown looked better, even though they cost clubs more than the slanted pulldown caps that previously gave ballplayers a pinheaded look. Shoes were better made and tighter fitting, too, than even the light kangaroo feathers of the immediate past. Players now move more quickly.

With pitchers charting opponents from behind the plate before they face them, managers charting defenses for opposing individual players, and, above all, gloves having come a long way from Biddy McPhee's and Fred Dunlap's bare-knuckle toughness to the early skintight, golf-style hand protectors, baseball most certainly has taken a step forward.

At least, as they say in football, in dee-fense.

4
Broken
and
Unbroken

Baseball has come, figuratively, farther than a flight to the moon —
not even those imaginative Baltimore Orioles of the Naughty
Nineties could have envisioned *that* "one giant step for mankind"—
but we believe that the legal eagles who took kinks out of the rules
over the years also missed one.

Even now, though the rules say a catcher must have possession before blocking off a runner at the plate, the split-second requirement
of a plate umpire to follow the flight of the ball and locate the position of a runner trying to score seems too difficult. Or, perhaps worse,
some arbiters just don't give a damn.

With a sweeping bow of admiration for men who've concocted, cor-
rected, and refined rules since Alexander Cartwright charted his first
set in 1845 for the 21-aces-and-out game, they've muffed one.

Many rules now, rudimentary to the fair play of the sport with the
foul lines, have made baseball what it is. So many of those were conceived in the 1893–95 era when John McGraw, Wee Willie Keeler, and
Ned Hanlon of the old Orioles were the "smart dummies." Smart
dummy was the height of baseball acumen as defined some years later
by a canny Cuban in cracked-ice English. Mike Gonzalez, that is, the
man best known for having telegraphed the most succinct description

of most of us who failed to fulfill our boyhood baseball dreams: "Good field, no hit!"

Gonzalez hadn't learned the difference between a "medicore" ball-player and a good one when the rulesmakers made their giant strides in the 1893–95 period. Most aimed at the cunning cutthroat characters whose "scientific" approach was winning ball games and ruining baseball.

Not only was the pitching distance increased 10 feet 6 inches (actually less when you consider that the horseshoe-pit, 5-foot pitching box was discarded), but the last primitive point of hitting was eliminated when the rule was changed in 1893 to abolish a flat side of a bat. Henceforth, the pitcher would have to toe a rubber, and the batter, as now, would have to hit with a round bat solely made of wood.

But here's where the subtleties of the game were changed: In 1894, a rule was written that a foul bunt would be classified as a strike, meaning, of course, that a bunted foul with two strikes meant "out." Until then, McGraw, Keeler, and other Hanlon henchmen would stand up there, using a bat flat-sided or round, and deliberately push bunts foul until they worked a weary pitcher for a base on balls or a base hit or, perhaps, until the poor "tosser" fella's arm fell off.

A year later, after the pitching slab was doubled in size to its current dimensions — 24 inches by 6 — and the length of the bat (42 inches maximum) and the width (2¼) standardized, the rulesmakers closed other more significant gaps in the mental machinations of the game.

They established the infield-fly rule, as basic now as three-outs-to-a-side. For too long, the wisest guys had permitted pop flies to fall, scooping up the ball to double up confused runners who didn't know whether to sit, stand, or go blind. At least, repeatedly, wiseacres afield were forcing off fast runners in favor of slow, creating unattractive chaos and detracting from the game.

By then, naturally, they already had prohibited a player from retaining a position as a baserunner if he was hit by a batted ball. (As far back as 1888, they even had credited the batsman with a base hit if a teammate was struck by his batted ball.) Years later when Jackie Robinson was starring as the spotlighted black pioneer of post-World War II, Robinson and Pittsburgh's Don (Tiger) Hoak were smart dummies who scooped up a ground ball as baserunners to avoid a certain double play. Umpires thereafter were given permission to decide on a two-out penalty rather than one if they felt a batter had deliberately been hit.

Back there in the Naughty Nineties the rulesmen reshaped the game like jockstrapped Pygmalions. They ruled in 1895 that a held foul tip was a strike. H'mm, they never did quite circumvent a clever catcher who dropped the third one if it suited his taste or his side's defensive strategy.

As the new century and the American League were about to intrude, these years were the most meaningful in the modern method of trial-and-error by which baseball prevailed. For instance, in 1899 the rules were changed requiring the pitcher to throw to first base in a pickoff attempt if he faked in that direction.

Years later, Hugh Duffy, the little leprechaun outfielder of the Boston Braves who had seized on that extended pitching distance and a bandbox ball park in 1894 to hit a record .438, made a decisive point with Paul MacFarlane. Mac, current archivist of *The Sporting News,* was a boy in Boston when Hughie, a venerable old man, coached for Joe Cronin's Red Sox. MacFarlane's fresh kid point to Duffy was that records of the distant baseball past had to be tainted if, as he had learned, runners were given a stolen base when they took an extra base on a hit. One such was Slidin' Billy Hamilton, the early day base stealing king. Hamilton would get a "stolen base" if he went from first to third on a single!

Duffy nodded, smiling, and said, "But don't take anything away from Billy or the rest of us in those days, because pitchers could fake a throw to first when you were about to steal. They could have you sliding back into the bag when they delivered the ball to the plate."

So the establishment of the balk in 1899 was a triumph for justice, even though most folks still don't understand the balk rule clearly. For that matter, many umpires vary in their definition of the foot fault, especially in a lefthander's stride "toward" first base.

In 1900, the year Johnson converted his Western League into the American and raided poorly-paid NL players, the National established the current rule designating the first and second foul balls as strikes. The AL didn't adopt that rule for two years.

Left intact, the previous rule that didn't penalize a hitter for fouling off pitches would have enabled the best fouling-off bat-wielders then and later—i.e. Luke Appling, Eddie Stanky, Solly Hemus, Harry Walker, Richie Ashburn, etc.—to stay up there forever, fouling off pitches and fretting both the pitcher and the home management.

Actually, the Americans' insistence in staying with the old rule was among the factors that aided the hitting of Napoleon (Larry) Lajoie, probably the best pure hitter before Ty Cobb and a graceful, sure-fielding second baseman if not a fast one. Recent statisticians act as if they've rediscovered a star in Lajoie, but the big Frenchman was superb most of his 21 years from 1896. For a time when he managed Cleveland, the Indians were named the Naps in his honor.

Lajoie, after hitting .328, .363, .328, .380, and .346, jumped from the Philadelphia Phillies to the new rival Athletics in 1901, the prized National League superstar whose jump to the infant AL merits more attention in a chapter on salaries and economics. Immediately, Nap tore apart the new league, hitting a record .422.

Prime researcher Lee Allen, later historian at the Baseball Hall of Fame in Cooperstown, noted that Lajoie was blanked just 17 of 131 games, collecting 229 hits. By contrast, when Rogers Hornsby had the "modern" high of .424 in 1924, the Rajah was stopped in 24 of 143 contests. But, Allen noted, Lajoie, who obviously faced more new (minor league) faces, also benefited in '01 from the new league's retained no-foul-strike rule.

The observation was typically Allen — honest and fair. Justice, if you will, is what we had in mind at the outset of this chapter when suggesting that for all the sophisticated rules' changes, baseball had missed one. Failure, that is, to grant a baserunner "air rights" over home plate, which is not really physically a base at all.

Too often runners have been hurt and, more often, lost runs because catchers who really didn't have possession of the ball blocked them off the plate. Or runners have been criticized, because they did not slide. For example, when Lou Brock, hitting hero of more than one World Series, went in standing up and was tagged out in the fifth game of the 1968 Series at Detroit, the St. Louis runner explained that catcher Bill Freehan's position made a slide impossible. Brock's point was that, if he had slid, his shoe would have been hooked off by Freehan's foot or shinguard.

Often, that's the way it has worked. On a bang-bang play, a sliding runner will spin off the catcher's shoe or shin protector, diverting the runner away from the plate. The catcher, often still catching the ball and bringing it down when the runner already has begun his slide, then reaches down or over and tags out the man who arrived first, yet hasn't tagged the plate. That's not just.

Why, then, as suggested, can't the runner have the "air rights," as they say in high-rise construction? That is, permission to slide so that his shoe merely passes *over* the plate. You can't hook the plate like a bag. It's a barely elevated white rubber 17-inch termination. A hook or leg-raised slide could clear the catcher's foot and protector, minimizing chances of injury or an unfair putout.

In football, a combat game, the distance between goal line and goal line is 100 yards precisely, not an inch more. Once a ball carrier crosses the horizontal plane of the opposition's goal, he has scored even if he immediately fumbles. The distance around the bases is 360 feet. Shouldn't there be, in effect, a horizontal plane at home plate, too?

Ah, well, it's only one man's opinion . . . oops, make that two . . . even though some umpires agree and others tell the professor to stick to his textbook and the sportswriter to get his nose out of the comic books.

In 1857, to take up the beat by which baseball took up the national heartbeat, the 21 aces were dropped in favor of the magical 27 outs, the requirement for victory in a game if it is not rain-shortened, prolonged by a tie score, or forfeit.

Before the National League was formed, changes were made that eliminated rules that smacked so much of cricket. By 1876, (1) baserunners couldn't advance on a foul, (2) the force play had been invoked, and (3) the fly ball caught had become an automatic putout. Also, first bounce no longer was out.

Pitches were called "balls" and "strikes," but even though progress was made in Henry Chadwick's establishment of scoring, and official averages were introduced (1865), pitchers (or "tossers") still could run forward like a cricketeer in his delivery, yet hitters had the luxury of requesting high or low pitches.

Over the years since '76, the same year Custer and his command fell at the Little Big Horn River in the Montana Territory, here's a capsule of the rules' cavalcade:

1877: Canvas bases were introduced, 15 inches square . . . The batter was not charged with a time at bat if he walked.

1879: The number of called balls was nine . . . The pitcher had to face a batsman before pitching to him . . . Official umpires were introduced.

1880: Eight called balls became a walk . . . The baserunner was out if hit with a batted ball . . . A catcher had to catch a third strike on the fly. The reserve clause was put into players' contracts.

1883: The pitcher could pitch from above his waist . . . The "foul bound" catch was discontinued.

1884: Six balls became a walk . . . All pitching-delivery restrictions were removed . . . Championships were to be decided on won-and-lost percentage.

1885: One side of a bat could be flat . . . Home plate could be made of marble or whitened rubber . . . Catchers and umpires wore chest protectors.

1887: The batter's request for high-or-low pitches was abolished . . . Five balls became a walk . . . The 10-foot pitcher's box was cut in half . . . Home plate became 12 inches wide . . . The batter was awarded a base if hit with a pitch . . . For this season only, the base on balls counted as a base hit and (again '87 only) four strikes were permitted . . . Base line coaching was recognized in the rules.

1888: The batsman was credited with a base hit when his batted ball struck a runner . . . Third strike became out.

1889: Four balls became a base on balls . . . A sacrifice bunt was recognized statistically as no time at bat.

1891: Substitutions were allowed at any time . . . Catchers were permitted to wear padded mitts.

1893: Pitching distance was increased from 50 feet to 60 feet 6 inches . . . Pitching box was eliminated in favor of a rubber slab, 12 inches by 4 inches . . . Pitcher required to put rear foot on slab . . . Flat-sided bat abolished.

1894: Bunted fouls were classified as strikes.

1895: Infield-fly rule was adopted . . . Also, held foul tip was classified as a strike . . . Pitching slab was enlarged to present size, 24 inches by 6 inches . . . Bat limits placed at 2½ inches in diameter, 42 in length.

1899: Balk-rule established.

1901: National League instituted current foul-strike rule . . . New AL refused to adopt it . . . Catchers were compelled to stay under the bat constantly, many having complained that the old requirement favored runners too much.

1903: American League adopted NL's foul-strike rule.

1904: Height of the mound was limited to 15 inches.

1908: Pitchers were prohibited from soiling a new ball . . . Sacrifice fly was adopted for run-scoring output only . . . Roger Bresnahan introduced shinguards.

1910: The cork center was introduced in the baseball.

1917: The earned-run average (ERA) was added to the rules and to statistical summaries.

1920: Freak deliveries were barred, including the spitball except for 17 registered spitball pitchers already in the majors . . . Only a given runner was out, none other, if one man missed a base . . . Runs-batted-in (RBI) became official . . . In reversal from previous rule that ended scoring with winning run, a homer leaving the playing field became officially four bases, and all men on base would add to final score . . . Frivolous ninth-inning steals by players uncontested on losing side in one-sided games were disallowed. Runners to be described as "taking second (or third) *unmolested.*"

1925: Pitcher was allowed to use resin bag . . . Minimum home run distance except for existing parks set at 250 feet.

1926: Sacrifice-fly rule liberalized to remove time at bat for batsman any time player moved up on outfield fly—to second, third, or, as previously, the plate.

1931: Sacrifice-fly rule eliminated . . . Glass buttons and polished metal were forbidden on uniforms . . . Except for existing parks, distance from home plate to backstop barrier reduced from 90 feet to 60.

1939: For one year only, sacrifice fly restored.

1954: Run-scoring sacrifice fly brought back . . . To rectify deliberate efforts to be hit by batted balls, rule changed so that infielders could commit interference as well as catchers . . . Players were required to remove gloves and all equipment from playing field and bat racks were to be established vertically rather than horizontally . . . No fielder could take a position in line with a batter's vision with the deliberate intent to distract batter or his batting view.

1959: Minimum boundaries were set for all new parks, 325-400-325 feet, foul line to dead center to foul line.

1963: Playing committee expanded strike zone, hoping to cut down bases on balls, theoretically raising and also lowering strike zone.

1968: Efforts made through rewriting rule to tighten restrictions against the illegal spitball.

1969: Pitcher's mound flattened 5 inches to 10 and standardized in slope . . . Strike zone, altered in 1963, lowered again and shrunk because of strikeouts, theoretically from the uniform letters to the top of the knee . . . The "save" rule, introduced by _The Sporting News_ in 1960, was added to the official statistics.

1973: To curb the growth of gloves and standardize colors, rules were rewritten . . . Guidelines set to determine cumulative performance records . . . American League experimented with the designated hitter, proposed by National League president John Heydler in 1929 and rejected by the AL and Commissioner K. M. Landis.

1974: The rule on "saves" was rewritten . . . Minimum standards for individual championships were outlined.

1975: The ball, always covered with horsehide and officially altered in 1910 and 1926, was changed to a cowhide cover because of shortage of horses and hides . . . Suspension set for three days if batter hit a fair ball with a filled, doctored, or flat-surfaced bat . . . Save rule again changed to provide save for last pitcher on winning side (other than actual victor) if game-saver (1) worked three innings, (2) pitched the ninth with less than a three-run margin or (3) came in at any time with the potential tying run at bat or in the on-deck circle.

1976: The American League adopted the DH as official.

Of the foregoing, for which Paul MacFarlane deserves credit with his rules' chronology in _The Sporting News,_ some have been explained more thoroughly and others probably could be, but won't.

It's enough to explain, we hope, that when the rule was established in 1954, threatening penalty for a fielder deliberately getting in a batter's vision to bother his concentration and batting background, it was an offshoot of the days when little Stanky, the slick second baseman, bothered batters. The Brat, as they called the mighty mite of "intangibles" with Brooklyn, Boston (Braves) and New York (Giants), was a clone of brassy, crafty Leo Durocher.

Stanky came to "play and to beat you," as Durocher would beam proudly. For one, Phil Rizzuto, former half-pint shortstop star of the New York Yankees, never appreciated the other little guy who would stand at second base in a hitter's sight lines and wave his arms as frantically as a fella trying to hail a cab in the rain near show time for a Manhattan theatre.

Rizzuto's peeve shows even on radio. He's a capable color man for Yankees' broadcasts. Phil is still riled over the time—in the 1951 World Series—when Stanky, sliding, kicked a ball out of the New York shortstop's glove. Phil resented Eddie's professionalism.

Reminds the guilty guys who've put this book together about the personal exasperation that the rulesmakers never have seen the wisdom of our air-rights' reasoning about a runner trying to score against a mask-and-mitt monster.

5
Of Real Estate
and
Unreal Hitters

Did only the fickle chicken-wire finger of fate keep Jimmy Foxx from hitting more home runs in a season than Babe Ruth or Roger Maris? As Branch Rickey would comment with the magical mind of one for whom the tongue was quicker than the eye or ears, "Possibly, probably and, under given circumstances, yes."

Mr. Rickey belongs in this tale of the tape and the tape measure, relative to hitting and to home runs, because baseball's organizer of the first farm system, the man who brought the blacks back into organized baseball, had a pet notion about power production. Said B. R. when he was trying in the early 1950s to resurrect Pittsburgh as he earlier had converted the St. Louis Nationals from nothing to something and helped boost Brooklyn, too, "It's not the rabbit in the ball, but, rather, the quail in the pitchers that's wrong with baseball."

Over the years good pitching has stopped good hitting most of the time except when batting burst its boundaries against a lively ball in 1929–30 or when, as this chapter will indicate, ramifications of baseball real estate affected hitting, especially home run hitting.

For this, a bow, please, to Lowell Reidenbaugh, senior editor of *The Sporting News,* for his research and to the artistry of sports cartoonist Amadee Wohlschlaeger, longtime chief artist of the *St. Louis Post-Dispatch.* Especially our tribute to Carl Schoen, a retired St. Louis postal clerk, whose genius in building miniatures of ball parks, past and present, is exceeded only by his dedicated research.

Before Schoen takes the reader back a century to prove why home run statistics were horribly distorted, particularly at Chicago in 1884 and Boston in 1894, let's reconsider the chapter's opening comment: Did only a screen hoisted in front of the right-field seats at St. Louis's old Sportsman's Park in 1930 keep Jimmy Foxx from breaking Babe Ruth's home run record two years later? And also from hitting even more than Roger Maris in 1961, a season in which Maris hit 61 and earned only an asterisk in the record books?

Double-X, as they called the handsome, bulging-biceped Foxx, or "The Beast," a mixture of his awesome physical appearance at the plate and off-the-field proclivities, was truly one of the most devastating power hitters ever. He hit 534 home runs, 12 times exceeding 30 homers, five times surpassing 40, and twice getting 50 or more.

At Baseball's Hall of Fame induction ceremonies in 1985, Ted Williams, top percentage hitter of the post-World War II era, saluted Foxxie this way: "When Jimmy or Mickey Mantle hit the ball, it *sounded* differently."

Foxx's most productive season was 1932 when, hitting .364 and driving in 169 runs, he hit 58 homers, just two fewer than Ruth had hammered five years earlier. By Reidenbaugh's research for *Take Me Out to the Ball Park,* a well-written, richly illustrated history of stadiums old and new, Foxx hit the right-field screen, Jimmy's favorite target, 12 times at Sportsman's Park, and the ball was in play. By contrast, Ruth, who batted left-handed, pulled four of his 60 homers into the pavilion, which then was unscreened from the right-field foul line, 310 feet to the 354-foot power alley in right-center.

A 30-foot screen was placed atop the 10-foot outfield concrete wall in 1930 so that, in effect, Ruth gained and Foxx lost by a whim of St. Louis clubowner Philip deCatesby Ball, saddled with poorer pitching than robust Brownie bats could overcome.

Actually, as Reidenbaugh acknowledged, research was questionable. Although he said Foxx hit onto the screen 12 times at a time when big league clubs played 11 games in each city, the figure was seven in Bob Broeg's *Super Stars of Baseball,* published previously by *The Sporting News.* In an interview with Neal Russo of the *St. Louis Post-Dispatch* in 1964, three years before Foxx died at only 60, Double-X also listed seven home runs lost by the screen. Some researchers calculate it as few as four, which still would be a record 62.

"I didn't worry about 'em when I hit 'em to left field because they were often long gone," said Foxx, a right-handed hitter who once broke a seat in the upper far corner of triple-tiered Yankee Stadium.

"But when they pitched me away, I liked to go to right field and St. Louis, short in right-center, was my favorite park."

So, presumably, Foxx did deserve the single-season home run crown. "Presumably" is used correctly because, with the screen up, pitchers *did* alter their style in St. Louis and probably other parks. For example, immediately after the screen was put up in June 1930, Heinie Manush, a left-handed hitter, banged three off the chicken wire.

When the feat was mentioned at a reunion of Hall of Fame members shortly before his death in 1971, Manush scoffed. "I didn't hit for much power, but was fast and hit the other way (to left)," explained the former outfielder. "I had a good career average (.330) going that way. So with the screen up, making the home run distance greater, the other side would pitch me inside more."

To illustrate further the circumstances affecting just one park, the tenant Cardinals, taking over ownership of the stadium when the Browns left for Baltimore in 1954, charted home runs at manager Eddie Stanky's request. That year the Redbirds hit the screen at a 35-to-18 ratio, meaning that, in effect, Stan Musial would have had 10 more homers, Red Schoendienst and Solly Hemus five each. So Anheuser Busch removed the screen for '55.

The result: Opposition, 28; St. Louis, 24. Taking over as general manager, Frank Lane ordered the screen reinstated post haste for '56. "The fans want to see the ball kept in play," said Lane in an observation that could be disputed. See 1987 homer *and* attendance heights.

Truth is, not until after the Los Angeles Dodgers' Maury Wills dusted off the stolen base, which had become a relic, did the offensive extremes live together.

Construction of sterile, symmetrical stadiums, built primarily to accommodate both baseball and football, has enlarged playing fields in most cases, particularly the power alleys. New covered stadiums have shortened others. As determined over years of research by Bob Kingsley, climatologist for government cartographers, the most homers are hit just left of the left-center field slot and just right of right-center.

So even though foul line distance can't and won't be ignored in this chapter about ball park idiosyncrasies, it's a fact that, as researched by Schoen, most older ball parks were built on real estate in proximity to streetcar tracks rather than with contemporary ample parking room. As a result, baseball stands often were rectangular, thereby creating a batting imbalance, one that usually favored left-handed hitters.

As Schoen learned in his research, two of the oddities of home run hitting in the 19th century, a period of dead ball play, showed just how much effect the size and shape of the playing grounds could have on the ability to hit for four bases. Back in 1884, playing for the Chicago Nationals, Ed (Ned) Williamson hit 27 homers, a heady sum and the high until Babe Ruth hit 29 for the Boston Red Sox in 1919.

Williamson hit only two home runs the year previous, just three the season after the 27 and, overall for 13 fragmented seasons in the majors, he hit just 63 home runs. Similarly, Bobby Lowe, whose career total of homers for nearly 18 seasons was just 70, became the first player to hit four homers in one game.

Not even the mighty Ruth, the greatest home run hitter, or Henry Aaron, the hitter of the most home runs, could match that mark. Truth is, Lowe, a second baseman nicknamed "Link," weighed only 150 pounds, scrawny for his height — 5-10 — and he hit for distance in only two seasons. He had 13 home runs in 1893, 17 the year he got four in one game.

At the time the pitching distance was increased to its current figures, favoring hitters, the Boston Nationals played in two bandbox ball parks. South End Grounds burned in May 1894, and most home games were played at the old Congress Street Grounds. Although the field had slightly larger dimensions, it also was a dollhouse. For example, Boston hit 78 home runs on the home field and visiting clubs 67, a handsome figure for that time. By contrast, Boston had only 25 on the road. Lowe, matching Hugh Duffy with 15 on his own field, hit just two on foreign fields. Duffy, who batted .438 in 1894, by far the highest average of 17-plus seasons (.328), homered only three times away from Boston.

In the case of Williamson with the White Stockings, as Cap Anson's Cubs originally were known, the facts are more precise. Schoen researched ball park distances at the Library of Congress where, armed with a letter of authorization from G. Greeley Wells, president of Sanborn Map Company, Pelham, New York, he was able to obtain Sanborn maps covering big league ball parks from 1872 to 1920.

Research and old photo sketches show Lake Front Park with a distance of only 196 feet to the right-field corner, because railroad tracks were located just outside the barrier. Estimated distance to center field was a mere 300 feet and to an angled left field about 260 feet not far from the foul pole.

In 1883 balls that cleared the fences in Chicago were ruled as doubles, not home runs. The White Stockings hit a record 277 two-base hits in 98 games. The home run high that year was 10 by Buck Ewing of New York in the National League, where Boston had the most team homers. In the American Association, then a major league, Harry Stovey of Philadelphia hit 14 homers, and Cincinnati led as a team with 35.

In 1884 Chicago changed ground rules to make any ball hit over the fence a home run. The White Stockings' total leaped dramatically to 142, three times the highest number for any other club. For the Stockings, Williamson hit that questionable 27, of which 25 came at Lake Front Park.

Chicago, posting a 39–17 record at home compared with 23–33 on the road, found Lake Front Park to have even "more friendly confines," as the Cubs' homer-hitting blithe spirit, Ernie Banks, would put it years later in glorifying Wrigley Field. Fred Pfeffer hit 24 of his 25 homers at home, and 32-year-old Adrian (Cap) Anson, the club's founder, hit 20 of 21 at home. Anson, a 22-year veteran as baseball's first 3000-hit player, batting .334, had only 96 career homers.

Over the years, seizing on agility, strength of arm, and indolence or slowness of runners, more than one rightfielder has thrown out a batter at first base on an apparent single. Brooklyn's Carl Furillo and Pittsburgh's Roberto Clemente, to name two. Once, Ken Wood, playing right field for the old St. Louis Browns, threw out two men at the plate in the same inning. But the extremely shallow (196 feet) distance down the right-field line at Chicago's old Lake Front Park enabled Mike (King) Kelly to perform some of his most crowd-pleasing diamond derring-do.

Kelly was the early glamour guy of big league baseball, a versatile seven-position star, a swaggering, handsome athlete who caught the crowd's fancy from 1878 at Cincinnati until he died at only 37 in 1894, eight clubs, 16 years, and too many drinks later. His batting average was only .307, not especially robust for his day, but he captivated early Hall of Fame voters as he had crowds in his day. Old "Slide, Kelly, Slide," the tippling Mick from Troy, New York, was the first "expensive" player sale, shipped to Boston by Chicago's A. G. Spalding in 1877 for $10,000.

The King used the cozy right-field corner for some crowd-pleasing plays of which, certainly, this had to be one: As ferreted by Schoen, Kelly had one of his dazzling days on July 5, 1884. To tie New York in the eighth, The King singled, stole second and third, and scored on a short fly ball.

When New York threatened in the 10th, one on, one out, Kelly fielded a sharp hit to right by Roger Connors and pegged out Connors at first. When the baserunner tried for third, Cap Anson's throw to Williamson retired the side. A double play on a "single" to right! Whereupon Kelly stole home with the winning run in the last of the 10th, 7–6.

No wonder The King's memory was fresh in the mind's eye of men who had grown up when or just after he played. When the Baseball Hall of Fame voting began in 1936, he was an early inductee of a pioneer old-timers' committee in '45.

Other players' Hall of Fame chances were helped or hindered by the size and shape of parks in which they played, particularly their home fields, but more about that feature down the (foul) line.

Along about the time the cork-center ball helped the game (1910), clubowners realized that the game Doubleday didn't invent nor probably Cartwright either, had a potential that made steel-and-concrete stadiums worthwhile successors to the old postage-stamp ball parks, which looked like oversized outhouses. They were, truly, wooden death-traps, obviously obsolete, and, ah, yes, Mr. Magnate, too small.

Even before Brooklyn's Charley Ebbets purred when his ball park opened in 1913—"baseball is in its infancy"—the Lords of Baseball, as the *New York Post*'s Dick Young liked to label them, were building their playing field monuments. As Philip J. Lowry romantically tabbed them in a 1985 publication of the Society for American Baseball Research, they were the "Green Cathedrals."

At Pittsburgh in 1909, Barney Dreyfuss opened Forbes Field, named for a Revolutionary War general. With beautiful Schenley Park as a backdrop, the rich field with an attractive archway opening in the city's Oakland section was most eye-appealing. Before a double-decked stand was opened in 1925, expanding seating capacity and cutting down the distance at the right-field line to 300 feet, the playing field was extremely spacious—376 feet to right field, 462 to center, and 360 in left. As a result, Forbes Field had the kind of dimensions that led it to be a haven for triples, not homers.

Wearing Pirates' black-and-gold colors, Owen (Chief) Wilson, then 29 years old, hit a record 36 three-base hits in 1912. The record seems to mock modern standards when a player able to hit 20 triples makes big news. If Forbes Field offered a supreme test for the three-base hit to the flying feet of a Wilson, a Paul Waner, a Roberto Clemente, or the kid from the Pittsburgh area who got away, Stan Musial, Philadelphia's Baker Bowl became the paradise that turned creampuff hitters into muscle men.

Baker Bowl, built by sporting goods executive A. J. Reach and Colonel John I. Rogers in 1887, actually survived the scurry to new stadiums just before World War I. In effect, that was part of the trouble of the ball park, located at Broad Street and Lehigh, that had a cozy 20,000 capacity and neat dollhouse dimensions.

At one time early in the going, before Grover Cleveland Alexander demonstrated a height of pitching craftsmanship in 1916, hurling 16 shutouts, the Phillies even had a bicycle track girdling the inside fence. Imagine a slight embankment at times to the right-field fence, only 272 feet from home plate at the foul line, making it more difficult to field drives off the wall.

The short right-field porch, coupled with only a 300-foot distance in the right-center field power alley, made Baker Bowl a shooting gallery, especially after the ball was juiced up and the club no longer had the ability of an Alexander, slyly dealt to the Chicago Cubs just before he put on his doughboy uniform for WWI.

By the time the ball sprouted wings, 1929–30, heaviest hitting era in the century, the rusty, rundown ball park should have gone to a junkyard grave as obsolete, archaic, and just too damned small. By then, Baker Bowl had survived fire and two disasters, one of which was a partial roof collapse in May 1927. A person was killed and 45 other spectators were hurt.

The third disaster was suffered by pitching staffs in the '29–'30 period, particularly the Phillies'. In '29 the Phils had a team batting average of .309, yet finished only fifth. A year later, their team hitting mark was higher, .315, but they finished *last*. In an unforgettable season of 50-plus batters hitting over .300, the *league* average in 1930 was .303. The New York Giants, leading with .319, finished only third. No wonder John McGraw was getting ready to give up the managerial ghost.

The anatomy of a ball park's impact on individual and team averages was a fascinating exploration undertaken by Carl Schoen. The St. Louis miniature-park-builder-and-researcher showed graphically what happened at Baker Bowl. In 1929 at the Phillies' fun field, with one game cancelled, the Giants, a .290 team overall, batted .340 and hit 17 home runs in 10 games. The Giants' hit totals were 14, 20, 18, 20, 17, 14, 12, 14, 4, 16, and 16. In nine games New York scored 11 or more runs. The one the Giants lost was the game in which they got only four runs. Philly southpaw Les Sweetland topped Carl Hubbell, 5–4.

"Sugar" Sweetland and righthander Claude (Weeping Willie) Willoughby were shellshocked after the 1930 season in which Sweetland had a 7–15 record and a 7.71 earned-run average and Willoughby was 4–17 with a 7.59 ERA. As they paraded in and out for manager Burt Shotton, to whom a second chance at Brooklyn in 1947 must have seemed hog heaven, a press box wag set up a hummed parody from "America." It wound up, "Sweetland and Willoughby, of thee we sing. . . ."

In particular, the right-field fence and myopic power alley in right-center were so short that not even a 60-foot high screen in right field could do anything more than set up more doubles than homers. Even so, as St. Louis hit .352 in 11 games, scoring a record 28 runs in one game, first baseman Sunny Jim Bottomley hoisted eight over the beckoning barrier.

The fence was so close that, as Pulitzer Prize-winning sports columnist Red Smith wrote, "It might be exaggerating to say the outfield wall cast a shadow across the infield, but if the right fielder had eaten onions at lunch, the second baseman knew it."

Although the Phillies had good power hitters, Baker Bowl obviously distorted their averages and helped delay induction of some into the Hall of Fame and deterred others from winning the honor. Frank (Lefty) O'Doul, whose outfielding never came within spittin' distance of his charm or his bat, led the National League in hitting with a .398 in the inflated 1929 season. At home he batted .453 compared with .341 on the road and hit 19 of his 32 homers. Young Chuck Klein, author of 43 homers his first full season, was .393 at Baker Bowl, .341 elsewhere. Twenty-five of his homers were lifted over the right-field screen at home.

A right-handed hitter, Fresco Thompson, an amusing infielder who became a Dodgers' executive, batted 53 points higher than on the road, finishing with the highest average (.324) of his nine-year career.

Of all the hitters who hated to grow old or to see Baker Bowl demolished, none could have missed it more than the New York Giants' Mel Ott. After the Phillies became tenants of the American League Athletics in mid-season, 1938, Ottie never homered at Shibe Park, where he played as a regular visitor and part time until 1947. Masterful Melvin, a 17-year-old schoolboy signed by the Giants' John McGraw in '26, hiked his front leg unorthodoxically high and hoisted 511 home runs before he retired.

Ott, a .308 career hitter who played the Polo Grounds' caroms with the billiard skill of Pittsburgh's P. Waner and Clemente, was one of the many New York Nationals' Hall of Famers who played parts or, as he did, all of their careers, in the most famous NL park. Most famous, at least, until Chicago's Wrigley Field lasted as an old-style ball park landmark.

By the time the "new" Polo Grounds was opened in 1912, St. Louis's Robert Lee Hedges had used profits from a close pennant race in 1909, enhanced by the screwball presence of eccentric lefthander George (Rube) Waddell, to improve and enlarge Sportsman's Park.

The same year Philadelphia received the first of what really were palatial parks, certainly from the exterior. Pittsburgh's Forbes Field had an inviting decoration and rotunda, but Shibe Park, not only the first completely steel-and-concrete stadium at its completion, had a solid smoked-glass exterior with a graceful cupola over its main entrance gates at 21st and Lehigh.

The Athletics' ball park, sold to the Phillies in 1954 before the A's were sold themselves to a Kansas City interest, became known eventually as Connie Mack Stadium. There, Mr. Mack turned out his great teams and bad ones for a half-century. Although Jimmy Foxx and others muscled home runs—and Foxxie even hit over the towering roof in left field—the American League ball park offered a tough target for hitters. After all, the distances to the fences were far enough from the plate; and, in addition, to cut out the free-admission gawkers from porches and rooftops behind the right-field fence, a 12-foot-high barrier was increased to a 50-foot louvered wall in 1935.

By then, Lou Gehrig had homered three straight times in a game in 1932. After Gehrig's third home run, manager Mack removed his giant righthander, scowling George Earnshaw, and urged the 20-game winner to sit next to him on the bench so that he could watch reliever Leroy Mahaffey pitch to the Yankees' Iron Man. Off Mahaffey, Gehrig homered over the left-field fence 360 feet distance. Earnshaw, angry at himself and at the manager for not having let him go directly to the clubhouse, was properly sarcastic. "Oh, yes, Mr. Mack," said big George, "I see—Mahaffey made Gehrig change direction."

Like Shibe Park, Chicago's Comiskey Park offered a firm home run hitting challenge. The park was built in 1910 by a man later accused of penury with his players at the time of the Black Sox scandal nine years later. Charley Comiskey outdid himself with his handsome brick ball park, described as the "Baseball Palace of the World." Like many another park of its time, the home of the White Sox has been increased in size over the years. Its foul lines, though changed from time to time in ownership whims over the years, including an eight-foot increase in 1986, were a robust 363 feet down each foul line. Comiskey would be pleased, certainly, that the whitened-and-brightened brick amphitheatre at 35th and Shields on Chicago's South Side was the majors' oldest park as this book was written (1988).

Comiskey Park had the distinction of becoming the site for the first major league All-Star game, 1933, a brainchild of *Chicago Tribune* sports editor Arch Ward as a sidelight to a World's Fair in Chicago. A Depression-era crowd of 47,595 paid $45,000 that went to the old-timers' baseball fund. Babe Ruth's home run gave the American League a 4–2 victory. The AL was managed by Connie Mack, the NL by John McGraw. McGraw had resigned from the Giants and ended a 30-year reign at the Polo Grounds on the same day Gehrig hit those four homers in Philadelphia—one to the "wrong" field. In effect, McGraw stole the headlines from the quiet hero whose death at only 38 from amyotrophic lateral sclerosis (1941) brought to public attention a rare, dread disease.

McGraw went so far back into New York baseball history that, in effect, the spunky railroad butcher boy from Truxton remembered three Polo Grounds, none of which ever saw a polo mallet. Yet the Polo Grounds became probably the most unusual name in baseball history. Certainly, the last of the three ball parks, removed briefly from athletic limbo as the first home of the expansion Mets, 1962–63, had the most unusual dimensions.

The first park, bought in 1883 by John B. Day from James Gordon Bennett, publisher of the longtime *New York Herald,* was located at Fifth Avenue and 110th Street and, as Lowell Reidenbaugh noted in *Take Me Out to the Ball Park,* had been the site of polo matches.

The second location, fortunately given that misleading, engaging name, too, was located beneath Coogan's Bluff at Eighth Avenue and 155th. Actually, briefly home of the Players' League for one season (1890), the second Polo Grounds had an open-ended center field, permitting horse-driven carriages to fringe the playing area. When the Giants and Chicago Cubs played their historic replay in 1908, a result of the delayed Fred Merkle force-out detailed earlier, angry fans eager to enter overran one section of the wooden fence. Fire hoses turned back the crowd that time, but fire crept in and destroyed the stands in 1911.

Owner John T. Brush suffered as a wheelchaired victim of locomotor ataxia, a degenerative disease of the spinal cord. He was a courageous man who risked his family's future with a steel-and-concrete stadium, noted by Reidenbaugh as third only to Pittsburgh's Forbes Field and Philadelphia's Shibe Park.

Over the years the Polo Grounds simply grew until center-field bleachers, closing off an open area unnecessary with the nearby subway and automobiles, brought park capacity in 1923 to 55,000. The same year the rival Yankees opened Yankee Stadium, the last privately built ball park until the transplanted Brooklyn Dodgers opened their own place at Los Angeles' Chavez Ravine in 1962.

Dodger Stadium is a beautiful baseball property. So, too, are many of the newer parks, products of a building era begun with Milwaukee's gambling effort with County Stadium in 1952 up through most recent additions, domed stadiums at Minneapolis and at Seattle. In the interval, as baseball prospered and pro football drew impetus and interest from television, symmetrical stadiums were built almost feverishly in San Francisco, St. Louis, Cincinnati, Washington, Pittsburgh, Philadelphia, and expansion cities — Houston, Atlanta, Montreal, San Diego. The park at Arlington, Texas, was rebuilt from minor league dimensions.

Additionally, Baltimore improved Babe Ruth Park to Memorial Stadium and, reflecting their interest as sportsmen, Tom Yawkey upgraded Boston's Fenway Park, Philip Wrigley face-lifted the family field, and John Fetzer completed the overhaul of Tiger Stadium begun by Frank Navin and Walter O. Briggs.

Major league lights appeared for the first time in 1935 at Cincinnati, instigated by Larry MacPhail, who knew a good thing when he saw one as St. Louis's Sam Breadon did, too, when MacPhail ran the Cardinals' ball club at Columbus, Ohio, in 1932. Said Breadon, unable to put up lights in St. Louis because he didn't own the park, "Night games make every day Sunday."

After MacPhail's similar success with his second set of lights in 1938, where Charley Ebbets had built a marble-tiled, theatrical rotunda, lights flickered like fireflies in big league ball parks. Detroit was the last to flip the switch in mid-season, 1948. The Chicago Cubs would have had lights, also, except that the war with Japan late in 1941 prompted patriotic Wrigley to turn over to the government the lights and steel bought for Wrigley Field. Following the war, P. K. changed his mind and stuck his gum and future on sunshine baseball.

Artificial turf, the next dramatic change in baseball real estate, resulted from a miscalculation in the bold venture of a former Houston mayor, Judge Roy Hofheinz, buoyed by his persuasive tongue and respondent ears of Harris County voters in Texas. When the Astrodome was built in 1965, three years after Houston was awarded a National League franchise, day games disclosed a glaring misjudgment. A transparent dome made it most difficult to judge a high fly ball on a sunny afternoon. A paint job killed the sun light, and, worse, the ball park grass. Monsanto Company of St. Louis produced the antidote for miffed Mother Nature in 1966 — ersatz grass.

For fresh-air stadiums that opted for Astroturf and other artificial services thereafter, the more sophisticated synthetic surface almost ended two traditions: The time-honored "No Game Today — Rain" and the distressing field announcement, "This game called because of wet grounds. . . ." Moreover, with the need for tougher turf because most of the newer, round stadiums housed football teams, too, the bright green substitute gave a June-in-January look to ball park playing fields.

Of ball parks built — past, present and probably future — none will be as unique as New York's old Polo Grounds, horseshoe-shaped as if they had in mind big time college and pro football when both branches of the autumn sport were played in rinky-dink stadiums. The shape and sightlines definitely were better for football, and in effect, created much of the charm in baseball.

The field was an east-to-west funnel, meaning that the foul lines were only 257 feet from the plate in right field and 279 in left, but center field was an unbelievable 483 feet away. Overhanging the field in left at the base of the first of two decks was a façade that jutted forward just enough to nick a looping fly ball for a home run almost as cheap as a popped fly into the fetching right-field stands.

The stingiest blooper to right at the PG—probably the most publicized—was a three-run chip shot pinch hitter Jim (Dusty) Rhodes hit off Hall of Fame righthander Bob Lemon to give the Giants a 5–2 victory over Cleveland in a 10-inning opener of the 1954 World Series. By startling contrast, the same game produced one of the longest outs ever made at the unusual ball park, and—again!—the Indians were the victims.

In the eighth inning of the opener with runners on first and second base, Willie Mays raced back near the center-field bleachers for an over-the-shoulder catch of Vic Wertz's blast off reliever Don Liddle. Mays' catch was great and best remembered, but probably not the fleet centerfielder's best defensive achievement. His wheeling, strong, off-balance throw probably was even more significant in preventing a runner, tagging up, from scoring from second.

The catch had to be nearly 438 feet, the distance to each of the center-field bleachers, divided by an open area that led up steps to a second-story home and visiting clubhouse. Except for Manager Mc-Graw, who had a secret exit in the back of the home (first base) dugout so that, en mufti, he could circle back under the right-field stands to his clubhouse, all entering or exiting players had to walk the distance from the bench or diamond to the clubhouse. For a pitcher knocked out, it was an extremely l-o-n-g walk.

Few players ever hit into the bleachers straight away, and none ever reached that 483-foot indentation to *dead* center. The Giants' giant centerfielder, Hank Leiber, gave it a lusty try in a Subway Series between the New York clubs, 1936–37. Leiber teed off tremendously, but, playing deep and loping with effortless grace, Joe DiMaggio ran back, caught the ball over his shoulder for a game-ending stop, and was about to bound up the stairway into the visitors' clubhouse. Suddenly, DiMag skidded to a stop. He remembered. Because President Franklin D. Roosevelt was at the game, no one was supposed to leave the playing field before the presidential limousine. As the chief executive's auto exited via center field, FDR winked at DiMaggio.

Although the mixture of extremely short fences at the foul lines and an incredibly deep center field created an element of injustice and plain-vanilla luck at the Polo Grounds, the historic old park's most famous homer was not tainted. That would be the savage line drive Bobby Thomson whistled into the lower left-field stands for a three-run, pennant-winning homer with one out in the home ninth of the 1951 playoff. Thomson's shot off Ralph Branca gave the Giants a 5–4 victory over the borough rival Dodgers and the National League pennant.

Actually, Thomson's sinking line drive, landing in the lower stands, might not have stayed up, to use a baseball expression, long enough to hit the seats in some parks, but the ball was struck so hard that it undoubtedly would have cleared any leftfielder's head and hit a fence for at least a game-tying double.

The Polo Grounds' vast center-field acreage created considerable challenge even though the U-shaped field permitted the left and right-fielders to bunch toward center, creating bigger gaps down the short foul lines. When Casey Stengel came over to the Giants as a veteran player in 1921, he was concerned about the territory. Frank Frisch, a cocky young second baseman, told him, in effect, not to worry, Pop.

Years later, then a double-talking, championship legend as a manager, Stengel would explain, "I haf-ta say Mr. Frisch treated me handsome. He told me to play deep and that he'd come back and catch the short ones and I haf-ta say he did. The man was so fast and so quick going to his left that he could play a deep second base and not only come back to center field, but he also could run diagonal down toward the right-field line and catch short flies near the fence."

Stengel was a 23-year-old rookie when Charley Ebbets opened the Brooklyn ball park, 1913. Ebbets Field became a baseball Camelot, a legend along with Flatbush's baseball faithful. From the Brooklyn Bridge to Sheepshead Bay, from the Gowanus Canal to Greenspernt . . . pardon, Greenspoint, there still are memories of Ned Hanlon's turn-of-the-century Superbas, the first Trolley Dodgers. Also, Uncle Wilbert Robinson's Daffiness Dodgers of the late 1920s and early '30s and Leo Durocher's battling "Bums," as the fans called their pets in disgust or delight.

Obliquely, we feel for any town that lost a franchise — most certainly Professor Bill Miller, whose affection for the old St. Louis Browns followed the ball club to Baltimore — but both agree that the unkindest cut of all was Brooklyn's loss of the Dodgers.

At Ebbets Field, a dollhouse in dimensions, especially after Branch Rickey installed a new ring of seats in left and center field in 1947, right-handed hitters joined the left-handed in taking advantage of altered size. In left field, where the distance became 348 at the line and did not fall back rapidly toward center, power guys like Gil Hodges and Roy Campanella found a favorable jet stream to left-center.

The right-field fence was only 296 feet from home plate, though a 20-foot screen caused Duke Snider and others to loft the ball for homers. Trickily, the wood fence sloped toward the infield near ground level. When the New York Yankees played the Dodgers in a pre-season exhibition there in 1951, Mickey Mantle's rookie year, Stengel sauntered into right field with Mantle in practice. The Switcher was playing right then because Joe DiMaggio was finishing up in center.

Stengel explained the defensive difficulties of the sloping wall to Mantle. The 19-year-old blond gaped at the veteran manager. "Did you play here, Casey?" asked the kid.

"Crissakes, yes," snapped Stengel. "You don't think I was born 60 years old!"

Before Ol' Case was the young kid from KayCee, Fenway Park was built in Boston (1912) by John I. Taylor of the distinguished newspapering Taylors. The name came because the park was located in The Fens, a marshy area of the city. Like Comiskey Park, Wrigley Field, and dramatically remodeled Tiger Stadium, Fenway Park has architectural character. It was best described by Lowell Reidenbaugh in *The Sporting News'* 1983 book about ball parks:

> . . . A monument to antiquity, distinguished by its irregular architecture, its infinite charm and its seven decades of memorable baseball. Seventeen facets and barriers mark its interior design, the "Green Monster" frowns frighteningly in left field and pigeons fly merrily throughout the premises. . . .
> . . . For (more than) 70 years the misshappen ball park at the intersection of Lansdowne and Jersey streets (a.k.a., Yawkey Way) has presented the good and the bad, the humorous and the humdrum of baseball. . . .

Uh-huh, and the presence of three of the greatest hitters ever—Ted Williams, Jimmy Foxx, and a cabbage-headed, broad-nosed guy who was a 19-year-old kid when he first toed a big league pitching rubber there in 1914: Of course, Babe Ruth, whose loss through sale to the New York Yankees ended the Red Sox's championship dynasty and began the Yankees'.

Before Harry Frazee dealt the Babe to save his first love as a theatrical producer, the proud Bosox were the American League's first and really only rival to the Philadelphia Athletics in the American League. From the time they played and won the first "modern" World Series, 1903, topping Pittsburgh, the Sox were superb.

With a title in '12, the year Fenway Park opened, they won four World Championships in a six-season stretch even though Frazee's front-office predecessor sold Tris Speaker to Cleveland after a salary tiff in 1916. Speaker in center field, Harry Hooper in right, and Duffy

Lewis in left formed perhaps the greatest defensive outfield, certainly of its time, and they could hit.

Boston's left field, the right-handed equivalent of the inviting right-field targets at Baker Bowl, the Polo Grounds, Yankee Stadium, Cleveland's League Park, and St. Louis's Sportsman's Park, was terraced in the early days. "Duffy's Cliff," they called it in tribute to the mountain-goat agility of Lewis, who wore a rakish Maurice Chevalier straw hat. Later, dapper Duff had a long career as traveling secretary of the rival Boston Braves.

By the time wealthy Tom Yawkey took over the ragged Red Sox in 1933, they were long since the doormat of the American League, as reflected in part by the experience of pitcher Red Ruffing, en route to the Hall of Fame with a 273–225 record. Ruffing was only 33–96 his first five-plus seasons pitching for the Fenways.

Before Yawkey spent so much money in the Depression period, building the Gold Sox into pretenders if not contenders, fire tore heavily into the park, by then as tattered as the team. In 1934 Yawkey began the improvements that made Fenway Park most attractive and virtually required spectators seated in the left-field grandstand, squarely facing home plate as deep third basemen in foul territory, to wear protective fielders' gloves or be able to duck, pronto.

As Yawkey added concrete bleachers in center field, he leveled Lewis's terrace in left field, and replaced the wooden wall with a metal fence. A 23-foot screen was added above the 37-foot high left-field wall, cutting down baseball buzz bombs into the Lansdowne Street, but not preventing home runs at the base of the screen. So the beckoning barrier leered menacingly at all pitchers, particularly Boston's when removal of advertising signs brought a solid paint job and the label of Green Monster.

In this Quasimodo of ball parks, left field is listed as only 315 feet from home plate at the line, and the target is inviting in the left-side power lane. Curious players, having walked the distance, question the 315 as fudging. Over even the good years, Boston teams have had trouble winning on the road because of that "Fenway Park swing" by right-handed hitters, including Bobby Doerr, Vern Stephens, Ken Harrelson, Jim Rice, and, of course, even Jimmy Foxx. Double-X hit 50 homers as a Red Sox in 1938, six years after his 58 with Philadelphia.

Managers seldom dared to use left-handed pitching at Fenway Park, though Mel Parnell had a healthy winning percentage of .621 for 10 years with the Red Sox. The center cut of his 123–75 achievement came in six seasons, 1948 through '53, in which he posted 15–8, 25–7, 18–10, 18–11, 12–12, and 21–8 records.

In the famed first American League playoff, a one-game showdown in which Cleveland traveled to Fens and beat the Red Sox, 8–3, preventing the chance for an all-Boston World Series, Indians' manager Lou Boudreau boldly pitched and won with a loosey-goosey rookie lefthander, Gene Bearden, a 20-game winner his first and only good season.

When the St. Louis Cardinals won a surprising pennant in 1985, a major factor was the superlative 21–8 season of John Tudor, whose earned-run average, an excellent 1.93, was indicative of 10 shutouts. Tudor, acquired from last-place Pittsburgh after a 12–11 season, never had been outstanding previously.

"But he'd broken .500 pitching in Fenway Park," explained St. Louis manager Whitey Herzog, who also had managed in the American League. "When a lefthander can come inside on a right-handed hitter with that big green 'thing' over his shoulder, I certainly felt he could pitch better in a bigger park (St. Louis) and with a standout shortstop (Ozzie Smith), third baseman (Terry Pendleton), leftfielder (Vince Coleman), and centerfielder (Willie McGee)."

Tudor himself acknowledged that he had pitched tight to right-handed hitters often at Fenway Park, observing "It's difficult to pitch differently in any park."

Then the *Boston Globe*'s crack baseball writer, Peter Gammons, now with *Sports Illustrated,* offered another interesting view. Gammons noted that aerial research indicated that the left-field fence was only 304 feet from home plate, just 380 to dead center. In recent seasons through 1985, said Gammons, left-handed hitters had hit the green monster in left more than right-handed hitters. He mentioned Mike Easler, Wade Boggs, Rich Gedman, and Bill Buckner.

"Too many right-handed hitters hit with arms extended so far from the body," said Gammons, "that they prefer the ball away from them. If they're pitched up and in, tight strikes inside, they can't pull the ball effectively."

Super-hitter Ted Williams, an authority on Fenway Park and just about every other stadium, good or bad, recalled ruefully that for a .344 hitter who had hit 521 home runs, he had hit only *four* home runs to the left side of the flag pole in center field. "But," he said, "late in my career when I didn't pull quite so much, I did hit home runs into the center-field stands."

When Williams hit a fabulous .388 at nearly age 39 in 1957, he broke up the severe right-side infield shift against him by swinging a heavier bat in the spring, choking the grip, and grounding hits through the vacated shortstop position. "Suddenly," he recalled triumphantly, "I faced a normal defensive alignment."

That is, they played the defense wide enough, but not high enough for Williams, who was what the Fenway faithful had awaited ever since Boston's loss of its brightest star, Babe Ruth. Although the ball wasn't nearly so lively in the Babe's day or even Williams', the physical-and-psychological impact was lost on the happy Baltimore industrial-school refugee who didn't know what it meant to be nervous. As a left-handed hitter, just beginning to zero in on outfield fences, the Babe was a left-handed pitcher who had a five-plus season of 89–44 in Boston, 1914–1919. He won three World Series games in three tries. Then he hit an eye-arresting 29 homers in 130 games in 1919, winning nine of 14 games. Suddenly, he was gone.

Once the Babe was sold to the Yankees and transferred to the outfield full time, not only did he hit more than 50 homers four times, including 60 in 1927, but he also *averaged* 46 a season over a 14-year period. True, even though he missed the equivalent of a full season (153) games with everything from a stomach abscess to suspension as a Peck's Bad Boy grownup.

For most of his career, Ruth was favored by short-porch fences at foul lines, including the two home parks in his New York career, the Polo Grounds and Yankee Stadium. Even so, one wonders what his career total of homers (714) might have been if he had spent his seasons in, say, Sportsman's Park, Tiger Stadium, or Cleveland's League Park. Probably better than his career rate, a home run every 11.6 official times at bat.

Until flamboyant Bill Veeck moved the Indians full time into Cleveland's huge stadium on the shore of Lake Erie in 1946, the Indians played full schedules for years at a stadium built in 1891 by a new owner, Frank DeHaas Robison, who held a streetcar franchise there. For Robison's financial benefit and customers' convenience, the ball park at Lexington Avenue and East 66th Street crisscrossed two of Robison's trolley lines.

Robison and his brother, Stanley Matthew Robison, can't be remembered fondly by anyone in Cleveland. The Cleveland Spiders were in the National League as the brothers Robby bought the St. Louis franchise and, disenchanted with their attendance at Cleveland, swapped complete franchises.

The Robisons' Cleveland park, named League Park and then Dunn Field until new owner James Dunn died in 1927, was a tidy place with a left field that was too long (376 feet) and a right field that was too short (290), even though a screen topped homer heights by 40 feet in right. How much effect could the chummy batting situation have had on, say, Earl Averill, a little left-handed-hitting outfielder? Averill batted .318 for 13 years, 1929–41, the first 12 at Cleveland.

When the Indians moved to Municipal Stadium for all games in the 1933 season, Averill dropped from two successive 32-homer seasons and 143 runs-batted-in and then 124. He hit only 11 homers and batted in 92 in the lakefront stadium, where the distances at the outset were 320 down the foul lines, 463 in the power alleys, and a whopping 470 to dead center. A year later, as the Tribe went back to League Park except for Sundays and holidays, Averill's homers went back up to 31 and his RBIs to 122.

Another heavy left-handed gunner at Cleveland was Hal Trosky, a first baseman, who teed off at the right-field screen at League Park from 1934 until he dropped out with severe migraine headaches in '42. Trosky returned briefly, yet he was only 32 when he finished with the Chicago White Sox in 1946. He had his biggest year in 1936, the year New York set a modern record with 1065 runs. Forty-one American League players in 10 or more games batted above .300. Cleveland, finishing fifth, led with .304. Trosky batted .343, hit 42 homers, and drove in a league-leading 162 runs.

You don't have to be an iconoclast to wonder about park dimensions' effects on records. For instance, even the great Tris Speaker stroked many of his doubles off the screen at League Park. Four of Speaker's five seasons of 50 or more doubles came at Cleveland, including 59 in 1923 when he was 35 years old and 52 his last season with the Indians, 1926, when he was 36 and batting .304, a figure 40 points below his career average. The Gray Eagle's record for doubles was 793.

The single-season high of 67 came off the bat of a rather undistinguished player, Earl Webb, a Red Sox outfielder who played for five clubs in seven major league seasons. Webb's 67 doubles in 1931 were 43 percent of his extra-base hits. That season with the Red Sox, the left-handed-hitting Webb took advantage of Fenway Park dimensions when, totaling only 14 homers, he batted .333 with 103 RBIs. A longtime *Boston Globe* baseball writer, Harold Kaese, remembered that, record conscious down the season's stretch, Webb slowed some potential late-season triples into doubles. Or is "slowed" the proper antithesis of "stretched?"

Ted Williams, stretching no imagination as one of the greatest hitters ever, never hit more doubles than in his rookie season at age 20. He had 44 in 1939 and even though, as mentioned, Fenway Park was not built for homer hitting by left-handed batters who were pull hitters, Williams homered 31 times. Only 14 were delivered at the Fens.

So a bullpen was set up extending from the foul line to deep right-center, cutting down the home run distance, but it had no positive effect for Williams, whose homers dropped to 23 as a big league sophomore. But Teddy Ballgame, who mixed torrid sinking line drives for singles with his big blasts, doubtless would have homered more than 43 times, his Red Sox maximum in 1949, (1) if he hadn't missed nearly five seasons in two wars and (2) if he had hit regularly in favorite parks, St. Louis's and Detroit's. Except for the 1946 World Series, when he batted with an injured elbow against crafty slow-curve pitching and Harry Brecheen's screwball, down and in to a left-handed hitter, Williams feasted in Sportsman's Park. He was equally torrid in Tiger Stadium, then Briggs Stadium.

Previously Bennett Park, named for a former Tiger catcher and hometown loyalist maimed in a railroad accident, seated only 8500 at Michigan and Trumbull, a magical Detroit location. There, Navin Park, Briggs Stadium and now Tiger Stadium have been rebuilt, enlarged, and changed drastically and dramatically to a ballplayer's ball park, double-decked with a good batting background and definitely reachable fences. As far back as 1938, a year Briggs double-decked the park completely around to achieve a capacity even more than the current 52,000-plus, the foul lines were moved in. Power hitter Hank Greenberg, reaching 58 homers, wasn't hurt at all, but then High Henry never was at a loss for expression, with or without a bat. Besides, the year before, Greenberg had knocked in 183 runs when homering 40 times.

You see, this real estate chapter really is not intended to debunk hitting statistics, but, rather, to explain now-and-then differences and, of course, the current realistic requirement that a ball club can't alter its outfield boundaries once a season begins.

The cat-and-mouse game was probably perpetrated at its amusing best by front office wag Bill Veeck at Cleveland. Veeck (as in Wreck) moved cyclone-style wire fences in and out daily depending on whether the muscular Yankees or pit-a-pat Browns were in town. That prompted the present standfast rule.

As far back as 1928, the Boston Braves sought to help hitters at a National League ball park, built in 1915 just in time to let the rival Red Sox have a larger World Series site. Braves Field had ridiculously long distances to the fences at the start: 402 feet at the foul lines and 550 in center field. No wonder it took 10 years before the New York Giants' Frank (Pancho) Snyder, never noted as a power hitter, whomped the first ball over the left-field fence.

Over the years Braves Field, a single-deck stadium, was noted for (1) construction that permitted streetcars and subway trains to loop inside its outer walls, (2) having just too damned many so-called "pavilion" seats, roofless and backless seats that stretched high-and-far in the wings fore and aft of the grandstand, (3) a tight, cute 2000-seat right-field bleachers called the Jury Box, and (4) a brisk wind that blew in off the Charles River, which flowed directly behind the out-field fences.

When Casey Stengel managed the Braves from the late '30s into the early '40s, a hitter complaining about the wind would get a chilling, sarcastic response from the Old Perfesser. "Y-a-s," he would say, dragging out the affirmative characteristically, "it *is* a shame. Mr. Hornsby played here one season (1928) and he hit *only* .387."

True, but early that year The Rajah did benefit some from an over-dose of fence maneuvering by Boston management. Bleachers were placed in the left-field fence to center, reducing the distance, left to center, to 353 feet and 387. As a result, Les Bell, the third baseman, hit three homers in one game and missed a fourth only because a ball struck a guy wire and fell short for an extra-base hit. The distances obviously didn't hurt Hornsby, acquired that season from New York to play and ultimately manage the Braves briefly, but The Rajah actually hit hardest to right-center. By mid-June the opposition was hit-ting the ball into the stands much more than Hornsby or any other Brave. The temporary stands came down.

Later, a wall-within-the-wall created more realistic distances for raw-boned Wally Berger, whose 38 homers as a rookie in 1930 were un-matched until Cincinnati's Frank Robinson equalled that high as a freshman in 1956 and Oakland's Mark McGwire bombed 49 in '87. Just before the Braves pulled up their tepees in 1953 for the nomadic move to Atlanta by way of Milwaukee, a 20-year-old third baseman named Eddie Mathews put in his first cuts toward a career 512 homers. In 1952 Mathews hit 25 at Braves Field, measured, left to right, at 337 feet, 390 and 320.

Crosley, where F. Robby first romped to a Most Valuable Player Award before winning a similar distinction in the American League, was a ball park that had more ups and downs than the aggressive outfielder's 586 home runs. The park, first Redland Field, was cozy for the customers, but, originally, too long from the plate at the foul lines. Among the many physical changes in the park of a city famous in baseball as the cradle of the first professional team, 1869, and of the majors' first night game, the most significant was in shortening the distance to the left-field barrier.

Cincinnati's Crosley Field, renamed for sportsman Powell Crosley, reduced the distance to the left-field fence to 328 feet in 1938, a year after heavy rains in which backwaters of the Ohio River flooded the park. A remarkable photo shows two Reds' pitchers (Lee Grissom and Gene Schott) rowing across the center-field fence. Left field had an annoying incline. Right field varied from 366 feet down the line to

342, depending on whether management of the moment put up or took down the "Goat Run," a screened-off bullpen area.

Over the years more than one right-handed hitter hunkered up and hit one across the street atop a laundry company's one-story plant beyond the left-field fence. Incongruously, a ball hitting the towering scoreboard on the edge of the field in left-center was in play, at a height considerably higher than the wall. The weakness of Crosley in the heavy power-hitting era of the 1950s was the short center field, only 387 feet from the plate.

If it's a rule of a baseball pitcher's thumb that to win, he must make the opposition hit the ball straight ahead, i.e., to the long field, center wasn't far enough away, not for hitters such as Robinson and Ted Kluszewski. But Klu, the genial first base slugger and former Indiana University football star, was a massive man whose arms were so big it looked as if he could have backhanded a ball out of there without a bat.

The Reds had a masterful groundskeeper, Matty Schwab, who, like a latterday George Toma at Kansas City, had a reputation for soft, lush grass and a dirt infield he manicured perfectly. When Bill McKechnie won successive pennants in 1939 and '40 with back-to-back 20-game pitching twins, low ball artists Bucky Walters and Paul Derringer, Schwab trimmed the grass just the way the manager wanted it—high enough to slow down enemy ground balls.

Just before the Cincinnati club moved down by the O-hi-o in mid-season, 1970, taking over Riverfront Stadium, a feisty, rusty-haired fella watched Henry Aaron reach the magic 3000-hit plateau at Crosley Field. Seven years earlier, the kid had played second base the day Stan Musial got his last two of 3630 hits, one to each side of him. Pete Rose already was seeing himself in the same class company, en route to topping Ty Cobb's astonishing 4191 hits.

At Riverfront Stadium, almost twice the size of Crosley Field in seating capacity, Cincy's Big Red Machine and the delightful stadium had a happy coincidental date with destiny in 1970. Rose led the hit parade. Johnny Bench performed like a Hall of Fame catcher, and a walk-wheedling second baseman, Joe Morgan, showed surprising power, too. The Reds took four pennants and two World Championships in the decade. Six times the city with the smallest metropolitan capacity drew more than 2,000,000 spectators.

For a fact, at least temporarily, the Reds played as if they were . . . well, the Yankees, the symbol of perennial power and success. If it hadn't been for sheer jealousy by John McGraw, envious that magnetic Babe Ruth and window-breaking buddies could outdraw his Giants, four straight pennant winners, 1921–24, it's a wonder whether Yankee Stadium would have been built.

As tenants at the Polo Grounds, a great target for a home run hitter able to hook fly balls and line drives around the fair side of the foul pole, the Yankees' owners were overjoyed when the Babe electrified the boroughs locally and baseball nationally. First, in 1920, he raised his own home run record of 29 as a Boston outfielder-pitcher to a startling 54. Next season, as the Yanks won their first pennant, the Babe hit 59.

Sure, the ball was livelier and others were hitting for higher averages and occasionally a Ken Williams or a Cy Williams or a Hornsby would hit homers in impressive numbers; but, always, it was the Babe.

For the Yanks' first 10 years in New York when they were known then as the Highlanders, they played at Hilltop Park, which seated only about 15,000 at a location on Broadway between 165th Street and 168th. When fire temporarily forced the Giants out and into the re-built Polo Grounds, Yankee owners invited their intra-city rivals to share their park.

So the Giants reciprocated in 1913, giving the newly christened Yankees a park eminently satisfactory in size and shape. The two colonels, Jacob Ruppert, the brewer, and Tillinghast Huston, might have been happy to stay put at the Polo Grounds, particularly when they acquired Ruth. Immediately, the Babe's bat beat the Giants' baserunning, even before Ruth and other Red Sox acquisitions set up the first Subway Series in 1921. In '20 when the Yankees became the first club to draw a million, drawing 1,289,422 or 350,000 more than the Giants, McGraw told clubowner Charles Stoneham to evict the prosperous tenant.

Said McGraw, "The Yankees will have to build a park in Queens or some other place out of the way and wither on the vine." Ruppert and Huston squirted cider in Mac's ear. They had paid $460,000 for the Yankees in 1915. They spent $600,000 for a 10-acre plot across the Harlem River, less than a mile from the Polo Grounds. Within a year, a triple-decked, reinforced-concrete and steel grandstand was built. Aptly, sportswriter Frederick G. Lieb called it "The House That Ruth Built." John Philip Sousa's Seventh Regiment band led the opening day procession to center field for the flag-raising.

At the Polo Grounds, the Yanks played and lost two World Series to the Giants, but in 1923, the year the Stadium opened, they tripped McGraw's men. The Yankees went on to win 22 championships. They knew how to take care of their home diamond, too, meaning, naturally, the Babe, *their* Hope Diamond.

They made the right-field corner just 296 feet from home plate and with a low wall, permitting a good pull hitter to have an inviting target, as Ruth proved, as well as Lou Gehrig and, later, Yogi Berra, Mickey Mantle, Roger Maris, Reggie Jackson, and Don Mattingly.

The distance down the left-field line was close, too, only 301 feet, but the fence fell away considerably sharper in left. The power alley, where little Al Gionfriddo motorcycled to take away a likely homer from Joe DiMaggio in the 1947 Series, was 405 feet from home plate. Center field behind the outfield monuments to Ruth, Gehrig, and Miller Huggins also was too far at 461.

When the Yankees, who had built the original park privately, convinced the city that the park needed replacement, the new Yankee Stadium in 1976 closely resembled the catywompus old park, including the same escalloped third-deck ornamental bric-a-brac. (Mantle once hit that towering facade deck, 109 feet above the field, 374 feet from the plate, presumably a 620-foot smash. Reportedly, black league star Josh Gibson hit one out of Yankee Stadium.) The seating capacity was trimmed to 57,545 and the foul lines were much more equitable in distance—310 in right, 312 in left, 430 in center. The left-field power alley was shortened in 1988. Center, too.

Still, how many more home runs would DiMaggio have hit—he had 361 in 13 fragmented seasons and missed three more in service—if he had faced a more reasonable power ally? Or Mantle, when the Switcher batted right-handed? Partly, because of a gimpy right (front) knee when he batted left-handed, he had more power right-handed and also hit for higher average. Mantle hit 536 homers, twice clearing 50.

Mickey's high, 54 homers, came the year teammate Maris hit 61, a figure asterisked controversially by Ford Frick, then commissioner. The point was, Maris had eight games more than the Babe, but probably more meaningful was the presence of watered-down pitching, a result that year of the American League's expansion from the traditional eight teams to 10. When the National League, a year later (1962) also went to 10 clubs, Stan Musial hit .330 when near 42 years old. Stan the Honest Man's observation was that he had benefited from the presence of some pitchers who otherwise would not have been in the majors.

For one who played in a left-handed hitter's apple orchard, as press box poets used to put it, Musial did not appear to benefit greatly by St. Louis's Sportsman's Park or, putting it another way, perhaps The Man Stan just didn't want to try to pull too many pitches, fearful he would lose his ability to line the ball to all fields. Typically, after a series at the Polo Grounds, he would lament that he had lost his proper batting stride in an effort to take advantage of the closest right-field fence.

When he hit his fourth straight homer at New York in 1962, he recalled his amusement and the amazement of New York Mets' left-handed Willard Hunter. Musial had homered pinch-hitting the day before and was seeking his third of the day when Hunter pitched to him. Musial promptly curved a pitch around the pole in right field for HR No. 3.

"The pitch was about a foot inside," Musial said in probable exaggeration. "I guess Hunter was trying to brush me back, but I never took an inside pitch at the Polo Grounds, figuring that the worst I could do would be to hook the ball foul or now and then, like this time, keep it fair. But I can't get over the look on the kid's face (Hunter's) as I circled the bases."

For another who presumably resisted home-field temptation to retain his career perspective, the Giants' big first baseman, Bill Terry, fought off John McGraw's blandishments. As a result, a left-handed hitter who batted with feet close together and stroked his hottest line drives to left-center, Terry averaged .341 for 13-plus seasons, tying Lefty O'Doul's record for hits, 254, in his .401 season in 1930. Terry had power, but his home run tops was 23 in '30.

Musial, standing deep in the batter's box, crouched like a cat about to spring, was favored by a St. Louis right-field fence of only 310 feet at the foul lines, screened to a height of 40 feet from there to the 354-foot power alley in right-center. The other distances at St. Louis were 405 in farthest right center, 424 straight away, 426 at the left-center field break into dead center. Left field was 351 at the line, 378 in left-center.

Despite the home-field advantage to a left-handed hitter, though demonstrating further that old-fashioned rectangular ball parks generally favored them, Musial had only a 10-point career edge at home, .336 to .326. His 475 homers were almost evenly divided, 252 in St. Louis to 223 on foreign fields. The swift player had 62 doubles more at home in 10,976 official times at bat in 21-plus seasons, again hardly startling.

More unusually, his triples were virtually the same—90 at home, 87 away—and in a rare tribute to a player's consistency, Musial had *exactly* the same number of hits in his Redbird whites and road grays: 1815! And if at Sportsman's Park he had achieved in 1948 a home season equal to 1946 and 1950, when he batted .370 each, or 1953, a year he hit .382 at home, he would have had a .400 season. The .331 career hitter batted .415 on the road in 1948 and hit 22 of his 39 home runs in away games.

Explaining factors in pulling the ball, Musial said he learned to become more selective over the years and, like the incomparable Williams, troubled by emergence of a slider as an effective pitch, Stan inched away from the plate in 1957, trying to avoid having a right-hander's slider dart in toward his fists. That year he won his seventh and final batting title, with .351.

As to vaulting into power when he climbed from 19 to 39 homers after five seasons in the majors, Musial explained, "After undergoing an appendectomy following the '47 season, I felt stronger and instead of choking my batting grip just a bit, I went down to the knob with my swing in '48 and thereafter."

Except, that is, when Musial suffered a hairline shoulder fracture in 1957, a year the Cardinals finished second to Milwaukee. Hurt with a savage swing, trying to protect a runner on a hit-and-run play, Musial was expected to miss the last several weeks of the season. Instead, he insisted that he could return within a couple of weeks, playing first base with a minimum of difficult throwing. At bat, he merely stroked the ball, widening his batting lead. When Henry Aaron's home run clinched the pennant for Milwaukee in late September, manager Fred Hutchinson told Musial, "Take the last week off, Stan, so I can look at some kids. Hell, they couldn't catch you if it took all winter."

Point is, the question of a batter's intentions at the plate as well as ball park real estate probably should be explored more, but how? In Musial's case, for instance, finishing the '57 season just 43 hits short of 3000 and aware through his injury of man's fragility and the caprices of nature, Stan began the 1958 season the way he had ended '57.

Just meeting the ball rather than mashing it, Musial got those 43 hits in only 22 games. "I guess," he said, grinning, "I was afraid I might get hit in the can by a cab." His average on May 13 was .483. Tailing off at nearly 38, he finished with .337 and his fewest homers (17) in 11 years. He had experienced a letdown, he acknowledged, and probably became tired, too, "but for the good of the club, I'd also swung harder and tried to pull the ball more (after Hit No. 3000)."

What was it Babe Ruth once said when asked if he could hit .400? The Babe, whose individual high was .393 in 1923, scoffed when asked if he felt he could reach .400. "Hell, kid," he roared, "bunting now and then or going to left field more often, I could hit .500!"

If Ted Williams had gone to left field more often also, especially in Fenway Park, where he estimated he hit the chummy wall only several times, gosh knows what he might have hit. Even more than a severe shift to the right side used by the National League against rangy Fred (Cy) Williams, a Phillies' pull-hitting slugger of the '20s, the American League shifted against Teddy Ballgame after, physically, he no longer was the Splendid Splinter. The St. Louis Cardinals adopted and improvised Cleveland manager Lou Boudreau's shift in the 1946

World Series, swinging all infielders to the right of second base except shortstop Marty Marion. Finally, frustrated, Williams bunted safely toward third base in one Series game at Fenway Park. Afternoon newspapers in Boston signalled the unexpected with 72-point type headlines, customarily used in catastrophic situations. The stark head shrieked: "TED BUNTS!"

A versatile hitter who needed no introduction to any part of a playing field took advantage of Sportsman's Park more than Musial, even though Rogers Hornsby hit right-handed. Standing extremely deep in the batter's box and away from the plate, Hornsby strode directly toward the plate and, in effect, right-center. As a result, The Rajah could tattoo the right-field area even before improvements in 1925.

Yet, Hornsby could pull with power even though Robison Field, where the Cardinals played until mid-season, 1920, had left-field distances so deep that it wasn't until September 1919, as reported by Dent McSkimming of the *St. Louis Post-Dispatch,* that Rog became the first batter ever to hit a ball over the fence.

Robison Field was built at Natural Bridge and Vandeventer by Henry Lucas as part of a one-year experience (1884) with the Maroons of the short-lived Union Association. The Maroons couldn't compete with the Browns, Charley Comiskey's four-time American Association Browns. The Browns were operated by a colorful saloon keeper—"Der Poss Bresident"—as Chris Von der Ahe called himself.

At Grand and Dodier, still a playing-field area for underprivileged kids as a result of a gift from August A. Busch, Jr. and the brewery that owns the current Cardinals, Von der Ahe inherited an area on which baseball had been played since the Civil War. St. Louis played at the first kindling Sportsman's Park in the National League's charter season, 1876. Sportsman's Park, improved by Von der Ahe, drew its first concrete and steel center section from Robert Lee Hedges after the 1908 season.

By 1920, after the death of the Robisons and sale of the ball club in 1917 to Helene Hathaway Robison Britton, the St. Louis National Ball Club was called the Cardinals, though the team was as drab as sparrows and the playing field, to quote an eminent old movie philosopher, Charlie Chan, as "empty as a robin's nest in January."

When a consortium of hometown men reluctantly kicked in $300,000 in 1916 to "Lady Bee," as the press referred to the woman who brought petticoat rule to St. Louis baseball, suddenly one man awakened to find that in his enthusiasm he had spent $2500 he didn't want to lose. Sam Breadon, a one-time New York kid who skinny-dipped in the East River, had gravitated to St. Louis as a proud grease monkey and automobile salesman. He became president of the Redbirds. He also lured law graduate Branch Rickey, a brief big leaguer who had coached baseball at the University of Michigan, to move over from the rival Browns.

Rickey became field manager and business manager with a novel notion. So that the rags could live with the riches, B. R. wanted to develop his own talent, aware that whenever a big league ball club scouted a young player and farmed him out for seasoning, the independent minor league operator often sold the developed player to a higher bidder.

Breadon, fast-talking the Browns as glibly as he might sell one of his sleek Pierce-Arrow autos, convinced Philip deCatesby Ball to let the Cardinals become Ball's tenants at Sportsman's Park. Sale of Robison Field, then rechristened League Park, and adjoining real estate for a public high school and a streetcar turntable, brought the Cardinals to Grand and Dodier in mid-season, 1920. It brought, also, $300,000 used more sagaciously than any windfall in baseball history.

With it, buying first a piece of the Houston, Texas League team and then the Ft. Smith, Arkansas, club in the Western Association, Rickey began the extensive farm system that paid off dramatically. Derisively labeled the "baseball chain gang," it brought St. Louis its first National League pennant in six years, then nine league titles and six World Championships over 20 seasons.

Hornsby, a hitting hero with a .400 *average* for a five-season stretch, managed the first title team in 1926, then was dealt away, controversially and yet successfully, winding up later as the linchpin to the Chicago Cubs' success in 1929.

Of the players The Rajah left behind, graduates of "the subsidiaries," as the nimble-tongued Rickey liked to call farm clubs, were young players who profited from the screenless right-field wall. Ball, having operated the St. Louis Feds of the Federal League the two years of the three-league war, had been allowed to buy the American League Browns and Sportsman's Park. He virtually doubled the 18,000-seat park in '25, just in time for the Cardinals to cash in as he thought his Browns would.

Replacing a chicken-wired outfield screen, fronting bleachers from foul line to foul line, was a concrete grandstand wall that gave a rebound effect, like the jai-alai rebote off marble. The 10-foot unyielding concrete wall, fronting the bleachers in left field and the roofed pavilion in right, claimed more than one outfielder's skull or knee or shoulder. And before Ball hiked up the right-field screen, mentioned at the outset of the chapter in relationship to Jimmy Foxx's unfortunate failure in pursuit of Babe Ruth's single-season record, the wall also took its toll.

The best example of the difference between 10 feet home run height and 40 likely was in the diminishing four-base output of Sunny Jim Bottomley, a swaggering St. Louis first baseman. Bottomley hit a league-tying 31 homers in 1928, a year he was the NL's MVP. He also had 29 in '29, but when the screen was put up before mid-season, 1930, his total dropped to 15. Even a year later when Bottomley lost the batting championship by only a fraction of a point to roommate Chick Hafey at .349, his homers dipped to nine.

By contrast, however, the record for St. Louis clubs, past and present, was set *after* the screen by Johnny Mize, who led the National League in 1940 with 43 home runs. The Big Cat, four times the league's home run leader, hit as many as 51 with the New York Giants at the Polo Grounds in 1947. Mize, like Ted Williams, a sharp-eyed hitter who merely leaned back from high-and-tight pitches without moving his feet, was described early by an admiring Casey Stengel as "slugger who hits like a leadoff man." For Ol' Case's victorious Yankees in 1950, Mize was a money-in-the-bank investment, hitting 25 homers in just 90 games or 274 times at bat, a homer every 10.9 swings. What if Mize had played his entire career at the Polo Grounds and/or Yankee Stadium?

By the time the Cardinals left Sportsman's Park for Busch Stadium in downtown St. Louis, mid-May 1966, the symmetrical contours and the below-ground-level construction of the playing field dictated that home runs would be difficult. Obviously, too, so did the distances to the fences, 330 at the foul lines curving back rapidly to 385 feet in the power lanes and 414 straight away.

Not even a 10-foot reduction with a lower, phoney inner fence in 1973 was satisfactory. No significant difference was noted. Also, with artificial turf, too many potentially exciting balls in play bounced into the bleachers for automatic and dull doubles. So the experiment was shortlived.

As a result, 20 years beyond Busch Stadium's opening, a product largely of private capital as used at Yankee Stadium and Dodger Stadium, the park has produced an assortment of two-legged jack rabbits, the speed-and-burn base stealing and defensive emphasis of manager Whitey Herzog. The place has known just two hitters able to bring Busch Stadium to its knees. In one season there, 1970, Richie Allen—before he rechristened himself "Dick"—hit 34 homers as a Redbird. And he did it in 122 games, sitting out September with a pulled hamstring. Jack Clark hit 35 in 131 games in '87.

Allen showed his power in 1972 later at Chicago's Comiskey Park, where he hit 37 homers and also a league-leading 113 RBIs, winning a Most Valuable Player prize. He had another robust home run season there, 32 in 1974, as the White Sox sought to capture the long ball glamour of the club's most capacious, more colorful North Side neighbor, Wrigley Field.

Over the years, as mentioned, the landmark parks have about them a nostalgia that grips the old man and a curious character that intrigues the young. Even if, yes, they've been face-lifted and enlarged as much as Detroit's Tiger Stadium or both Boston's Fenway Park and Comiskey's white-painted, scoreboard-dominated athletic arena. None, though, catches the fancy as much as the brick-walled, ivy-covered park at Chicago at Clark and Addison Streets, Wrigley Field.

Oddly, Wrigley Field was built first for Federal League play in 1915 by Charley Weeghman, a Chicago cafeteria king. When a judge sympathetic to the two-league balance of the National and American, Kenesaw Mountain Landis, dragged his feet in a pending lawsuit by the Feds, the "third" league threw in the towel. But it was only a technical knockout.

Of the Federal League that had been seeking a ruling challenging the sanctity of so-called "baseball territory," the legality of the restrictive reserve clause and the harsh 10-day release clause by which baseball could give the back of its proprietary hand to players insufficiently servile, there were some demands reluctantly met by the existing majors. They paid off oil king Harry Sinclair for a wooden-plank park at Newark, New Jersey, happy he wouldn't try to give the New York borough a *fourth* big league club. They paid off in Pittsburgh, too.

As for the ice-and-coal curmudgeon in St. Louis, Phil Ball, they permitted him to buy the Browns and Sportsman's Park. In Chicago, they arranged for Weeghman to buy the Cubs and to move them to his park. Weeghman called it Cubs' Park, but when William Wrigley of the chicle-and-chew company bought the club in the early Roaring Twenties, Wrigley renamed the park and with good reason. The Wrigleys double-decked the park, enlarged it, and then reduced seating as Phil Wrigley, taking over after his father's death, sought to make the park a comfortable playground for his customers.

At the present, seating only 36,755 and owned now by the *Chicago Tribune,* a vast newspaper holding company, Wrigley Field has the largest old-fashioned, hand-operated scoreboard. From a flagpole flaps a daily win-or-lose sign for late-afternoon viewers—blue with a white "W" if the Cubs win, white with a blue "L" if they lose.

Indeed it flaps because Chicago wasn't called the Windy City because of gabby politicians or the hot air off the guns in the hoodlums' Prohibition heyday. With the wind blowing out, you don't have to be an Ernie Banks to take advantage of the currents of the "friendly confines," to catch the jet stream for a home run to left field. If the wind is blowing in off Lake Michigan, h'mm, even Banks or Hack Wilson or Rogers Hornsby or Andre Dawson might have trouble cleaving the climatological opponent.

By the time Bill Veeck, Sr. obtained Rogers Hornsby from underprivileged Boston for five players and $200,000, the 1929 Cubs and Chicago were drooling for a winner. The Toddlin' Town turned out a record 1,400,000-plus to watch Hornsby hit .380 with 39 homers, 155 runs and 149 RBIs. The Rajah was the National League's MVP.

Matching swings with Hornsby then, however, and actually improving on the perennial batting champion's output, was a sawed off right-handed slugger, built like a fireplug. Hack Wilson, who ballooned over only a 5-6 frame, hit 39 homers and drove in a league-leading 159 runs in a .345 season.

In 1930 Hack was probably the most destructive hitter, a result of 56 homers, still a National League high, and 190 RBIs, the uncontested major league record. Ask modern major leaguers how they relate to individual-season peaks — Hornsby's .424 average, George Sisler's 257 hits, Earl Webb's 67 doubles, Chief Wilson's 36 triples, Roger Maris's 61 homers and even Joe DiMaggio's 56-game winning streak — and they exclaim the most over Wilson's 190 RBIs the year he hit .356.

Maybe it's because in a time of lower averages and bigger parks — except for, say, George Brett's .390 in 1980, George Foster's 52 homers in 1977, and Wade Boggs's 240 hits in 1985 — they can only be in awe of Wilson's RBIs. When 100 runs-batted-in still is a target of achievement, a figure almost double that amount would double a Cub fan's pleasure as much as Banks did.

Hitting 512 homers, a high for a player who began his big league career as a shortstop, Banks was twice MVP with a losing ball club, 1958–59, and a sunny, personal joy. Mr. Cub, they called him, as he chirped, "Welcome to the friendly confines. It's a lovely day. Let's play two. . . . "

The team's success was far less, but the clubhouse cheer, too, compared with the end of the Roaring Twenties when the Cubs established a happy rhythm of pennants every three years — 1929, '32, '35, and '38. They won even though Hornsby and Wilson were long gone. The Rajah's problem was a broken leg and inability to handle men, from many of whom the inveterate horse player borrowed money. Wilson's argument was that Hornsby "took the bat out of my hands," a baseball bromide based on a sign from the bench not to swing at a 2-and-0, 3-and-0, or 3-and-1 pitch. Truth is, a heavy drinker, Wilson could have been caught up by rot-gut gin or, as suggested elsewhere in this book by former catcher Al Lopez, by a slight decrease in the 1931 resilience of the ball.

Wilson's best shots were from left-center to right-center in a park that was 355–400–353 down the lines, but, with bleachers bellying out, a target for power hitters in the power lanes. In 1930, Hack hit .381 at home, .324 on the road. Of his 190 RBIs, 115 were knocked in at Wrigley Field.

Past the mid-1980s even with the caprice of Jack Frost blowing in on cool days or Ma Nature swishing her skirts toward Waveland and Sheffield outfield avenues on warm days, Chicago remains the National League's No. 1 homer hitter's park.

The most publicized homer at Wrigley Field undoubtedly was Babe Ruth's alleged "called shot" in the 1932 World Series. Strongest indication is that, in rebuttal for his riding the Cubs for cutting manager Hornsby out of World Series money when he was fired in August and for giving Babe's old Yankee teammate Mark Koenig only a part share after he played spectacularly down the stretch, Ruth was heckled heavily by the "cheapskates." The Babe presumably pointed that he had one swing left, rather than to the spot where he would hit it, before he homered off Charley Root. But, hell, why spoil a good story?

Even better, truly, was the drama of the 1938 pennant race when the Cubs rallied to win under Gabby Hartnett almost as spectacularly as when Jolly Cholly Grimm's 1935 Cubs caught St. Louis's Gas House Gang with a 21-game winning streak in September. The '38 Cubs, overtaking Pittsburgh, were only a half-game behind in the ninth inning of a 5–5 tie. The game was about to be called because of darkness. With two strikes, two down, manager Hartnett hit a September shot, aptly labeled "the homer in the gloamin'!"

"I couldn't see it, but I could feel it," recalled Hartnett. "I knew it was gone. Blood rushed to my head and I felt dizzy."

The dramatic shot that helped Hartnett toward the Baseball Hall of Fame must have made a little 70-year-old man wince back there in both men's home area, New England. Years earlier (1921), Jesse Burkett, three times a .400 hitter in the gaslight era of the 1890s, was a baseball coach at Holy Cross. John McGraw asked him to appraise a kid catcher for a wire company team close to "Crab" Burkett's home in Worcester, Massachusetts. The old Crab watched young Tomato Face and wired McGraw: "HARTNETT WILL NEVER BE BIG LEAGUE CATCHER. HIS HANDS ARE TOO SMALL."

6
Westward Ho!

Except for Yankee Stadium, built only because the landlord Giants told Babe Ruth and buddies to haul their pinstriped bottoms out of the Polo Grounds, no new big league ball park was built until a half-century freeze in franchise motion was ready to thaw.

Almost overnight then, expansion followed. Westward ho, the wagons, as frontier pioneers used to say in the gutty trek of the prairie schooners. It was an exciting development by which the majors went from regional to national, from the Atlantic to the Pacific rather than barely to the Mississippi.

Wouldn't you believe it, Bill Veeck, who certainly would have been a wagon master if he had been born a little earlier, was front and center in the baseball thaw. Veeck was the maverick, the hair shirt among stuffed shirts; the man who brought the midget into the majors; the rough-hewn intellectual; a promoter whose ball park surprise packages tried to make every day or night at the ball park fun, win or lose.

Veeck, who crammed 2,600,000 into Cleveland nearly 40 years ago when 1,000,000 was a lot, was a man of courage, character, and humor as he proved shortly before his death in 1986. He regretted sleep because he might miss something. "I now have a lung and an eighth, a leg and a quarter, 40 percent of my hearing and one legal eye. I figure I've given the rest of the world as much of an edge as I'm going to give."

He gave it imagination and movement, too, with the help of Milwaukee, which gambled and won. Milwaukee, scene of the last big league shift to St. Louis (1902), broke the geographical ice and a half-century of frozen franchises. Who knows, really, how soon Veeck felt the Browns might have to be the Brewers again? The burghers of Sudsville, USA, showed their civic gumption at the outset of the 1950s by building a 35,000-seat stadium (later increased to 53,000) even before they had a major league team to play in it. County Stadium beckoned to hitters with a reasonable target for home run hitters — 320, 402, and 315 — but, above all, Milwaukee's efforts to reverse 1902 caught front office eyes, especially Veeck's.

Perhaps, egotistically, as he suggested, Veeck thought he could coax, cajole, needle, and rattle real estate operator Fred Saigh out of St. Louis with Saigh's Cardinals, coveted by Houston and Milwaukee, to name two. Anheuser Busch's purchase of the Redbirds from Saigh, convicted of income tax evasion, furrowed Veeck's corrugated forehead in February 1953.

Saigh and Robert E. Hannegan, a prominent Democratic political figure close to Sam Breadon, had bought the ball club from the ailing Breadon in November 1947, inheriting cash-drawer riches, most presumably earmarked for a new stadium. A year later, Saigh bought out Hannegan, who was ill. Then, heeding Commissioner Ford Frick's request to sell when he encounterd personal troubles, Saigh preferred the hometown brewery to potential out-of-town investors.

As Veeck related even before showing brisk August A. Busch, Jr. around rusty, rundown Sportsman's Park, for which Veeck had no money for repairs, the Browns' owner knew he was licked. So he quickly cast a covetous eye on Milwaukee, where he and Charley Grimm had operated a minor league club with fun and delight.

Trouble was, under baseball law, territorial rights to Milwaukee belonged to the Boston Braves, who had spiraled badly from crowds of 1,400,000 in a pennant-winning season of 1948 to only 280,000 in 1952. Lou Perini, a construction man who had gained control of the Braves, asked the National League to grant him permission to beat Veeck to Milwaukee. They did on March 18, 1953.

The tradition-shattering franchise switch was a rousing success from the time Bill Bruton's first and only home run of his rookie season tipped off a leaping Enos Slaughter's glove in the 10th inning, beating visiting braumeister Busch and his Redbirds in the opener, 3–2. As the young Braves romped home a robust third in '53, they drew a record 1,826,397.

Before that first season was over, a handsome, apple-cheeked third baseman, Eddie Mathews, only 21, celebrated his second season in the majors by hitting a league-leading 47 home runs. Thus began a home run punch that, for production if not reputation, surpassed Babe Ruth and Lou Gehrig: Mathews—and Henry Aaron.

Aaron came up to the Braves a year later, barely 20, and, though he would homer quickly off former Yankee standout Vic Raschi, then winding down with St. Louis, he showed little of the power production that would make him, if you please, the greatest hitter of home runs with 755.

But by the time the Braves won their first of two pennants in a World Championship season, 1957, Aaron's high was 45 in 1962. Hammerin' Hank and Home-Run Mathews were a peach of a slugging pair. Before a bad back began to take its toll on the third baseman in 1966 at Atlanta and he was dealt to Houston, Mathews and Aaron combined for 857. By the time they—and the Braves—packed up at Milwaukee and moved to Atlanta, Mathews had 477 homers, Aaron 396.

By then, of course, it appeared likely that Aaron would win the race between the two men, but not that the lithe, rawboned Aaron, who broke in playing for the black Indianapolis Clowns, would pound enough homers to break Babe Ruth's magical 714. At Milwaukee, for instance, Mathews led twice with 47 homers and also 46 (1956), but Aaron's high had been that aforementioned 45.

Over the bulk of 12 seasons at Milwaukee, Aaron had been a line drive hitter, gifted at hitting to all fields. He was a .325 hitter in round figures, a brilliant outfielder who played and ran with deceptive grace. But it just didn't seem to be in the cards for a 32-year-old player not only to play 11 more seasons, including two more back in Milwaukee as an American Leaguer, but also, actually, to improve his home run production. Hitters just don't improve with age—period.

With a bow to a new ball park, higher altitude, and his own strategic style change, plus a devotion to conditioning probably second only to Pete Rose's, Aaron got better as he got older. Even without the rarefied air that has made Fulton County (Atlanta) Stadium a home run hitter's park, the fence distances were encouraging—325 on the foul lines, 375 in the power alleys, and 402 in center field.

To aid Aaron further in his assault on Ruth's record and as a box office attraction, the left-field fence was moved closer to the plate. In the early '70s *after* Aaron broke Ruth's record on April 8, 1974, homering off Los Angeles's Al Downing before a national television audience, the power alleys were lengthened by 10 feet.

Aaron, who went back to Milwaukee to finish up with 755 homers, actually averaged 36.5 homers at Atlanta compared with a 33 average his first lengthy stay in Milwaukee. Seven times he hit 40 or more homers, reaching his peak with 47 at age 37 in 1971, a pivotal year in his assault on the home run heights. Four times, including three at Atlanta, he hit precisely his uniform number—"44."

As a hitter for average, Aaron declined to .305, not at all indicative of his batting prowess or consistency, but as he explained, "As a black man going into the South, I wanted to please the crowd. Left field was an attractive target, so I stopped going to right field, but relied on my quick wrists to pull the ball. No, I didn't hit for average any more, but. . . ."

But the statistics stand out, just as—in reverse—they stand out almost flukishly in the career of Davey Johnson, later manager of the New York Mets. Johnson played a fragmentary 13 seasons in the majors with a total of just 136 home runs, including an American League high of 18 with Baltimore in 1971. But in his first of two-plus seasons in Atlanta, the 30-year-old Johnson, a .261 career hitter, took advantage of the proximity of Chief Noc-a-Homa's tepee in left field. Davey hit 43 homers and —poof!—there went Rogers Hornsby's 51-year-old record for most single-season home runs by a second baseman. If you please, a tear! Long live the king or, at least, The Rajah!

The Braves' nomadic trip to Atlanta came by way of Milwaukee, more understandable as an exit from Boston, a two-team city, than from Milwaukee. The beer-and-bratwurst city had supported the team royally most of the time despite aloof absentee ownership. Milwaukee's spectacular box office success early prompted musical chairs with baseball franchises. Not since Sutter found gold in California in 1848 or the Oklahoma Territory was opened for a land rush in 1889 had there been anything like it.

The American League, too stuffed-shirted for a colorful, collarless character like Bill Veeck, refused to permit Veeck to move the Browns to Baltimore in 1953 after Perini and the National League blocked his plans to move to Milwaukee. A year later when the lame duck operator was *persona non grata* both in St. Louis' riverbank and at the financial banks, the AL approved sale of the Browns to Baltimore. So the Orioles, a storied name of the Naughty Nineties, returned to the majors.

Through heavy early spending for free agents, but largely through capable scouting, good managing, and good overall operation, Baltimore turned the bashful Browns into a winning franchise. Thirteen years after the franchise shift, the Orioles had their first World Championship and for a quarter-century thereafter owned the best won-and-lost record in baseball.

The Birds of an orange-and-black feather, kingpins in the International League for seven successive seasons through 1925, the era in which Lefty Grove was a major league star in the minors, played in myriad parks. Jack Dunn, the longtime operator who discovered that

Catholic reform-school big kid, the George Ruth they named "Babe," flourished after the Federal League's days in Terrapin Park. But Fourth of July pyrotechnics in 1944, unexpected and unappreciated, reduced rechristened Oriole Park to past tense.

Could the Orioles rise like the mythical Phoenix from its ashes? You can bet the best Maryland crabcakes they could. At hastily redesigned Memorial Stadium, a football layout, they crammed in 52,000 for a Junior World Series game with Louisville. As Lowell Reidenbaugh noted in *The Sporting News* book, *Take Me Out to the Ball Park,* the contrast with a 31,000 crowd for the Streetcar Series in St. Louis between the Cardinals and Browns that same year (1944) wasn't lost on the civic or monetary minded.

By 1950 Baltimore had opened a new facility—gee, why didn't they let it be officially Babe Ruth Park?—and with a return to the majors close at hand, city fathers double-decked newer Municipal Stadium in 1953. As the new major league Orioles, the old Browns played Baltimore's first big league game in 52 years at the Maryland metropolis's home opener in 1954.

Over the years of six division titles, five pennants, and two World Championships, most of them won under the stormy leadership of Earl Weaver, the Orioles flourished with topflight pitching. The pitching prevailed even though field dimensions remained relatively unchanged—309 at the lines and 410 to center field—and, in effect, Memorial Stadium was a hitter's park.

Actually, however, Frank Robinson, obtained from Cincinnati in a 1966 deal that took a superstar out of the National League, didn't need too much help for so many of his 586 home runs, 179 of which were struck in six seasons with the Orioles, and one completely out of the stadium enclosure. F. Robby was a Triple Crown winner as the American League's MVP his first year when he hit 49 homers, drove in 122 runs, and batted .316.

If a return of Baltimore to the bigs was popular and a reduction of two-team towns in Boston, St. Louis, and even Philadelphia was justifiable because of burgeoning Sun Belt cities crying out for a chance and older cities unable to support a pair of clubs, the situation in Philadelphia was unusual. Over the years the Athletics had brought much more baseball fame and glory to Philly—and venerable Connie Mack was more discussed and respected than even cussed—but the phutile Phillies, as the Nationals were called, had come a long way under a new owner, Robert R. M. Carpenter, Jr. An aggressive young guy who ran foot races with his first manager, Ben Chapman, Carpenter poured money into the Phillies. It was well spent. The Phillies'

Whiz Kids won a pennant in 1950, the club's first since Grover Cleveland Alexander was a young whiz in 1915.

Connie Mack, a former catcher turned manager and eventually part owner, was a founding father in the American League, building a ball club that won six pennants and three world titles the first 14 years of the AL. Even after four flags and three championships, 1910–14, he lacked funds to meet a winning team's payroll. So he sold some of his best players and languished in the lower latitudes until he came up with a ball club that finished first three times and took two championships, 1929–31. A similar sale of talent ensued.

So by the time he gave up the managerial scorecard with which he wig-wagged his defense, he had spent exactly 50 years as manager of the A's or, as they once were called, White Elephants. He was 88 years old when he finally stepped down and, having finished last 17 times, Mr. Mack proved that the only way to avoid being fired is to own the club you manage. In 1955, sadly, five seasons after he turned over his team to Jimmy Dykes as manager, Mr. Mack sold the Athletics to Kansas City. A year later, age 93, the spare, erect man with the kindly blue eyes and lifelong New England accent died.

Kansas City, living up to Oscar Hammerstein's lyrics in one of the rousing numbers from the musical *Oklahoma,* was trying to make certain everything was up to date, flexing its civic muscles along about the time Arnold Johnson and associates brought the Athletics to Kay-Cee in 1955. A Chicago canteen vendor, Johnson found that Muehlebach Field (renamed Ruppert Stadium), an old 17,500-seat park built on an ash heap at 22nd Street and Brooklyn Avenue in the early 1920s, could be double-decked. A record Kansas City crowd of 32,844 turned out for the 1955 opener.

The man from Independence, former President Harry S Truman, threw out the first ball, and legendary ol' Connie himself came out. Slugger Jimmy Foxx was there. It was a far cry from 10 years earlier, the war year of 1945, when, even managed by native son Casey Stengel, the American Association Blues drew only 38,000 for 77 home games.

Johnson paid $100,000 for the scoreboard from idle Braves Field, but as Kansas City poured out enthusiastically at the gate, Johnson took much more than he gave. The city paid him $500,000 for the improved ball park, and he siphoned off seasonal profits, proving in more than one deal that the A's were what they had been for years: That is, a subsidiary of the New York Yankees. Sent to New York was extremely popular Enos Slaughter, a hustler well-regarded when sister Missouri metropolis St. Louis was the westernmost major league franchise. Additionally, a kid with a blond crewcut was dealt to the Yankees — Roger Maris.

Whether Maris ever would have hit 61 home runs, which he did two years later in New York, is unlikely because, by any name, Municipal Stadium offered a formidable target for hitters, especially left-handed batters. Left field was a reasonable 330 feet, but right field was 354 at the line, and the power distance bowed out deeply to 422 in center. Still, as he evidenced with his playing field professionalism as a good fielder who threw well and ran well, Maris was a complete ballplayer. He was always a hidden asset, twice MVP in the AL.

Kansas City dwelled in the depths of the second division in Johnson's era, exhibiting stout box office support. Even when Johnson died unexpectedly early in 1960, leaving the question of the ball club in doubt, KayCee had a warm spot but it wasn't the gee-whiz, golly-ain't-you-great enthusiasm that greeted Johnson. New boss Charles O. Finley missed it. The Chicago insurance executive who bought the ball club for $2,000,000, proved to be an argumentative eccentric. Later niggardly, Finley spent money wisely and well. Facing a spend-it-or-give-it-to-the-government, Finley benefited also from a reverse-order draft in 1965. The draft gave losing ball clubs first crack at high-rank selection of college and high school graduates. Finley's farm system, headed by Hank Peters, later general manager at Baltimore, profited from good scouting and the owner's good timing.

Finley, a poor man's Bill Veeck as a promoter eager to please the fans, was thwarted in part, we believe, because he had not been greeted like Johnson, meaning as Ajax prancing into town on a white horse. As the club continued to lose despite his gimmicks and support dwindled, he became increasingly controversial, spiteful, almost as stubborn as the long-legged Missouri mule he shepherded into his ball park. Miffed at the league for its insistence that he sign a four-year lease agreement in 1964 when he began to flirt with other cities, Finley even took on the commissioner, Ford Frick.

To flout modern foul line standards, Charley O., as he became known, even built a phony fence inside his right-field barrier in 1964, calling it "Pennant Porch." The low fence, curving into the right-field corner, was designed to resemble the size and distance of the right-field corner at Yankee Stadium, just 296 feet at the foul pole. The "porch" was there for pre-season exhibitions with St. Louis, but Frick ordered it dismantled before the American League season began.

Finley was muleheaded, all right. Next, he built an overhanging roof in right field, purportedly to protect fans, but it, too, overhung the home run area in a manner most similar to New York's. Opening night, American League umpire Cal Hubbard made the Athletics dismantle the roof.

A fuming Finley, annoyed at the Yankees' domination of the American League, a condition that was totally opposite to the subservient footsies Johnson played with the perennial titleholders, couldn't help his own side, but he made it difficult for *all* hitters in right field. He put up a 40-foot screen in right field. As a result, a tough enough target became even higher and more difficult.

Now, Finley feuded and fussed openly with the town. Despite passage of an incredible Jackson County bond issue in 1967 for what seemed a frivolously expensive project—*two* stadiums, one for baseball and one for football—Finley . . . well, as Lowell Reidenbaugh put it, "With his mule in tow, Finley trucked off to Oakland."

By then, the West had been won. Used as an excuse was the fact that Brooklyn couldn't get enough folks into small Ebbets Field and the novelty of home televised games was being felt at the gate. Walter F. O'Malley noted that the Dodgers couldn't compete with the attendance drawn by the former Boston Braves at Milwaukee. O'Malley opted for Los Angeles, which, indeed, became the land of milk and honey for the Dodgers.

Except, however, for World War II and a previous decision by the L.A. Coliseum committee, the St. Louis Browns might have won the flight to the Pacific palisades. Back in late 1941, the Browns apparently had sympathetic ears and favorable railroad schedules to prove at an American League meeting that teams could leave Chicago on the crack Super Chief train and make it to Los Angeles for games. The day before the planned December 8 American League meeting, a "date that will live in infamy" brought the United States into war. Restricted transportation shelved a move to L.A.

In 1953 when Veeck opened the Pandora's box by making eyes at Milwaukee, bringing the Braves on the gallop from Boston, Los Angeles interests wanted the Browns. The story then was, as Lowell Reidenbaugh reported in his ball park book, the L.A. Coliseum's governing body turned thumbs down. At the time the Coliseum, home of the University of Southern California Trojans and Los Angeles Rams and expanded for the 1932 Olympics, saw itself only as a football and track-and-field stadium.

By the time The O'Malley was ready to make his move, the shrewd Irish lawyer had (1) bought out his Brooklyn partners, (2) swapped his Fort Worth (Texas League) franchise for Phil Wrigley's Los Angeles (Pacific Coast League) Angels, and (3) even played a series of "home games away from home," as they phrased the Dodgers' limited series of games at Jersey City's Roosevelt Stadium, a Works Progress Administration landmark of the Depression. By then, Jersey City had lost its Triple A International League franchise.

So it was not surprising, but only disappointing, that O'Malley moved to L.A. with the National League's blessing after the 1957 season. Not surprising because, certainly, Los Angeles deserved major league status in baseball. Disappointing only because the franchise was a plump plum, Brooklyn, a team whose quaint affection and dialect made Dem Bums and Flatbush a standby for radio comedians. If you were laying a standup egg, merely cackle "Brooklyn." Yuk!

At L.A., bringing in 1958 a team that had been a championship force since 1941, O'Malley cast a frowning look at junior-sized Wrigley Field, a 20,000-seat miniature of the Chicago Stadium built by the Wrigleys in 1925, and not even the 100,000-seat Rose Bowl in nearby Pasadena appealed to Sir Walter. But, now, the L.A. Coliseum was ready to talk and The O'Malley was ready to do business.

As a result, O'Malley created the most unusual big league ball park since the National League's Ed Williamson took pot shots at that pigeon-coop fence at Chicago's Lake Front Park in the last century. With the Dodgers footing the bill for more lights, sunken dugouts, a backstop, and a press box at a flag-pattern northwest corner of the football end zone, L.A. was ready for ersatz big league baseball in 1958.

Oh, yes, the Chinese Wall or Bamboo Curtain was constructed in left field, a 40-foot high screen fronting the left-field stands from home plate, only 251 feet away, if that far. It extended 140 feet toward center field. Right field was s-o-o far away that Duke Snider, who had been taking happy whacks at Ebbets Field's clubby right field, luxuriating as the only left-handed hitter in a right-handed lineup, nearly wept with frustration. Imagine, 440 feet distance to right-center and too far, also, down the foul line.

When The Duke boo-hooed to Stan Musial as St. Louis came to town for the second series of the '58 season at L.A., the Man soothed him at the batting cage. "If you can't beat 'em, Duke, go the other way," said Musial, who went 4-for-4 his first game in the Coliseum, avoiding trying to pull toward the far-away barriers in right.

O'Malley was indeed a favored son in baseball. For one thing, NL owners, aware of a chance to attract bigger crowds, agreed to a disaster plan, distributing talent, if one of the teams were involved in a plane disaster. Basically, NL clubs left railroad stations behind forever in favor of airports. For another, Commissioner Frick tuttutted the suggestion that the fetching fence in left field ridiculed big league rules.

"I don't think (Babe) Ruth's record is in particular danger," said the commissioner, a former sportswriter and broadcaster. "Foul lines are not especially important where home runs are concerned. The other distances in left-center and right-center determine the number of homers."

Yeh, jeez, Commish, but the power alley in left-center, though high, was only 320 feet from the plate. But Frick proved correct if not logical. All that four-year stint in the Coliseum did, other than to make O'Malley a rich man and visiting clubs happy, too, was to turn into a hero a journeyman ballplayer named Wally Moon.

Moon, who had a master's degree from Texas A&M, was an intense player, a defensive player of limited ability with only a mediocre throwing arm, but in playing half his schedule in the short field requiring a short throw, his defense improved automatically. At bat, a left-handed hitter using an "inside out" swing, almost like a golfer pronating his drive, Moon arched balls on or over the fence. It wasn't that he hit tremendous numbers of homers or even doubles or triples, but how he hit them and chip-shotted singles off the screen. His homer high was 19 in four seasons at the Coliseum, and his RBI total reached 88. He was a clutch player averaging over .300, a most significant contributor to a seventh-to-first pennant in 1959 and a close call second in '61.

By the time the Dodgers moved into their own stadium at Chavez Ravine in 1962, Moon had lost his glass slipper. His batting averages, homers, and RBIs were modest his final four seasons in the majors.

Although a medium-height screened fence in right-to-center (added in 1959) cut down the disparity, the Coliseum still was a park built for a right-handed hitter quick enough and courageous enough to get out in front of the ball. In other words, the batter had to avoid being tied up inside, the way the Dodgers' sidewheeling and intimidating right-handed pitching star, Don Drysdale, could menace a hitter.

For one, Terry Moore, captain and center-field star of St. Louis's 1942 and '46 World Champions, gaped in his first look at the Chinese Wall as a Redbirds' coach. Moore smiled and said, "I just wonder how great right-handed pull hitters like Chick Hafey and Whitey Kurowski would have liked this. And just think: If poor Campy (Roy Campanella) hadn't had that disabling auto accident, how many would he hoist over that screen?"

At Brooklyn, hitting with an open stance and an uppercutting swing, Campanella hit as many as 41 homers in one of his nine-plus seasons in the blue-and-white of the Dodgers. Gil Hodges, at 34 a couple of years younger than Campanella, also flicked home runs into the jet stream at Ebbets Field, hitting 40 homers twice and averaging around 30 most of his 11-plus seasons there, but Hodges couldn't take advantage of the ridiculous rectangle. Maybe Gil was just homesick.

The size of the football stadium and the weather, which produced a heady 92,500 attendance for each of three 1959 World Series games against the Chicago White Sox, made the Coliseum a financial if not artistic baseball success. (A current high of 93,103 gathered on a May night in '59 for a salute to paraplegic Campanella, now a goodwill lecturer who also teaches catchers from his wheelchair and is a member of the Baseball Hall of Fame's Veterans Committee.) The Dodgers in '58 drew 1,845,000 as a seventh-place club, contrasted with their bare million the final third-slot last season at Brooklyn. In 1959 they went over 2,000,000 for the first time.

The Dodgers then were en route to their status in the late 1980s as the first franchise ever to draw 3,000,000 people, a result in part of The O'Malley's wisdom in holding ticket prices in line and a beautiful stadium. He built Dodger Stadium with his own money after a controversial swap with the city of Los Angeles and a close call with a referendum in 1958.

O'Malley swapped Wrigley Field at 42nd and Avalon for a hilly, depressed region two miles from the center of the vast city. The area was inhabited by squatters and goats, as Lowell Reidenbaugh explained it, but the 166 acres had potential value O'Malley turned into gold with his 56,000-seat park, unique because it was six-layered and had an al fresco driving-garage effect that permitted spectators to park on the same level as their seats.

Built privately by the perspicacious, jolly man with the jowls and neatly held constant cigar, Dodger Stadium traditionally has been a pitcher's park, one in which two great lefthanders, Sandy Koufax and Fernando Valenzuela, burst the ample amphitheatre's seams. Keeping home game television at arm's length most of the time, leaning largely on attractive concessions goods to augment reasonable seat prices, the Dodgers have had to tamper only lightly with the distances to the fences—330 on the lines, 385 in the power alleys, 400 feet in center.

With a Hollywood audience included regularly, the old Brooklyn bums have won eight pennants and three World Championships in 26 years at Chavez Ravine. And the Taj O'Malley glows as happily in tribute to the Irishman as The O'Malley did annually on St. Patrick's Day.

By painful contrast, the transplanted New York Giants, coaxed by O'Malley into removing National League baseball from the Big Apple in 1958, had only limited and painful success in San Francisco, a charming place on the Bay, but, because of the brisk trade winds, the

North Pole of baseball. As a ball club, well-bundled in the early going, the Giants showed close championship contention and then an
annoying habit of finishing second. A collapse in attendance and the
standings followed. It wasn't cute.

Horace Stoneham really hadn't wanted to leave the Polo Grounds,
even though the Giants' attendance began to flounder in the '50s in
competition with the Dodgers and Yankees. The Giants suffered financially despite the Little Miracle of Coogan's Bluff, the playoff victory
in 1951, and a four-game World Series sweep in 1954 of Cleveland,
which had won an American League record 111 games.

If there was any place to go, Stoneham felt it ought to be the Twin
Cities, Minneapolis and St. Paul. The Giants had a farm club in Minneapolis, which was gnawing away at progress like an eager beaver.
Still, The O'Malley's persuasion was not only good ol' blarney, but,
truly, it made sense to the rest of the National League and, indeed,
to Stoneham himself. Horace had other family investors to consider,
and even if SanFran didn't have Toots Shor's bistro, Lefty O'Doul's
joint was a pretty good watering hole. The man in the green suit had
helped the Giants to a World Championship (1933). O'Doodle was
the sports king of Frisco, visibly, even more than the city's favorite
baseball son, the silent, shy hero, Joe DiMaggio.

San Francisco, where the game had been played at least since 1860,
perhaps when Alexander Cartwright passed through the Barbary Coast
en route to Hawaii, was for years the strength of the Pacific Coast
League. With week-long stays in the city for economy purposes, yet
train trips necessary because of distances, the temperate weather favored former big league players and also promising kids. If Jigger Statz
and Frank Shellenback were Coast League legends because of so many
seasons, so were 17-year-old wonders named Ted Williams and DiMag.
Wonders, in part, because the Coast could only wonder about their
proud graduates playing back East.

But now in 1958 major league ball had come to Seals Stadium,
built in 1931 by owner Charley Graham and associates. The 18,600-
seat facility at 16th and Bryant streets would serve temporarily as home
of the Giants, awaiting San Francisco to fulfill a promise to build a
new stadium if, as finally achieved, the lovely city finally won a big
time suitor. San Francisco also won one of the greatest players ever—
Willie Mays.

At 27 a National League batting champion and with one season
of 51 homers at the Polo Grounds, Mays was a remarkably capable all-
around player, maybe the greatest ever, but he was faced first with San-
Fran's view that he would be like, say, DiMaggio, who hit safely in 61
straight games when playing 184 in the expanded Coast League of

1933 or like Paul Waner. Waner, hitting .401, had 280 hits in 170 games in 1925.

Initially, Willie couldn't win. Seals Stadium offered a reasonable target to left field, all right, 340 feet, but a 30-foot fence ringed the portion to center, 400 feet away. The right-field bleachers were a distant 385 feet from the plate, a problem more for left-handed hitters.

Mays hit .347 that first year on the Coast, including 29 homers, and drove in 96 runs, but San Francisco was captivated more by a 20-year-old rookie first baseman from Puerto Rico. They called him the Baby Bull—Orlando Cepeda, a good-looking big guy—and Cha-Cha, as he became better known with St. Louis's championship El Birdos several years later (1967). Cepeda caught the community's fancy. He hit 25 home runs his rookie year, en route to 46 three years later when he drove in 142 runs. Oddly, later in a pouting match with Willie Mc-Covey, another first baseman who really didn't want to play outfield, either, Cepeda lost out and McCovey stayed. Big "Stretch," really neither as gifted as Cepeda defensively nor as fast, spent most of his 22 years in a Giant uniform and hit 521 home runs.

McCovey, like Mays a first-round selection for the Hall of Fame, was a left-handed hitter favored by the severe crosswinds when Candlestick Park opened in 1960, a travesty to a game intended to be played in pleasant circumstances. Although the sun might be shining, cold winds whipping from left to right in the baseball hours, 1:30 to 3:30 P.M., held up fly balls hit to left field. Worse, it chilled the players and crept into the bones of spectators as shadows fell in the stands.

After drawing nearly 2,700,000 in the skimpy seats of Seals Stadium, nearly four times their final season's draw in New York, the Giants felt as if they had a windfall at Candlestick Park, named by area sports editors because it jutted in a piece of land named Candlestick Point, virtually surrounded by San Francisco Bay.

If, for instance, San Francisco had opted for old and vacant areas downtown near the cable car turntable at Market Street and Powell, chances are the Giants would have had much of the good fortune of centrally located ball parks, such as St. Louis's Busch Stadium and Cincinnati's Riverfront Stadium.

Instead, with contractors and civic fathers aware at the outset that Candlestick Park would be uncomfortable, a radiant heating system was installed in the 20,000-seat reserved section of the stadium, which initially seated nearly 44,000. But it didn't work. Candlestick Park was not, as proclaimed, "the only heated open-air park in the world." It was, instead, the only park completely constructed of reinforced concrete and, yes, the coldest.

Colder than the Giants became after their one pennant-winning season on the Coast (1962) when, with veteran American League left-hander Billy Pierce unbeaten in a dozen home games, San Francisco nipped bitter rival Los Angeles in a three-game playoff. What the season proved, as Yogi Berra would say, is a race or a game isn't over until it's over. The Giants rallied to tie on the last day. Then in the best-of-three playoff, submerging a startling performance of four hits, three stolen bases, and two great fielding plays by L.A. shortstop Maury Wills, they scored four times in the ninth. Their 6–4 victory gave them the unexpected pleasure of a World Series against their old New York neighbors and rivals, the Yankees.

Mays, struggling pridefully to hit and to obtain in San Francisco the kind of affection he knew in New York, realized that if the best shots to left field were stonewalled by the wind, he'd better try to go to right-center. The crosswind drift, diagonally from foul pole to foul pole, swept left-field concessions' debris into a neat end-of-the-game pile at the right-field pole. It had one beneficial effect. For a ball hit tight to the right-field line? No. For one to right-center that drifted toward a shorter distance near the foul pole? Yes.

That's the way Mays hit over the years. He didn't beat Candlestick Point, but he certainly joined it, improving home runs from 29 the first year there, 1960, to 40, 49, 38 47, and finally 52, giving "Say Hey" the rare distinction of achieving 50 or more twice. Finally, reluctantly, his finances strapped, Horace Stoneham sent Mays back to New York with the Mets in 1972, unable to meet the player's contractual nut at a time Willie really was no longer a wonder.

Mays, finishing at 40 in 1973, played nearly 20 full seasons, missing nearly two in military service. He wound up third to Henry Aaron and Babe Ruth in career homers with 660. If he hadn't been in khaki rather than flannel and if he had played his entire career at the Polo Grounds rather than Candlestick, would he have challenged Aaron for batting's Mt. Everest beyond Babe Ruth? A good question.

For the Giants, Candlestick Park just didn't work, and neither did diminishing finances. Partly because SanFran offers so many exciting diversions and, again, because night games are played in a penetrating chill, Stoneham retained his Polo Grounds policy of night ball only on Tuesday and Friday. When Mayor Joseph Alioto proposed that Candlestick be scrapped and a $50,000,000 multi-purpose stadium built in midtown, His Honor didn't get enough public support. So he opted for expansion and improvements.

Before the 1971 season, the seating capacity was increased to 58,000, most helpful to football. Double-decked, the stadium was converted to a bowl in the hope that the bigger barriers would diminish the winds. An escalator up the grade from Cardiac Cliff, the climb from the parking lot, reduced heart attack incidents. Briefly, artificial turf replaced grass.

Removal of the thick, dewy turf made contact hitters who stroked ground balls breathe easier, but natural grass was returned by 1979. By then, new owner Bob Lurie had tackled the task of trying to improve the Giants on the field and at the box office. As the Giants continued to do a shivering and limited business at Candlestick Park, with more and more major leaguers rejecting Jack London's town as a place to play, only one thing was certain: The wind had changed directions—and now it came in trick crosscurrents rather than, like a newspaper photo cutline, reading from left to right.

Back in the good ol' days San Francisco's inferior neighbor, labeled as "sleeping quarters" for Frisco, Oakland, rescued San Francisco at the time of the catastrophic earthquake-and-fire in 1906. The Oaks permitted the Seals to play in their park. For years, too, the San Francisco-Oakland rivalry was a fascinating, money-saving Pacific Coast League delight.

But once Brick Laws moved the Oaks in 1955 from their weary old park to Vancouver, British Columbia, Oakland was without baseball for 11 years, most of them spent watching and envying the National League Giants at San Francisco. So Oakland paved the way for big league ball by its enterprise building Oakland-Alameda County at Nimitz Freeway and Hegenberger Road in the city's southern section. This was, if you will, Circe in cement.

When Charley Finley came to town in 1968 with the other "Charley O.," the mule, enthusiasm, and young ball club about ready to roll, a former film pitcher who had a bigger date with destiny, Ronald Reagan, governor, threw out the first ball.

By 1971 when the major leagues had expanded and split into divisions, Oakland won the AL's West Division. A year later, under Dick Williams, they won the World Championship. They repeated again and again, gaining four division titles and three successive World Championships, the best dynasty since the Yankees' record five in a row, 1949–53. But, naturally, they didn't do it under one manager, a most difficult achievement under Finley even when winning. Alvin Dark, who had given jealous San Francisco its one pennant winner, won two pennants and extremely heady victories over the Mets and Dodgers in World Series play.

Eccentrically, paying his players more and enjoying it less, Finley tightened his front office staff, the smallest in the majors, and, charming as always could be his wont, Charley O. picked the mental pockets of men he esteemed, like St. Louis's cerebral Bing Devine, and served as his own general manager.

In changes that probably should be mentioned in our final chapter on traditions, Finley changed baseball shoes from funereal black to wedding-gown white, to borrow one of his adjective expressions about the kelly green and Fort Knox gold with which he interspersed pants and shirt or jersey combinations. Similarly, he cultivated his "Mustache Gang," flouting a baseball clean-shaven tradition. The champion with a villainous pointed 'stash was baseball's winningest relief pitcher, Rollie Fingers.

Fingers was a low draft choice who hit the jackpot for himself, Finley, and the fellas in the "softball uniforms," as baseball first derided Charley O.'s playing field haberdashery and then copied it. Finley, also first to advocate night game play in the World Series, was both good and lucky.

When the profitable medical insurance gimmick he designed for doctors paid off so handsomely in 1964, shortly after Finley had a close brush with death as a young man, the executive faced a handsome tax bill. So he directed astute farm director Hank Peters, later general manager at Baltimore, to distribute some $800,000 to good prospects. Sharp scouts sniffed talent and money talked. Signed early were Jim (Catfish) Hunter, Johnny (Blue Moon) Odom and Chuck Dobson.

The reverse-order draft, installed to avoid such extravagance as Finley just had exhibited, found Kansas City still last so that Charley O. was favored with the first choice. He tabbed Arizona State outfielder Rick Monday as No. 1 and also signed third baseman Sal Bando. A year later Reggie Jackson was KayCee's second draft choice.

In 1967 those able Kansas City scouts sniffed out as No. 27 a left-hander named Vida Blue, described by Whitey Herzog as the "Dwight Gooden of his day." Correct. At only 22, Blue was 24–8 with a brilliant 1.82 ERA for Oakland's division-winning team in 1971.

Smiling, Herzog, a highly successful manager later at Kansas City and St. Louis, recalled having scouted a standout pitcher, Don Sutton, at a time Finley tired of putting out bonuses to teenaged wonders. Sutton, who would pitch better than two decades in the majors as a constant winner, wanted only $16,000 and the equivalent of a college education. Finley drew the line at $10,000. To Sutton, Herzog lamented, "Charley likes those unusual nicknames and first names— Catfish, Blue Moon, Vida. Couldn't you come up with something catchy or fancy, kid?"

Before Finley wearied enough to get out in 1979, unhappy with free agency's impact on salaries, he was checkmated by Commissioner Bowie Kuhn, a personal rival. Critics still believe, however, that if Charley O. had kept his mouth shut and accepted a throw-in player or two as a smokescreen, he might have gotten away with six-figure sales of

Blue to the New York Yankees, Fingers and outfielder Joe Rudi to the Red Sox, and, ultimately, his whopping offer from Cincinnati for Blue at a time the Big Red Machine already was rolling.

When Finley brayed about those million-dollar sales of valuable baseball bric-a-brac, Commissioner Kuhn stepped in and, mindful of the promiscuous sales in the past of Babe Ruth and other Red Sox to the Yankees and later extravagant athletic rummage sales by the A's Philadelphia forerunners and also the financial hari-kiri of the old St. Louis Browns, the commissioner drew a line. At a time $400,000 was a more sizable amount than later, he would authorize no cash amount above that figure in a player deal.

As a deep thinker, Herzog questioned the right of even baseball's highest office to help a man run or ruin his business. "Why," asked Whitey in logical rhetoric, "couldn't a more generous price tag be placed on a player by the commissioner and a reverse-order draft be applied, giving the lowest-standing club first chance to bid?"

Maybe Finley wouldn't have gone out when he did. Possibly, too, he might have left his calling card in the game's history another way. When Finley reneged on a clause in Hunter's contract, Catfish took the case to arbitration. The arbitrator, Peter Seitz, not only found for the player, but he also surprised by declaring him a free agent. Hunter's consequent switch to the Yankees in 1975 tore off the last shackles of baseball peonage. Thereafter, the inmates took over the asylum.

Just before Finley bowed out unhappily, a modern day Chris Von der Ahe who couldn't stand the sweet smell of success, Finley's follies had dipped in defeat to as few as 653 spectators for a game. But Bay area roughneck Billy Martin turned the team around. Although Reggie Jackson would become a bigger, better bomber when a free agent at Yankee Stadium, hitting October homers like Babe Ruth and Mickey Mantle, the A's profited by ignoring the fences. Like Herzog at St. Louis, Martin designed a game called BillyBall, emphasizing speed and daring. One of his speedsters Rickey Henderson, quickly broke Lou Brock's fresh single-season, stolen-base record with 130 in 1982.

If you want to suggest that money talked when Henderson wound up with the same Yankees in 1985, be our guests. Money never was more articulate than since free agency came along, though in Henderson's trip to Baghdad-on-the-Subway, he was swapped in a multiple-player deal in which the dollar sign wasn't so obvious.

By 1986, a grand ol' name of the game was gone. The family Griffith reflected not only a long-standing term in Washington, but also in the Minneapolis-St. Paul area, marking a new era in real estates, i.e., ball parks. That is, expansion.

Back in the late 1950s New York attorney Bill Shea, at the behest of New York mayor, Robert Wagner, sought to bring pressure to bear on the National League to return to New York. Indignantly, not wisely or well, NL president Warren Giles had huffed, "Who needs New York?" Silly talk. They needed each other.

One way to convince Giles and all was to threaten formation of the Continental League by Shea, using as front man the unctuous master of cunning and polysyllabics, Branch Rickey. B. R. could convince any or many in Denver, Buffalo, Atlanta, Houston, Dallas-Ft. Worth, and many other major-sized metropolises, including Montreal and Toronto, that they belonged in the bigs, too.

Alarmed at a potential recurrence of the Federal League war before WWI and perhaps fearful of the sanctity of their one-sided player contracts, the majors sought to nip the heart out of the Continental, i.e., New York. Unilaterally, the National League acted the October day (1960) Bill Mazeroski's ninth-inning homer gave Pittsburgh a dramatic Series victory over the Yankees, 10–9. Justifiably, the American League was miffed.

So when the NL said it would expand to 10 teams in 1962, returning a franchise to New York and awarding one to Houston, the American League announced at the winter meeting in St. Louis that it would expand immediately (1961). The AL would buck the Dodgers in Los Angeles, permit Clark Griffith's heirs to move the Senators to the Twin Cities, and grant new ownership to operate in Washington.

The cynical suggested that Joe Cronin, president of the American League and a former star shortstop-manager at D.C., had permitted the Griffs to hopscotch to Minneapolis-St. Paul, virgin territory, because he was a member of the family. True, Joe was married to Calvin Griffith's sister, Mildred. Undoubtedly, Cronin felt family fealty for the tight financial operation in Washington, which had few good ball clubs to cheer and with fewer fans cheerful enough to turn the turnstiles. Obviously, however, membership clubs had to share in the president's view, no matter how persuasive the aldermanic Irishman could be.

So, diplomatically labeled as the Minnesota Twins, the Senators moved to the Midwest. Even more diplomatically, Minneapolis and St. Paul, bitter rivals in everything from opposite banks of the Mississippi, buried their differences to win major league favor. Minneapolis's Millers had played most of their years at Nicollet Park, where pitch-and-putt distance to right field made a 69-homer-hitting legend out of Joe Hauser. As American Association foes, St. Paul played at Lexington Park.

Almost simultaneously each built a new park in the mid-1950s, but they agreed, finally, to use the Millers' expanded facility at Bloomington, Minnesota, located between the two cities. When Metropolitan Stadium hiked its seating to 30,000 and the Senators moved from Griffith Stadium in 1961, two questions were unanswered: Would the young Washington team improve with the enthusiastic backing of the upper Midwest? Would Harmon Killebrew expand there the home run stroke he had displayed the last couple of seasons in the nation's capital?

The answer was the same—yes and yes.

Yes, thanks to Washington-transferred scouting, always capable even when the Griffiths didn't have the scratch of most clubs, the Senators—or, Twins—still had their Cuban connection, one that over the years brought them good material at cut-rate salaries. By 1965, an American League pennant fluttered over Bloomington—the ball club's first since AL president Cronin player-managed D.C. in 1933.

Immediately, too, Killebrew, a muscular man from Idaho, continued in the new park the home run punch he first displayed at Griffith Stadium. With no disrespect to Killebrew, who gave it the old defensive college try at first base, third base, left field, even briefly at second base and then as designated-hitter at the tail end of his 22-year career, the mild-mannered man wouldn't have had too great a chance if the Griffiths hadn't altered their old park.

Griffith Stadium, built back in 1911 just off the Florida Avenue streetcar line in Washington, had much of the crazy quilt "character" of fields over which young observers rhapsodized well into the '80s— even if they hadn't seen them. The park had a left-field foul line that was *deeper* than center field. Right field took a jagged left turn in right center, a result of the park having been built around five homes and backyards of property that, like others in the alleged good ol' days, created too big a purchase problem. The wall in center to the right-field corner was 31 feet high.

So Washington really had no home run tradition until Killebrew came along. "Killer," they called the son of an old Illinois wrestler. Harmon the Charmin' had the muscle, all right, but not the disposition that fierce nickname would indicate. But the sturdy right-handed hitter, who came up when he was barely 18 in 1954, had a home run bat that almost matched Pittsburgh's Ralph Kiner's among more modern right-handed power men.

By the time Killebrew came up, Old Fox Griffith and his heir-apparent guardian and nephew, Calvin, had installed extra seats (1950) in left and left-center. As a result, the target was trimmed from 405 feet to 386 down the left-field line, still an outrageous distance. But the fence not only shortened the distance to the left-center power alleys more than its original cockeyed design, it also trimmed center field's 391 to a most inviting 372 feet.

Inviting, indeed, but still far enough from the plate and high enough that when Mickey Mantle teed off mightily from the right side against lefty Chuck Stobbs, April 17, 1953, the Yankees' publicity director, Arthur (Red) Patterson, trekked out of the park to a yard behind a three-story tenement. A woman pointed out where the ball landed. Patterson measured it and came up with a good guesspert's estimate of 563 feet. Thus was born the tale of the tape measure, still employed by others now as enterprising as Patterson, a former New York newspaperman who later went west with the Dodgers and the California Angels. Today computers calculate distance immediately as a delightful scoreboard message tidbit.

Killebrew, becoming a regular with Washington in 1959 at nearly 23, slugged 42 homers that first season in revised Griffith Stadium, and then, playing 29 fewer games in 1960, he still hit 31. He would doubtless have done extremely well in District of Columbia Stadium, opened the year after the first Senators carpet-bagged to the Minnesota tundra. RFK Stadium—Robert F. Kennedy Stadium, as the park was renamed after most unfortunate circumstances—was a modern, symmetrical, two-sport stadium. The dimensions were not only reasonable—335 to 335 with a 410-center-field mezzanine overhang—but the ball also traveled well.

Killebrew, however, wore only visitors' gray in the 10-year term of the ersatz Senators, later transferred to Arlington, Texas, as the Texas Rangers. He hit the bulk of his 573 home runs at Bloomington's Memorial Park, where the ball carried so well that the 330-foot foul lines later were lengthened by 13 feet. Killebrew hit more than 40 homers there seven of his first 10 seasons with the Twins. His top figures were 49 in 1964 and again in 1969.

Killebrew, driving in 100 runs seven times, did not finish with the Washington-Minnesota varsity for which he had been a 21-year letterman. He ended up at Kansas City in 1975 at 39, hitting his last 14 homers.

By then, just before collapse of the reserve clause broke the bank for some clubs with a rush to free agency, Calvin Griffith was having the same financial shorts experienced by "Unk," as the family tenderly referred to Clark Griffith, who had died in 1955 at 86. Calvin, hale, hearty, and considerably outspoken and more profane than the waspy pioneer from whom he inherited a surname and club control, had the same Griffith loyalty to filling the payroll with family and faithful retainers.

Now and then, the second Griffith would stick his foot in his mouth, too, with a thoughtless racial expression or over a contractual crisis, but he had the smarts. Even though he kept the Twins out of the free-agent market and flatly refused to play can-you-top-this financial contest for players, his and yours, the Twins were decent if not dandy for years. The old grow-your-own farm-system concept lived with a ball club that offered a short-cut chance to the majors. Has-been pickups also came back. By 1985, however, Calvin ran up the white flag. He sold out to Minneapolis interests, hopeful that an investment and the three-year-old downtown stadium, Hubert H. Humphrey Metrodome, might bring back glory experienced seldom by the Twins and the Senators, old and new. In 1987, they did.

The same year Minnesota got into the majors, 1961, movie cowboy-actor-singer, Gene Autry, and associates were awarded the American League's answer to the National League Dodgers, a franchise in Los Angeles. As mentioned earlier, the AL acted, in part, in angry reprisal for the National League's private decision to return to New York, in effect contesting the Yankees. Obviously, as the saying goes, the Angels read the small print. Still—.

In this informal backside approach to baseball, past and present, we don't pretend to be calling 'em unemotionally and without prejudice. Hopefully fair as in "just," not as in "mediocre," but with occasional amusement or annoyance, as, for instance, in the ramifications of expansion. Or, as the *St. Louis Post-Dispatch*'s Kevin Horrigan put it in quarter-century reflection of the Houston ball club in 1962, "organized extortion."

Actually, of course, a robust membership "fee" was merited, as much as any golf club or other private preserve, and, to be sure, no ball club was going to expose its fair-to-good talent in expansion draft. That's why it's still incredible that New York made it from misfit "Mutts" to World Champion Mets in eight playing-field seasons, 1962–69.

But sportsman Autry, the former semipro outfielder who had thumped a railroad telegraph key in Oklahoma, tolerated stern ground rules when Commissioner Ford Frick gave him the bad news: A newly enacted major league rule would prohibit the Angels' playing in the Dodgers' temporary and hefty home, the Coliseum.

Why was that rule suddenly enacted if, aware that the AL would move into L.A. the only city other than New York and Chicago with the logical population base for two teams, the Dodgers hadn't thrown The O'Malley's ample weight and oral persuasion into the scenario? Surely, with Bill Shea having got exactly what he and New York wanted, a new National League franchise in 1962, the proposed Continental League hadn't even reached first base.

Yet, despite years of coexistence by two St. Louis and two Philadelphia ball clubs in one park and with Boston's Fenway Park and old Braves Field just a good sprint from Kenmore Square up Commonwealth Avenue, why that new provision prohibiting a second major league club from playing within five miles of the first? Oh, yes, as Frick explained, the Angels "also agreed to play at least two years in Chavez Ravine."

H'mm, that Dodger-owned new park wasn't even completed. So even if Autry and associates liked junior-grade Wrigley Field, which seated only 22,000, they couldn't stay there after Dodger Stadium opened. If they had, you would have to wonder what might have happened to home run records over the years. After all, Wrigley Field No. 2 had power alleys *only* 345 feet from home plate, but the opposition hit more homers there than did even aging Ted Kluszewski, Leon (Daddy Wags) Wagner, or Steve Bilko. Bunky Bilko, once hailed by St. Louis clubowner Fred Saigh as "the next Jimmy Foxx," hit 20 in just 114 games at Wrigley Field. At Sportsman's Park, where the barriers were deeper, big Steve's best too often was a long fly to center field.

To prove that this really isn't a regional bias, Saigh figured only as a tenant in what appeared an impractical lease arrangement. In St. Louis, operating the Cardinals when they outdrew the rival landlord Browns by as many as 5-to-1 in 1949, Saigh successfully held the brothers DeWitt, Bill and Charley, to a 29-year-old lease signed by Sam Breadon with Phil Ball. Even though the Cardinals obviously created much more need for concessions' cleanup, etc., the Browns were unable to get courtroom relief. The Redbirds' rental was not only most modest, $35,000 a year, but the Browns still had to pay for half the daily rubbish pickup, etc.

Actually, though O'Malley took $200,000 for the Angels' rent or seven and a half percent of net receipts, the Dodgers' boss was a mite more understanding than Saigh. He shared half of the concessions' income with his tenants, though none of the parking, and when Autry wondered why he had to pay for half the toilet paper when the Dodgers' patronage used 76 percent of it and when the Angels in the windowless basement were required to pay for half the washing of the Dodgers' windows, The O'Malley relented in both protests. But not when the Angels didn't want to pay half the bill for watering the grass.

By the time the 1965 season ended, the Los Angeles Angels had a new name and a new home. As announced by executive Bob Reynolds, the former Stanford football All-American, they would play at a new stadium at Anaheim, California. A good thing, actually, because their one-time 1,100,000 attendance at little Wrigley Field had dwindled with poor play to 566,000 in larger Dodger Stadium. Lowell Reidenbaugh noted "little profit" after four years.

At Anaheim, often regarded as a bedroom for Los Angeles, yet a fast-mushrooming area of Orange County, home of Disneyland and Knott's Berry Farm, the name would be bush league if not the area. So the haloed athletes were christened the California Angels. Given half of the concessions, two-thirds of the parking, they've lived happily ever after in Big "A," the Anaheim Stadium that now also houses football's Los Angeles Rams. The stadium, built originally to seat 43,000, has been double-decked all-around, and now handles 65,000.

With shrewd judgment, playing field dimensions were determined by air density and wind tests at normal game times, 1:30 and 8 o'clock. From climatological judgments, foul lines were established at 333 feet, 370 in the power alleys, and 404 in center.

Reggie Jackson, the most glamorous of expensive talent assembled by Autry, paying off at the box office even more than in the standings, had an immediate MVP season in 1982, a division-winning year. Jackson hit 39 home runs. Aging Rod Carew was not quite the same bat-wielding master who won seven batting titles at Minnesota, where one year he stole home seven times. A 3000-hit player, Carew priced himself out of baseball in 1986. The biggest disappointment other than in near-misses in '79 and '82 was Fred Lynn.

To more than one observer, Lynn, who looked like a latter-day Stan Musial when he came up at Boston late in 1974, missed Fenway Park, tailor-made for left-handed shots to left-center that banged off the convenient Green Monster. Lynn hit .419 in 15 games in 1974 and batted .331 his first full season, a pennant-winning year for the Bosox. He contributed 21 homers and drove in 105 runs. Fact is, he once hit a league-leading .333 (1979), belted 42 doubles, 39 homers and knocked in 122 runs. By the time he was dealt to California after the 1980 season, then at a hitter's presumed prime, 28, Freddie had hit over .300 four times in six seasons and averaged 34 doubles, 20 homers and nearly 90 RBIs.

In five seasons since, including 1985 in which he played out his option at California and went to Baltimore, Lynn never reached .300 in batting. His doubles dropped 16 a year, his homers dipped five, and his RBIs 35. Except for a spectacular 1982 playoff in which he went 11 for 18, .621, in a five-game set lost to Milwaukee, Lynn hasn't been the same hitter who took a bead on the opposite-field barrier at The Fens.

When the National League rushed its two new members a year later, 1962, new ball parks weren't ready. The Mets' move was logical. They occupied the briefly vacant Polo Grounds, which, like too many former parks, later became a site of high-rise apartments. Houston prepared for its historic baseball-under-glass, the domed stadium, with a 32,000-seat stadium hastily constructed on South Main Street.

Colt Stadium, they called it, in tribute to the ball club's original name, Colt .45s, for which the Colt Firearms Company granted permission. The symmetrical park wasn't helped by the semi-tropical Houston humidity or the mosquito mass. The old wind blowing in out of right field was the same problem it had been for years at Buffalo Stadium, the Texas League park put up in 1928 by the St. Louis Cardinals.

Houston's pear-shaped former mayor, Judge Roy Hofheinz, peering owl-eyed through spectacles over a Churchillian-sized cigar, orchestrated the domed stadium, a classic concept and one that made particular sense in Houston because of the heat, the humidity, the bugs and those thunderclouds that so often threatened rain around the dinner hour even if there was no precipitation.

The Harris County Domed Stadium, the initial name for the "Eighth Wonder of the World" as Judge Hofheinz brazenly called it, took two bond issues for public passage. Total cost was $31,600,000 for which the ball club guaranteed an annual lease of $750,000 plus all operating expenses. When other clubs about to build learned that it cost $1000 a day in utilities—proper air conditioning was necessary to prevent "inside rain" condensation when the place was empty—the Astro-Dome stood uncontested as covered.

AstroDome became the stadium's name, in part, because the Colt .45 people drew a line when the ball club began to market novelties under the same name. Judge Hofheinz, never one to be found inattentive, switched gears and used a proud new name of space exploration, most indicative of Houston because of its headquarters of NASA.

The Astros had perfect 72-degree weather inside, at no little expense, and soft theatre seats that wouldn't last or be practical outdoors. Their fences were too far for considerable slugging, a problem management still sought to alter by reducing distances in 1985, but the biggest problem was one evident when the 48,000-seat facility opened in 1965. Bless the Judge's Pullman-sized, six-floor playhouse hidden behind the right-field fence and his startling $2,000,000 animated scoreboard, but the outfielders and infielders just couldn't judge fly balls. The problem was a transparent dome.

Obviously, a rainout is an attractive no-no in the AstroDome, which celebrated Houston's quarter-century in the majors with just one division title. No, they'll never rain *out* a game at the AstroDome, but they rained *in* one game, June 15, 1976. The ballplayers made it before a torrential rainstorm struck Texas' south-central metropolis, then a downpour flooded streets. Not even the umpires or stadium personnel could make it, much less the fans.

"It was," as Lowell Reidenbaugh put it so aptly, "baseball's first postponement because of wet grounds *outside* the park."

When the New York Mets moved from the Polo Grounds into their own stadium, named for corporate lawyer Bill Shea, who had worked hard in the project, the Mets still were amusing or, as Casey Stengel put it when managing for the first four years through 1965, the "Amazin' Mets." The field, originally called Flushing Meadow Park, was built on the Grand Central Parkway close by the World's Fair area of 1939–40 and 1964–65.

With the whir of planes from nearby LaGuardia and Kennedy Airports making even more noise than the banner-waving Mets' fans — obviously many of the Dodgers' faithful must have forgiven if not forgotten — the laughable team was a box office success. So successful, in fact, that 15,000 seats were added to 57,000-plus after the woeful ball club drew 1,700,000 its first season there, 1964.

A joyful toy for Joan Whitney Payson, a jovial, wealthy woman fan intensely interested in baseball, the Mets turned into an immediate moneymaker when, as a result of their lease with the city-owned stadium, they scored heavily in concessions revenue as the football Giants and Jets and even the Yankees themselves moved in briefly. (Yankee Stadium was torn down and rebuilt.) The football clubs later moved by tunnel to a handsome complex at Meadowlands, New Jersey.

With 341 feet at the foul lines, 410 to center field, but a fetching 358 in left-center, Shea Stadium offered a home run target. Gil Hodges, returning as a player, was too old to take advantage of it, then became a shortlived storybook manager. Even when the Mets peeled off a nice round $2,000,000 a year to obtain free agent George Foster, a few years after his brow-raising 52 homers at Cincinnati, Foster's diminishing home run spiral continued. And George never was a first-rate player defensively.

But then crazy things happened at Shea. On Father's Day, 1964, Philadelphia's Jim Bunning, a sire of six with a political future ahead, pitched the majors' first perfect game in 43 years. A doubleheader with San Francisco lasted 9 hours and 52 minutes until 11:25 P.M. And a 25-inning game with St. Louis went until 3:12 A.M., just after Bake McBride's infield hit, a wild pickoff throw, the weary runner's speed, and a return errant peg decided the game for the Cardinals, 4–3.

That marathon match in 1974, effected by a game-tying, ninth-inning home run by St. Louis's Ken Reitz hours earlier, brought Reitz the typical Star-of-the Game recognition — in the shortest salute ever. The Redbird flagship broadcaster, Jack Buck of KMOX, said simply: "Tonight's Star-of-the-Game is Ken Reitz. Congratulations, Ken. Thanks and good night."

For the Mets, combining a strong second-half surge with a Chicago collapse, a pennant in 1969 was a most pleasant surprise and a tribute to baseball expansion. A World Series upset over Baltimore was frosting on the cake. Four years later in an Eastern Division race, neither St. Louis nor Pittsburgh seemed to want to win. The Mets slipped through to the title with an embarrassing 82–79 record, then surprised Cincinnati's powerhouse in the National League's Championship Series and nearly knocked the Oakland A's off their Series dynasty.

With pitching prowess probably unmatched anywhere except from Sandy Koufax, Don Drysdale, and then Fernando Valenzuela at Los Angeles, the Mets achieved box office boffo from two toeplate talents. First, Tom Seaver. Second, Dwight Gooden.

If Shea Stadium didn't produce anticipated eye-opening individual home run achievements, Atlanta's did, as explained in part in the delightful twilight of Henry Aaron's career and in Davey Johnson's single-season assault as baseball's greatest homer-hitting second baseman. More recently, Dale Murphy, a gifted all-around athlete, and Bob Horner, injury-hexed before departing for Japan in a holdout huff, have indicated that if there's a hitter and a park that might produce a new champion, it well could be at Atlanta's stadium.

At Philadelphia, where 65,000-seat Veterans' Stadium opened in 1971, with foul lines 330 from the plate, 408 to dead center, and favorable air density, a brilliant multi-talented player, Mike Schmidt, gave it the old college try, but age and ailments were closing in on Hall-of-Fame-bound Schmidt in 1987.

Size helps, as illustrated by Babe Ruth, and of course, by Frank Howard, the 6-7 giant from Ohio State who must have been dehydrated the day they listed his weight at 255. Hondo could hit the darnedest line drive homers, like one for the Dodgers in a 1963 Series sweep over the Yankees. At Washington in old Griffith Stadium, he hit more than 40 homers three straight seasons, topped by 48 in 1961. But when RFK Stadium opened in 1971, Howard dipped to 26.

The Senators were switched to Texas in 1972 by Bob Short, who once owned basketball's Minneapolis and Los Angeles Lakers. Howard creamed the first homer at Arlington Stadium, built in stages from 1955 as Turnpike Stadium to 1978 with a current 41,000 capacity. The foul line distance is equitable, 330, and dead center, too, at 400. The distance to the power alleys, 380, is, as indicated elsewhere, just a bit too tough.

Still, when Frank Robinson found the home run downs in September 1973, F. Robby established a record by hitting a home run in his

32nd major league park. If nothing else, friends, that accomplishment speaks not only for Robinson's power, but also for the fact that baseball was played in just 16 parks when he came up in 1956.

Movement and expansion have become magic carpets in baseball. From San Diego to Seattle, California alone and the Coast have had a remarkable growth in franchises. Not that the western shoreline state wasn't shut out for too long, but California zoomed from no major league club in 1957 to *five* in 22 years. Make that six, too, when you include Washington's pride-and-joy at Seattle.

Seattle needed two chances to make it. Kansas City, which also got there a second time in the American League's double expansion in 1969, really hadn't failed at all.

Seattle's flop in '69 was unfortunate, a result probably of underfinancing as well as civic failure to enlarge and spruce up Sick Stadium as required in agreement with the club and the AL. The Pilots, as the team off Puget Sound was called, paid a $6,000,000 ante fee for the franchise. Only 18,000 of the contemplated 25,000 seats were ready for the opener. Things went from bad to worse when an anticipated 850,000 fell nearly 200,000 shy, and the Pacific Coast League, having lost a dominant member, demanded $1,000,000 in damages.

Despite a $650,000 loan from the American League, the Pilots kept gurgling in red ink. Virtually at the 11th hour, the way Milwaukee got that National League franchise from Boston in 1953, the AL approved the Pilots' move to Bud Selig and associates at Milwaukee. The Brewers, ach, himmel, did handsomely at the gate and soon had a pennant-winning ball club (1982).

Kansas City, aided by the injustice of having lost Charley O. Finley's ball club when a new park was under construction and with pressure exercised by a distinguished statesman, Sen. Stuart C. Symington, came back swinging with only a year's delay. The financial angel was Ewing Kaufmann, owner of a pharmaceutical company.

With Kaufmann spending generously—he even unloaded millions in a fruitless experiment to develop ballplayers from unsigned athletes with no baseball background—the Royals soon became as luxurious as their park. The smaller twin entry of the opulent Harry S Truman Complex opened in 1973, its estimated cost escalated from $43,000,000 to $70,000,000.

Royals Stadium, scene of a constant championship contender's happiest moment, i.e., 1985 victory over St. Louis's rival Redbirds in an all-Missouri World Series, sparkled in color and display. The 40,000-plus stadium, with seats facing second base and arranged in tiers of maroon, gold, and orange, had two spectacular showcases for which

Kaufmann shelled out more than $3,500,000 — a giant Royal-crested scoreboard and a cascading 10-foot center-field waterfall.

Kansas City displayed the American League's first all-synthetic playing surface. And though no one took advantage of sizable home run distances — 330-385-410-385-330 — with a 12-foot high outfield wall, Royal fans were treated to royal batting. In 1980 KayCee's brilliant third baseman, George Brett, produced a .390 average, the highest since Ted Williams broke the .400 barrier 39 years previously.

San Diego and Montreal entered the major leagues in 1969. Montreal, a strength of the International League as a Dodgers' farm club, brought an international flavor to baseball. Some lamented that the two Canadian rival cities, Montreal and Toronto, couldn't be in the same league.

Unfortunately, with Montreal reeling from financial boondoggling of the 1967 World's Fair, efforts by Mayor Jean Drapeau to add 12,000 seats and a roof for the 25,000-seat Autostade were rebuffed. Only Drapeau's efforts and fast-talking to National League president Warren Giles turned a 3000-seat playground ball park into a 30,000-seat stopgap. Like Houston's Colt Stadium, Jarry Park wasn't the answer, but the single-deck structure sufficed. The park had boundaries of 340 at the lines, 420 to center field.

The problem was that despite unhappy clucking from Expo club management and the National League, the wait was eight years. Then, instead of a domed stadium as promised and necessary since Montreal is hardly a summer resort city, the outrageously expensive $770,000,000 Olympic Stadium had to do. Montreal would not pay more for a dome, mon dieu.

With 325-foot foul lines and a center field 404 feet away, the stadium has deep shadows from a large overhang, almost as somber as the city's attitude after close-call races. The queen of Quebec still draws amply and hopefully, roof or no, but — eureka! — the crown finally was placed in 1987.

Roofed stadiums became the "in" thing after Houston put up the Astrodome. Seattle got its second chance with a group headed by Danny Kaye, movie comedian. The showcase just south of downtown Seattle in 1977 was the Kingdome, built for nearly 65,000 in football and almost 60,000 in baseball. With reachable fences removed from the steady, thin rain of the Japanese Current, somebody there might break the record.

At Minneapolis, too, a hefty Kent Hrbek or another might find the target often enough in Hubert H. Humphrey Metrodome, a 55,000-seat stadium protected by an air-supported fiberglass roof, a 340-ton cover harnessed by steel cables and 90-horsepower generated fans. The 10-acre construction opened in 1982 on Chicago Avenue South offers an enticing target of 343 feet in left field, 408 in center, 327 in right.

When Toronto narrowly missed luring the San Francisco Giants in 1976, the American League acted quickly, going its own way unilaterally now, to add the Maple Leafs and also Seattle in 1977. At long last, after rejections to expand the Canadian National Exhibition grandstand, where the football Argonauts played, CNE was enlarged to 40,000 for baseball and 55,000 for football.

The time-honored Toronto nickname—Maple Leafs—was junked in favor of a new name, the Blue Jays, and Toronto rose quickly from leftover material to championship caliber. The Blue Jays won their first division title in a short eight-year span.

Why leave San Diego for last in this quick trip around the big league baseball country? Not because the Padres haven't come a long way, as Lowell Reidenbaugh described, from the time of old Lane Field in the Pacific Coast League when a curious groundskeeper discovered that first base was only 87 feet from home plate, rather than Alexander Cartwright's magical 90. The fact that the same fellow discovered that the right-field foul pole was 10 feet shorter than the posted 335 isn't surprising. Too many outfield-fence measurements even now might belie the yardage or metric figures.

But San Diego is mentioned, again with respect to the Padres having come up in reasonable time with a contending team, because Jack Murphy Stadium, as the new athletic arena was rechristened, was named for a sportswriter, not many of whom (ahem!) ever get their name on anything except a laundry list or a police citation. Eat your heart out, Ted Giannoulas (the San Diego journalism student who became "*The* Chicken," the fair San Diego fowl).

San Diego is listed last because the man who saved the 1969 franchise when they wanted to move it to Washington did what more than one clubowner must have wanted to do. At Ray Kroc's first home opener as owner of the Padres in 1974, he grabbed the public-address system and told nearly 40,000 fans, "This is the most stupid ball playing I've ever seen."

Kroc, you see, had grown up in Chicago rooting for the slugging Cubs of the late '20s and early '30s and this ineptitude, if you'll forgive the expression, was to Kroc a crock. Oh, sure, he apologized, but the McDonald hamburger king had made his point.

Just as Mrs. Kroc did after his death when the Padres won an AL West title in 1984, easing her pain. She remembered to kiss manager Dick Williams goodbye with thanks when Williams set a record in 1986 by quitting even before the rooster came up or The Chicken.

Now that you've read the sites and seen the distances of modern two-sport parks—330 at the lines, 370 in the power alleys, and 410 in center at Jack Murphy's joint—it's easy to see why if guys hit longer home runs and more guys hit them, they hit fewer of them, and why the stolen base came back to baseball after the quick kick went out of the companion sport, football. Obviously, parks are now bigger in capacity and field measurements.

With westward-ho the expansion, why not to the Far East? Japan has an interest in baseball and, obviously, too, the money, much of it ours. Too far away? Heck, no. With the highest-powered, most-sophisticated jets, Tokyo wouldn't be any farther away than, say, Los Angeles was by train from Chicago on December 7, 1941.

7
Alone in
a Crowd

The umpire, baseball's cop on the corner and judge without a black robe, often is hard-headed and dictatorial, hypersensitive and egotistical, even rabbit-eared. But the ump is as necessary as the ball and the bat. Evidence was recorded as far back as 1846 when the game's possible inventor and definite innovator, Alexander Cartwright, umpired and fined a Knickerbockers' player "six cents for swearing."

Although once-upon-a-sandlot, many of us called our own kid games, with or without arguments, professional ball would be a survival-of-the-foulest without the presence of neutral supervision.

Umpires are unsung. Until recently, they also were underpaid, a reflection as far back as when they were required to work as fashionably as old-fashioned, top-hatted funeral directors. They worked with dignity from a position off to one side rather than behind the plate because, actually, neither the ump nor the catcher had the equipment to stand up and face the music of a batter's solid foul tip.

If they could be killed thusly as innocent victims, at least two were killed outrageously as a result of drastic overreaction from spectators. As noted by Ira L. Smith and H. Allen Smith in *Low and Inside,* an umpire was bludgeoned to death at Lowndesborough, Alabama in 1899. Two years later at Farmersburg, Indiana, another umpire was killed similarly.

If there's one startling statistic as umpiring's brightest hour, it's that only one game official ever was cashiered out for dishonesty. He was Richard Higham of the National League in 1882. The mayor of Detroit, an NL city at the time, was also president of the Tigers. Mayor W. G. Thompson charged that Higham and another umpire, John Doscher, colluded with pool gamblers to manipulate game outcomes. The league expelled Higham and, momentarily, dropped Doscher for dishonorable conduct.

To suggest that at no time before or since an umpire "fixed" a game might be as naive as belief that umps were treated fairly financially from the $5-a-game fee outset until recent times. Far more than players indulged by proud, enthusiastic fans with perquisites of playing, umpires were vulnerable when sponging for free or cut-rate meals or having extremely short arms when asked to pay for an open-date golf game, etc. By 1988, senior umpires finally got up to $100,000 a year, a result of a threatened second strike at the beginning of the 1987 season. At long last, they were catching up to, if not really surpassing, inflation and their importance in the game.

This is, indeed, a far cry from 1876 when the National League was organized at New York's old Park Central Hotel. Not only was the pay limit the thin fin mentioned, but not until the third season was the home side denied the right to pick one of the league's 20 nominees to work a game. If you wondered where the slur "homer" began — and it's enough now to make the men in blue and gray see red — it obviously was when the traveling team was given the backhand of the white-suited side's choice.

Fact is, as researched by Lee Allen for his 1955 book, *The Hot Stove League,* the upstart American Association did more than anyone else to help the status and stature of the umpire until, perhaps Ban Johnson, founder of the American League. Johnson, former Cincinnati newspaperman, was a stickler for protecting his umpires. Actually the National League's second president and true league organizer, Chicago's William Hulbert, also was sympathetic to the cause of umpires, usually poorly educated as well as poorly paid.

When the Association came in as the National's major league competitor in 1882, the NL sneered because the new league charged only 25 cents admission, not 50, and because the Association had so many saloon-and-distillery owners. They jeered it as the Beer-and-Whiskey League. But the "saloon" circuit selected league-appointed, full-salaried umpires.

At Hulbert's behest, the National retaliated in 1883 by ordaining that umpires could not work in their native city or live in any league town. Later, both regulations were relaxed, but the one-umpire system, almost unbelievable when four umpires still can't see everything, continued as a farce until Johnson came along with the AL in 1901. The Association dropped out in 1892 and returned later as a minor league.

With only one ump in action, the official hunkered up behind the plate when the catcher did and both wore protective equipment. With a man on base, the umpire stationed himself directly behind the pitcher, but he would have needed eyes in the back of his head to keep up with the hocus-pocus of legal-eagle, eager-beavers such as the Naughty Nineties' shrewd Baltimore Orioles.

When the ball was in play and the umpire forced to look one way, the Orioles' footpads would sneak shortcuts between bases. Defensively, they would hip a runner off a bag or just plain obstruct him by forcing a detour. Wily, tough John McGraw, who had one legitimate kick coming that will be explained later, was crafty at third base when, as the umpire looked skyward to make certain a fly ball was caught, Mac would hook his fingers into the belt of a runner tagging up to score. The only time Muggsy caught crabcakes in his eye was when a wise guy loosened his belt. So McGraw wound up with the evidence in his hand—the other guy's belt.

Johnson, who hated umpire-baiter McGraw so much that McGraw jumped over to fame and fortune as manager of the Nationals' New York Giants, upgraded umpiring. By 1906, he hired his league's *fifth* umpire, its first swing man, 22-year-old Billy Evans, just out of Cornell University.

By 1912, each league already had contributed two umpires each to work a World Series. Then, they made it official—two for every league game—with a couple of spares. By 1933, even though times were tough, salaries smaller and player rosters trimmed from 25 to 23, the majors had seen the wisdom of using three-man umpiring crews. Four men became standard in 1952. Finally, also, the extra Series umpire provided by each league was moved out of the stands onto the outfield foul lines.

Here, differences between the two leagues' umpires began to manifest themselves. For one, graceful, dexterous Jack Sheridan of the AL worked for years wearing only a mask, disdaining the protector and shinguards of catchers and umpires. Stubbornly, umps followed their league's two top men, the National League's Bill Klem and the American's Tommy Connolly.

Employing Connolly's technique, American League umpires wore a blown-up protector and stood directly behind the catcher, peering over his shoulder. National League umpires used Klem's style. They wore a horsehair-padded, neck-to-vest dickey under their plate coat, umpiring "inside"; that is, between the left shoulder of the catcher and right shoulder of a right-handed hitter and the right shoulder of the catcher and the left shoulder of a left-handed batter.

Before the four-umpire crews were standardized in 1952, the two leagues' umpires worked the bases differently, too. The American would station its two umpires on the bases near second and third when a runner was on first, creating a situation where the runner or runners would come to them, counterclockwise. By contrast, with one man on base, the NL kept an umpire behind first base and the other at second, relying on the plate umpire to come down to third, clockwise, if there was a play at third. If the play continued beyond third, the first-base umpire would swing back to make the call at home.

One remaining difference, resolved when Lee MacPhail replaced Joe Cronin as American League president in 1973, had the AL umpire at second base working _behind_ the bag. The NL stationed its second-base umpire at a point _between the pitcher and the infielder,_ hopefully out of the batter's concentrating eyes. A difference lay in the playing rules. If an umpire is hit by a batted ball _after_ it has passed an infielder, the ball remains in play. When the umpire is in _front_ of an infielder, the ball is dead and the runners advance a base.

When the two-league umpiring differences were eliminated, a grandfather clause permitted the last AL umpire wearing the outside protector to work that way until he retired in 1986. Unfortunately, the uniformity included adoption of the other NL decision that moved the second-base umpire into the infield rather than behind it.

Now, the two leagues' umpires even dress alike after years of variety, mainly in the American League. Back in the 1930s, the NL let umpires depart from the traditional blue-serge suit with white pants on Sundays and holidays. More recently, NL men were permitted by Warren Giles, who became president in 1951, to shed their coats and also ties on hot days favoring open-throat, light-blue shirts. Finally, small uniform numbers were added to the left shirt sleeve.

The American League, often regarded as stuffier and slower to react, moved more dramatically, thanks in part to Charley Finley. For television purposes, aided by the Yankees' George Steinbrenner, Finley urged color. So the AL went first (1969) to blue coats with gray pants, now the colorful combination worn by _both_ leagues. Next, the AL switched to a royal-blue coat, then to a burgundy blazer with blue pants, blue shirt, and red cap. Finally, in 1976 the AL went to the gray pants that the NL adopted when the leagues agreed not to disagree. The AL also added numbers.

So now umpires in the majors are much alike. The NL, which used to have umps straddle the foul lines, exposing them to a fair-hit ball, stand in foul territory as the AL did. Also, adopting the American's method, National arbiters hold hands high, then point into foul territory when a batted ball is foul. Previously, they immediately gestured foul. At the plate, using the inside-shoulder technique invented by Klem, AL umpires also position themselves lower to get a good look at a low pitch.

Trouble is, as rules' definition of the strike zone changed, umpires have gone above, yet below, the description. Once, the rule required a strike from *between* the shoulders and kneecaps. Next, from the uniform letters to the *top* of the knees. For a time in 1963, answering beefs about the length of games, rulesmakers sought to liberalize the strike zone, seeking to reduce bases on balls. Instead, more strikeouts created less action and fewer runs.

So the strike zone was lowered when the mound height was reduced from 15 to 10 inches after the run-scoring drought in 1968, the Year of the Pitcher. But apparently from habit, not edict, umpires have shrunk the strike zone so that it's difficult for pitchers to get a strike *barely above belt high.* Check your own ball park scene or television set. Gobbledygook language designed for use in '88 won't help.

Financially, a result of the 1987 strike threat, umpires get up to $100,000 a season and retain virtually a rotation system for working All-Star, League Championship and World Series games. The extra pay, ranging from $2500 upward to $15,000, is nice, but debatable because it discourages a merit system. Back when league presidents used their own judgment, a Bill Klem, for instance, would work the World Series every other year. So would a Tommy Connolly or a Charles (Cy) Rigler. Klem had 18 Series assignments.

Hotel and meal money, nearly $100 a day, is adequate, but with umpires required to retire at 55, several years before Social Security opportunities, an improved pension plan of up to $30,000 a year still needs tinkering and improvement. If we seem to be spending baseball's money freely, the umpire's integrity and independence is essential — *always.*

Umpiring is better and, also, unfortunately, bigger. Yale's former president, A. Bartlett Giamatti, succeeding retired Charles S. Feeney as president of the National League in 1987, urged several broad-beamed, pot-bellied umps to lose weight.

Thanks to the late Fred Fleig, former National League secretary, umpires no longer wrestle their heavy umpire equipment or even, if desired, personal luggage. It's shipped air special from ball park to ball park.

Uniforms now are provided by each league, a fringe benefit, and the cute, white-trimmed black umpiring shoes are provided by Pony

Shoes, an endorsement approved by the Major League Umpire Association. Courteously, ball clubs provide a sandwich or two before the game and afterward a soda or a beer.

So umpiring is a far better job now, attracting college graduates rather than coal miners or former players who often weren't qualified. But it's still a poor-paying, tough-traveling job in the minors. Appointment to the bigs always will be a matter of judgment—personal choice of someone in each league's office. So major league umps, out on strike in 1979, were out of bounds when they stonewalled then and too often later their replacements from the minors as "scabs." Most of them would have taken the same opportunity because it would be a political no-no to turn down the chance. And politics plays perhaps too great a part in picking umpires.

Even so, there have been great umpires. For instance, two of the five Hall of Fame umpires, Bill Klem and Billy Evans, thought the greatest was Jack Sheridan, the gutty guy who wore only a mask in his era in the American League, 1901–14. To us, Cy Rigler, who introduced the foul-strike motion as part of his ability and durability, merits a bow. So do Hall of Famers Jocko Conlan and Cal Hubbard. Also, Al Barlick, Bill McGowan, John (Beans) Reardon, Larry Goetz and Nestor Chylak.

Chylak, a war-wounded old soldier, was the last big league umpire to forfeit a ball game. Back in 1974 at Cleveland, where the Indians were offering a boomeranging promotion, i.e., beer at only 10 cents a bottle, a crowd of more than 25,000 overindulged in liquid enjoyment. When Cleveland's Ed Crosby hit a game-tying outfield fly to rightfielder Jeff Burroughs in the ninth inning, overzealous fans leaped out and swarmed the Texas ballplayer.

In defense of the beleaguered lone Ranger, manager Billy Martin and teammates rushed out, brandishing bats. Cleveland fans' fury mounted. A chair hit Cleveland pitcher Tom Hilgendorf on the head. Chylak also was hit. The Indians' manager, Ken Aspromonte, winced. He knew what was coming. Chylak forfeited the game. Five persons were arrested. Seven spectators were hurt. The next night after the lakefront fiasco, Johnny Carson cracked on his TV show that the crowd was so unruly because the Indians sold beer for a dime and then forgot to unlock the rest rooms.

Protests and forfeits aren't funny, but they are necessary if only rarely. The most prominent protest was in 1983, Lee MacPhail's last year as American League president. It was the famed Great Pine Tar Case at New York's Yankee Stadium. When Kansas City's George Brett hit an apparent game-winning, two-run homer in the visitors' ninth, Yankee manager Billy Martin—yeah, Billy and trouble got around a lot together!—challenged the amount of pine tar Brett used on his bat. Pine tar helped hitters grip the bat better.

Plate umpire Ed Tim McClelland, to whom Martin appealed, conferred with umpiring crew chief Ed Brinkman. The umpire measured and found that the pine tar extended an inch or so farther than the 18-inch limit prescribed in baseball rule 1.10 (b). Brinkman upheld New York's protest, declared Brett out, nullifying the home run and giving the Yankees the ball game.

An enraged Brett rushed out and had to be restrained from assaulting Brinkman. When the late Dick Howser angrily protested the defeat, veteran Royals' pitcher Gaylord Perry sneaked into the pandemonium at home plate, grabbed the bat, and rushed it into hiding in the visitors' clubhouse. There, a uniform guard intercepted Exhibit "A." Four days later, league president MacPhail upheld Kansas City's protest.

Overturning his umpires, MacPhail exonerated them and, instead, criticized the playing rules, which he said "should be rewritten and clarified." MacPhail's point, supported by most baseball men, was that the pine tar restriction had been written into the rules not because a batter's contact or batting-power potential was improved by the gooey substance, but merely that the pine tar upon the presumed hitting surface of the bat defaced the ball, an unnecessary expense because the ball had to be thrown out.

The Yankees' owner, George Steinbrenner, took the reversal with extreme discourtesy. First, he said, "If the Yankees lose the decision by one game, I wouldn't want to be Lee MacPhail living in New York. Maybe he should go house-hunting in Kansas City."

Next, when ordered to finish out the game with Kansas City leading, 5–4, Steinbrenner obtained a Bronx borough justice's grant of a preliminary injunction barring the replay. Later, when a New York State Supreme Court appellate division stayed the grant, Steinbrenner tried to set a 2 P.M. replay for the fragmentary five-out finish for which MacPhail had ordered a 6 o'clock start. Finally, before the Royals preserved their lead and victory in just 12 minutes and 16 pitches before only 1245 persons admitted at the wrap-up six weeks later, Martin placed left-handed first baseman Don Mattingly at second base and pitcher Ron Guidry in center field.

Before pitcher George Frazier delivered the first ball to Hal McRae, the Yankees tried appeal plays at first and second base. When the umpires waved off the appeal plays, Martin approached a new crew chief, Dave Phillips. Forearmed if not forewarned, Phillips whipped out a notarized letter signed by the four umpires in the previous game, testifying that batter Brett and the Kansas City runner had touched all of the bases. For the Yankees' shameful spoil-sport reaction, Commissioner Bowie Kuhn slugged Steinbrenner with a $250,000 fine for "certain public statements." In addition, King George was directed to pick up the $50,000 legal fees the commissioner's office had incurred.

The National League's most recent protest upheld came a few years earlier (1980). It was more amusing than serious, the inadvertent absence of a ninth man on defense, as required by the rules.

With the Mets' Pete Falcone only one out away from a shutout over visiting Houston, a ball came out of the left-field bullpen and onto the infield. An instant before the pitcher delivered to Jeff Leonard for a game-ending out, umpire Doug Harvey called "time." So the umpires had to shoo the retreating New York team back onto the field.

When play resumed and Leonard this time singled, Mets' manager Joe Torre came out with a complaint. His side had left the field and been forced to return to it so fast that his first baseman hadn't reached the diamond in time. On Torre's appeal that play should not been resumed, the umpires agreed. Leonard was required to return from first base and to bat again.

As a result, Bill Virdon, Houston manager, protested on the grounds that his side had lost a baserunner through no fault of its own. The umpires overruled. However, seated with administrative assistant Blake Cullen, in charge of umps, league president Chub Feeney recognized Virdon's protest. So he erased Leonard's putout the second time up in the ninth and, next morning, he ordered the game resumed before the regularly scheduled action, two out and—yeah!—Leonard at bat again.

"Imagine," said Cullen, "Leonard batted four straight times."

An all-time oddity, of course, and, in addition, Falcone, unable to come back, won a game, but lost credit for a complete shutout.

Forfeits have been more rare than protests, but they run the gauntlet in the National League back to 1907, a year the Philadelphia Phillies won by forfeit at New York's Polo Grounds. On an opening day obviously too cold for baseball, the grounds crew had cleared the field, banking snow around the edges. Bored as the Giants were losing a one-hitter to the Phillies' Frank Corriden, fans began firing snowballs at the players. One whizzed past Bill Klem's ear. The "Old Arbitrator," as he was self-styled, was young then, but still pretty salty. He halted the game and awarded it to Philadelphia.

The American League had a forfeit its first season, 1901, Detroit over Chicago, when the White Sox were accused of stalling. The Sox also were involved in the most recent oddity, 1979. Bill Veeck's son sweet-talked the sport-shirted iconoclast, a big band devotee of the

1930s and early '40s, into permitting a rock concert at Comiskey Park when baseball still was in season.

For a fact, Comiskey Park's field looked as corrugated as Veeck senior's furrowed forehead, but, even though the White Sox advertised games with Baltimore each of the next two days and traditionally the home club has authority to begin a game, the umpires would not permit play. For unhappy cash customers who had trekked out to the park, the arbiters said of the Disco Demolition:

"Blame the umpires!"—and, for once, they meant it.

Now and then, far less often than the field or fans believe, umpires *do* make mistakes, particularly when they give opposite calls on the same play or try to make a decision with two baseballs in play at the same time.

If the St. Louis Cardinals and Chicago Cubs, old rivals, occur often in here, they bring out the beast and the best in each other and the worst in the umpires. When they get through—and it's probably true, too, when the New York Yankees play the Boston Red Sox—none would believe that Irish umpire Tim Hurst meant it when he crowed years ago of "empiring":

"You can't beat thim (sic) hours!"

To the umpires it was a l-o-n-g night at St. Louis in 1953 when Tom Gorman, a young umpire, and Hal Dixon, a rookie, gave a conflicting safe-and-out call that caused a traffic problem and classic confusion. With bases loaded, St. Louis's Wally Moon hit a low liner to left, where Chicago's Ralph Kiner caught or trapped the ball.

When the third-base umpire ruled no catch, the two lead runners broke. Meanwhile, headed for second, the runner on first saw the second-base umpire's "out" sign and retreated to his bag. Confusion reigned and reigned. Both teams protested.

Ultimately, shooing away the players, veteran Larry Goetz huddled with his two young red-faced associates. He decided, finally, that the second-base umpire had jurisdiction. Therefore, the catch call stood and the runner was doubled off second base. Curiously, the umpires permitted the runner on third to score, ruling he had tagged up on the fly ball and scored before the man on second was doubled off.

The run was a questionable sop to a double out on what would have been a decisive hit. Afterward, Goetz humanized it magnificently. The jut-jawed, red-necked codger wouldn't let the press reach his fledgling officials. Instead, he stepped out and, answering a question, put it rhetorically?

"What was it? Lousy umpiring, that's what it was."

At times the conflicting calls can be made at the same base, as reflected in a prize-winning photo taken by the *St. Louis Post-Dispatch*'s

Lynn T. Spence in 1969. With shortstop Steve Huntz and second baseman Julian Javier ranging back for a looping ball off Bill Sudakis's bat, third baseman Mike Shannon alertly broke to cover second base. As a result, taking a throw from centerfielder Curt Flood, Shannon tagged Sudakis sliding into second.

Retreating from the outfield, second-base umpire John Kibler called the runner "out." Trailing the play from first, figuring Kibler couldn't get back, Ed Vargo signaled "safe." The double decision was a prize. So was Spence's photo. Los Angeles' protest, in a game won by the Cardinals, 6–2, was overruled.

No decision was necessary because St. Louis won a 1959 game at Chicago's Wrigley Field when two baseballs were in play. On a full-count pitch from Bob Anderson, Stan Musial walked as the ball whizzed to the backstop, and catcher Sammy Taylor whirled to argue with plate umpire Vic Delmore that Musial had swung at the ball. Anderson also stormed toward the plate as Musial, loping toward first, was urged by coach Harry Walker to speed up for second.

Meanwhile, sensing the situation, third baseman Alvin Dark charged in and fielded the ball, which already had been touched by the batboy. Wisely, the Cubs' field-announcing perennial, Pat Pieper, rejected the ball as if it were a hand grenade. Just as Dark scooped up the original ball, Anderson stuck out his glove. Absentmindedly, Delmore plunked another ball in it.

With Musial running and the Chicago bench shouting, Anderson whirled and threw wildly toward second. Musial, seeing the wild throw, rounded the bag and headed toward third. Halfway, taking Dark's throw, shortstop Ernie Banks stood grinning. "Look what I got, Stanley," said Banks, applying a tag.

The umpires defended Delmore as St. Louis protested. The Cardinals then won the game. Said Giles, sighing in relief, "I'm glad I didn't have to make that decision."

Later, easing out Delmore, just as other umpires quietly are retired when not regarded sufficiently competent, Giles reversed his umpires in a game that created another unusual situation—three teams on the same field.

With Milwaukee leading Cincinnati in a 1954 game in the ninth inning, two on, one out, Bob Borkowski struck out as the runners broke off base. When catcher Del Crandall dropped the ball, Borkowski headed toward first base, though officially out because first base had been occupied with fewer than two out.

Crandall, recovering, threw too late to Eddie Mathews at third base in an effort to flag down the leading runner, Gus Bell. Mathews, seeing Borkowski run, threw to first and errantly. The ball struck the batter and bounced into right field. As Bell and Wally Post scored, the jubilant Reds thought they had tied the score.

No! The umpires ruled that because Borkowski was an illegal base-runner, he had interfered with the play. Therefore, messrs. Hal Dixon, Al Barlick, Lee Ballanfant, and Bill Jackowski ruled that because Borkowski already was out, a double play was demanded, ending the game—they thought.

On a protest from the Reds' Birdie Tebbetts, Giles acted with dispatch, ordering a replay, justifiably in this opinion. Cincinnati, which had gone to Chicago, was ordered back to Milwaukee, where the Braves were to play St. Louis. This feeling, apparently shared by the man who counted, Giles, was that Borkowski's reflex action in running on an automatic out, after seeing the ball dropped, was at least as excusable as the action of the third baseman or any other defensive player in making a play on him.

Presumably ruling each side is supposed to know the rules, Giles made a Solomon decision. Rather than permit the two game-tying runs to score, he arbitrarily stopped the action after Crandall threw late to third to head off Bell. So Cincinnati had men on second and third, two out, and darned if Johnny Temple didn't hit safely, tying the score, but only briefly. George (Catfish) Metkovich singled to win it in the home team's ninth, 4–3.

As National League president, Giles hated to reverse an umpire which is, in effect, par for the course. When Chub Feeney resigned as National League president in 1987, noting he could go back to rooting for the team with whom he'd grown up, the Giants, Feeney suddenly stepped in as president of the San Diego Padres. "Now," he said, "I can't root for the Giants, but I don't have to love the umpires any longer."

As a former football referee, Giles had been pretty tough on umpires when he ran the Cincinnati Reds, but he quickly became a defender of the faith. So he was wounded to the quick when his prized protégé, Gabe Paul, who had batboyed for him at Rochester and followed Giles to the majors, sent him a scorching telegram about umpiring.

Giles, who established the league office in Cincinnati, called Paul, then GM of the Reds. "I'm hurt, Gabe," he said. "I don't see how you can be so terrible to the umpires, to the league or to me."

Paul couldn't suppress a chuckle. "Gee, I'm sorry, Mr. Giles," he said, "but angry and in a hurry, I just copied down a letter you sent to Ford Frick a few years ago about the umpires and the league office."

For umps, other than good eyesight and good judgment, a tin ear, a willingness to trade profanity with managers or players and, especially, a sense of humor is most helpful. The American League's patron saint of umpires, Tommy Connolly, elected into the Hall of Fame with Bill Klem, was a model.

Connolly, only 5–6, 130 pounds, was a British import who grew up from age 13 in Natick, Massachusetts, and never played baseball, yet became a whiz on the rules—a gee whiz. As noted by Jim Kahn in his book, *The Umpire Story,* Connolly had a way with words and with men.

The imp, who umped two years in the NL and then the first 31 of the American's existence, was chastised profanely one time by Babe Ruth. Without raising his voice, the stately little man cooled him off. "Babe, you ought to be ashamed of yourself, a big fellow like you acting like this. Now, run along to the clubhouse."

Sheepishly, the Babe went. The episode, reportedly 1922, was said to be the last time that Ruth ever was run or that Connolly ever "chased" anyone.

Once, Detroit's Bobby Veach, hard-hitting outfielder, stormed at the umpire that a line drive he hit down the left-field line had been fair, not foul. "Hit fair, Tom," Veach insisted. "I can see the mark on the foul line."

Connolly, brushing off the plate, shrugged. "Well, Bob," he said, "I'll tell you what you do. You run out and bring in the foul line so I can look at it."

By comparison with Connolly, Klem was a noisy fellow, though not much larger. He was fog-horned, wide-mouthed with a pouting lower lip that made him look, caricaturistically, like . . . well, like a catfish. And, oh, oh, if you (or anyone) ever dared call Klem "Catfish," you— or he—would be gone. After all, the Old Arbitrator had his own mirror and sensitivity.

Klem, originally Klimm, tried everything before he became an umpire, even tried to play ball professionally. Only reluctantly he turned to umpiring, he told author Kahn, because umpires weren't "gentlemen" in those days. "And I," Klem insisted, "always was a gentleman—a gentleman steelworker, a gentleman bartender and, on occasion, even a gentleman bookmaker."

Truly, Klem dressed like a gentleman, too. On the field, bow-tied, he wore a uniform tailored for him, pleated horizontally across the back. His cap, somehow, seemed neater, nicer, too, like latter-day players' caps, indicating he had his own caps made. Off the field, he dressed with a breezy neatness, favoring sports jackets, light-colored, pleated slacks, two-tone shoes and the newest Nassau straw hats. He lived liked a well-to-do Floridian, spending most of his winters there, including many at the race track. His trips to the track, a no-no with Judge Landis, infuriated the commissioner, who called him Will-yum.

Although astute Tommy Connolly wanted Klem for the American League, Bill opted for the NL in 1905 even though he knew Ban Johnson was a stronger president and also trying to live with the Giants' John McGraw would be extremely tough. Intimidating umpires was one of the forces in baseball's Little Napoleon, who hated to be called "Muggsy," nickname of an unsavory Baltimore politician, Muggsy McGraw, when the manager played there.

One time early, McGraw threatened to get Klem's job. "If you can get it," Bill sniffed, "I don't want it."

Years later, 1928, after blistering oral battles with McGraw, Klem indirectly cost his old forensic foe a pennant chance. Late in the race when the Giants were only a half-game behind St. Louis, a Giants' player, Andy Reese, was caught in a decisive rundown play against the Chicago Cubs. Ultimately, locked in a bear hug with Gabby Hartnett, hefty Chicago catcher, Reese was tagged out by third baseman Clyde Beck. A rooftop newspaper photograph, blown up at McGraw's request, was introduced in evidence the next morning at NL president John Heydler's office.

Because, even if wrong, it was a judgment call, not a rules' interpretation, Heydler threw it out. The Giants fell back and lost the pennant by two games. McGraw's attack this time was so vitriolic that the umpire told Heydler he thought he would quit.

Still, he stayed on through 1940, a year when he was struck by a batted ball and decided that, at 66, it was time to step down. Although he had umpired World Series regularly, he had been turned down five straight years by Judge Landis as a reprimand. In an elevator in the 1934 Series, Klem had a salty exchange of words with Detroit outfielder Leon (Goose) Goslin. National League president Ford Frick persuaded the commissioner to give Will-yum a graceful farewell.

When Klem no longer umpired with both hands grasping his coat lapels, like a powder-wigged judge holding his robe on the British bench, he became supervisor of umpires. One afternoon at Brooklyn, inebriated and fuming loudly at the umpires, the Dodgers' general manager, Larry MacPhail, sought to upset the superintendent, seated close by in the press box. He succeeded admirably. Suddenly, Klem walked down behind MacPhail and intoned in his deepest bass, "You, sir, are an *applehead!*"

Klem could be tolerant to a point. He liked "John McGraw Jr.," as they called Frank Frisch, probably in part because Frisch was tough on the American League in World Series play. In addition, Frisch, as first player and then manager, was funnier than his old New York boss. When Klem drew a line with his spiked shoes and pulled his watch, a tell-tale sign not to follow him and to get the hell back into action,

Frisch amused him by stepping *around* the line. But when the Fordham Flash keeled over in a latter-day argument and fell backward,
Klem leaned over him and roared:

"If you ain't dead, Frisch, yer outta the game!"

Frisch was involved one time when Klem was overruled by Heydler
in 1934, upholding Frisch's protest as player-manager of St. Louis's
Gas House Gang. In a game at Chicago, bases loaded for the Cubs,
breezing to victory behind Lon Warneke, Chicago's Chuck Klein lifted
a high wind-blown pop foul.

Retreating backward into fair territory, the Cardinals' catcher, Bill
DeLancey, fell down and the ball landed. Each runner advanced a base
and Klein reached first. Apocryphally, when Frisch argued for applica-
tion of the infield-fly rule, Klem is supposed to have retorted, "Since
when is a catcher an infielder?"

But, come now, Will-yum knew better. It's just that he probably
was right when he reasoned the ball couldn't be handled by an infielder because no one was near it. But Heydler upheld Frisch's protest, ruling that Klein should have been declared out. To Klem's embarrassment, the game was ordered resumed at the same point with
an extra put-out in Chicago's seventh inning. The Cubs still won the
game.

Klem's colleague, Cy Rigler, invented the right-handed strike motion at Evansville, Indiana, in 1904, a year before Rigler and Klem
came to the majors. Previously, coaches had used a hand signal to let
deaf mute outfielder William (Dummy) Hoy (1882–1902) know when
a pitch was a strike.

Klem apparently invented the fair-or-foul hand signal, a result of
a letter of complaint from a Milwaukee lawyer who had seen a runner
and batter continue to run because they couldn't hear even the sten-
torian call of the umpire. At first, Klem conceded he thought the bar-
rister ought to stick to his torts, but his better judgment told him the
man was right.

Of Klem's contribution, one that must appeal to all umpires of integrity was misunderstood. "I never said 'I never missed one in my
life,'" he explained in Kahn's book. "Silk O'Loughlin said it and meant
it. I meant it as not having missed any here."

The Old Arbitrator pointed to his heart.

A fairminded man, Klem thought his old antagonist, John Mc-
Graw, had been victimized by an umpiring call in an historic 1908 decision. The call cost McGraw what would have been his 11th pennant
in 30 years, he insisted until his death in 1934. It was, if you will, the
most significant of all the safe-and-out, fair-and-foul, yes-and-no decisions in baseball.

This was the technicality by which plate umpire Hank O'Day called out Giants' rookie first baseman Fred Merkle for failing to touch second when running from first on a teammate's apparent game-winning single in 1908. The delayed decision, made as New York fans poured happily onto the field with the belief the Giants had won the game, 2–1, resulted in ultimately calling it a tie, to be replayed only if necessary.

When the Chicago Cubs, seeking a third straight pennant, ended the season exactly even with the Giants, a replay was necessary. Chicago won it at New York, 4–2, as Mordecai (Miner) Brown, working in long relief, outdueled the great Christy Mathewson. Light-hitting Joe Tinker, Chicago shortstop, hit a key triple that broke down Matty, a 37-game winner.

Previous to the play in which young Merkle, relieving an ailing Fred Tenney that day, followed monkey-see, monkey-do custom, runners often failed to go through the formality of touching the next base when forced to move up on a decisive hit. Al Bridwell's single scored Moose McCormick with two out, but Merkle, heading for second base, peeled off and ran to the clubhouse.

Earlier, Johnny Evers, the Cubs' second baseman, had argued with umpire O'Day at Pittsburgh. That time O'Day hadn't seen the runner's oversight. This time, though the call was base umpire Bob Emslie's, Emslie had to dive out of the way and didn't see the mishap. O'Day saw it.

Evers yelled for the ball, got one, and touched second base. With the crowd on the field, O'Day made no decision, but hours later he confirmed the force, a third-out play, ending the game with no runs. National League president Harry Pulliam upheld the umpire.

"Bad umpiring and gutless thinking at league headquarters," reflected Klem, aware that league president Pulliam, badgered by McGraw and others, committed suicide the following year. O'Day, Chicago-born and favoring the Cubs, managed his hometown team four years later. He died in Chicago in 1935 at age 72.

Ever since, as you'll note, players do complete the formality of touching the bases in a potential force-out situation. To this day, though time has dulled the sting, a mental mistake often has been called a "Merkle."

The 20-year-old kid's faux pas, yukked up by a vaudeville comedian who quipped, "I call my cane 'Merkle' because it has a bone head," became a dunce in defeat, a negative common noun like Quisling. (Vidkun Quisling, Norwegian war minister, a Nazi party member, traitorously instructed waterfront patrols not to oppose German invaders in 1940.)

McGraw defended Merkle stoutly. The player lasted 16 years as a great fielding, fair hitting first baseman. When the Giants brought back old heroes for a reunion in 1950, Merkle, then 62, went reluctantly and was given a standing ovation at the Polo Grounds. When he died six years later at Daytona Beach, Florida, his family expressed bitterness of his deep, longtime hurt.

Umpiring *is* difficult, but umpires are not *infallible*. They don't always know the rules or, at times, fortunately, the timetable.

Back in 1968 in a St. Louis-San Francisco game at Candlestick Park, as Willie Mays broke for second base on a two-strike pitch, Willie McCovey swung and missed, striking out. As Tim McCarver threw to second, McCovey jerked his bat into a backswing that deflected the throw. Under baseball rule 7.09(f), Mays also should have been declared out.

The rule reads, as ample as one author's red nose, "It is interference by a batter or runner when any batter or runner who has just been put out hinders or impedes any following play being made on a runner. Such runner shall be declared out for the interference of his teammate."

Plate umpire Bill Jackowski made the call correctly, a double penalty, but when the Giants protested the call because McCovey's backswing had been *unintentional* interference, young third-base umpire Harry Wendelstedt persuaded Jackowski to permit Mays to stay at second base.

Just a few days earlier, as the youngest member of Jackowski's umpiring crew, Wendelstedt made the plane assignments for a trip from Cincinnati to San Francisco by way of a stopoff at Houston for a series. The rookie umpire had the crew booked out of Houston to Dallas on a late Braniff flight that wouldn't get them into San Francisco until a few hours before game time.

The older arbiters grumbled and, as they strolled through the airport lobby into Houston, Frank Secory glanced at a schedule board and did a double take. There was an earlier flight to SanFran on National.

So Jackowski overruled Wendelstedt then and, as author Broeg joshed old friend Bill at lunch shortly afterward in St. Louis, it's a wonder Jackowski ever would let Harry *ever* overrule him again.

After all, the umpires took the National flight Secory spotted casually. The Braniff flight on which Wendelstedt had scheduled them crashed and killed all 85 persons aboard.

8
S-C-A-N-D-A-L-S

Athletically, all of the U.S.-of-A. might have been a single Mudville if the mighty Casey had struck out in an early 1927 confrontation of right versus wrong. By comparison, the infamous Black Sox scandal and the plight of Shoeless Joe Jackson would have seemed a kindergarten crime—for impact.

If baseball's first commissioner, a crusty, profane old federal judge named Kenesaw Mountain Landis, who learned from a ballplayer (Pepper Martin) to spit tobacco between his teeth and never lost a fan's interest in a game he policed. . . . If. . . .

If Judge Landis had thumbed Ty Cobb and Tris Speaker into the Hall of *Shame,* what would have happened to baseball? To the memories of two of its top superstars? Would the Hall of Fame have begun 10 years later?

More than 60 years after Cobb and Speaker retired in tandem, two frequently listed with Babe Ruth on the "all-time" All-Star outfield, the terrible tempered Georgia Peach and graceful Gray Eagle are immortalized by the masses and the media, most of whom never saw either man swing a bat, cut a base's corner, or grab a fly ball.

After all, Cobb and Speaker hung it up in 1928, no longer able to play with the skill of old because Ty was nearly 42 and Tris 40, ages that were more impressive even then because players basically bowed out earlier. Speaker died at 70 in 1958, Cobb at 75 in 1961.

Cobb, premier base stealer and batting champion, whose career average of .367 seemed certain to stand as a monument to the man's drive and fury even if his 4191 hits didn't, was chosen first by members of the Baseball Writers' Association of America for the Hall of Fame in 1936.

Chances are that with the passage of time, Babe Ruth, a close second then, would be remembered better and by more, if only because of personal charisma and the popularity of sheer batting power. But Cobb had held the honor as No. 1 for many years in which he won 12 American League batting championships, nine of them in succession, and stole 892 bases.

Speaker, elected to Cooperstown the second time the BBWAA was polled (1937), was a close second to Cobb in the peak of their playing heyday, which covered the dead ball to the quivering horsehide of the 1920s. "Spoke" hit .344 in 22 seasons, two fewer than Cobb. He broke Ty's string of batting championships in 1916, and set a record of 793 doubles. Speaker also was perhaps the greatest defensive outfielder ever, the one who played the most shallowly and still was able to hightail back for deep drives.

So, between them, Cobb and Speaker represented for the double decades of their playing period and the years of worship that followed a grandpa-to-son-to-grandkid reverie. What if DiMag was great and Teddy Ballgame and Stan the Man and Wonderful Willie or Hammering Hank or Pete the Rose? You should have seen the Georgia Peach and the Gray Eagle!

But what if, as suggested earlier, Judge Landis had turned thumbs down instead of up when Detroit's Cobb and friendly foe Speaker, a standout for both Boston and then Cleveland, were accused of having conspired to bet on—and help throw—a ball game?

Would they have disappeared into the myths and mystique of Joe Jackson? Shoeless Joe was a hard hitting illiterate who was the most prominent of eight Chicago White Sox players barred by Landis from baseball for having conspired to throw the 1919 World Series to Cincinnati.

For all the recently surfacing sympathy for Jackson, a sweet swinging South Carolinian who had a career record of .356, Shoeless Joe has probably just two chances to have a bronzed plaque placed in his name in the Hall of Fame—little and none.

Cobb, who hated Ruth with apparent jealousy even more than the Babe disliked him, agreed with his box office rival on one thing: Both thought Jackson had the best batting stroke they had ever seen. The

Babe even tried to copy it. Jackson, hitting a .382 at age 31 when side-lined in 1920, died in disillusionment at 62.

Barred by Landis with Jackson, even though they were acquitted in a comic opera trial from which their signed confessions "disappeared," were four other regulars, two pitchers and a handyman off the 1919 White Sox, considered by many as one of the best ball clubs ever. Uh-uh, and most underpaid, too.

Blackballed by the white-haired little geezer, Landis, brought in to restore fandom's faith in baseball, were two other potential future Hall of Famers, pitcher Eddie Cicotte and third baseman George (Buck) Weaver. Also, first baseman and ringleader, Charles (Chick) Gandil, shortstop Charles (Swede) Risberg, centerfielder Oscar (Happy) Felsch, pitcher Claude (Lefty) Williams, and utility infielder Fred McMullin.

Obviously, McMullin, a wallflower as the Chisox won their second pennant in three years, was as necessary to a clubhouse conspiracy as only an eavesdropping wallflower can get, just as Weaver, of whom more will be written, was a victim in the commissioner's purge only because he'd had the ignoble thought that to tattle would make him a squealer. Buck never got a buffalo nickel out of the defiant disaster.

This one, outlined briefly above, was the granddaddy of all baseball scandals—certainly any ever disclosed—but there have been enough unsavory moments, not to mention damned fools who made horse's necks out of themselves in actions on and off the field. That is, as far back as before even the National League wet its infant diapers.

Investigation disclosed back in 1865, the year Yankee bluebellies and confounded Confeds quit shooting at each other, that the New York Mutuals conspired to throw a game to the much weaker Brooklyn Eckfords, 29–11. (Scores and errors were so high in that early era of rudimentary rules, underhand pitching, and gloveless play that when the St. Louis Browns and Syracuse Stars played a scoreless 15-inning game in 1877, a game of no errors in which St. Louis's Tricky Nichols pitched a two-hitter, the pre-season exhibition was saluted with a senti-mental dinner of revered recollection 30 years later.)

Although the Brooklyn Mutuals and Philadelphia Athletics did not finish the National League's first season, 1876, pleading financial in-ability to make the last western swing, the rubber-stamp first presi-dent, Morgan G. Bulkeley, a Hartford banker and later mayor there, reportedly wanted both teams expelled for throwing a game.

The man to whom the NL is most indebted was William A. Hul-bert, a Chicago baseball executive who took charge of what he really had been, i.e. a founding father virtually anonymous in comparison with the man who began the American League, Ban Johnson. Hulbert had only one weakness, as devilish Lee Allen related in *The National League Story,* published in 1961 when Allen was baseball historian at Cooperstown. Said Hulbert, "I'd rather be a lamppost in Chicago than a millionaire in any other city."

Gosh, Jimmy Walker, New York's flamboyant mayor of New York in the Roaring Twenties, couldn't have said it any better when he wondered why anyone wanted to be president when he could be mayor of New York!

Hulbert had an immediate handful in 1877 when the Louisville Colonels, a charter National League club, lost seven straight on an eastern swing, blowing the pennant. Club president Charles E. Chase received anonymous telegrams that tipped him several players were throwing games. In addition, John Haldeman, *Louisville Courier-Journal* sportswriter whose father, Walter, actually owned the club, also provided tell-tale tipoffs from the road.

Chase trapped confessions of players that served to have a said domino effect on two franchises. When star pitcher Jim Devlin and several other players were involved, they were drummed off the team that folded. Innocently, John R. Lucas, first St. Louis clubowner with the Browns, as the National League Cardinals then were called, lined up Devlin, catcher Charley Snyder, shortstop Bill Craver, and leading hitter George Hall, the leftfielder. Public disclosure that the players from the suspended franchise were tainted angered Lucas, embarrassed most by implications that he and his associates were aware of the stigma. He turned back his franchise to the league. St. Louis was without a professional franchise until the American Association Browns of 1882. The National League returned in 1892.

Thundered Hulbert when Chase's research became public, "You are banished from baseball for life. There's no place in our national game for crooked players." Devlin sought reinstatement for years. No sale. At only 34, he died in his hometown, Philadelphia.

An umpire was even involved in overt dishonesty in those seasons of infancy and infamy. Curiously, appointment of Dick Higham as an umpire showed questionable judgment, which marred National League progress. Higham, English-born and son of a prominent cricket player, had been a member of the Mutuals when the New York–Brooklyn club was suspect for dubious effort.

"Scandals" in baseball have been large and small, minor and major, serious and almost frivolous. For instance, as recently as 1976 George Brett, Kansas City's great third baseman, won a questionable batting championship over teammate Hal McRae when outfielder Steve Brye of Minnesota loped indolently and late after a late-inning fly ball on the final day of the season and acknowledged that, yes, he preferred to see Brett win the championship. Brett did, .333 to .332.

Harmless? Maybe. Yet back in 1910, there was all hell to pay after an episode at St. Louis. Highly favoring Napoleon Lajoie over Ty Cobb, who by then was a batting star despised for his temper and furious all-out effort, the Browns contrived to help Lajoie toward the batting title on the season's last day.

First, using a rookie third baseman, manager Jack O'Connor directed the kid, John (Red) Corriden, to play extremely deep for Lajoie. Nap tripled his first time up, but, next, Lajoie, a great and graceful player, yet not noted for running speed, bunted toward third base. The ball was not properly placed so that shortstop Bobby Wallace fielded it. Wallace, a great defensive player, reacted slowly and threw too late to first.

Thereafter, theoretically needing nine-for-nine to beat Cobb, who had knocked off the final two days of the season, Lajoie bunted again and again toward third and, except for one instance, beat out the ball to the deep-playing Corriden. Years later, Red was a grand old guy as a big league coach, affectionately called "Lollipop." But that black comedy afternoon in 1910 he was just a lamb.

Except for one bunt, a fielder's choice, all were base hits, giving Lajoie eight-for-nine, maybe enough, but maybe not. The Browns' dislike for Cobb was so great — several of Ty's Detroit teammates even sent Lajoie a congratulatory wire when they thought the Cleveland second baseman had won the title — that coach Harry Howell strolled over to the ground-level press box to inquire about the official scoring. Next, a note was sent with a batboy to offer St. Louis scorer E.V. Parrish a suit of clothes if he changed his ruling. Parrish refused. Bless him in the name of every underpaid newspaperman!

Graciously, aware that even the St. Louis crowd had applauded the popular Frenchman, the Chalmers company offered to give *each* player, Cobb and Lajoie, a new car. After both Ban Johnson and National Commission chairman Garry Herrmann of Cincinnati ruled out future awards, Johnson declared that Cobb had won the championship after all. Alleged official figures had Ty at .38444 to Nap's .38404. To this day, researchers aren't sure.

Angry and offended at the poor sportsmanship and doubtful ethics, the Browns' owner, Robert Lee Hedges, fired both manager O'Connor and the overzealous coach, Howell. Later, O'Connor won a lawsuit for his 1911 salary, $5000.

The point is, you see, effort over a 154-game schedule (now 162) is difficult to maintain at full level keel, we are aware. Baseball is played daily like a regular lunch pail working job, even if it isn't blue collar, and the reward is much greater than in the past. But even if achievements are inconsistent—and they obviously are in a game in which the good batters are out seven of every 10 times up and only the best pitchers win six of every 10 decisions—the effort must be there.

That's why, with no reflection on Bob Feller, author of the first major league game with 18 strikeouts, last day of the season records are suspect; for instance, the record for fastest games. The National League record of only 51 minutes was set in a final day game won by the New York Giants over the Philadelphia Phillies in 1919, 6–1. The AL shortest game by time was set seven years later on the final day, too. The Browns beat the champion Yankees in just 55 minutes, 6–2.

Pardon the suggestion, but even Mike Witt's perfect game for California against Texas on the last day of the 1984 season loses a bit of luster because it *was* the last day.

As Casey Stengel would say, look it up: To illustrate further, when the dethroned World Champion Cardinals floundered home in 1932 in a tie for sixth place with the New York Giants, the Redbirds played second-place Pittsburgh in a final-day doubleheader at St. Louis. The Pirates won the opener in one hour and 29 minutes, 7–1. The Cards took the second one in just two minutes longer, 7–4.

A doubleheader completed in one minute past three hours! Do you think they played that one with their cars packed and the engines running?

Similarly, when Feller, then flame-throwing fast with a jagged curve and just wild enough to keep the hitters loose, fanned 18 on October 2, final day of the 1938 season, maybe no Detroit hitter except Hank Greenberg wanted to take a serious toehold. Why die so young when the beer is cold and the kielbasa hot? The Tigers' Chet Laabs struck out five times. Greenberg, hoping for two homers with 58, could double once before darkness shortened the second game. No lights.

This is not intended to disparage efforts and/or records, but merely to emphasize the attitude that can lead to scandals. By the time Uncle Sam went into World War I, baseball had lowered its guard. Baseball was 99.44 percent pure at least, begging Ivory's pardon. Oh, sure, now and then the boys bet the horses, but they weren't betting on ball games any more or throwing 'em. Ah, but weren't they?

Take Hal Chase, for instance. If you believe the oldest old-timers, "Prince Hal," as they called the good looking, red-haired Californian, was perhaps the most graceful, finest fielding first baseman ever, indeed a high tribute. He was an oddball, even in a rare physical approach to the game. He threw left and batted right, a circumstance that, except for pitchers, is most unusual. Maybe a Rube Bressler, a Johnny Cooney, a Herman Reich, a Carl Warwick, a Cleon Jones, but how many others?

A good hitter, though not a great one when averages were higher, Chase once won a National League batting title (.339 for Cincinnati in 1916), but not before he had established himself as an individualist, a free spirit. One time, 1908, he jumped the New York Yankees to play outlaw ball in Stockton, California. Reacquired, he apparently undermined George Stallings as Yankee manager, obtained the job, then saw the Yanks plummet.

Sold to the White Sox in 1913, Chase jumped to Buffalo in the shortlived Federal League. At Cincinnati, even when hitting well for manager Christy Mathewson, he was apparently guilty of transgressions that, testimony later indicated, included seeking to urge others to throw games—pitchers Pol Perritt and Jimmy Ring.

In August 1918, immediately after John K. Tener resigned as president of the National League and was succeeded by John Heydler, Chase was suspended without pay "for indifferent playing." Indifferent, in Prince Hal's case, often meant strangely inconsistent, not poorly, because even then he was hitting .301.

Dropped by the Reds, Chase sued Cincinnati in late August 1918, for $1650 of his $7800 salary. Management was handicapped, as Allen noted, because Mathewson not only was in France, where the former great pitcher would suffer a poison gas attack that shortened his life, but also Heydler was only acting league president.

Most damagingly to Chase, Jimmy Ring, 23, a second-year Cincinnati pitcher, testified that when he had come up in '17 and entered a ball game with men on bases and the contest at stake, Chase walked over from his first base and said, "I've got some money bet on this game, and there's some for you if you lose."

Wise enough to recognize trouble, Ring shooed away Chase, but the pitcher still was unable to prevent a Redleg loss. Next day, he recalled, when he was seated in a hotel lobby, the first baseman walked past him and tossed $50 into his lap. The pitcher then told Mathewson.

Still, after a lengthy private hearing at which Chase appeared with three lawyers and a shorthand expert, Heydler gave a delayed decision in which he acquitted Prince Hal. Immediately, John McGraw gave two players for him.

Prophetically, *The Sporting News* editorialized, "The Cincinnati club learned its lesson along with other ball clubs that have harbored Chase, and it doesn't matter whether he is innocent or guilty of the charge of throwing games. Experience with him is no more than it deserves, just as Charley Comiskey got no more than was coming to him for ever taking the player to his bosom. Now it seems that John Mc-Graw wants to try it for a spell. So let it be."

Mathewson, back from service and with the Giants as a coach, re-fused to speak to Chase in 1919. After having played in 110 games, hitting .284, the 36-year-old Chase disappeared in late season. Mc-Graw explained lamely that Prince Hal had not been feeling up to par.

When the Chicago Cubs released Lee Magee, a 30-year-old out-fielder who batted .270 in 1919, Magee sued the Cubs for the sec-ond year of his contract. Trial testimony in a U.S. court at Cincinnati brought forth detailed testimony, faithfully reported by Allen, that showed a gambling tie-up between Magee and Chase. The jury needed just minutes to find for Cubs' management in its unconditional-release decision.

Neither player played major league baseball beyond 1919. Magee, who was born Leopold Christopher Hoernschemeyer, lived to 76. He died at Columbus, Ohio. The mysterious Chase, a talented and per-verse man, became a legend of outlaw ball in little western copper towns where, years later, Allen found hotels where they said he'd stayed. Eventually, an alcoholic drifter, suffering beriberi, Harold Homer Chase died at Colusa, California, in 1947. He was 64.

The point is, its guard down and housing rents up in a crazy finan-cial inflation after World War I, baseball was ripe and ready for the Black Sox scandal, as it became known, the classical infamy of baseball best described by the *New York Times* as generically "one of the most amazing and tangled tales of graft and bribery and interlocking double-crossing." Indeed.

To backdrop briefly, it's easy and probably just to finger Charley Comiskey as Eliot Asinof did in *Eight Men Out,* a magnificent job of research and writing published by Holt, Rinehart and Winston, Inc. in 1963. Comiskey was a villain. In truth, the "Old Roman" was like the proverbial mystery story butler. He did it, at least helped contrive the 1919 scandal by underpaying his players. But, in fairness, there is a necessary preface.

Baseball had a short, scarred 1918 season, bobtailed by government orders, and the situation was so uncertain that the World Series be-tween the Chicago Cubs and Boston Red Sox, which had a big blow-'em-down pitcher named Babe Ruth, almost wasn't played or, at least, was nearly not finished.

The work-or-fight edict, issued by the government's provost mar-shall, forced a Labor Day cessation of a season in which many top stars had gone to France. The hastily arranged Series was poorly attended, the worst since 1910. As rules were changed for the first time to in-clude payments to the top four teams in each league, the angry pennant-winning clubs, the Cubs and Red Sox almost struck before the sitdown-delayed fifth game.

With that rascal named Ruth winning two games and playing a bit of left field, too, Boston won the championship in six games. A skimpy payoff, reduced by a war tax, was a pitiful $890 for each member of the Red Sox and only $535 for each Cub. By contrast, in 1917 when Comiskey's White Sox beat the New York Giants in the World Series, the payoff to New York was $2442 each and to Chicago $3669 a piece.

So a Comiskey, even if more tightfisted than most other clubowners, had reason to wonder and worry immediately after the war when the major leagues scheduled only 140 games for 1919, rather than 154. But Commy, who had earned as much as $8000 as player-manager of the champion St. Louis Browns in the 1880s and once struck in sympathy with underpaid players in 1890, had forgotten. . . .

Yes, forgotten the players of whom defense attorney Ben Short said later when the soiled Sox were tried, "The magnates led the public to believe the ball players got about $10,000 a year, and here we find out they got as little as $2600. At the end of the season, they have nothing left but a chew of tobacco, a glove and a few pairs of worn out socks. . . . "

Dramatically done, of course, and overstated, but with elements of the way it was when Charles Arnold (Chick) Gandil, the strapping first baseman who had boxed a bit and could intimidate a person as well as outtalk him, decided on the 1919 World Series "fix." Although the gamblers profited most, apparently Gandil, who hatched the plot from which the players received much less money than promised, had to like it or lump it because, after all, any act of oral reprisal would be self-accusatory. The payoff was almost as pathetic as the entire experience — period.

Discontent was reasonable, all right. Except for Eddie (Cocky) Collins, the college-educated superstar second baseman, all White Sox were underpaid. Collins, who had joined the Sox a few years earlier under economic circumstances described in another chapter, earned $14,500, good money for the times.

But, to illustrate, Eddie Cicotte, a 35-year-old pitcher who had posted a 28–12 record in 1917, writhed with a $5500 contract in '19, a season in which he was 29–7 with a 1.81 earned-run average. Sure, he'd dipped to 12–19 in 1918, but he'd been a consistent winner, as testified by a 210–148 record for 14 seasons. Time was running out on Cicotte.

Shoeless Joe Jackson was no kid, either. At 32, he had been in the majors for 13 seasons and once hit .400. The sweet swinger was just coming off a .351 season, but he earned only $6000.

So it went with the others—Lefty Williams, Swede Risberg, Happy Felsch, and, of course, the eavesdropper, Fred McMullin, and the good guy who listened, but who foolishly wouldn't squeal—Buck Weaver.

The gamblers to whom ringleader-and-paymaster Gandil talked, with Cicotte apparently confirming the ballplayers' interest in doing business in the World Series with Cincinnati, aren't important except, probably, for former featherweight boxing champion Abe Attell, a little welsher, and for notorious Arnold Rothstein, a big cigar of gambling who declined to participate. But, cripes, a high roller like Rothstein merely had to know that the players could be had.

One "honest" gambler, as he was called, Boston's Joseph (Sport) Sullivan, ponied up $70,000, and Attell, who should have provided plenty, came up only with $10,000. How much the players realized is still a question.

Gandil apparently got away with the most loot, $35,000, and at age 31, a nine-year veteran, the first baseman quit baseball and surprised friends with his opulence as reflected in a new car, a new home in California, and a few assorted diamonds.

Risberg, 25, a light hitting, slick fielding shortstop, received $10,000 or $15,000, take your pick of reports. Cicotte, who sobbed that he'd done it "for the wife and kiddies," found $10,000 under his hotel pillow one night.

That's presumably all he got. One report is that Jackson received the same and the others, too, but the other account is that Shoeless Joe got only $5000, as did the other players. Except, that is, for Weaver, who had passed before and after the payoff. Buck was 30 then, a master third baseman who, once he'd learned to switch-hit, had made his offense almost as good as his defense. Felsch was 28, Williams, 26, and McMullin, 28. Those were and are center-cut athletic years.

The Black . . . er, White Sox lost that 1919 Series in an apparent upset, five games to three as, briefly, the post-season attraction went to best-of-nine. And despite heavy betting on the 1919 Series and mounting rumors that finally compelled Comiskey to offer $20,000 reward if anyone could prove that his athletes had dumped to the Reds, the Sox still were showing in 1920 that they were a great ball club.

Gandil, displaying championship chutzpah, had asked for a $10,000 raise, then had quit in a predetermined huff. The gifted illiterate, Jackson, had been sweet-talked into a three-year increase at $9000 per. Weaver signed for $7500. Cicotte also had been upgraded, but, though the soiled Sox individually and collectively did extremely well in a head-to-head drive down the stretch with Cleveland in 1920, Cicotte was the most troubled, emotionally.

Jackson was hitting .382, Weaver .333, and Cicotte had a 21–10 record in 1920. Chicago just had closed out its home schedule as reports of the thrown series mounted. When Hugh Fullerton couldn't get a Chicago paper to report his account, he went to Joseph Pulitzer's *New York World.* Jim Crusinberry, a Chicago reporter, heard Abe Attell apologize to manager Kid Gleason. Gleason baited the barroom trap for reportorial eavesdroppers Crusinberry and a man who would win other literate letters, Ring Lardner.

Finally, Jimmy Isaminger of the *Philadelphia Inquirer* persuaded an unhappy former ballplayer-boxer-tinhorn gambler, Billy Maharg, to sing about the double-cross, naming names, etc. So a weary Comiskey, looking older than his 60 years, agreed with a sigh that manager Gleason was right. Call in Cicotte, as the Kid had suggested. Eddie was spooked, anyway, and. . . .

Summoned into Comiskey's lawyer's office, Cicotte croaked: "I know what you want to know—I know," he sobbed, as Asinof reported the confrontation dramatically. "Yeah, we were crooked . . . we were crooked. . . . "

That "done" it, as Eddie said. Confessions fell into place like dominoes. With the Grand Jury of Chicago ready to conduct hearings, Comiskey suspended the eight players with three games to go, killing off the Sox's small chance against Cleveland, which had prevailed over the loss through death of shortstop Ray Chapman. Chapman, freezing at the plate, was killed accidentally with a pitch thrown by Carl Mays of the New York Yankees.

That sole death on a diamond in a major league game was as rare as the drama that unfolded. A comic opera drama, if you will, because signed "confessions" disappeared from the Cook County district attorney's office, reportedly a result of the cash-and-clout of the man who knew too much, Arnold Rothstein. Rothstein was gunned down in a card game in New York several years later.

The only threat apparently made at the time was one Jackson related. Risberg had told Shoeless Joe he'd kill him if Jackson talked, but, though acknowledging misplays in the World Series as Cicotte had confessed, Jackson didn't really seem to understand quite what he'd done. Sure, questioningly, he'd let a couple of fly balls fall in, but he'd hit .375.

After the Grand Jury exonerated the players without confirmed confessions—the hero-worshippers even went out to drink with the "free" men—baseball took steps necessary to clean its dirty linen. No one would know that a big guy sold from the Boston Red Sox to the New York Yankees—Babe Ruth—would ease the mental pain by making the home run as exciting as a streetcar rider's first automobile. But baseball men hoped that the first full-time commissioner, Judge K.M. Landis, would bring respectability.

A pithy national columnist, Will Rogers, cowboy-actor-humorist, wasn't trying to be funny the day they hired the Judge. Rogers wrote: "Baseball needed a touch of class and distinction. So somebody said, 'Get that old boy who sits behind first base all the time. He's out there every day anyhow.' So they offered him a season's pass and he jumped at it. But don't kid yourself that the old judicial bird isn't going to make those baseball birds walk the chalkline."

Right on, Will, the chalkline and the foul line.

Barely had the comically cleared White Sox and the jury that cleared them hoisted their last speakeasy salute when Landis issued the kiss of death in 1921. In a decision that forever more should have scared the conscience out of the most crass professional, the commissioner doomed the eight men to exile. He ruled: " . . . Regardless of the verdict of juries, no player who throws a ball game, no player who undertakes or promises to throw a ball game, no player that sits in conference with a bunch of crooked players where the ways and means of throwing a game are discussed and does not promptly tell his club about it, will ever play professional baseball."

What happened to the Black Sox? Old Roman Comiskey, the Irishman whose niggardly pay created temptation, died in 1931 at 71. The players had mixed-bag futures that averaged out to age 70.

Jackson, for whom most recently sentiment has been the greatest, died the earliest, apparently drinking quite a bit of the liquor he sold in Greensville, South Carolina. He was only 64 in 1951, ignorant of most things except one of the most difficult. That is, how to hit a round ball with a round bat. Perhaps apocryphally, yet understandably, a choked-up kid is supposed to have cried, "Say it ain't so, Joe."

McMullin, an obscure figure, died at only 61 at Los Angeles in 1952.

Weaver, to us the most sympathetic because his guilt was only the macho one of not snitching, thought for a time that Landis might yield. He had taken nothing and had hit .324 in the infamous Series. He even sat and talked to the Judge. Landis listened patiently, then later issued a chilling statement: "Birds of a feather flock together. . . . "

Buck, declining to join the conspirators in outlaw semi-pro games, drifted from job to job, the last of which was as a parimutuel clerk. Weaver was 66 when he fell over dead in 1956 of a heart attack in the city he loved, Chicago.

Williams, crudely ineffective in the crooked Series, losing three times with a 6.61 ERA, died at 66 in 1959 at Laguna Beach, California. He had a seven-year record of only 82–48 when he sold out.

Felsch, still running a bar in Milwaukee and trying to laugh off a drunk's snide remarks now and then about his past, died at 73 in 1964. He had been a brilliant defensive centerfielder who batted .293 for six years.

Cicotte went back to Michigan, became a game warden, and then worked as a security guard at an automobile plant. Retired and alone, sweeping off snow for neighbors and raising strawberries, he was interviewed by the *Detroit Free Press*'s Joe Falls. Cicotte, 85 when he died outside Detroit in 1969, said that, yes, he still received letters, most of them from kids, and, yeah, they asked occasionally about the Black Sox.

Wiping his glasses thoughtfully, the little white-haired man said, "I tell them I made a mistake and I'm sorry for it. I try to tell them not to let anyone push them the wrong way. I did wrong. . . . "

Gandil died so quietly at 82 in his Shangri-La of California's beautiful Napa Valley in northern California (1970) that *The Sporting News* didn't catch up to it for three months. It was December 1970. The ringleader had become a plumber after he settled down. Ironically, in view of the circumstances of exile, the sleepy little town in which the perpetrator passed away was St. Helena. Coulda been Elba!

Risberg, a light hitting, sharp fielding shortstop when he was trying, spent years as a dairy farmer in Minnesota before heading to California, where he died at 81 in 1975—last man out of the infamous eight of 1919!

If it brought about any results other than to whitewash baseball for the prosperous period ahead, the Black Sox scandal, notably through Buck Weaver's misfortune, should have kept players as clean as Landis wanted them to be when he had ball parks post "No Betting Allowed" signs and tried to keep athletes away from gambling situations, such as race tracks. Truth is, in hard times particularly when attendance was low, gamblers were the best customers. They would congregate in isolated ball park areas where they could continue their betting on every pitch and every play, much less every game.

But where ballplayers directly were concerned, the specter of Weaver unearthed the last two episodes involving players. Actually, one of Landis's last acts in 1943—the old Judge was too ill to attend the all-St. Louis World Series in 1944 and he died shortly thereafter—was to require young William B. Cox, owner of the Philadelphia Phillies, to sell out. Cox had committed a no-no. He bet on ball games.

Chances are, now clubowners or even players might challenge a Landis edict in court and win because times, tide, and civil liberties have changed, but not back then when the craggy commissioner held forth in a suite on Michigan Boulevard at Chicago's lakefront. He ruled out the Giants' Benny Kauff because the overrated former Federal League player was cleared of car stealing in a decision the arbitrary arbiter thought was odiferous (1920).

Back in 1922 when lanky New York Giants' pitcher Phil Douglas wrote an indiscreet letter to a St. Louis outfielder, Les Mann, the Redbird player immediately thought of Weaver. Knowledge wasn't innocence. Douglas, obviously drinking and having the best start of a nine-year career in the majors, had an 11-and-4 record when he wrote Mann that if the Cardinals made it worth his while, he could "go fishing."

Mann reported the letter to Branch Rickey, then manager. The wheels spun rapidly. Landis finally got the message. Douglas got a hearing. Although Shufflin' Phil had been mentally fuzzy and obviously was miffed at manager John McGraw, an easy man at whom to get miffed, drunk or sober, the 30-year-old pitcher's answers didn't satisfy that Judge. Out!

Two years later, at a time Weaver was suing and getting a measure of satisfaction in partial settlement of his three-year contract from Comiskey, Buck's good-guy silence boomeranged for another player. In the final days of the 1924 season, as the Giants sought a National League record fourth-straight pennant, their borough Brooklyn rivals, the Dodgers, led by McGraw's former close friend and bitter foe, Wilbert Robinson, threatened to nip New York.

Winding up the season, the Giants played Philadelphia. In practice, a second-season outfielder, Jimmy O'Connell, a handsome kid from California who had batted .317 as a part-time outfielder and pinch hitter, approached Phillies' shortstop, Heinie Sand, also a second-year big leaguer from San Francisco and a personal friend.

"Hey," O'Connell cracked at the Phillies' batting cage, if Sand would "take it easy" on the Giants, it would be worth $500 to him. Sand growled, "Get away, Jimmy."

If Weaver hadn't been found guilty by association, Sand might have forgotten that conversation and maybe that Irish kid from the Coast might have wound up a longtime big leaguer. But, disturbed, Heinie told the Phillies' manager, Art Fletcher.

Fletcher recognized also that silence no longer was golden. He phoned John Heydler, National League president. Heydler phoned

Judge Landis and told McGraw. Before you could say Jack Robinson or Uncle Wilbert Robinson, the news was out.

Huffily, having begun his private war with Landis for high-command supremacy, American League president/founder Ban Johnson insisted that they either should call off the World Series or, although the Giants had won the pennant, designate Brooklyn as the National League champion. Good ol' Ban, who had been a giant of strength for the refreshing second league, for clean parks, cleaner play, more respect for the umpires, and for women spectators, too, was beginning to wear thin. Earlier, he had been rebuffed when he sought—probably correctly—to bar Carl Mays because Mays had insisted in 1919 that he no longer wanted to pitch for Boston. Oh, no you don't. Free agency liberty was 57 years later.

As much as Johnson wanted to see the Yankees competitive with the Giants in New York, which they would become in a deal for Babe Ruth the winter after May's stubborn sitdown strike, the AL founder didn't want a player dictating for whom he could play. A dangerous precedent, Johnson reasoned wisely. But Boston defiantly sold Mays to New York, and the clubs took Johnson to court. The Yankees won. Mays did, too. He won 62 games and lost only 23 the next two and one-half seasons and helped the pinstripes win a third straight pennant in 1923.

To suggest that if Johnson had prevailed over the surly Mays and prevented the sale of the recalcitrant pitcher to New York, he might have saved Ray Chapman's life in 1920 would be unfair, of course, but it's not unfair to suggest that Ban Johnson tried to decide imperiously for Landis in the 1924 O'Connell case.

For the Judge, a chin-on-the-rail fan, it must have been nearly as tugging as the Ty Cobb–Tris Speaker crisis just a couple of years down the road. First, the Judge called in O'Connell. Sure, the kid had made the offer, he said, innocently. Around the Giants' batting cage, Cozy Dolan had told him to do it; and, sure, Frank Frisch knew it and also Ross Youngs and George Kelly.

All Jimmy was doing, leaving aside Dolan, a coach, was to mention three men who had Hall of Fame credentials, especially Frisch, a great second baseman and later player-manager of St. Louis's Gas House Gang, and Youngs, a brilliant all-round outfielder who would be stopped only by an early death.

The Judge, moving rapidly with the Series just ahead, called in Frisch, then Youngs, finally Kelly. Their answers satisfied, if not pleased him. They had been kidding around, they insisted, because they knew O'Connell and Sand were good friends. They didn't intend for Jimmy to ask Heinie to lay down. Honest, Judge!

Now, Alvin James Dolan — the second "Cozy" Dolan in major league history — was called in. Cozy, 40, a former well-traveled infielder-outfielder, had been coaching for John McGraw for two years. Landis asked him about O'Connell and the $500 bribe:

"I don't remember," said Dolan.

By then on the eve of a World Series in which Ban Johnson lost and Walter Johnson won Washington's first and only championship, Commissioner K.M. Landis barred O'Connell and Dolan from baseball.

Cozy lived 34 more years until 1958 in Chicago. At his death he was 76. O'Connell, for whom we have considerable compassion, lived until 1976, then age 75. Gosh, how many times he must have wished he's read more about the Black Sox, especially about Buck Weaver!

For Landis, the most vexing case of his career obviously had to be the one involving box office veterans Ty Cobb and Tris Speaker. Cobb, not successful as a manager, had resigned as both manager and player at Detroit, creating only a mild surprise. But when Speaker, who had won a championship in 1920 and finished a close second to the Yankees in 1926, also quit at Cleveland, buzzing began. What gives?

The "what gives?" was Hubert (Dutch) Leonard, a capable left-handed pitcher many of his 11 years in the majors, 1913–1925. He had come across country from California with letters he showed Ban Johnson and Detroit's clubowner, Frank Navin. The letters indicated obliquely that seven seasons earlier (1919), Cobb and Speaker had been involved with a couple of other players in getting bets down on a late-season game.

Cleveland had clinched second place, but Detroit still needed to win to finish third. So as long as they were going to scratch backs by helping the Tigers win one from the Indians, why not bet on it? The letters to Leonard, who was in on the plot, were reasonably damaging, all right, but a tough thing to resolve was the fact that, though Cobb got only one hit when trying to win, Speaker got two triples and a single and did not falter afield when reportedly trying to lose.

"Spoke" liked to play the horses in the old days and even let his players gamble, but how do you adjust involvement when hitting so hard in a game ultimately lost 9–5? Still, Johnson and Navin bought the evidence from Leonard as dynamite to the baseball structure.

When the American League moved at a secret meeting to notify Landis, the Judge hushed gossip by making the information public, then went west to California when a reluctant Leonard, who must have seen too many hoodlum movies or watched Cobb sharpen his spikes too often, thought he might get "bumped off" in Chicago.

The Judge wasn't satisfied completely, aware now that Leonard was miffed that Cobb had released him in 1925 and that another teammate, Speaker at Boston, had brushed him off at Cleveland. Besides, as press box patriarch Fred Lieb intimated, Landis didn't like o-l-d messes. Also, the Judge had thrilled as a fan for years watching Cobb and Speaker.

Obviously, the public outcry impressed Landis, too. Besides, even many of Cobb's teammates who didn't like the Captain Bligh of field foremen, rallied around him. It was easier to say nice things about Speaker. Of Cobb, umpire Billy Evans, who had fought Ty physically, spoke up:

"It is a crime that men of the stature of Ty and Tris should be blackened by a man of this caliber with charges that every baseballer knows to be utterly false."

Cobb, denying involvement other than to know that there had been betting in the pre-Black Sox episode, asked, in part "Is there no decency left?" Both Cobb and Speaker wanted Leonard to attend a full-fledged hearing in Landis's office. Leonard refused to come. To the great sportswriter, Damon Runyon, the former pitcher gloated, "I have had my revenge."

Landis, aware finally that he had backed high-command rival Johnson against the outfield wall, preened in his own new seven-year contract and an indefinite leave of absence prescribed by American League clubowners for their floundering founder. The Judge, knowing that Cobb and Speaker had threatened to sue, came out for—in effect, motherhood—the baseball immortals.

Reviewing Leonard's case, the Judge wound up, "This is the Cobb-Speaker case: These players have not been, nor are they now, found guilty of fixing a ball game. By no decent system of justice could such a finding be made."

"Phew! That had to be Landis's toughest. The Judge ground Johnson's florid nose into the ground when he told John McGraw to "lay off" an attempt to hire Cobb. The commissioner wanted the Georgia Peach and Gray Eagle to finish where Johnson said they couldn't—the American League. No wonder Ban's 26-year reign ended that fall.

Gracefully and financially flattered, Cobb and Speaker finished up the next two seasons. Cobb, already a millionaire through propitious investments in General Motors and Coca-Cola, received about $70,000 from Philadelphia's Connie Mack. Speaker got $35,000 from Clark Griffith at Washington.

A year later, 1928, Speaker joined Cobb with Mr. Mack. At Washington, Tris had hit .327. Now 40, he finished with .267 in 64 games. Cobb, who batted .357 his first season for the Philadelphia fixture he admired, got into 95 games. At 42, he hit .323.

As for "scandals," back in 1947, a couple of years after Landis's death, A.B. (Happy) Chandler, former Kentucky governor and United States senator, suspended the Brooklyn manager, Leo Durocher, for a full year.

Durocher, colorful, capable, and controversial, had gotten into a hissing match with his old boss, Larry MacPhail, then operating the New York Yankees. MacPhail had been strong for Chandler in the difficult assignment of replacing Landis. Through a column for Durocher ghosted by Harold Parrott, a Brooklyn sportswriter who had become a Dodgers' front office man, Durocher had wondered about gamblers seated in MacPhail's box at an exhibition ball game.

Lippy Leo, you see, had been chastised for association with gamblers and for letting movie actor George Raft use his apartment for games of chance. To top it off, Durocher had been involved as the "third party" in actress Laraine Day's sticky divorce. Leo and Laraine circumvented a California judge's decision directing them not to marry for a year by hopping across the border into Mexico.

About the time the Brooklyn Catholic Youth Council discussed boycotting the Dodgers' Knothole Gang over manager Durocher's marital indiscretions—bless Branch Rickey's bow tie and bushy brows, that WAS a blow to the new Brooklyn boss—Chandler thumbed the Flatbush field foreman to a prolonged honeymoon. Moral turpitude, you know.

But 40 years later, we wonder. That was hardly a "scandal," certainly not with a capital "s," particularly in view of recent developments in baseball. Now, despite former commissioner Bowie Kuhn's vigilance about the game's integrity, two of the most prominent players in recent times, Mickey Mantle and Willie Mays, were cast out temporarily because they were working directly for gambling casinos. The Mick and Say-Hey were reinstated by newest commissioner Pete Ueberroth.

Above all, flouting the law of the land, well-heeled ballplayers have been involved illegally with possession and/or use of drugs. Some even have served jail sentences. Drugs have become baseball's No. 1 problem.

To borrow an expression used by a most pleasant Pittsburgh baseball writer, the late Charles (Chilly) Doyle, if Kenesaw Mountain Landis were alive today, he'd turn over in his grave!

9
Press Box
Poets and Pests

I f the Baseball Hall of Fame had been built before a bearded old
man died in 1908 at age 83, chances are that, like Emmett Ashford,
who was big league baseball's first black umpire, Henry Chadwick
could have been buried by request in Cooperstown. Father Chadwick,
as they called him with proper awe, is the only sportswriter or broadcaster ever elected directly to the Hall of Fame.

Chadwick, born in Britain, son of a journalist who liked sports,
came over here in 1837 at age 13 and from the first time he saw that
game the bloody colonials played — time and place unknown — he
thought cricket belonged to the wickets.

By 1847 Henry was playing amateur shortstop in New Jersey. By
1856, when he quit teaching music to follow in his father's footsteps,
he had invented the box score and perhaps the first system of scoring,
too. Thereafter, he would serve as a gadfly of the game, urging rules'
changes and improvements as common sense dictated.

Always, though, from the time he joined the *New York Times* in
1856, then moved to the *New York Clipper,* the *Herald-Tribune,* and
ultimately the *Brooklyn Eagle,* he pestered editors with newspaper
pieces about baseball.

Chadwick's enthusiasm as a rules' buff and writer continued to the end. The "father of baseball," as they labeled him, served officially on the rules' committee and for the last 27 years he edited the annual *Spalding Guide*. The *Spalding Guide*, which early competed with one published by a sporting goods rival, Reach, was replaced in 1942 by the *Baseball Guide*, published by *The Sporting News*.

In part tribute to that vital step in the history of baseball continuity, as well as for J. G. Taylor Spink's forceful years as a colorful editor and publisher, the name of terrible tempered Taylor, the soft-hearted Spink, was given to an annual award. The winner, chosen by members of the Baseball Writers' Association of America, is honored on the program at the annual Hall of Fame induction at Cooperstown.

But the Spink Award for meritorious contributions to baseball writing is not membership in the Hall of Fame. That distinction alone in the Fourth Estate belongs to Chadwick, who as an observer and reporter, if not unfortunately a sufficient string-preserving researcher, had really only two weaknesses.

Pop . . . er, sorry, about that . . . Father Chadwick couldn't stand to see a pitcher unable to finish what he started. He couldn't stand it, either, when some broad-beamed lout stood up there and, as Chadwick wrote in the 1895 *Spalding Guide*, hit "what the groundlings (fans) call a homer."

Truth is, at the time Chadwick was annoyed at the heavy hitting of Philadelphia's Sam Thompson, who didn't have the decency to bunt and hit-and-run with the scientific skill of the time. Thompson, by the way, definitely a sizable man for his century at 6–2, 207 pounds, hit 16 home runs in 118 games that year. Pretty good outfielder, too, and, as research has indicated, probably the first to use the one-bounce throw from the outfield for more speed, accuracy, and better handling at the plate.

If Big Sam bothered Chadwick, the press box patriarch probably would have developed a rectal rash over the arrival several years later of a guy named Babe Ruth. Quite likely, watching a newer, whiter, livelier ball, he probably would have quit questioning the courage of pitchers who couldn't go nine innings. If, however, he'd learned that a "replacement" pitcher named Mike Marshall would become the first reliever to win the Cy Young Award, christened for the complete-game czar, it undoubtedly would have been too much for him. Young was the durable dude of Chadwick's day. *ANY* day!

Chadwick's "day" was, of course, more than a half-century of contributions, including his efforts first to establish an association of baseball writers in 1887. The first meeting of the Base Ball Reporters' Association at Cincinnati's Grand Hotel on December 12, 1887, was one at which George Munson of *The Sporting News* presided. Chadwick, graciously serving as vice-president, sought even then to clarify a fuzzy scoring rule covering credit for stolen bases.

Unfortunately, the association didn't last because baseball was suffering growing pains even more than newspapers that began to feature sports rather than merely tolerate them. Formation in 1890 of the Players' League, by which athletes sought a better share of the baseball buck, was costly. The "Brotherhood," as the players called it, lasted only a season before the National League sucked it up, but reporters took sides in the struggle and the writers' association collapsed.

So by recognized standards the organization of the Baseball Writers' Association of America didn't occur until 1908, the year Chadwick died. Emerging as the first hero of the BBWAA, which still used the stuttering double "B" even after baseball decided the twain should meet, was a man named Joe Jackson.

No, not Shoeless Joe; but, first, as they would say in radio or television, time-out for a commercial or at least a digression. In the Hall of Fame's files, Ernest Lanigan, the first historian at Cooperstown, left a memo expressing the opinion that both Cincinnati's Jack Ryder and New York's Sid Mercer deserved credit for having tried in both 1906 and '07 to unite baseball writers.

For Mercer, a distinguished man who once wrote in St. Louis and served as traveling secretary of the old Browns, the Lanigan memo served as one more tribute. Mercer, like Grantland Rice, the bald eagle of American sports journalism the first half of the Twentieth Century, also had a daughter good enough to win some movie recognition. (They were Frances Mercer and Florence Rice). Sid Mercer, a posthumous recipient of the Spink Award at Cooperstown, also is the man in whose honor the New York baseball writers present their annual meritorious award at their traditional January dinner.

When John McGraw once disavowed an interview given to Mercer, backing down after having lashed out too strongly at league authority, the high-minded writer immediately quit covering the New York Giants. He switched to a "lesser" club, the Yankees. Another writing old-timer, Jack Ryder, could be equally stubborn.

Ryder, a gifted scholar, graduate of Phillips Exeter Academy and Williams College, covered the Cincinnati Reds for the *Enquirer* for 32 years. In fact, he died on the job of a heart attack in 1936. He wrote with talent, but with some prejudice, as, for instance, when he failed to cast a vote for Rogers Hornsby in his top 10 players in 1924. That year was the first in which the National League awarded $1000 in gold to the Most Valuable Player. Hornsby, who had batted a record .424 for St. Louis, was nipped by pitcher Dazzy Vance, a 28-game winner with Brooklyn. Asked how 'n hazes he could have omitted Hornsby, Ryder huffed, "How can you call 'MVP' a guy whose team finishes sixth?"

Writers are human. They proved as much when, getting back to scrivener Joe Jackson, they found enough was enough. Over the years they had been pushed around by thin-skinned clubowners. For example, when a Tammany Hall politician named Andrew Freedman owned the New York Giants at the turn of the century and traded young Christy Mathewson to Cincinnati for old Amos Rusie, clever writer Charley Dryden chided him. Freedman barred Dryden from the Polo Grounds.

Dryden played a dirty trick on the minor league politician. He quoted him directly when Freedman said, "You're standing on the brink of an abscess (sic). If you ain't careful, I'll push you in."

Barred from the ball park, Dryden sat outside, fed the pigeons, listened to the roar of the crowd, talked to his fellow reporters afterward, and wrote with the same amusing skill that had prompted him to suggest once that Washington was "first in war, first in peace and last in the American League."

Not all writers were as amusing as Dryden. Chicago had a feisty little baseball writer, an astute man named Hugh Fullerton, who found one of McGraw's actor friends, Louie Mann, sitting in his seat when Fullerton came in for the famed 1908 Giants-Cubs' replay game. Actors and others were filling the ground-level press box seats too often. The report for years was that even when Mann wouldn't move, Fullerton plopped onto the actor's lap and dictated his play-by-play. Ernie Lanigan said in Cooperstown memoirs that it wasn't so. But Hughie was blazing mad when he improvised by sitting in an aisle.

By the time of the World Series between the Cubs and Detroit Tigers, the writers had had it up to here and beyond. At Chicago, where even with a former writer running the Cubs, they sat so far back that they couldn't recognize Tinker-and-Evers-and-Chance, much less the unremembered third baseman, Henry Steinfeldt. And at Detroit, they were forced to climb a rickety ladder and to sit on the roof, uncovered, in rain and snow.

Enter Joseph Stansfield Jackson, sports editor then of the *Detroit Free Press* and eventually with the rival *News*. As a baseball writer, personally "favored" at the home park, Jackson was embarrassed at poor working conditions at Bennett Park, the site now of Tiger Stadium. Urged by Ryder and Henry P. Edwards, Cleveland writer who later served as longtime secretary for the American League, Jackson arranged for a room at Detroit's Hotel Pontchartrain.

The date was October 14, 1908, the one on which Jackson, a convivial, gentle man, a teetotaler helpful to young writers, set in motion the standards of the BBWAA, an organization heralded by its own emblem, a green-designed baseball diamond with the initials on it and, criss-crossed in gold, a bat and a pen.

Even though in recent times newspapers have shrunk in the face of financial costs and the pressure of radio, television, and changing times, more than 400 regular 10-year members and retired veterans vote in the annual Hall of Fame election. So, considering the many more youthful members, enrollment is much larger. Yet, present young and old BBWAA members—and future ones, too—owe their status to Jackson and 20 others who gathered that night after the fifth and final game of a World Series in which Orval Overall pitched a three-hitter that gave the Chicago Cubs their second straight World Championship.

The honor roll of ink-stained wretches who put up a silver dollar each to begin the (headache) ball a-rollin' for clubowners were: Tim Murnane and Paul Shannon, Boston; Charles A. Hughes, Hugh E. Keough, Malcolm A. McLean, Hugh Fullerton, W. A. Phelon, and I. E. Sanborn, Chicago; Ed F. Bang and Edwards, Cleveland; Ryder and Charles H. Zuber, Cincinnati; J. W. McConaughy and Sid Mercer, New York; William G. Weart, Philadelphia; George L. Moreland, Pittsburgh; Jackson and Joseph Smith, Detroit; James A. Crusinberry, Hal Lanigan, W. G. Murphy, and J. B. Sheridan, St. Louis; and J. Ed Grillo, Washington.

By the time the newly organized BBWAA met in December in New York at the time of baseball's winter meetings, the wheels were in motion. Thereafter, the BBWAA would consider the Detroit pioneers as founders. The New York winter additions and the first season men (1909) were labeled charter members. They were all gone before the BBWAA celebrated its 75th anniversary in 1983.

Of the ancient and often honorable order, though occasionally cantankerous, the principles and purposes of the BBWAA are contained in three objects listed in Article 2 of the writers' constitution:

(1) To encourage the square deal in baseball.
(2) To simplify the rules in scoring games and promote uniformity in scoring.
(3) To secure better facilities for reporting baseball games and better regulation of the scorers' boxes during both championship seasons and the World Series. . . .

At the 1984 Baseball Hall of Fame ceremonies at Cooperstown, New York, the heart-and-soul of the BBWAA was spelled out by Charley Segar, a BBWAA member for more than 65 years. Segar joined the

BBWAA in 1920 with the old *New York Mirror.* He later assisted Ford Frick when Frick was president of the National League, and was big league baseball's national secretary in Frick's years as commissioner, 1951–65.

Often regarded as crabby by young colts of the press, Segar, an outspoken member of the Veterans' Committee that selects old-timers for the Hall of Fame, put it fairly and forcefully: "Despite helping themselves with better working conditions and, ultimately, gaining stature through official scoring, official selection of Most Valuable Players, and Hall of Fame balloting, baseball writers did the most with that first objective: To encourage the square deal in baseball."

Segar grimaced a smile—or smiled a grimace—and emphasized, "Whether it's square now to use 'square' as George M. Cohan did in musical lyrics and as we used to mean it as 'fair' and 'honest,' that's exactly what the BBWAA did. Especially before Judge Landis as commissioner—and even after—the baseball writers were the watchdogs. They kept the game honest."

From too little authority to almost too much eventually, from no control of poorly-placed plank seats to well-located comfortable press boxes over which they had the presumed vigilance of St. Peter, the baseball writers gained an authority unmatched in the game's labor ranks. That is, until the players themselves marshalled their forces as an association under Marvin Miller and won free-agency and an arbitration coup.

The peak period for newspaper impact came obviously before radio emerged from clumsy crystal sets early in the 1920s to clubs' independent networks in the years after World War II.

The baseball writer was the swaggering cock of the ball yard in those days, the key man of the sports department, often outstripping the columnist (if there was one). Sports pages mushroomed after World War I. Sports staffs soared in the Roaring Twenties. Staffs doubled, tripled, and quadrupled as America sped into the Golden Age of Sports.

The gee-whiz era of purple-prosed-and-poetic, put-'em-on-a-pedestal writing was accompanied by personal observation, the kind that enabled veteran reporters to view and review ball games as if they were theatre critics and/or movie and book analysts. Writers weren't encouraged to come into baseball clubhouses, and they usually didn't need to.

Ball games were played generally at 3 P.M. local time, based on the belief that only the wealthier, white-collar workers could make it. Bosses signed business mail in the early afternoon and then hit the ball park en route home. (The Chicago Cubs reinstated the philosophy in 1987.) The afternoon newspaper play-by-play was the way for others to find out quickly who won.

Maybe the morning paper would expand with a better why-and-wherefore, but if the A. M. man didn't, the P. M. reporter would in his early-edition "second-day" story. In newspaper haste to stay current, too often better written post-mortem stories next day were pitched in favor of skeletonized play-by-play of the new day's game. If you missed either the era or the opportunity to see an older paper, the play-by-play might cover only one inning.

Say, to illustrate, it's the 1927 St. Louis Browns playing the New York's famed Murderers' Row at Yankee Stadium. The felt-hatted or straw-hatted or maybe capped reporter, shedding his coat, but not his tie, would sit next to a veteran Western Union operator fingering the dot-and-dash Morse Code of an electronic telegraphic instrument. The reporter would dictate after each play:

"FIRST INNING—St. Louis—Melillo struck out. O'Rourke grounded out, Dugan to Gehrig. Sisler singled to left, but was out trying for second, Ruth to Lazzeri.

"Yankees—Combs walked. Koenig sacrificed, O'Rourke to Melillo covering first. Ruth hit a home run into the right-field seats, scoring behind Combs. Gehrig doubled off the right-field fence. Meusel flied deep to B. Miller, Gehrig taking third after the catch. Melillo made a good stop to his right and threw out Lazzeri. TWO RUNS."

As soon as the game ended, with "dummy" lead paragraphs having been written, meaning a hold-for-release "win" or "lose" or "extra innings" introduction, a typesetter merely had to set a final scoreline that was dropped in the hot-metal page by a printer as a single-sentence insert.

With the sports pages invariably printed on colored paper then—peach or pink or green or salmon—rather than color-photoed, which was years down the road, the late-breaking, baseball-headed newspaper would be whisked by trucks to key traffic points and, ultimately, even as far as some fortunate homes. The night-sports specials, as they usually called the late-breaking, day-game editions, were read as hungrily as the giant-sized, handset box scores that were kept abreast of game developments.

As a result, taking that make-believe first inning of a Browns-Yankee game out of New York, which had a two-hour edge in time zone then, a St. Louis Knothole Gang kid could watch the Cardinals beat the Giants that afternoon at Sportsman's Park. Not even allowing for a lagging look afterward to get Frank Frisch's autograph or Sunny Jim Bottomley's as the Cardinals hurried out of Sportsman's Park, a guy would inch along by streetcar through midtown traffic. Within a half hour of game's end, he would stick two or three pennies out of the streetcar window at Grand Avenue and Olive Street. A hawking newsboy would have the line scores of all afternoon games and the play-by-play of the two St. Louis games.

The newsy's wily oral salesmanship told the story even before the peach-shaded, black-bannered headlines in the *Post-Dispatch*: "Cardinal victory . . . Brownie box score!"

The romance of writing waxed and then waned. From the time the BBWAA became policemen of the press box and, as Charley Segar suggested, of baseball, too, until recently when writers have established what seems a tug o' war individually over whether the players now get too much money, the questions are: Will mum become the word for most players, many of whom now zip the lip, and will the BBWAA suffer further from lack of interest or inability to control press boxes? Will the writing craft suffer further because radio and TV help pay the increased front office freight?

The BBWAA was feeling its literary oats back in 1910, for instance, when Melville Webb, *Boston Globe* writer, reportedly expelled club-owner John I. Taylor from the Red Sox press box. Even if it was only a gag, Webbie was the kind of salty, old soul who could have done it. And Jackson held sway for 10 years as president, a lengthy stint that made the man from Detroit regarded as the Great Emancipator of the press. Oddly, Jackson got religion or, at least, he wound up a church editor in San Francisco.

For years thereafter, the BBWAA president held forth a couple of seasons at least. But at the 1931 World Series, incumbent Bill Slocum, who sired sportswriting sons before becoming General Mills's baseball liaison (Wheaties), suggested that it would be wiser to move the presidency around each year. After all, the strength of the BBWAA lies directly in the role of the secretary.

Over the three-quarters of a century, there have been only six secs— William G. Weart and Joseph M. McCready, both of Philadelphia; Henry P. Edwards, Cleveland and Chicago; Ken Smith, New York; Hy Hurwitz, Boston; and Jack Lang, New York. Nearly 40 years on the baseball beat, Lang, who switched from the *Long Island Press* to the *New York News* when the *Press* bellied up, was senior traveling baseball writer in the majors until reduced to part road coverage in 1987.

The baseball beat obviously has lost glamour. In the old days, traveling by train with the ball clubs at a time St. Louis was the western terminus in the two leagues, writers socialized more with players and clubowners. Truth is, for too many years newspapers permitted writers to travel with the teams at the club's expense.

Too many newspapers, that is. Now, refreshingly, it's a rarity, but now, too, newspapers take a view that serving as official scorer is a conflict of interest or a distraction for reporters. Additionally, younger writers themselves don't want the cheek-to-jowl conflict with angry athletes.

Probably from the time the Great Scorer made the decision that paradise was lost, Adam and the others have squawked that Eve made the error or the apple took a bad hop. There does not seem to be any greater visibility of discomfort or display by players even though incentive contracts, providing for performance clauses that were prohibited in the era of the reserve clause, can make a player crankier. After all, the official scorer *can* be taking the new fur coat away from the wife of the well-heeled jock.

Sadly, it seems, even where allowed to serve as scorer, once a badge of responsibility and authority, the baseball writer is losing part of his input into the game and, incidentally, $50 hard-earned daily pay in the majors. Traditionally, appointed by the major leagues on a basis of the number of daily newspapers in a city, writers took turns scoring the game and then filling out the much more detailed official sheet for league offices and statisticians.

Over the years, especially in view of the need to hire retired baseball writers and others, baseball has sought ways and means of solving the problem. To travel an extra umpire and utilize him—or a regular arbiter on a day off—would be expensive, but maybe necessary. Former athletes as scorers often have blind spots, i.e., an ex-pitcher favors pitchers too much; a former hitter is either too liberal to the modern men at bat or, jealous of their salaries, too severe.

For one, Seymour Siwoff, longtime head of the Elias Sports Bureau, has offered to train official scorers because of the reduction of baseball writers eligible—or willing—to stay in the kitchen and stand the heat. Siwoff, statistician for both major leagues and for the National Football League and National Basketball Association, is a man of competence and judgment.

So it's merely for old times' sake and press prestige that we lament disinterest in scoring by baseball "beat" men and also feel distress that newspapers can be so concerned about conflict of interest. Uh-huh, especially those papers that took the free ride for so many years, some of them even *after* they told the writers to give up the outside income.

About scoring, defined thoroughly in Rule 10 of the official baseball rules, we feel that some restrictions are in effect because of implied pressures by which scorers necessarily would favor the home team or a favorite player, or, even worse, treat unfairly a less pleasant person. The human element can become involved.

For one thing, if complete objectivity were involved, we believe that, leaving aside the strait-jacketed mumbo-jumbo utilized in determining a game's winning pitcher, a sound scorer—like an objective boxing referee—merely could raise the hand in victory of the pitcher whose work any given day justifies the decision.

Similarly, common sense must prevail on a close play when an umpire, reacting too quickly, flashes an "out" call before bang-bang action ends. If, to illustrate, a catcher takes a throw and applies a tag, just as he's hit and before he has possession, he shouldn't be given an error merely because the umpire signals a put-out prematurely.

For all of the trial-and-error between Henry Chadwick and now, the adoption of meaningful and helpful statistics, and an obvious improvement in scoring rules, the effort to establish a game-winning RBI has fallen short of justice. Couldn't there be a point system? One point for an early game winner on up to five points for hitting a late-inning jackpot?

The baseball writers' association resurrected the Most Valuable Player Awards in 1931 after the majors had dropped them. The American League had given that glamorous white bag filled with $1000 in gold pieces ever since 1922 when George Sisler of the Browns won the prize. The NL began a similar award in 1924, the year Dazzy Vance of Brooklyn finished first.

The writers couldn't come up with the necessary scratch, but they began the award with Lefty Grove of the Philadelphia A's and Frank Frisch of the Cardinals. They used a three-man committee in each league city, now reduced to two with a third baseball writer selected at each franchise to pick the winner of the Cy Young pitching award. The writers also began Rookie-of-the-Year selections in 1947 with the pioneer black performer, Brooklyn's Jackie Robinson.

Ever since 1936, the BBWAA has had the honor of picking Hall of Fame members, a result of a decision made by a so-called centennial committee, one headed by Judge K. M. Landis, league presidents Ford Frick and Will Harridge, former NL president John A. Heydler, and the minor leagues' two top executives, Judge William Bramham and George Trautman.

Over the years, changes have been made in balloting procedure. By 1944, the BBWAA choices were narrowed to players only. A year later a nominating system was installed, followed by a vote on only the top 20. That experiment was shortlived. By 1947, the current rule of 10 years' membership as a baseball writer was required and the rule limiting the number of years a player could be retired before becoming eligible for consideration was adopted. Always 75 percent approval was required.

Hall of Fame voting responsibility, exciting and controversial and dramatic, is one the writers have handled not only well, but almost admirably. Basically, meaning with rare exception, it's not how many the BBWAA lets in that *might* not belong, but how many the picky members, ranging from aged, retired greybeards to youthful members barely past 30, keep out of the bronzed-plaque corridor at Cooperstown.

If the game has changed, from regional to national, trains to planes, natural grass to artificial, plus sizes and styles of uniforms, gloves, and even ball parks, too, so have baseball writing and baseball writers.

They are younger now, largely, because they don't or won't stand the gaff as long as they used to. Maybe their wives won't let them. Maybe their own health or the pressure of the job. They work longer and later and at more irregular hours because planes fly by night, the wee hours of the night.

Shortly before Red Smith died in January 1982, the most literate of sportswriters, a syndicated *New York Times* columnist who had spent years on the baseball beat in St. Louis and Philadelphia, was asked about changes in writing. Smith began by quoting Blackie Sherrod, brilliant Dallas columnist who had this amusing twist: "Blackie said it used to be that you moved into a hotel and the first thing you checked was the bathroom. If there was a bottle opener on the wall, it was an acceptable hotel. Now, the first thing you look for is a three-prong outlet for your electric typewriter, or word processor."

Most certainly a proper place is needed for the video display terminal a traveling reporter now carries in place of the typewriter. The Western Union operator and his "bug" are long gone, replaced first by a woman operator and her teletype, but then by the copying machine the reporter used to transmit his own material through telephone connection. This, forerunner of the VDT, was a print-material offshoot of the wirephoto system the *Associated Press* first used to relay photographs from town to town in the mid-1930s.

As for Red Smith himself, lamenting the loss of trains that gave a writer a chance to have a cold beer and a long talk with athletes, he noted that press critic A. J. Liebling once had said of himself (and most others) that "I can write faster than anybody who can write better than me and write better than anybody who can write faster than me."

Commented Smith wryly, "Well, I can't write faster than anybody," an amusing comment from a painstaking slowpoke who said once that writing a column was like opening his veins and bleeding a little. His punchline, though, in the interview about now-and-then of writing, was simply this: "I simply can't write as good a story at midnight to make a morning edition as I could in the old days after an afternoon game." Especially, Red, when from the quiet of your lonely room, you might curl the wall's ears with profanity if the VDT computer sputters and fails in telephonic communication with the home office and you wind up wet-nursing the temperamental electronic gadget half the night.

So there is apparent reason for briefer stints as baseball writers, in addition to a more difficult and dissident athlete with whom to talk. In part, the problem is one that writers brought upon themselves by relying too much on the post-game interview for their stories.

Sure, greater use of radio and TV coverage required more jockstrap sniffing, to use the vulgar Anglo-Saxon of clubhouse coverage. But, still, aren't there games in which trained eyes see a key situation that can be converted into a readable tale of victory or defeat? Or, just for a change of pace, wouldn't a well-written narrative stand up by itself?

Seems as if it would beat, hands down, the wearying pitching response, "He hit a hanging slider." Or the same story told by the hitter, "I hit a hanging slider."

C'mon, fellas, if imagination and a let-up are so good in the game, why wouldn't the same be true out of an observer's typewriter . . . er, VDT?

Perhaps deflatingly, though doubtfully no one reading this is holding his breath, there will be no attempt to chart a course of writing greats. Maybe readers wouldn't care, anyway. For what it's worth, the Spink Award at Cooperstown has been given, posthumously or in person, to: Ring Lardner . . . Hugh Fullerton . . . Charley Dryden . . . Grantland Rice . . . Damon Runyon . . . H. G. Salsinger . . . Sid Mercer . . . Heywood Broun . . . Frank Graham . . . Dan Daniel . . . Fred Lieb . . . J. Roy Stockton . . . Warren Brown . . . John Drebinger . . . John Kieran . . . John Carmichael . . . James Isaminger . . . Tom Meany . . . Shirley Povich . . . Harold Kaese . . . Red Smith . . . Gordon Cobbledick . . . Edgar Munzel . . . Tim Murnane . . . Dick Young . . . Bob Broeg . . . Tommy Holmes . . . Joe Reichler . . . Milton Richman . . . Bob Addie . . . Allen Lewis . . . Si Burick . . . Ken Smith . . . Joe McGuff . . . Earl Lawson . . . Jack Lang . . . Jim Murray.

In the view of one honored at the Hall of Fame, other candidates are close because of personal talent and also because, we agree, writing basically is better than it used to be. Reporters are better educated.

The color basically is still there in the printed word, but, happily, the clichés, unless the writers insist on letting the athletes, managers, and coaches resurrect them, have been laid to rest by most of the modern press.

The era of the "chipmunk," as a Runyonesque character named Jimmy Cannon called chattering press box dissenters of the Uncertain Sixties, has pretty well run its course. A writer still can have his awnuts negative rather than gee-whiz pep pills, but there are limits, as a player properly objected one day. Interviewed by a writer, he excused himself because his wife had to nurse the baby.

"Breast or bottle?" asked the press box busybody.

Actually, as brother Broeg found out a quarter-century back, writers can have a lot of fun if they don't take themselves or their jobs too seriously. You don't have to do what Warren Brown did. The acerbic Chicago wit would sit in the White Sox press box in the course of losing, which the Chisox did often in his day, and flip peanuts down at the fans following the losing side.

"Go home, you silly people," Brownie would smirk.

Or it's not even necessary to play games, as J. Roy Stockton could in the era when he was chief chronicler of the Gas House Gang for the *St. Louis Post-Dispatch*. When the guys would try to decide which occupations certain players' surnames indicated, Stockton was a sure winner.

For instance, Rogers Hornsby? "An orchestra leader." James Bottomley? "A butler." Stanley Bordagaray? "An interior decorator." Baxter Jordan? "A stagecoach driver." Gordon Slade? "A riverboat gambler." Red Lucas? "A cowboy."

Take it from one who was there, sweating under the rusty-roofed, low-slung press box in the Polo Grounds or shivering in the open-air trade winds of San Francisco's Seals Stadium or when the wind whipped in off Boston's Charles River into Braves Field, it *does* help to be a little punchy.

Like, for instance, Bill Phelon, a gifted writer and poet when they all turned a fair-to-worse verse. Phelon, long gone (1925), had a crazy sense of humor. We'd have loved to meet the man who wrote for the *Cincinnati Times-Star.*

One time, walking down Broadway in New York, Phelon spotted W. A. (Bill) Hanna headed toward him. Hanna was a gifted Manhattan writer, slightly hypochondriac. Phelon passed Hanna, who was headed for his office, and greeted him cheerfully:

"Hi, Bill."

Hanna, deep in thought, looked up and smiled, "Oh, hi, Bill."

Phelon barely cleared Hanna when he located a streetcar headed back in the direction from which he had come. Phelon rode merely a block, jumped off and headed again in the original direction so that once more he approached Hanna.

"Hi, Bill."

Hanna, startled, blinked. Slowly, he stuttered in disbelief, "H-i-i, Bill."

Phelon, as soon as he was certain Hanna's eyes no longer followed him, hailed a taxi headed back from where he had come and moved down another block in front of Hanna, who was walking more slowly now, head down, bewildered.

Phelon approached as if seeing his fellow baseball writer for the first time that day.

"Hi, Bill."

Bill Phelon never got an answer from Bill Hanna, though later the press box got a helluva laugh out of it. Hanna turned off his trek to the newspaper office. He hailed a cab and hurried to see his doctor. "You wouldn't believe this, Doc, but . . ."

10
The Eyes
of the Fan

If baseball ever wild-pitched in dreams and schemes, it was early in the Depression, at a time when turnstiles understandably were as slow as the economy. Baseball feared radio's impact on attendance then. Most ball clubs went through a season or more with no game broadcasts. It seems hard to believe that baseball once feared radio as a competitor.

In 1932 *Baseball Magazine,* then a red-rimmed monthly widely read, questioned editorially, "Will Radio Kill Baseball?" Even the more perceptive baseball bible, as J. G. Taylor Spink called *The Sporting News,* wondered whether it was plausible to try to sell seats when, in effect, "the game" was giving them away.

You see, even though broadcasters then were basically not so well-trained as later, still the listener's mind's eye, if you don't mind the confusing, mixed metaphor, could conjure up playing fields and situations. Why go to the ball game, especially if you didn't have the dough?

That's the way most of the ball clubs saw it. The broadcast was too close to the real thing. They would say the same later about television, probably with more justification, but it's unbelievable now when anyone considers the impact radio has made. The revenue is nice now, though not so hefty as TV, but Mr. Marconi or Mr. Tesla and Mr. DeForest, the pioneers of the old sidebar crystal set that evolved into the stick-it-in-your-ear privacy of the pocket-sized transistor, probably would wince over the great use baseball makes of its own personal hucksters.

At times some of the broadcasters will bristle at uncomplimentary comparisons with the print media, noting that the radio-TV men make more money and are certainly better known than the writers. But if it's true that the newspapers and their reporters or columnists have more freedom of expression and criticism of ball clubs and ball games than the men of the microphone, that's *all* the press has left.

As this book's authors, one of whom has made his primary living proudly in the newspaper game, having the rare opportunity to triple up in radio and TV, it's not easy for an academician or a writer to give the spoken word priority over the printed one. After all, in the basics of the King's English, the ABCs of education, learning to read and to write does take more formal effort than speaking.

But to disavow with ostrich lack of grace the change of life and communications caused generally, first by radio and then by television, would be stupid and, above all, unfair. Objectivity and honesty are twin pillars of a proper press, along with that old standby—accuracy—so it's fundamental to give the broadcast art full due for its important part in baseball development. And, of course, to express amusement that the game once sought to suppress the best asset it has other than a winning team.

For all the drum-beating broadcasters can do to help sell beer, automobiles, cigarettes, blades, deodorants, and other necessities or luxuries and for all the men of the mike can do to push tomorrow's pitching pairings, next week's free cap day, or other assorted promotions, the biggest impact is this: Day after night, the radio and the voice on it offer great entertainment and even friendship for the lame and the halt, the blind and unemployed or the aged, the persons who can't get there and who need more detailed pleasure than a game story or printed commentary can give.

The club that deserves the most sweeping bow for having given baseball broadcasting its biggest boost is the Chicago Cubs, now owned by a newspaper, the *Chicago Tribune*. Factually, of course, the tribute is one that properly goes to the Wrigleys, William and son P. K. In the era when others quit the airways fearfully, the Wrigleys expanded and encouraged radio's participation in baseball reportage. Also, Larry MacPhail at Cincinnati, then Brooklyn, was a clairvoyant about radio.

Pittsburgh deserves special attention, too, and not because, later, cadaverous Rosey Rowswell would chant "Open the window, Aunt Minnie" when Ralph Kiner hit a home run over the fence at Forbes Field or puckish Bob Prince would become another Pirate institution, using

"How sweet it is!" even before Jackie Gleason "originated" the expression on television. Prince, the king of jesters, once put the owner of St. Louis's Chase Park Plaza Hotel into a state of shock by diving out of a third-story window into a swimming pool—and just skimming the concrete perimeter to make it.

No, Pittsburgh made it first with a man considerably less colorful than Rowswell or Prince. KDKA at Pittsburgh, owned by Westinghouse Corporation, originated radio broadcasting in 1920. Just winging it one day the next year, August 5, 1921, a Westinghouse foreman by day and an announcer by night, Harold Arlin, lugged radio equipment into Forbes Field and, perched in a low grandstand seat, broadcast a game between the Pirates and the Philadelphia Phillies.

In this book that likes to explore "firsts," Mr. Arlin deserves other recognition because he also first introduced on radio the voices of Will Rogers, Herbert Hoover, William Jennings Bryan, and Babe Ruth. The booming-voiced Babe himself must have suffered the first mike fright because, Arlin recalled, Ruth froze when asked to deliver a prepared speech. (Why didn't he just ask the Babe a few questions?) So Arlin read Ruth's lines. Uh-huh, and KDKA got letters praising the "quality" of the Babe's voice.

The firsts continued. For the 1921 World Series, Giants versus Yankees, all at the Polo Grounds because Yankee Stadium was two years away, KDKA combined with two other Westinghouse affiliates, WJZ in New Jersey and WBZ, then in Springfield, Massachusetts, and later in Boston. The intracity games were broadcast regionally by sportswriter Grantland Rice. A year later when the same clubs met, another New York sportswriter, W. O. McGeehan, did the announcing.

By 1923, New York's WEAF introduced a voice that would become the first nationally known for sports broadcasts, Graham McNamee, whose coverage of the Cardinals-Yankee Series in 1926 was the first coast-to-coast. By 1924, Chicago's WMAQ had become the first station to undertake regular local broadcasts, airing home games of the White Sox and the Cubs.

First daily broadcaster was Hal Totten, later a minor league president. At a time when the only compensation a ball club got was a free spot plug occasionally about that day's upcoming game or the next one, the Wrigleys recognized the more the merrier. At one time a half-dozen stations competed for the audience at Wrigley Field and then Comiskey Park behind such names as Totten, Quin Ryan, Pat Flanagan, Johnny O'Hara, and Jack Brickhouse.

Brickhouse's "Hey, hey," easy-does-it approach led to 30 years of Chicago broadcasting, most of it eventually with the Cubs, for whom he even wound up on the ball club's board of directors. Brickhouse was

1983 winner of the prestigious Ford C. Frick award given for meritorious service at the annual Hall of Fame Day ceremonies at Cooperstown.

Chicago, as mentioned, was the early leader, not New York. For that matter, Cincinnati, where Red Barber got his start, and St. Louis, where Thomas Patrick (Convey) crowed "Oh, the score!" when the Cardinals often or the Browns occasionally led, were more prominent early than New York. Flaming redhead Larry MacPhail would take care of that. Make that *two* redheads, MacPhail and broadcaster Barber.

Along the way in the Windy City, Bert (Windy) Wilson, who said he didn't care which team won "as long as it was the Cubs," caught the fancy. So did Jack Quinlan, killed unfortunately in an accident early in his already-bright career. But the premier early day favorite of ability and durability, the Midwest's answer to New York's Barber and Mel Allen, was Bob Elson. "Braggin' Bob," his critics called him.

Elson, like Barber, Allen, and Brickhouse, a winner of the award at Cooperstown, broadcast both Chicago clubs' games and then just the Sox for 40 years through 1970. He also continued celebrity interviews at the ball park and at the famous Pump Room at the Ambassador East Hotel. He had won from the first commissioner, Judge Landis, the right to an on-the-field interview. Elson's choice in 1931? Connie Mack.

Elson did 12 World Series and nine All-Star games, acknowledging with a smile when honored at Cooperstown in 1979, then 74, that it didn't hurt having Judge Landis as a friend, but actually Braggin' Bob had the talent and the clarity. His color men at times were such giants of the industry as Gabriel Heatter, Boake Carter, H. V. Kaltenborn, and Fulton Lewis, Jr.

"The Commander," a preening nickname for Elson from his duty in World War II, was a Chicago-born man who attended Loyola and Northwestern University. As a boy, he had been a member of the world-famous Paulist Choristers. The experience didn't hurt his voice training.

Visiting in Minneapolis, invited as an amateur to participate, he won an announcing contest. Next, aware that Tom Convey's Station KWK in St. Louis was conducting another on-the-air contest, matching applicants for skill in sports, news, disc-jockeying, Elson won that one, too. Trouble is, a sour-grapes contestant screamed "foul!" So Convey, who had Chicago connections, landed Elson a job with powerful WGN.

By 1929, Elson was on the air and teamed with St. Louis KMOX's France Laux, a former football coach from Tulsa, to broadcast the World Series for Columbia Broadcasting System. He was on his way, a gin-rummy sharpie, pool-playing expert who, though personally a nervous guy, had a technique of sounding relaxed. And he was a masterful interviewer.

Elson had a knack of using occasional silence on radio, considered deadly by many, as an effective change of pace. The manner in which he raised inflections for a swinging strike or an umpire's decision against a sprinting runner at first base simulated the race of man against ball. Most effective, and it occasioned many announcers, some of them extremely good, to copy his style.

One mimic, Milo Hamilton, who later worked with his idol in Chicago, could imitate Elson delightfully, whether Hamilton was working in St. Louis, Atlanta, Pittsburgh or Houston. If you ever had heard The Commander, you would swear he was seated in a team bus or wherever Hamilton would parrot the old master. For instance — and, unfortunately, the printed words can't catch the nuance of the intonation — Elson would say: "This week's ice cream special at Walgreen's — tutti-frutti . . . Ball two!" Tutti-frutti never sounded — or tasted — any better than when Elson's voice rose and fell in "tootie-frootie!"

One who obviously listened to Elson when working his way up through the ranks in small stations at Joliet, Illinois, and Kalamazoo, Michigan, was Harry Caray, a St. Louisan.

Carabina, a name he shortened for air purposes, became first on St. Louis radio and then in Chicago as regionally popular as Elson even if he never earned so many World Series assignments. A barechested bleacher broadcaster at times, using a giant net to snatch fouls in his press box seat, Caray is a hardworking announcer whose flamboyant, imaginative style could excite a crowd even more than an actual game. With the Cubs making a run for it in 1984, Harry had a ball on WGN's national cable TV network. His seventh-inning stretch, as he stood to lead the crowds in "Take Me Out to the Ball Game," became as legendary as his home run chant or his pet substitute for an expletive — "Holy Cow!" His return to the airways from a stroke in 1987 was a dramatic, widely acclaimed salute to the "Mayor of Rush Street."

For a fact, working big league baseball play-by-play since 1945, Caray was sanctifying a bovine when New York's Phil Rizzuto still was scooping up ground balls for the Yankees. (Rizzuto later used "Holy Cow" on radio.) Caray's home run promise of "might-be, could-be, it IS!" was dashed only when — too often — he groaned, "Foul ball!" or even worse, "He caught it!"

Caray, like two former St. Louis associates, highly talented Jack Buck and Joe Garagiola, would seem a warm candidate for the Frick Award at the Hall of Fame. Buck was honored in 1987, Lindsey Nelson in '88. Previous winners for meritorious baseball broadcasting included Mel Allen and Red Barber at the outset, Russ Hodges, Ernie

Harwell, Vince Scully, Curt Gowdy, Brickhouse, Buck Canal, Bob Prince and, as mentioned, "The Commander."

Elson's great moment, Bob conceded, previous to the distinction of stepping up on the library steps to receive the Hall of Fame award from a Hall of Fame player, Ralph Kiner, New York Mets' commentator, was when he covered the Battle of Produce Row, i.e., Detroit's anger at Joe Medwick in the 1934 World Series.

Delightfully, Elson related at Cooperstown, shortly before his death of a heart attack, "I gave it to 'em, tomato by tomato, pie by pie, without missing a lemon, banana, cabbage, or whatever. It would be only a matter of how long the garbage and Medwick would hold out, because I had reached my best crescendo. Then Judge Landis spoiled the fun. He ordered the umpires to get Medwick the hell off the field. . . ."

By 1934, the Ford Motor Company had come along with $100,000, a sizable sum for that poor-penny period, to broadcast the World Series, the first underwritten. But, actually, most ball clubs had not participated in broadcasting that summer. If gum guys Wrigley hadn't urged a live-let-live attitude, every-man-chew-his-own-cud, radio would have been banned completely.

At New York, the Giants, Yankees, and across-the-bridge Dodgers agreed on a five-year ban, home and road games. As Red Barber noted in both his books, *The Broadcasters* and *1947 — When All Hell Broke Loose in Baseball* by Doubleday and Company, New York, the stiff ban wouldn't even permit Western Union to re-create the games for popular make-believe broadcasts elsewhere.

In St. Louis, too, among others, Sam Breadon drew the line, prompting an old Scotch-drinking partner, Convey, who broadcast under his first two names, Thomas Patrick, to try to defy an old friend. Thomas Patrick Convey propped a ladder atop the North Side YMCA, looking down over the center-field fence. There, with binoculars, Patrick planned to pirate the action, sorry to give up the free cakes and other goodies women guests on "Ladies' Day" used to provide him at his balcony chair perch beneath the ball park press box.

Wisely, Patrick catered to the fair sex. He was almost as much a Ladies' Day favorite as Sunny Jim Bottomley until, weakened by too many bouts with the bottle, he was felled in '34 by a burst appendix, but he lost the bout also to air 1934 games.

When Breadon prevented bird's-eye piracy, Patrick quickly followed the 3 P.M. game with a brief newspaper-style, play-by-play as soon as the contest ended, but the skeletonized catch-up wasn't the same. The colorful Gas House Gang drew only 334,000, a good 100,000 of whom came the final week of the season when the Cardinals caught and passed the Giants.

Before the '34 World Series, Will Rogers, already a legend as a cowboy-actor-newspaper humorist, took young friend Dizzy Dean to breakfast with radio sponsor Henry Ford, urging Dizzy to show proper respect for the aged automobile pioneer. You know, Diz, call him Mr. Ford. Ford himself answered the door at Grosse Pointe, greeted Rogers, and welcomed "Mr. Dean."

"Hiya, Henry," Dizzy beamed, shaking an old hand with extra vigor. "Nice to meet ya, podnuh. Sorry I'm a-gonna hafta make pussy-cats out of your Tigers."

Will winced the way Walter Lanier Barber's father did when Red, a University of Florida graduate eager to get farther in his broadcasting career, went "big league" for less money. After scrimping to get by, Red rode busses at night to save the cost of hotel rooms, working for fly-by-night stations as a student for 35 cents an hour to $135 a month. "Always, always, always," as Red put it, he sought a spot on Cincinnati's WLW. WLW then, truly, was the Babe Ruth of broadcasting stations with 500,000 watts and a staff as big as a network's.

Finally the offer came, but it was only $25 a week, and Red's father questioned the arithmetic. Pop could have saved his breath. Red was going. Powell Crosley, Jr., who owned WLW and also a company that made radio sets, refrigerators, and later the Crosley car, then owned the Cincinnati Reds. He just had hired Larry MacPhail from Columbus to general manage the sickly ball club.

MacPhail and Barber, the two redheads, did almost as much to turn things around in baseball as the minor league "gimmick" MacPhail brought to Cincinnati a year later — night games.

By the time Irish MacPhail got in Dutch with Crosley over his fighting three years later, Larry liked the other redhead's softly cornponed accent, knowledge of the game, and an objectivity only lightly salted with home team loyalty.

By the time MacPhail got out of the one-season doghouse and into the Dodgers, almost as downtrodden as the Reds had been, the flaming former football official knew exactly what he wanted: More than money for lights for Ebbets Field, one redhead wanted the other — *and* radio.

To General Mills, the company that produced Wheaties, the "Breakfast of Champions," which showered its boxed flakes on ballplayers who hit home runs, MacPhail made it plain he would break away from that no-radio nonsense in New York. He wanted $70,000, a 50,000-watt station — and Red Barber.

As Barber recalled ruefully in his books, Red wished he had known how *much* MacPhail wanted him. Maybe Red would have gotten more than the $8000 he was offered and accepted, considerably less than the $25,000 estimated in print by a sharp newspaperman, Bill Corum, the Broadway boulevardier sports columnist. Corum himself would become Gillette's radio fight commentator and also part-time president of Churchill Downs at Kentucky Derby time.

Barber's quaint comments about "rhubarbs" for playing field fights and "the catbird seat" for supremacy, i.e., eatin' high on the hog, were refreshing novelties, but Red was basically just a darned good reporter. He lasted until he made a mistake when working with the New York Yankees in the mid-1960s. He had his TV camera crew pan what the emaciated Bombers of old had acquired too many of: Empty seats. So Red wound up back in Florida, retired at Tallahassee, turning out occasional newspaper columns and books. He had so much to remember, as recounted by Ron Powers in *Supertube,* published in 1984 by Coward-McCann, Inc., New York.

Powers's book is highly recommended for exciting detail, depth, and skill. Powers, a University of Missouri graduate from Mark Twain's hometown, Hannibal, was a *St. Louis Post-Dispatch* sportswriter who won a Pulitzer Prize for his television criticism with the *Chicago Sun-Times.* He became a New York novelist and national TV critic on the tube.

Powers points out in *Supertube,* geared more to television than radio, that a turning point came in 1939, the same year MacPhail (and Barber) freed New York fans from their roaring radio silence. Larry and Red forced the Giants and Yanks to lift their blackouts, but, as usual, Mac stayed one up. He not only immediately put his man on the road, which others didn't in the time of economy, but he also aired spring training games.

Meanwhile, when Ford decided to drop World Series broadcasts after its five-year contract, so discouraged by inability to pick up auto sales that it didn't even use commercials in the Yankees' 1938 four-game sweep over the Cubs, Gillette's A. Craig Smith stepped forward.

Smith, a University of Michigan man, former police reporter, and at one time a door-to-door brush salesman, put Gillette's reputation and money on the line. Even though Craig personally didn't give the same hang for baseball as big boss Joseph P. Spang, he talked the company president into letting him spend $203,000 for the World Series broadcast.

The tab included $100,000 to baseball and the rest to the Mutual Broadcasting System for line charges and other costs. This was nearly one-fourth of Smith's annual advertising budget at a time King Gillette, as the founder was named, struggled with only 18 percent of the safety-razor market it created at the turn of the century.

Gillette skeptics frowned at the investment. How many blades would the project sell? A million? Ah, good, *if* achieved. But the Series lasted only four days, not seven, cutting public exposure. Red Barber, obviously a better announcer than personal salesman, didn't like it, either, because Smith had committed himself to only $90 a game for Red's southern-fried zeal.

The first bold venture in 1939 sold brilliantly. Not only 1,000,000 blades, but 4,000,000. Gillette was off and running. A. Craig Smith, too, and Barber—and Melvin Israel.

Melvin Who?? Mel Allen, that's who, bless his syrupy southern tones. Born of Russian immigrant parents in 1913 at Birmingham, Mel attended the University of Alabama, graduated in law, and became a speech teacher at Tuscaloosa. The football coach then was Frank Thomas, a Notre Dame man who combined with Wallace Wade previously and Bear Bryant later to give the Crimson Tide three of the greatest coaching careers ever. Thomas urged speech major Allen to become field announcer at 'Bama games.

Quickly, the exposure had Allen on a station in Birmingham, en route to New York, where he already had done three World Series before he went into the army. Powers put it well when he wrote, "Allen's huge success was due in large part to his vibrant speaking style. He let his sense of startled, schoolboy enthusiasm loose on the big plays, and his deep-voweled southern phrasings seemed to add a natural drama to a crucial moment."

Allen's exclamation—"How a-bout that!"—became a part of, as Powers phrased it, Mel's "on-air persona."

Funny thing, the South turned out some great baseball broadcasting talent even though St. Louis was the southern-most and western boundary until Kansas City in 1955 and Atlanta in 1966. In other words, most of the media gentlemen from below that famed "battery," Mason and Dixon, didn't have the chance regularly to hear major league broadcasts, much less see the big leaguers play.

Still, until television's Game of the Week followed radio's Game of the Day into homes outside territorial big league boundaries, meaning largely in Dixie, barnstorming ball clubs found a small mint annually in the South. All clubs toured back from spring training. A master at picking the most obscure pockets for the longest junkets was Bill Terry as manager of the New York Giants, traditionally trekking with the Cleveland Indians.

From Terry's adopted state—"Memphis Bill," they called him for years—came a young man who, like Allen at Alabama, was influenced by a famed football coach. That was Lindsey Nelson, a student spotter thrust into action at the Tennessee-Vanderbilt football game in 1939 when the regular announcer became ill.

By the time World War II ended, Nelson, who had tutored Tennessee players as student manager for the great coach, General Robert R. Neyland, approached the stern military man, powerful in discipline and physical frame. If "The General," as they all called him, would give Lindsey a chance to set up a private radio network for the Vols, Nelson would promise the athletic department the first $10,000.

"If you can *raise* or *sell* $10,000," said Neyland in combined amusement and annoyance. But he liked Nelson, which is easy to do, especially if you like loud, flamboyant attire, which Lindsey wore as he moved quickly into national prominence as an all-around broadcaster, a craftsman whose years included lengthy baseball stints with the New York Mets and San Francisco Giants.

Still going strong, though saddened by the unexpected death some years ago of his wife, Nelson quit at his peak, if not his prime, and went back to the old campus. He bought a condominium in the mountains overlooking Knoxville, translated his energy into writing three newspaper columns a week and teaching a course in communications at the grateful university. On autumn weekends he still headed out to do football.

Oddly, Nelson and Jack Buck, whose excuse for his dashing dress is color blindness, have things more in common than their attraction to rococo haberdashery. Both were wounded on the same day in World War II in the same European action, the bridge at Remagen.

Buck, born in Holyoke, Massachusetts, early a fan of the Boston Red Sox, moved as a young teenager to Cleveland in a large family that lost its father. So Jack struggled in many menial jobs, ranging from mundane drive-in car-hop to Great Lakes' steamer deckhand. The GI Bill of Rights paid his way through Ohio State, i.e., paid in pain by the Purple Heart. He earned Hall of Fame recognition in 1987.

To get his professional baseball start, Jack sat in the outer office of Al Banister, general manager of the St. Louis Cardinals' Columbus farm club, so that Banister could hear, but not see him. Banister gave Buck *The Sporting News* 1949 annual guide, asking him to re-create the play-by-play of a World Series game between Cleveland and the Boston Braves.

Buck got the job, and when a better one opened at Rochester, New York, Banister recommended him to perceptive Bing Devine. As a result, when the Cardinals needed a replacement to help Harry Caray in St. Louis, the Redbirds auditioned Jack the Buckeye in a most unusual game in 1952 at New York's Polo Grounds. The Cardinals trailed No. 1 righthander, Sal Maglie, by an 11–0 score, yet rallied for a remarkable 14–12 victory.

Buck's professional aplomb is second only to his wit. He's even funnier than another former St. Louis assistant, witty Joe Garagiola, who gave up a $16,000-a-year playing job at 29 with the World Champion New York Giants to join St. Louis's KMOX for $12,000 in 1955. Joe's gutty gamble paid off.

Garagiola, moving ultimately to New York, became a household word through years on National Broadcasting Company's *Today* show as well as NBC's *Game of the Week,* which he retained after deciding to cut back and move west to the Phoenix area. Like Buck, Yogi Berra's pal "Joey" is in demand as an emcee or speaker.

The ability to tell a story interestingly and well is a gift. Before Waite Hoyt retired at Cincinnati after nearly 30 years doing Reds' broadcasts in a quaint, past-tense style, unlike the common present-tense technique, Cincy fans rooted for rain so that Hoyt would reminisce about his career, especially his escapades with a colorful old Yankee teammate, Babe Ruth.

Of all former athletes, the one who made the greatest impact on both radio and television, as Ron Powers noted in his history of radio and television sports, was Dizzy Dean. A folk hero as a lean, gangling, cocky, blow-'em-down guy with the Gas House Gang, Ol' Diz became a second legend as an overstuffed, brassy, warm, language-mangling personality on radio in the 1950s and the first half of the '60s.

Teamed first with another former ballplayer, Buddy Blattner, and then another, Pee Wee Reese, Dean was the Jubilation T. Cornpone of the airways, voiding the sound with a lusty rendition of the old railroad ballad, "The Wabash Cannonball," and himself with barbecued ribs and catfish. He became a mountain of a man in size as well as in memory.

His beer, Falstaff, fell far into the second division after he quit hustling it. Dean had a magic best remembered by Blattner and Diz's longtime producing friend, Gene Kirby. As Blattner said, "We'd be at a beer convention and a drummer or distributor would come up to shake hands. Dizzy would pump his arm warmly, grin and say, 'Nice to see you again, *Podnuh*,' and, so help me, the guy would go away in a daze, shaking his head, and tell the next guy, 'Imagine, he remembered my *name!*'"

When World War II ended, all ground rules of sportsmanship were dispelled, particularly in two-team towns. In St. Louis, for instance, Dean and Johnny O'Hara had been competing against Harry Caray and a former catcher-manager, Gabby Street, and at times, also, France Laux and ex-athlete Cy Casper. Now, to make a decision for the formation of an area network—and the Cardinals could go the farthest without overlapping into another club's—owner Sam Breadon had to make a choice. He chose Caray and Street, impressed with Caray's youthful enthusiasm and effort.

Dean, bitter, had to move over to the rival Browns. A couple of years later when the American League club was last, Dizzy was tee-heeing about how lousy they were. Cleverly, Bill DeWitt, club president of the Browns, challenged him to do better. Of course (ahem!) DeWitt would throw in "X"-number of dollars to make it worthwhile. Graciously, Phil Wrigley released Dean, who had been on the Cubs' retired list for six years.

Already ballooning, Dizzy worked out a bit and then pitched against the White Sox the last day of the 1947 season, drawing a pretty good crowd. For four innings he pitched scoreless ball, using an exaggerated windup and changing speeds, throwing slow and slower. At bat, he hit one deep to left field, rounded first safely, pulled an overstuffed hamstring, and limped painfully back to the bag.

Dizzy's protective wife, Pat, leaned over from her box seat and, looking into the dugout, she located manager Muddy Ruel. "Crissake, Muddy," she ordered, "get him out of there before he kills himself."

Over the years former ballplayers have gone from mask to mike, bats to batteries, especially since television and cable have increased the need for numbers and for expertise. First, in this research, was Jack Graney, little Cleveland leadoff man-outfielder of the Indians' 1920 champions. When Graney retired, he would have done well in the automobile business, but, oops, the Depression drove him into radio with Cleveland in 1932. He lasted for 30 years.

One of the more difficult tasks came when Frank Frisch, fired as manager of the Cardinals, was hired in Boston in 1939 to replace a popular broadcaster, Fred Hoey. The old Flash was glad a year later to give up the live lobsters at Scituate and beery nights with old teammate, Casey Stengel, for the bench perch as pilot of the Pirates.

Later, though, Frisch was back in the press box at the Polo Grounds, helping Russ Hodges with the Giants. Frisch's managerial lament, "Oh, those bases on balls," became a groan the neighborhood kids out in suburban New Rochelle chanted when they passed Frisch's house. He loved their oral riposte.

One day when Frisch was occupying the low-ceilinged coop attached to the upper deck of the Polo Grounds' grandstand, he was droning away at the microphone something like this: "The count on Musial is '2 and 2' and here comes . . . J-e-s-u-s C-h-r-i-s-t!"

The Lord's name never had been used in vain so loudly or before such a large audience, but there was a reason. A prankster seated just above the press box had lowered a life-like toy tarantula into Frisch's eye level as the pitch was en route to the plate.

For years, announcers played pranks on each other, trying to break up co-workers' professional aplomb, because, after all, until TV, the announcer was as anonymous as The Shadow. You had to have considerable poise and resistance to pain to continue as your jollying self if someone was applying the hotfoot, i.e., a match wedged surreptitiously into your shoe seam and lighted.

Traditionally, a Western Union report from a big league ball club would send a skeletonized account to a WU representative taking the dots-and-dashes in clickety-clack form. Such as, "B-1, low" or "S-1, foul," requiring the announcer to use his imagination in the trappings of the situation, such as windup, location of the pitch and the foul, etc.

As one who liked to romance about his early sportscasting days en route to Hollywood and the White House, President Ronald Reagan recalled that when broadcasting in Iowa re-creations of Cubs' games in 1935, the year Charlie Grimm won the pennant with a remarkable run of 21 straight in September, he came up to the inevitable crisis. A wire breakdown or, as they used to crack, "wire trouble east (or west) of Buffalo."

With the pitch en route when the operator's keyboard went dead, Reagan said he had the hitter, shortstop Bill Jurges, foul off innumerable deliveries, describing in detail how fans scrambled for the ball, stalling imaginatively. Suddenly the wire trouble was resolved. The key click-clacked again. "And," the President remembered, more than once, smiling, "I learned that Jurges had popped out—on the first pitch."

Too many re-creations sounded exactly like what they were, as unappealing as cold mashed potatoes, but some announcers were ingenious, none more so than a gutty kid from Dallas who took that $27.50 Western Union play-by-play ticker service and turned it into a mint.

After World War II, young Yale graduate Gordon McLendon, calling himself the "Old Scotchman," moved from live minor league ball to set up the Liberty Network in Dallas, buying that $27.50 bargain from WU and offering it re-created for $10 a game to 300-plus stations, which also absorbed the telephone line charges.

Using Lindsey Nelson as an announcer and also Jerry Doggett, later a longtime broadcaster with the Dodgers, McLendon did it so professionally that sound effects included taped organ music and the National Anthem from each park, as well as crowd noises, batting effects, and the echoed background noise of field announcers.

Nelson, in a recollection once for Hubert Mizell, recently sports editor of the *St. Petersburg Times,* said the muffled voice of a studio lackey from the men's room did nicely until someone flushed a toilet. Then, quipped Nelson, "We'd probably have to say, 'The game now is being played in a downpour. . . . '"

Liberty Network apparently made a millionaire out of the "Old Scotchman" before McLendon retired to his Texas ranch, his re-creations replaced by Mutual Broadcasting System's traveling, live *Game of the Day,* featuring Dizzy Dean and Buddy Blattner.

By then, too, major league ball clubs had begun to show the acuteness of Larry MacPhail, the first to broadcast games live on the road as well as at home. After all, radio did more to make fans of women customers than anything, probably even more than Ladies' Day, a tradition that filled many a ball park for free or at two-bits or 50 cents a head in the Depression when the half-buck bleacher seat or $1.10 general admission and $1.35 reserved seat was too steep.

Television, now offering a grand slam on regional or national networks and on cable, too, particularly as offered by superstations (Chicago's WGN, Atlanta's Turner empire, and New York's WOR), has risen dramatically from the first overall exposure. That was the 1947 Yankee-Dodger World Series.

Back then, reflecting the Baptist belt reaction of his own area, new commissioner A. B. (Happy) Chandler, former United States senator and governor of Kentucky, rejected beer sponsorship and took less money for Series TV. Ultimately, with the player-pension plan and their own desire for a dollar comparable with just about anyone's, baseball capitulated. Miller Brewery might be first nationally if only Anheuser-Busch, which has owned the St. Louis Cardinals since 1953, hadn't got there first with the most in the number of radio-TV beer sponsorships.

The battle of the breweries, in which St. Louis leads Milwaukee, Budweiser over Miller, brings to mind the part they played in molding the radio-TV career of two former players who, as a result of wit and warmth, became nationally known. One was previously mentioned, Joe Garagiola, whose book *Baseball Is a Funny Game,* published when he announced for the Cardinals a quarter-century ago, still sells well.

The other, Bob Uecker, for some years a member of Milwaukee's baseball broadcasting team, became, like Garagiola, a frequent guest on Johnny Carson's *Tonight* show. In addition, "Kroo-gah, the Oo-Boat commander," as he liked to call himself in low-Dutch comments when catching, became a star in Miller Lite beer commercials and television's "Mr. Belvedere" sit-com.

Once upon a time when Harry Heilmann and others such as Graney, Frisch, Jim Bottomley, Charlie Grimm, and Waite Hoyt sat in the press box, former ballplayers were novelties behind a microphone, but no longer.

In 1987, for instance, with Tony Kubek teaming with a brilliant wunderkind broadcaster, award-winning Bob Costas, on one weekend network for NBC and Joe Garagiola working with award-winner Vince Scully, regarded by many as the top play-by-play broadcaster, more ballplayers on radio and/or TV included:

Brooks Robinson and Rex Barney, Baltimore; Ron Fairly and Joe Torre, California; Don Drysdale and Ken Harrelson, Chicago White Sox; Herb Score, Cleveland; Al Kaline and George Kell, Detroit; Bob Uecker, Milwaukee; Harmon Killebrew, Minnesota; Phil Rizzuto, Bill White, Bobby Murcer, Billy Martin, and Jim Kaat, New York Yankees; Ray Fosse, Oakland; Steve Busby, Texas; Ernie Johnson, Atlanta; Lou Boudreau and Steve Stone, Chicago Cubs; Joe Nuxhall, Cincinnati; Larry Dierker, Houston; Duke Snider and Claude Raymond, Montreal; Ralph Kiner, Fran Healy and Tim McCarver (also ABC Monday Night Baseball), New York Mets; Richie Ashburn, Philadelphia; Steve Blass and Jim Rooker, Pittsburgh; Mike Shannon, Al Hrabosky, and Bob Gibson, St. Louis; Jerry Coleman and Dave Campbell, San Diego; and Tito Fuentes, San Francisco.

Over the years radio and then television seemed higher-risk jobs than the newspaper baseball beat, but, truth is, more recently with fewer papers and fewer men willing to make a career of it, radio-TV talent has turned into the one (or two) town durability of Washington's Arch McDonald; Pittsburgh's Rosy Rowswell and Bob Prince; New York and San Francisco's Russ Hodges and Lon Simmons; Boston's Curt Gowdy and Ken Coleman; Baltimore's Chuck Thompson; Chicago's Bob Elson and Jack Brickhouse; Brooklyn–Los Angeles's Vince Scully and Jerry Doggett; St. Louis's Jack Buck, Mike Shannon and predecessor Harry Caray, who established the same fanatical following in Chicago; Cleveland's Jack Graney and Jimmy Dudley; Atlanta's Skip Caray; Cincinnati's Marty Brennaman; Houston's Gene Elston; Los Angeles's Ross Porter; New York Mets' Bob Murphy; Philadelphia's Byrum Saum and Gene Kelly in the past, Harry Kalas and Andy Musser at present; Detroit's Ernie Harwell and Paul Carey; and ABC's Al Michaels.

Michaels learned his craft well at Cincinnati before settling into network broadcasting. Harwell, a reformed sportswriter and a Ford Frick Award winner at Cooperstown, finished his thirty-fifth year with the Tigers. Harwell's tender typed salute to baseball, "The Game for All America," like the famed yes-Virginia-there-is-a-Santa Claus editorial, is resurrected annually by *The Sporting News* as a season opener.

Oh, yes, Harwell is one announcer who got to where he is because he was traded by Atlanta, then a minor league town or, more accurately, a town with a minor league team. Ernie was swapped to Brooklyn for a ballplayer, Cliff Dapper, a catcher. But that's not bad. Atlanta once traded a ballplayer for a turkey! Yeah, a gobble-gobble *bird*!

If newer broadcasters or more recent with a given franchise will forgive omission here, please remember: An author who is a sportswriter didn't go nearly so far trying to spell out the guys in his game in the baseball writing chapter.

There's a lot more that could be written about broadcasters, only some of which can be accommodated in a book trying to touch virtually all of baseball's bases. It must be reported that from a sport which once gave away its product to any station that would be willing to air for free bartered game plugs to an attraction that once almost barred radio entirely and was slow about seeing television's potential, baseball has prospered at the gate and also in the treasury from radio-TV and now, daringly, from cable.

Most recently, each team totes to the bank $5,000,000 a year for its share of national television—Sunday, Monday and always, meaning All-Star game and World Series—and each club then pockets separately its local radio-TV network funds. The range is from an additional $1,000,000 to $2,000,000 a year—and that doesn't include income from cable superstations or individual clubs' private closed-circuit coverage.

So they've come a long way together, radio and then television, with baseball as well as with football, basketball, boxing, and two sports that were hidden except from, as Joe Garagiola would say, the high-rent view—golf and tennis.

As Curt Smith's *Voices of The Game,* a bright, 607-paged book published by Diamond Communications in 1987, would indicate, it's a far cry from the original days when the unctuous voice was infant radio's initial offering. Graham McNamee, who sounded as if to the manor born, was Mr. Radio at the outset, and his "How do you do, ladies and gentlemen of the radio audience, this is Graham McNamee speaking" rolled off his tongue like a trumpet's bringing the palace guard to attention.

McNamee, born in Washington, D.C., schooled in Minneapolis and a one-time railroad clerk for Rock Island, wanted to become a concert baritone when he signed as an announcer-singer with New York's WEAF in 1923. McNamee was at his best when serving as a staff announcer for big name variety shows, but he really didn't know much about the sports he broadcast nationally with the first coast-to-coast aired World Series, 1926.

After all, in glee, describing, say, a three-base hit, his favorite word was a girlish squealed "Whee!" And acerbic wit Ring Lardner, whose humor translated into short story success, summed it up after one Series game when, seated near McNamee, Lardner wrote they just had watched a doubleheader . . . the game he *saw* and the game he *heard.*

When the expert arrived, when knowledge transcended pear-shaped tones, Mr. Radio was just another announcer before he died prematurely in 1942, aged only 53, but the *Cleveland Plain-Dealer* probably put it best for any fortunate to have witnessed—or listened—first hand to the *Voices of the Game:*

" . . . We wouldn't have wanted to miss the Graham McNamee period of radio any more than we would have wanted to have skipped our childhood."

11
Follow the Leader

From the Wright brothers, meaning from George and Harry, not Wilbur and Orville, and from "A" to "Z"—from Cap Anson to Chief Zimmer—from the first rose of baseball summer to Pete Rose, baseball has had player-managers, a little or a lot.

Mostly, they were in the Depression Thirties when hard-pressed clubowners, trying to get two jobs for the price of one and to showcase their superstars, turned pellmell to the playing-field foreman. The National League opened the 1934 season with seven player-managers.

For a guy alive then, wide-eyed at major league box scores and rabbit-eared to radio accounts, this was the best of times. After all, the player-manager was as swashbucklingly romantic as the follow-the-leader in World War I. Then, wearing the washbowl-shaped helmets of the so-called "last" war, fighting trench-to-trench ridiculously for little bits of real estate, first lieutenants would climb to the top of the dugout, straighten up, blow a whistle, and shout, "Follow me."

Too often the young fighting man would be shot between the eyes, but the inspirational impact could not be lost in sheer statistics. If the kid in mummy-legged khaki lasted, he was sheer inspiration.

That's the way it was with the baseball manager who could step up there in a pinch and deliver a key hit or turn a top defensive play. After all, it's more meaningful to tell 'em to do it as I do, not as I say.

Not even Burt L. Standish, whose pulp fiction spurred many a kid, could have been so fanciful as, for instance, the first American League playoff game, 1948.

As manager of the Cleveland Indians, then a seven-season straw boss at only 31 years old, Lou Boudreau shortstopped the Cleveland Indians. Over the winter, promotion genius Bill Veeck, building up the Indians into record ticket buyers, had threatened to trade Boudreau to the St. Louis Browns for Vern (Junior) Stephens, throwing in a little cash to ease the Brownies' financial pain. But strong fan support in a public poll delayed Veeck's action.

So Stephens was dealt to the Boston Red Sox, instead, and Boudreau, the handsome dark-haired former University of Illinois basketball star, was tremendous in 1948. Playing short shallowly, cutting down the batting angle because he had a quick start and no speed, Lou fielded well and hit spectacularly. He batted .355 with 18 homers, scoring 116 runs and driving in 106. He struck out only nine of 560 official times at bat.

In the American League's first one-for-the-money tie, Boudreau took his Indians into Fenway Park to play Joe McCarthy's Red Sox, who had tied the Tribe on the final day of the regular season. The winner would play the Boston Braves, National League champions for the first time in 34 years.

An all-Boston World Series had appeal, all right, but not to Boudreau. The shortstop played with ankles bandaged and, though not heavy, a bulge at the belly, a lusty trencherman who ate too heartily. He had a hot stick in '48, physically and mentally. Even though Allie Clark never before had played first base, Boudreau substituted Clark for Eddie Robinson in that spotlighted game. To get one more right-handed shot at the beckoning green barrier in left field, Boudreau boldly played Clark out of position.

In what facetiously might be called the greatest managerial job ever, Boudreau himself got four hits, two of them homers; and the Indians won the pennant and World Championship. Boudreau richly deserved the Most Valuable Player Award and *The Sporting News'* Player-of-the-Year designation.

Even though he played four more years and managed nine more, before huffing up into the radio press booth at Chicago's Wrigley Field as broadcaster, Boudreau never came close again to .300 or a pennant.

The effect of the player-manager, at least most of them from the tough-times era when more served as player pilots, was probably expressed best some years afterward by Frank Frisch. Frisch, of the St. Louis Cardinals' colorful Gas House Gang, never recaptured as a bench manager his impact when he could throw his aging, chunky body in front of a hot smash or slide hard headfirst, or range back so that his cap came off and exposed his bald spot as he camped under a tough pop fly. And, of course, they didn't call him "a money player" for nothing at the plate, but. . . .

"I think managing shortened my career," Frisch summed himself up after he also managed Pittsburgh and the Cubs. "I was a better manager when I was playing, when I could lead like a platoon sergeant in the field rather than as a general sitting back on his duff in a command post."

Turning the introspection into self-defense, the Old Flash added, "But I won't apologize for having wanted my players to be as good as I was supposed to be. If intolerance of mediocrity is a crime, I plead guilty."

To be sure, that's the way Adrian Anson must have felt about it when he went from "Cap" to "Pop" in a 19-year managerial career with the Cubs or White Stockings, as the Chicago Nationals were known. He quit in 1898, one year after he finished playing. Anson, first 3000-hit player, was 45 when he hit .303. As a manager, Anson won five pennants over a seven-year period, 1880–1886. By then, he was baseball's first major league legend, a career .339-hitting first baseman.

The Wrights, meaning the ballplayers, not the aviation pioneers, were pioneer pilots, too, though neither George nor Harry put in the time in a uniform that Anson did. Fact is, George, a shortstop from the time of the first professional Cincinnati Red Stockings in 1869, managed in only '79 at Providence.

Harry Wright, born in 1835 in Sheffield, England, 12 years before George, managed the Boston Nationals, Providence, and Philadelphia for 15 years, playing only briefly the first two seasons of the National League. He died in 1895.

Brother George, named to the Hall of Fame its second year, 1937, died that same year at the ripe old age of 90. Anson, 71 when he died in 1922, was named to Cooperstown posthumously in 1939.

Cowardly, we will make no attempt to list all player-managers in the first 115 years of major league baseball. We learned from Ben Walker of the *Associated Press*. He gave it a noble try when Pete Rose brought back the athletic skipper in 1984, five years after manager Don Kessinger had played shortstop briefly for the Chicago White Sox.

Walker tried to list all player-pilots of this century and came up with 96. Good try, all right, but he omitted two from St. Louis alone—catcher Bob O'Farrell, 1927, and Billy Southworth, 1929, both Cardinals. O'Farrell also caught briefly when managing Cincinnati in '34.

Of the early day player-managers, a few even rose to ownership, a status that ended in 1984 when, hard-pressed to keep financially afloat after free agency drove up salaries, Calvin Griffith sold majority interest in the Minnesota Twins. In 1920 his uncle, Clark Griffith, had acquired controlling interest in the Twins, then Senators. In 1961 the team had been moved from Washington to the Minneapolis–St. Paul area.

From the virtual era of the frontier to well into the 20th century, grand old names gravitated from the playing field to management to franchise operation.

Connie Mack, born in the Civil War, was an eight-year professional when he caught at Pittsburgh and managed there in 1894. Switching to the American League in 1901, he lasted a half-century. Mr. Mack, as they called the tall, skinny Philadelphia patriarch, was an incredible 88 years old in 1950 when he put down the scorecard with which he had wig-wagged players en mufti, straw-hatted and high-collared in the dugout.

Five years later, again facing the financial problems that had forced him twice to break up winning teams, the Macks sold the Athletics, a ball club over which the former catcher had gained control over the years. For the first 13 years of the American League, Connie's White Elephants, as the Philadelphia Americans were nicknamed, won six pennants.

After he sold his talent to keep the franchise in existence, the A's finished last seven successive seasons. Under part-owner Mack, the Athletics rebounded and rebuilt. They won three more pennants and two World Championships, 1929–31. Then, the Depression and a dwindling gate forced the old man to sell off his talent again.

When the A's finally were sold in 1955 and moved to Kansas City, en route to Oakland, as the majors began to play musical chairs with franchises, Mr. Mack made Ft. Myers, Florida, his permanent rather than winter home. He died a year later at 93.

Mack and also Griffith, who will be covered in more detail later, came into flower with establishment of the American League by Ban Johnson in 1901. At the time the eldest of the group, Charley Comiskey, born in 1859 at Chicago, had turned over player-managing to Griffith. The Old Fox, a salutary sobriquet because Griff practiced pitching chicanery, was a most successful manager. He had a 24–7 record as a pitcher and batted .303 for the AL's first pennant-winning ball club.

Comiskey—"Commy," before the expression became a nasty capitalistic no-no—had paid his own dues as first baseman-manager of the old St. Louis Browns, then in the American Association, regarded as major league rivals of the National. Comiskey won four straight pennants, 1885–88.

Of the famed foursome of big name, turn-of-the-century pioneers who flourished for years, only John McGraw officially was not a club-owner, too, though he did have stock in the New York Giants and obviously exercised far more than customary managerial authority.

Muggsy McGraw was still a sharp, scrappy third baseman when he took over the Baltimore Orioles at 26 in 1899. McGraw hit a torrid .390 that year. When the Baltimore franchise folded and he was sold to St. Louis, McGraw went with almost admirable reluctance and a resistance that would do present day players proud. First, he wouldn't sign a contract because he knew that Ban Johnson was building up his Western League into a new major, the American. Second, he agreed to play on a piecework basis, $100 a game.

So in 1900, McGraw saw fit to pull on the red-trimmed St. Louis flannels just 98 times, collecting $9800, obviously a handsome sum for that era. At times he was thrown out of the game early at Robison Field, located directly across Natural Bridge Road from a jockey club at Fairground Park, where Mac loved to invest an idle horse racing buck.

Soon as the season ended, McGraw and his old Baltimore buddy, catcher Wilbert Robinson, a dear friend who became a bitter rival through a misunderstanding as Brooklyn manager, hopped a train back east. Ceremoniously, as the train crossed the Mississippi River, Mac and Robby dropped their Redbird duds into the river.

McGraw would last just long enough back at Baltimore, then a city briefly returned to the majors with the new American League, to find that he couldn't tolerate Johnson's stern support and defense of umpires. Muggsy loved to bedevil the men in blue. So, still playing briefly then and the next few years, McGraw went to New York with the Giants. He was the best thing to hit Broadway other than his dear friend, song-and-dance man George M. Cohan.

If you will, more about McGraw later in this saga about men who managed from between the foul lines rather than from the bench. First prominent in this century was Fred Clarke, fiery left-handed-hitting outfielder with Louisville, i.e., Pittsburgh.

The Colonels became the Pirates in 1900, six years after Clarke broke in as a player, five after he became field foreman in 1897 at only 25. When Clarke was at his peak, batting .316, .321, and .351, the Pirates won three straight pennants, 1901 through '03.

The first World Series was played in 1903 against the Boston Red Sox, who upset Pittsburgh. For 13 years, Clarke's teams never finished out of their first division, lower than fourth in the eight-team National League. The Bucs won another pennant and the World Championship in 1909 with an aging yet agile Clarke still playing the left-field foul line. Fred had sharp ability to turn potential doubles into singles. Honus Wagner and company beat Ty Cobb and Detroit in the World Series.

Clarke had taught Wagner well in Honus's rookie season. The bow-legged, barrel-chested shortstop with the jut jaw of sculpted granite was gentle as well as versatile. When in the loosely played one-umpire era, Wagner hit an apparent triple against Baltimore, first baseman Jack Doyle hipped him as he rounded the bag. At second Honus was forced wide because shortstop Hughie Jennings strategically stood in his way. At third base, John McGraw blocked him off the bag, then knocked the wind out of him by tagging Wagner hard in the stomach.

The 23-year-old rookie dragged himself to the bench, where Clarke blistered him. "Listen, Dutch," the ruddy-faced manager bit off the words, "let that happen again and you're gone."

Two versions of what followed became part of the Wagnerian legend. One, next time up, Honus grounded to McGraw and ran right over Doyle at first base, racing to third as the throw sailed over the bag. Two—and this one is juicier—was told years later by Wagner: "I hit another to deep center for extra bases. I dumped Doyle on his behind at first, left Jennings in the dirt at second, and trampled all over Mc-Graw's feet coming into third. Clarke was so tickled to see McGraw fuming and cussing that he strolled over from the coach's box and said, 'Nice day, ain't it, Muggsy?'"

By the time Pittsburgh played Detroit in 1909, Wagner and Cobb were the two biggest names in baseball. When Ty reached base the first time, the Detroit star snarled, "Look out, Dutchman, "I'm coming down."

If Tyrus intended intimidation, my, what a waste of time. "I'll be here," quietly responded Wagner. He was. As Cobb slid in, hard and spikes high, ham-handed Honus grabbed a catcher's throw, reached down, and tagged Ty in the mouth, splitting his lip. Wagner hit .333 that Series and stole seven bases, a record until Lou Brock 58 years later. Cobb batted just .231.

Clarke, a prosperous rancher at Winfield, Kansas, until his death in 1960 at 88, had obvious affection for Wagner, who filled in only five games as manager at the end of the 1917 season.

Clarke had other unusual accomplishments aside from the rare one as a Grade-A player who managed well and long. He introduced modern flip-style sun glasses for outfielders in 1914, as much to protect their eyes for batting purposes when fighting the glare of the sun as for obvious help in picking up the flight of the ball. Oh, yes, still a favorite of Barney Dreyfuss, longtime Pittsburgh operator, Clarke sat without official portfolio on the Pirates' bench much of the 1925 pennant-winning season under Bill McKechnie.

McKechnie, quiet and dignified, was called "Deacon Will." McKechnie, only manager until Dick Williams to win three pennants in three cities, was a psalm-singer, but you can bet your Bible that he didn't like old hero Clarke's presence on his bench.

Typical of many big stars, Napoleon Lajoie was a washout in five seasons as manager at Cleveland, 1905–09. The Indians even were called the "Naps" in that era, a reflection on the popularity of the big handsome player. Lajoie, a graceful second baseman, hit .339 for 21 years through 1916, but he never played in a World Series. "Larry"—his nickname—generally was regarded as the hardest right-handed hitter prior to Rogers Hornsby.

When Nap was flopping as manager at Cleveland, the Frenchman was extraordinarily phlegmatic. First baseman George Stovall hit him on the head with a chair in 1907, but Lajoie shrugged it off. "He's a good player and we need him."

Three years later, noting that for once he had hit under .300 as a manager, Lajoie stepped back into the ranks as gracefully as he played his position. He jumped to .383 his first year back in the ranks and in 1911, playing for Stovall, the same man for whom he'd taken the knock on the conk, he hit .365.

By contrast, Frank Chance and Fielder Jones, taking over as managers of the Chicago ball clubs at the time Lajoie nose-dived, had considerably more success. Chance, all-around, had the better of it. Jones—honest, his first name *was* Fielder!—had the better of it in a remarkable World Series.

Chance, a strapping right-handed first baseman, was a good glove man, anchor of the double play combination—Tinker to Evers to Chance—that lilted through New York columnist Franklin P. Adams's poetic lament. "Husk," they nicknamed the big guy, was a .297 hitter for 17 seasons, 11 of them as a manager.

By the time Chance's Cubs reeled off three straight pennants through 1908, they called him "The Peerless Leader," which seems like a tongue-in-cheek come-on now, but, fact is, the Cubs did win 322 games and lose only 136 those three years. For a truth, too, they won 490 and lost only 275 in Chance's last five seasons (1908–12).

Chance's personal batting average dipped each year when his defensively sharp team of pitching depth breezed to pennants, except in the 1908 replay with the New York Giants. But it is doubtful Husk ever forgot the '06 Series.

The Cubs had won that year with the best record ever, 116 victories and only 36 defeats, a .763 percentage. By contrast, Fielder Jones' rival White Sox had won with a horrible .228 team batting average. Jones, only a .230 hitter that season, 57 points below his 15-year career record, saw his Sox become the famed "Hitless Wonders" as they upset the Cubs in a six-game World Series. Jones hit only .095.

Fielder managed through 1918, including trips into the Federal League with the St. Louis Terriers and then with the American League Browns, but he never again matched the marvel of that single season of '06. He died at 60 in 1934. Chance, bombing out with the New York Yankees in 1913 and '14, was only 47 when he died in 1924. The year before he had managed the Boston Red Sox—a dead last.

Most of the time player-managers didn't win pennants. Bill (Rough) Carrigan won, catching part-time for his Boston Red Sox in 1913–1916. Even though he weakened and came back later to help poor Bob Quinn try to resurrect the pitiful Boston Red Sox, after theatrical owner Harry Frazee had sold Babe Ruth and all of his other stars, Carrigan was a hardy man. A survivor of those earlier years trying to keep a leash on rover-boy Ruth and three last-place seasons with the Dead Sox in 1927–29, Carrigan went back to Lewiston, Maine. A successful banker, Rough was a neat 86 when he died in 1969.

Cocky Johnny Evers—call him "The Trojan" if you're majestic, "The Crab" if you're realistic—couldn't make it as Chance's successor with the Cubs or elsewhere. Joe Tinker could win once with three clubs, but the only winner was the Chicago Whales of the Federal League (1915).

Roger Bresnahan, unloaded by McGraw on the Cardinals when he slowed as a catcher, couldn't do well enough on the field or in conversation that was too abrasive and salty for the Redbirds' woman owner, Helene Hathaway Robison Britton. The former Robison inherited her ball club from her father and uncle. She seemed to have—ah!—greater affection for Bresnahan's successor, Miller Huggins.

Hug was a pasty-faced little man, a slick, walk-wheedling second baseman. A University of Cincinnati law graduate, he was a class guy. No wonder Mrs. Britton, whose husband was on the prowl, might have wanted to turn over the Cardinals to Huggins. The little man was finishing up at 37 that last year. His Cincinnati friends, the Fleishmann yeast family, were willing to help him raise the dough—if you'll pardon the pun—to buy the Cardinals, but the Cardinals' lawyer, James C. Jones, was concerned about absentee ownership.

Actually, Huggins apparently had no intention to move the Redbirds, a rag-tag team until Branch Rickey's grow-your-own, farm-system method took root several years later. But Jones thought local money should be involved. So they scrounged up the money, $375,000, a pittance now, quite substantial then.

Angrily rebuffed, Huggins listened when J. G. Taylor Spink, publisher of *The Sporting News,* told him that the New York Yankees, rebuilding, were interested in Hug as a manager. "But, crissake," snapped Spink, "don't wear that damned cap. Jake Ruppert already thinks you're a jockey (5–4, 140 pounds)."

Miller Huggins became a giant with the Yankees, manager of six pennant winners in the Roaring Twenties until he died, barely 50, of erysipelas in the final week of the 1929 season. He was second that year.

The fulfillment of the player-manager drama really began when Tris Speaker, the Gray Eagle, took over as manager at Cleveland late in the 1919 season. A year later, staggered by the death of shortstop Ray Chapman, struck by a pitched ball, the Indians were hanging to a slender lead late in September.

The soiled part of the Chicago White Sox, seeking a second successive pennant, hadn't yet been uncovered as they played a pivotal third game of a series between the 1–2 clubs. Chicago had the bases loaded, two out, at old Dunn Field, as Cleveland's cozy League Park then was called. Shoeless Joe Jackson hit an apparent game-winning shot to right-center. Speaker, the master fielder, turned quickly and streaked for the exit gate. There, timing a tremendous leap, Tris plucked the ball off the concrete as he charged into the wall. Speaker was unconscious, but they had to pry the ball out of his game-saving hands.

The thrill of winning as a player-manager in a season (1920) in which he hit .388, belted 50 doubles, and drove in 107 runs, would have seemed the top thrill of the player's career. After all, he also hit .320 in a World Series victory over Brooklyn. But Speaker, 32 then and a manager until the 1926 "scandal" and a big leaguer for two more years, always regarded his greatest thrill in an era when he hadn't yet become a manager. The occasion was the home 10th of the 1912 World Series wind-up, New York Nationals versus Boston Americans.

The Giants just had broken through for a 2–1 lead behind the great Christy Mathewson. Even though, first up in Boston's last chance, pinch hitter Clyde Engle reached base on an error by centerfielder Fred Snodgrass, Mathewson appeared to pitch around the misplay. First, Harry Hooper flied out. Next, Steve Yerkes walked, bringing up Speaker.

"Spoke" always thought he could hit Mathewson because great hitters, like great pitchers, have confidence. Besides, a .383 hitter with 53 doubles, Speaker had won the Most Valuable Player Award that year. But—oops!—the great left-handed hitter popped a foul off the great pitcher's fadeaway, i.e., screwball.

Disgustedly, but, hopefully, Speaker was about to call frustratedly for Chief Meyers, the catcher, aware that the ball was much closer to the New York first baseman, Fred Merkle. But, to his delight, he heard Mathewson yell, "Meyers, Meyers!" The pitcher's commanding call was confusing, calling off the first baseman. The ball was blowing away from Meyers. The catcher couldn't catch it. The ball fell—untouched!

In the batter's box Speaker, then only 24, was overjoyed. In his throaty voice he needled Mathewson. "You just blew the championship, Matty," he rasped. Speaker's single scored Engle with the tying run and, after Duffy Lewis walked, Larry Gardner hit a sacrifice fly that gave the Red Sox a 3–2 victory and the World Championship— and Tris Speaker his most memorable recollection.

Personal perfection often is a hindrance rather than a help to a playing manager. Too often, as Ty Cobb indicated, they expected too much from the men under them and were too demanding. Even a much milder mannered man, Stan Musial, said years later that he had entertained no thought of becoming a manager because he would be—surprisingly to most!—too tough on his team, not too tender. "I would expect too much of them," said the man called Stan.

Cobb, more irascible, did expect too much, and even though he batted .389, .401, .340, .338, .378, and .339 in his six seasons as manager at Detroit, 1921 until released in the 1926 cloud covered in another chapter, he had finished as high as second only once and twice had drifted into the second division. Fiercely self-assured, Ty might not have had proper pitching, but he was tough on his talent. One consolation, about which he crowed in an autobiography, showed the physical effects of managing when playing and, also, the cunning character of a Cobb.

In a tense situation against the Yankees, hoping to show up his personal anathema, Babe Ruth, Cobb called time from the outfield, walked in and talked to his pitcher, visibly directing an intentional base on balls. After the catcher stepped out for three wide pitches, the Detroit pitcher threw a called strike against the relaxed Ruth. Cobb screamed "Time!" and charged in from the outfield, presumably to berate the pitcher for his laxity. When Ty trotted back out to his position, the crestfallen pitcher nodded and fired another strike past the Babe, still surprised.

Louder and longer, Cobb stopped play and rushed in from the outfield, red-faced, and shook a warning finger in the face of the head-hanging hurler. When Cobb returned to the outfield, everyone, including most definitely Mr. Ruth, was certain the pitcher wouldn't let the slip happen again. But, oops, he did. Strike three called!

Cobb, who had set up the situation, cackled with glee as he raced in and a crestfallen Ruth trotted out to his defensive position. "How, d'ya like that, Nig," drawled Ty to the Babe, aware that Ruth resented a racial slur aimed at his physical features.

The Babe, of course, would have liked to manage, and he made nasty noises about it as his career wore down, particularly after Joe Mc-Carthy had not been able to win a pennant Ruth's last two years as a player. The Yankees' clubowner, Jacob Ruppert, and general manager, Ed Barrow, a stern man who as field manager had converted Ruth from pitcher to outfielder at Boston, suggested he first show he could manage New York's nearby Triple-A ball club. That would be Newark of the International League, just across the Lincoln tunnel.

Ruth refused and was released, signed with the Boston Braves as "vice-president, assistant manager and player," a title almost as ludicrous as the overweight, over-aged athlete's efforts before he retired in May 1935. He would return only briefly to uniform as a coach and batting-practice exhibit under colorful Larry MacPhail at Brooklyn in 1938. Obviously, perhaps unfortunately because he was baseball's greatest hero, the implication was stated clearly in the cliché about the Peck's Bad Boy: "How's he going to handle 25 men when he can't handle himself?"

The player-management vogue, though most frequent in the '30s, got its greatest impetus in the mid-'20s from the bushy-browed little man at Washington, born in a log cabin at Nevada, Missouri (1869), shortly after the frontier went west. Not too many years after Custer lost his command at the Little Big Horn in the Montana Territory, wiry Clark Calvin Griffith was spending his winters working crap games in western casinos.

The Old Fox was a sharp codger. He had defaced baseballs, legally then, to help record a brilliant 21-year pitching record of 240–140 through 1914. As mentioned earlier, he had player-managed Chicago to the first American League pennant in 1901, and he was shrewd enough to keep managing until he maneuvered control of Washington in 1920. Uh-huh, 20 years when finishing in the second division eight times.

So Griff had the background, the knowledge, and the cheek in 1924 to turn over his Senators or Nationals, as they called 'em more often in Washington, to his curly-haired, four-year second baseman, a quiet, scrappy kid named Stanley Raymond (Bucky) Harris. Bucky was only 27. The "Boy Wonder," they called him.

Before Harris would quit managing 32 years later at 60, he managed eight different times in five cities—Washington, Detroit, Boston, Philadelphia, and New York. He won only three pennants and didn't even win as many games as he lost. But to the end, he was the quintessence of managerial ability, a label later hung on Gene Mauch, who never won anywhere.

But it all began because hard-nosed kid Harris from the Pennsylvania coal mining country was a self-made second baseman who, though he hit .300 just once, was an early day Eddie Stanky, a guy who "came to play," as Leo Durocher would say. When Harris achieved the polish he never lost, he dined at the home of a United States senator whose daughter he wooed and won.

A spectator at Washington's ninth-inning victory that day was a fellow diner who gushed over the gutty play of the field leader Griffith had picked from the ranks. Said the man, "I do believe, Bucky, that when you came up with the bases loaded in the last inning, you deliberately allowed yourself to be hit with the pitch that brought in the winning run."

The senator rose to his future son-in-law's defense. "Why," sputtered the solon, "Stanley wouldn't do such an unsportsmanlike thing."

Bucky smiled. He'd paid the price—sore ribs—but, as the old saying goes, the flanneled Senators had put one more in the old bat sack, en route to the first of two straight pennants.

Harris was no hitting hero in either the regular season or the World Series, but, though he managed just nine career home runs through 1931, he hit two in Series play. In addition, young Bucky and old boss Griff put their heads together and connived to finesse John McGraw out of his hottest Series hero in 1924, left-handed-hitting Bill Terry.

Terry had alternated with right-handed-hitting George Kelly at first base. The Nats' two commanders wanted Terry in and out of the seventh-game lineup at Griffith Stadium as quickly as possible. So they started righthander Curly Ogden. Warming up, however, was lefthander George Mogridge. The idea was to use Ogden only against the New York leadoff man, Fred Lindstrom, but when he struck out the Giants' third baseman, Harris permitted him to face Frank Frisch, who walked.

When the switch then was made, McGraw didn't bite at first. He stayed with Terry for two times at bat, but, ultimately, Little Napoleon lifted Terry for a right-handed pinch hitter. So big Bill was out of there as Washington's first-ever World Series went to a dramatic climax.

Walter Johnson, Washington's premier pitcher, perhaps the best ever or certainly the most victorious with perpetually poorest-contending teams (416 games), had toiled for the Senators for all of his 21 major league seasons. At 37 he had bounced back with his best season in several, winning 23 games and losing only seven. Sir Walter, the Maryland fox hunter from the Kansas wheat fields, was everyone's sentimental favorite.

Later, himself a manager whose serenity soured through seven seasons when he no longer could play, Johnson faced goat's horns as the 1924 Series wound to an extra-inning close. He had lost two games as a starter, and when Frisch tripled, first to face him in seventh-game relief, it looked as if Johnson would lose a third time. But Walter escaped scoring. And in the 11th, when the Giants again had the winning run on third, this time with only one out, Johnson fanned the clutch-hitting Frisch, who seldom struck out, and also struck out Terry's replacement, Kelly.

Manager Harris had set up the overtime with a sharp eighth-inning grounder that bad-hopped over Lindstrom's head at third base. In the home 12th after catcher Muddy Ruel lifted a pop foul on which New York catcher Hank Gowdy caught his tossed-aside mask on his foot like a bear trap, Gowdy couldn't get free enough to snare the ball. Reprieved, Ruel doubled. With one out when Washington centerfielder Earl McNeely hit sharply toward third, reserve Giants' outfielder Billy Southworth recalled he had reached behind him in the dugout for his glove.

"I knew the game was over," Southworth would recall years later. "As one of our guys (Jack Bentley) said, 'The good Lord couldn't let Walter Johnson lose *again!*'"

McNeely's grounder hit a pebble or whatever and, like Harris's earlier, bad-hopped over Lindstrom's head. Ruel scored, and Washington won the championship, 4–3. The capital was so happy that even President Calvin Coolidge, a low-key person, seated with wife Grace, a dedicated fan, did a brief jig of joy.

A year later at Pittsburgh, playing the seventh game of a Series in which Johnson already had won twice after posting a 20–7 season and hitting an astonishing .433, the Senators backed down from a decisive three-to-one lead in games. But certainly in game No. 7, the Big Train, as they called Johnson, would throw his express past the Pirates.

Playing that day was questionable judgment as adjudicated by Commissioner Judge Landis. The Series already had been twice delayed by rain, including the day before. So they began the game in a cold drizzle, first dolloping Forbes Field in circus sawdust. Umpires blotted game balls repeatedly. Pitchers slipped at the mound when not caking off mud from their spiked shoes.

With Johnson leading early and Pittsburgh having a prominent right-handed-hitting lineup, Harris stuck with "Barney" too long.

Johnson and other Washington pitchers had been handicapped because shortstop Roger Peckinpaugh, the American League's Most Valuable Player in '25, had committed a record eight Series errors. With two on, two out in the eighth, Pittsburgh rightfielder Hazen (KiKi) Cuyler clipped a game-winning double down the rainsoaked right-field line.

After Washington's 9–7 loss, the American League president sent Harris a tart telegram: "YOU SACRIFICED A WORLD'S CHAMPIONSHIP WHICH THE AMERICAN LEAGUE SHOULD HAVE WON TO MAUDLIN SENTIMENT."

Actually, not counting on the questionable grammar in the former newspaperman's wire, we liked Harris's reply, delivered to the press. "No man is going to tell me," snapped Bucky, "that when I need a pitcher in a pinch, Walter Johnson isn't the man for me. I'll go down the line with him until they carry either of us off the field."

They did just that with Johnson after a spring training mishap in 1927, when a broken leg ended his pitching career. By then, Bucky Harris could remember many things about Sir Walter, including the time back in 1919 as a rookie when he'd kicked a ground ball behind Johnson, who had been delayed in reaching the ball park by the illness of his five-year-old son. Phenomenally, under personal pressure, Johnson pitched a no-hitter, but Harris's error cost him a perfect game. Bucky apologized. "Goodness, kid, forget it," was Johnson's gracious reply.

Harris was a standup guy, as he proved again the only other time he was in a World Series, 22 years after the sawdust clown climax in 1925. In an unforgettable moment of the fourth game between the Yankees and Dodgers at Brooklyn's Ebbets Field in 1947, Harris defied baseball percentage and tradition.

Behind Floyd (Bill) Bevens, pitching what perhaps would have been the most ragged no-hitter anywhere ever, the Yankees led into the home ninth, 2–1. Bevens walked Carl Furillo with one out. Two were down when Al Gionfriddo, running for Furillo, stole second. With the tying run in scoring position, Harris directed Bevens to put the potential winning run on base. The intentional walk to Pete Reiser, batting for relief pitcher Hugh Casey, was Bevens' *tenth* that day.

Here, Brooklyn manager Burt Shotton sent up veteran utility infielder Harry (Cookie) Lavagetto to bat for Eddie Stanky. Lavagetto came through with one of baseball's most memorable hits. His long fly ball to right field, a short distance at Ebbets Field, hit the base of the sloping fence and skidded back past rightfielder Tommy Henrich for a decisive double.

So, held to one hit, the Dodgers won the game, 3–2, though they then lost the Series in seven games. Harris, asked about going against "the book," the abstract do's-and-don'ts of baseball, was aware he had flouted standards. "But I'd do it again," said Bucky. "I have great respect and admiration for Reiser."

Indeed, Reiser, a wounded warrior regarded by Leo Durocher as a close second only to Willie Mays among the players he managed, was a batting champion at only 22 in his first full major league season (1941) and was a speedy, strong-throwing outfielder who stole home plate seven times in one season. By then, he had weakened his throwing arm and his injury-hexed career by jousting bravely with concrete outfield walls as if he were a Don Quixote in baseball flannels. But when he pinch-hit in the World Series and Eddie Miksis pinch-ran home the winning run, Reiser was limping with an ankle injury that was more serious than believed—a broken leg!

If Harris could manage so well and so long despite limited success—he won more terms in Washington than Franklin D. Roosevelt—another player-pilot who had early achievement couldn't keep winning or a job, either—Rogers Hornsby.

Hornsby, the dimpled darling of St. Louis, was a tough-talking Texan who won opposing pitchers' respect and the umpires', too, even though he didn't bother too much with the men who played for him. Hornsby, averaging .400 for a five-year period, was named manager of the Redbirds on Memorial Day, 1925, succeeding Branch Rickey. Rickey had combined the field and front office operation of the St. Louis Nationals.

Clubowner Sam Breadon couldn't convince Rickey that he was doing B.R. a favor by kicking him upstairs as general manager. Rickey, who once had fought with Hornsby, didn't like it. Huffily, he wanted to sell his minority stock, which Breadon arranged for Hornsby to buy in a transaction covered in another chapter.

Hornsby, who sneered at college "rah-rah guys" in general, didn't like the football-style chalk talks Rickey used in an effort to improve his players' understanding of baseball techniques and strategy. First thing The Rajah did was to order "that Ohio Wee-zee-lan bastard's" blackboard thrown out of the Cardinals' small Sportsman's Park clubhouse. Next, proving responsibility really didn't bother him, Hornsby hit .403 in 1925, including 39 homers among his 203 hits. He drove in 143 runs as the young Cardinals, several of them products of the Rickey-inspired farm system, finished fourth.

A year later, though strangely one in which an injury-handicapped Hornsby hit the lowest (.317) of any full season from 1918 until he became a part-time player in 1932, the Cardinals gained their first National League pennant. The teetotaling Hornsby, whose only abuse was favoring a slow horse often and a fast woman occasionally, urged the Cardinals to claim on waivers an overaged rummy whom new manager Joe McCarthy felt he couldn't handle at Chicago.

Grover Cleveland Alexander—"Old Pete"—had been one of the greatest pitchers ever, a master of a pinpoint-controlled fastball, a short slider they called a "nickel curve" in those days, and an occasional screwball. But the great pitcher was a victim of epilepsy and a deep thirst.

Hornsby didn't worry that Alex drank or that, unlike most hitters, himself a right-handed batter who strode directly to the plate and into the pitch, he had hit solidly against Old Low and Away. "The old guy gets enough of those other guys out," Hornsby argued. So 39-year-old Alexander helped pitch the Cardinals to a pennant and won two World Series games over the favored New York Yankees. After he tied the Series in the sixth game, Hornsby said to him, "Go easy on it, Pete; I might need you tomorrow."

When Jesse Haines filled the bases with two out in the seventh inning of the seventh game on a raw, rainy October Sunday at Yankee Stadium, he looked down at his knuckles, rubbed raw. In recent times the "knuckler" is misnamed, delivered now with the fingertips, but Haines actually squeezed the ball off bowed knuckles. Hornsby came in from second base. The knuckles were red and bloody. Haines was a gamer, but. . . .

Hornsby looked out at the left-field bullpen, where his staff was warming up. Rog wig-wagged. Naw, naw, not those guys. He wanted the old guy seated. Reserve catcher Ernie Vick recalled that Alexander was taking a catnap.

Was Old Pete drunk? How high is up? Chances are, he was just relaxed, which is the way Alexander was when he had a couple of belts under his belt. Traditionally, when traveling, he'd take a snort or two after brushing his teeth, and, if the hotel elevator took too long to pick him up, he might mosey back to the room. You know, one more for the road or the breakfast table.

Without ever warming up in the bullpen, Alexander began his slow Grand Circle tour to the mound, well aware that (1) he never needed many throws to get ready and (2) that New York's kid second baseman, Tony Lazzeri, must be pretty jumpy waiting. (Curiously, Lazzeri was also epileptic.) When Alexander reached the infield grass, carrying his red woolen sweater, the jacket of the times, Hornsby walked over to meet him, looked at the sleepy gray eyes, and handed the ball to the knock-kneed veteran.

Alex's cap perched on top of his head like peanut shell, his neck turkey-wattled from a life as fast as the manner in which he pitched. "Bases loaded, Pete," Rog reminded him.

"Well, there ain't no place to put him, is there?"

Lazzeri struck out on four pitches. As demonstrated by filmed highlights, Alexander swaggered toward the bench and flipped his glove into foul territory with the haughtiness of a pitching king, which he was. After all, Alexander and Christy Mathewson share the National League record for victories, 373.

There was one postscript to the 1926 Series scenario, so dramatic that Alexander's strikeout of Lazzeri is immortalized on Old Pete's bronzed plaque in the Hall of Fame at Cooperstown. With two down in the ninth, protecting that 3–2 lead, Alexander faced Babe Ruth, who had hit three home runs in one game of the Series.

Carefully, working away, Alex got the count to "3 and 2." Now he tried for the outside corner with his short, semi-sidearmed delivery. Plate umpire George Hildebrand called it Ball Four. Alexander, starting down off the hill, continued toward the plate, reaching for catcher Bob O'Farrell's return throw. "How close was it?" he asked.

Hildebrand spread his fingers a fraction of an inch apart. "If," said Old Pete softly, "it was that close, you could have given it to an old guy. . . ."

The Yankees' No. 4 hitter then was Bob Meusel, rangy, right-handed-hitting outfielder. (Lou Gehrig, No. 5, moved up to cleanup the next season.) Meusel, though only a .238 hitter in the Series, was a .315 batter in 1926. He'd had three of the Yankees' 12 hits off Alexander in 20 innings, including a triple and single the day before. But the Babe had stolen second in that 10–2 rout. So . . .

Surprisingly, Ruth tried again. Some baseball men, including Ed Barrow, knew Babe best and his instinct for doing the right thing. They thought it was the only mental mistake he ever made in uniform. The Babe figured scoring position would increase scoring chances. True, but Alexander used a short, quick delivery. O'Farrell had a great arm, and both members of the battery remembered Ruth had run the day before.

So when the Babe broke for second on the first pitch, low and away with a right-handed batter at the plate, O'Farrell had a good chance for a quick, accurate throw. His throw beat the Babe by five yards.

Hornsby, then 30, would live another 37 years and manage four other major league clubs for an assorted 11 seasons without success, but he always came back to one thrill. "My greatest thrill," he would say, "was in taking O'Farrell's throw, putting down the ball, and letting the Big Monkey tag himself out, so we were World Champions."

Hornsby, hurrying from the ball park to Penn Station, caught a train alone for the long ride back to Hornsby Bend, Texas, where they had held up his mother's funeral.

Traded shockingly to New York as batting star and manager of the World Champions, Hornsby led a nomadic baseball life from 1927 until he ran baseball schools at Chicago playgrounds for the late, lamented *Daily News* after he had made his final managerial move in 1953. From the time he was ousted by the St. Louis Browns in 1937 until the second Bill Veeck brought him back there in 1952, mindful that Hornsby's name had particular impact and also that Bill's "Daddy," William Veeck, Sr., had sealed a pennant for the Cubs in 1929 by acquiring him from Boston, Hornsby had a hard time holding even minor league managerial jobs.

It wasn't because, as at the finish, he'd wave a pitcher coldly out of the box with a gesture from the dugout, like an old vaudeville stage manager using a hook to jerk a bum off the boards. It was many things, notably that Rog no longer could play. After he'd suffered a broken ankle sliding at Chicago in 1930 and developed heel spurs, the same devilish ailment that troubled Joe DiMaggio, Hornsby could help his own cause too infrequently.

Like the time the Cardinals, whom he had rejoined in 1933 as a pinch hitter short on cash, helped him move across the hall as manager of the rival Browns in July. For the Brownies he got into only 11 games, but there was an early time at bat in the American League when he was coaching at third base against the mighty Yankees. The lowly Brownies had a chance to win when he walked off the coaching lines to pick up a bat as a pinch hitter. The truculent Yankees chortled, "So here's the great National League hitter, *MR.* Hornsby!"

Rog hit the first pitch onto the roof in right-center for a game-winning homer, and he trundled around the bases, reaching home plate just as the sober, head-down Yankees trudged across the field to the home (third base) dugout, closer to the clubhouse. Although essentially a live-and-let-live guy with the opposition, Hornsby couldn't resist. "Yeah, you bastards," he said, "that *was* the famous National League hitter, *MR.* Hornsby."

The show wasn't the same for The Rajah when they took away his bat or didn't quite appreciate his talent, for instance, when he managed briefly in Mexico for the Pasquel brothers, whose impact on baseball's post-war financial improvements will be reserved for a chapter on economics. By World War II, then in his mid-'40s and fat because he loved thick malted milks even more than thick steaks, Rog had been persuaded by mucho dinero to take over as manager of the Vera

Cruz Blues. Jorge Pasquel, feeling his fortune, paid enough pesos to lure Hornsby south of the border.

After Hornsby's team had won the Friday opener of a three-game series, Vera Cruz trailed in the ninth inning of Saturday's game. From a box seat, Pasquel urged Hornsby to pinch-hit, and spectators who knew Spanish a helluva lot better than Rog joined in the chant.

Hornsby shrugged. Okay, so if this is what they want. He walked up and hit the first pitch over the fence for a home run that won the game. Smiling after scoring, he turned at the plate toward Pasquel's box. He found the Mexican clubowner troubled. "But Rog," the accented rich man lamented, "now you've ruined tomorrow's (rubber) game!"

Hornsby turned away in a quick exit. See you at Arlington Park, George, or any other race track across the border!

Over the years after Hornsby won in 1926 at St. Louis, many a player-manager failed to grab the brass ring. To wit, Eddie Collins, Rabbit Maranville, and Ray Schalk in the 1920s; Mel Ott, Bill Dickey, Billy Herman in the '40s; Tommy Holmes, Marty Marion, Fred Hutchinson, Harry Walker, and Solly Hemus in the '50s.

From then until Pete Rose returned to Cincinnati hell-bent for Ty Cobb's 4191 career hit total, banging out eight base hits in his first three games, the player-manager became a diamond dodo.

Hank Bauer had played briefly at Kansas City in 1961; Joe Torre had two times up with the New York Mets in 1977; and Don Kessinger had played a short time at shortstop for the Chicago White Sox in 1979. The only one who had achieved the old-time managerial touch—and he didn't win in his first two chances—was the first black big league field boss, Frank Robinson.

F. Robby, a distinct difference as the Most Valuable Player in each league (Cincinnati 1961, Baltimore, 1966), took over as manager at Cleveland in 1975. Opening day, first time up, Robinson made the huge-stadium lakefront ring with a home run. That was the way to do it, the way they'd done it in . . . in . . . oh, hell, the tough times of the Depression '30s.

Throughout that decade there were 15 player-managers, most of whom didn't last long or make it, like Lew Fonseca or Marty McManus or Jim Bottomley or Pie Traynor or even Jimmy Dykes or Leo Durocher, whose most successful seasons were after they finished playing, but the entire theme of this chapter is dedicated to the men whose playing ability inspired their teams to unexpected heights.

First off, an ailing, prematurely aged John McGraw had seen enough of seven barren seasons between pennants. The man who had won 10 pennants, four of them in a row, 1921–24, finally had enough one miserable Sunday in St. Louis in June 1932.

That lanky, popoff pitching kid of the Cardinals, Dizzy Dean, popped a bunt over the third baseman's head and charged into second base with a double. And when there was a wide throw from the outfield, the long-legged skinny kid lit out for third. Even one of the old man's personal joys, rightfielder Mel Ott, retrieving the ball, overthrew third base. So Dizzy never stopped—a "home run" on a bunt!

Next working day in New York, McGraw called first baseman Bill Terry into his office at the Polo Grounds and told him to shut the door. Oh, oh, thought Terry, this is it. The old man is trading me. After all, they hadn't spoken to each other for two years.

McGraw had a bad habit of using someone as a whipping boy, usually his captain. He'd driven Frank Frisch, his pet, off the ball club in anger. He'd driven Travis Jackson to drink. Terry, big and menacing, backtalked. One day when McGraw picked on Terry for an error, the first baseman told him bluntly that McGraw had been picking on other people for 30 years for his own mistakes. Terry had urged the timid Jackson to tell McGraw to relieve a tiring pitcher.

A disbelieving McGraw followed Terry toward the shower. Turning, Bill glowered. "Oh, nuts!" he said, cutting off the conversation. Despite the silence, the last National League .400 hitter (.401 in 1930) thought he had performed extremely well in the clubhouse cold war. With the ball dejuiced, he hit .349 and .350. He was too much a professional to let personal feelings affect his play.

Like the time earlier when Bill and Emil (Irish) Meusel were just a couple of minutes late, sprinting from a Chicago legitimate theatre, yet not quite making an 11:30 curfew. McGraw, standing in the lobby as they hurried in, sent word that each had been fined $50. Terry, a businessman ballplayer who had grown up in hunger in Atlanta, boiled over losing money unfairly.

Next day, compounding the difference, McGraw benched Terry against the Cubs, even though Bill hit well against Old Pete Alexander. Terry took off his baseball spikes, carried them down to the far corner of the dugout, crossed his ankles and feigned sleep. In the ninth a teammate nudged him. The Giants were a run down with a man on, and the old man wanted him to pinch-hit.

Slowly, Terry picked up the shoes and stalked down to the end of the dugout. Perching himself on the steps, glaring down with big brown eyes at McGraw seated on the bench beneath him, Bill slowly tied his shoes. Finally, he went up to the plate and hit the first pitch for a game-winning homer.

Afterward, back at the hotel, Terry found himself in an elevator with McGraw. A grateful McGraw told him he had cold beer, a Prohibition delicacy, in his suite. Pick up a case, Bill!

Terry would grin delighted as he retold the story. "So I called up Meusel, Jackson, and a few other guys," he said, "and ordered up enough ice to fill the bathtub. And I charged the ice to McGraw's suite."

But when McGraw called him years later into that private clubhouse conversation, yeah, Terry expected to be traded. McGraw, beating around the bush, told him he had come to an important decision. He wanted Terry to replace him as manager, but that he felt as if Bill should think it over.

Terry, leaning on the backside of a chair he had turned so that he could face McGraw cheek to jowl, broke in. "Hell, Mr. McGraw," he said, "I don't have to think about it. I'll take the job right now."

So McGraw, ending his legendary term as manager of the Giants, pinned a message on the clubhouse bulletin board and walked out. He would be dead within two years and would return to the clubhouse just once. "To congratulate me on winning the '33 pennant," Terry recalled softly.

As player-manager, a slick-fielding, hard-hitting first baseman, Terry emphasized defense. He wanted a good low ball catcher to handle his sinkerball staff. So he obtained Gus Mancuso from the Cardinals to hunker down behind the plate, and Carl Hubbell emerged from good to great as a pitcher.

The Giants won the World Championship in 1933, climbing from a tie for sixth and seventh. Terry hit .322 that year, not great by his standards, but he was physically sounder and better the next two years, hitting .354 and .341, as the Giants blew the 1934 pennant to St. Louis and also slipped earlier down the stretch in '35, passed first by St. Louis and then by Chicago.

By 1936, nearly 38, his knees troubling him, Terry could play only infrequently. This time the Giants did not break fast from the barrier. By the time New York was 10½ games out, Terry took his doctor's advice and announced he had retired. But he changed his mind and put himself in the starting lineup.

When he limped up to home plate with the starting lineup, veteran plate umpire Ernie Quigley urged him to reconsider. Even the National League president, Ford Frick, visiting Pittsburgh that day, hurried out of the press box in an effort to convince Terry to stay on the bench. "One more bad twist and you might be crippled for life," Frick argued.

But Terry played. He tripled home the winning run. The inspired Giants, picked up by the pain-wracked old skipper, won 15 successive games. As a result, with Terry hitting a gutty .310, the Giants won the pennant that had escaped them. Terry retired as a player. Thereafter, though he managed five more years, the Giants won just one more pennant. By 1985, 87 years old, the Hall of Fame first baseman finally needed a cane to help him at Cooperstown.

The World Series of the mid-1930s were the private preserves of the player-pilots. In Terry's first year, for instance, Washington was managed by Joe Cronin, 26-year-old shortstop. Handsome, jut-jawed Cronin was wooing Clark Griffith's niece and ward, Mildred Robertson, but that had little to do with Griff's shrewd judgment. In the competitive Irishman who later would manage Boston, general-manage the Red Sox, and then become American League president, the Old Fox must have seen obvious leadership.

Cronin, tapped for the job after six full seasons in the majors, knew what he needed: More outfielding and, especially, left-handed pitching to stop the perennial contenders, the defending-champion Yankees. Without decimating his ball club, Griff did it, acquiring outfielders Goose Goslin and Fred Schulte from the Browns, lefthanders Walter Stewart from the same club and Earl Whitehill from Detroit, and catcher Luke Sewell from Cleveland.

Sewell figured in a pivotal play, as Cronin recalled it. The Yankees were at Griffith Stadium and, after losing one game of a doubleheader, were closing in with Lou Gehrig on second base, Dixie Walker on first as Tony Lazzeri lined a shot to right-center.

Gehrig, fearing a catch, held up temporarily, but Walker had a better view. He got off quickly, younger, faster, in hot pursuit. By the time Gehrig reached third and Walker closed in on him, coach Art Fletcher couldn't separate the runners. Strong-armed Cronin, hurrying out for the relay, took the throw, wheeled, and his pulse pounded as he saw the prospect. Cronin unfurled a powerful peg to Sewell at the plate.

Big Gehrig, barging in, tried to dislodge the catcher from the ball. All he did was topple Sewell onto Walker, sliding in from the other side of the plate. A double play on a double!

"That day," remembered Cronin, "I realized anything could happen. That '33 could be the year Washington would win a pennant." Indeed, its *last* pennant.

Cronin's move to Boston (1935), which also can be categorized in the chapter on economics, brought life back to his bat. As field foreman for Tom Yawkey, a sportsman and close friend who followed Cronin into the Hall of Fame as the only enshrined clubowner, Joe hit over .300 seven times in 11 seasons, the last four of which were as a part-time player. He also added three of his eight seasons as a 100 RBI shortstop.

Afield, Joe had one shaky spell at Fenway Park. Briefly, he lost confidence and dropped to a knee to field ground balls, prompting the unsympathetic to label it as "the $250,000 squat," a reference to the incredible Depression amount paid for his contract. But Cronin was a professional, touched to the quick and to reality when his second baseman, Oscar Melillo, suggested gently, "If you're going to miss 'em, Skip, miss 'em like a big leaguer."

At 37, beginning to flesh out into the form that later made him look like an alderman from his native San Francisco, Cronin limited himself largely to probably some of the most magnificent pinch hitting any manager ever perpetrated. He was 18 for 42 in 1943, pinch-batting .410. Included were four doubles and five pinch home runs.

Philadelphia's Connie Mack saw enough of that good looking Irishman coming off the bench, that oversized chin thrown defiantly into the air, neck arteries strained, swinging three bats like dumbbells as he hit in the pinch. "Even better in a pinch," said Mr. Mack, "than the best I ever saw—Al Simmons or Ty Cobb or anyone else."

Frank Frisch was a great clutch hitter, too, but by the time his Gas House Gang overhauled the slumping Giants in 1934, setting up a World Series with Mickey Cochrane's Detroit Tigers, Frisch was almost as tired as the fighting, raven-haired, catcher-manager of the American League champions.

Over the years as the Fordham Flash, captain of the football, basketball, and baseball teams, a top-flight skier and bobsledder, Frisch was a remarkable all-around athlete. However, he had become heavier with the years, especially when trying to play and manage, too, doubling as a boxing promoter, breaking up fights among his Gas Housers, and serving as a confused, not amused, critic of Pepper Martin's Mudcats. Frisch, who cut his teeth on a silver spoon and a brass cuspidor, loved Wagner—Richard as well as Honus—but the musical depreciation of his merry men bothered him.

So did his advanced athletic age, 37, and the fact that as a rough-sliding infielder who had stolen many a base and been hacked in return, he had aching feet. Over the years the Old Flash, as he had begun to call himself, was a showcase star, best before big crowds. He had played in more World Series than any other National Leaguer (eight) and then owned the most Series hits, too (58). Even in the first All-Star game the year before, he had hit a home run left-handed off Detroit's Alvin Crowder at Chicago. Also in the summer of '34, he'd called a shot with a first-pitch homer right-handed off the Yankees' Lefty Gomez at the Polo Grounds.

But the morning of the final game in the 1934 Series at Detroit, where wife Ada ordered room service tomato juice, bacon and eggs, toast, and coffee for him, he had been able only to drink the juice and sip coffee. In six games Frisch had only five singles, and also was concerned he might be asking that lanky drink o' water, Dizzy Dean, to go back to the well too soon. Down to the pennant wire, Dizzy and brother Paul had appeared in seven of the Cardinals' last nine games. In the Series, Paul, the 21-year-old rookie, had two victories and Dizzy, just 23, had won one and had been skulled with a throw as a pinch runner and was knocked out. Next day he went nine innings and lost only 3–1.

Sure, Frisch had personal pride, lots of it, but, hell, that money-player proficiency was a result of nerves bound up in the beagle-eyed, crooked-nosed cat. As only the Cardinals' equipment manager, Butch Yatkeman knew, the Fordham Flash was so tense before a Series game that—ah, yeah!—he would wet his pants, and The Butcher would have to get him a new jockstrap.

By the time Frisch batted in the third inning of the scoreless seventh game, Dean had jolted the Tigers a couple of times. Walking through the runway, Redbird jacket slung over his shoulder, Dizzy paused behind Eldon Auker, warming up with his underhanded delivery. "Hey, podnuh, you don't expect to get anybody out with that shit, do you?" laughed Dean, promptly ordered away by a profane Cochrane.

Next, leading off the third, Dizzy singled to left and, slinging his bat in joy and momentum, rounded first galloping like Ichabod Crane, and slid magnificently into second, stretching the hit into a double. As a result, when Pepper Martin grounded to first baseman Hank Greenberg's right, the sure-thing force-out was removed. Pepper beat Greenberg's throw to first, then stole second.

Frisch, crouching on deck, watched and winced as Detroit pitched deliberately to his rightfielder, Jack Rothrock, walking Rothrock. Obviously, with the old man next up, Cochrane hoped for an inning-ending double play. Oh, if only Frisch could pull the ball, get it into the air, and knock in a run or, at least, give "Joey"—Joe Medwick—a chance to swing that big brown bat.

Auker's underhanded shoots were puzzling, but Frisch didn't strike out much. Still, as the count reached "3 and 2" and stayed there, Frank fouled off pitch after pitch—seven. He wasn't going to let that tall American League umpire, Harry Geisel, call him out.

The next pitch was up and in. Frisch swung and pulled a line drive, just a few feet fair, and as the ball skipped into the right-field corner, the Flash went into his old victory gallop. Looked like a prize trotter. But he was sightseeing, too. Dean scored. Uh-huh, and Pepper, and, yeah, now Rothrock.

As Frisch hit second and Cochrane called time to change pitchers with the heart and horse both out of the barn, a result of a three-run double, springboard to a seven-run inning and 11–0 cakewalk, the Old Flash squatted at second base. The legs were trembling.

"I'd rather have that damned double than eight hits, all homers," he chortled to himself, then came back to earth. "But, hey, what am I doing here at second? I ought to be on third. If one of my men had run the bases like this, sightseeing, I'd have fined him 50 bucks. . . ."

In 1935, spiked accidentally by Gus Suhr of Pittsburgh, Frisch missed much of the season, his last meaningful one as a player. But, refreshed, he came back strongly. In September, when Charlie Grimm's Chicago Cubs put together a remarkable 21-game winning streak, the oldest regular, Frisch, 38, and the youngest, Terry Moore, the 23-year-old rookie centerfielder, were the hottest Redbirds. Then Moore suffered a broken leg, cutting into the heroic efforts of the old-and-new.

Meanwhile, as explained, Grimm's Cubs were phenomenal. Jolly Cholly was out almost all of that season, his next-to-last, but he had been impressed by a hometown kid at first base. Phil Cavarretta, only 18, joined the Cubs late in the 1934 season. It was "Philabuck," as Grimm called him, who delivered the key blow by which Lon Warneke and the Cubs beat Paul Dean and the Cardinals in the final week of the season, 1–0.

Cavarretta's homer to the right-field roof in St. Louis was re-created in all of a future actor's talent by a young Davenport–Des Moines radio announcer called Dutch—Reagan. Yes, Mr. President.

Curiously, the Cubs, though they never lost again from the second game of the Labor Day doubleheader until they clinched the pennant the third-from-last day of the season, were caught with their front office pants down. They didn't print World Series tickets in time. So the Series couldn't begin at Wrigley Field. It began at Detroit and, as a result, ended there.

Poetically, the winning run in the sixth game was scored by Cochrane, the jug-eared catcher and former football hero of Boston University whose aggressive play, speed, and batting ability at Philadelphia and then Detroit made him rank with Bill Dickey and Gabby Hartnett as the greatest catchers of his day or maybe any day.

Cochrane, a .320 hitter, came over to Detroit not because Connie Mack wanted to get rid of him, but because Mr. Mack needed the money. Originally, Frank Navin, Detroit clubowner, had opted for Babe Ruth, but an astute veteran sports editor, H. G. Salsinger of the

News, noted that the Tigers' biggest playing need was a catcher. So the money, ponied up by Walter O. Briggs, was well spent for the 31-year-old Philadelphia catcher. Black Mike was named ringmaster of the Tigers.

In 1934, the year Detroit won its first pennant in 25 years, a frazzled Cochrane hit his career average, but he was so tired in the World Series that he spent his nights in a hotel bed. The opponents in a rough-and-ready Series, the Cardinals, really let the red-faced Cochrane have it in his jug ears when a newspaper photograph labeled him "Our Stricken Leader."

But Cochrane laughed last in 1935 when his famed "G-men"—Charley Gehringer, Hank Greenberg, and Goose Goslin—came through for him in beating the Cubs. Cochrane singled to begin the ninth inning of the sixth game, moved up on Gehringer's sharp out, and scored when Goslin singled.

Mickey reached home plate and, like a kid, jumped on it for joy. Afterward in the excitement of the clubhouse, he was needled good-naturedly by the commissioner, Judge Landis. The Judge, who thought he had heard enough profanity between the Cardinals and Tigers in 1934, was appalled early by the rough language in '35. He'd issued through the umpires a crisp cease-and-desist order. Annoyed, Cochrane sang out to the Cubs' bench, sarcastically, sweetly: "Hurry up, sweetheart. Tea will be served at 4 o'clock."

The Judge had heard that crack, and, congratulating Cochrane, Landis teased Black Mike by calling him "sweetheart."

If ever a ball club reflected its reliance and personality on the leadership of a player-manager and, in turn, the same man showed himself completely lost when confined to the bench rather than able to assert command on the field, it was Detroit and Cochrane—sadly.

Injuries limited Mickey to 44 games in 1936, but the Tigers did well and finished second to the Yankees, who began a four-season surge under Joe McCarthy. Then, early in the '37 season when Cochrane was back in harness, the Yankees' Irving (Bump) Hadley hit him in the head with a pitch, apparently accidentally. As Cochrane rolled into the dirt, clutching his head before lapsing into unconsciousness, catching rival Dickey heard him groan, "Oh, my God."

Oh, my Cochrane and the Tigers. Mickey's skull was fractured in three places. When he returned, new clubowner Briggs refused to let him risk further injury. As a bench manager, the Tiger was a caged, lower-cased tiger, unable to tolerate confinement. He was released in August 1938, and had a troubled life. He was only 59 when he died, a leader who lost because he couldn't follow.

Catchers do make good managers, especially when they can lend more than their intelligence to a team. Take Charles Leo (Gabby) Hartnett. Old Tomato Face, who looked as if he should have been mayor of Chicago, was a grinning, cigar-chewing Irishman who had a great throwing arm and home run power.

He joined the Cubs in 1922, and for most of his career he hit right at .300, threw out runners and hit for muscle that manifested itself best in the "greatest managerial move" other than Lou Boudreau's playoff production in 1948.

Gabby was 37 and had hit his highest if not his hardest in 1937, .354. Then he was asked to step in as manager in mid-season of '38 when P. K. Wrigley decided to release Charlie Grimm. Like Clark Griffith with Bucky Harris, Wrigley had this mutual love affair with Grimm, an ability to hire-fire-and-rehire with no hard feelings. So with the Cubs third that year when the chicle-and-chew magnate thought it was their timetable to be on top again, he switched in mid-stream to Hartnett.

Bless his doublemint, Mr. Wrigley was right. The Cubs had won in 1929, '32, '35, and, so help Gabby's midriff goiter, they did it again when Pie Traynor's Pittsburgh Pirates slumped in the stretch and the Cubs came on.

Down to the final week, Chicago had closed the gap so that Pittsburgh led by only a game and a half as the Bucs came to town. At Forbes Field maybe they paused, before nailing down the last planks for their new World Series press box. Hartnett, who hadn't played as much or hit as well (.274), was behind the plate now, and he had a hunch.

For the Pirates' opener at Wrigley Field, he would start Dizzy Dean, who had been acquired as acknowledged damaged goods from St. Louis in April for $185,000 and three players. Troubled by a bursa injury that took away his three-quarter motion and his fastball, Ol' Diz was only 27, but almost through. He was sidearmed now and had only good control and just a 6–1 record. He hadn't pitched for two weeks and hadn't started for a month, but. . . .

"I banked on his heart," Gabby related. "I knew they wouldn't scare him."

Dean upset the Pirates, 2–1, helped by bellwether Bill Lee in the ninth. So the Cubs were only a half game behind. Next day the score was tied in the ninth. The umpires huddled. They would have to call it because light was fading.

Two were out in the last inning before darkness. Pitching for the Pirates was relief ace Mace Brown, a curveball specialist. Hartnett, who liked to signal for the old No. 2 often as a curveball catcher, went up there looking for the breaking ball. He swung, missed. Again, he swung and fouled one off.

Maybe Brown should have deliberately wasted a pitch, but he tried to go down and away with his curveball, but he caught too much of the plate. Hartnett swung, and the 38-year-old gaffer knew it was gone.

"I got the kind of feeling you get when the blood rushes to your head and you get dizzy," said Hartnett, recalling his start around the bases. The ball cleared the ivy-covered brick wall in left field and landed in the bleachers.

The "homer in the gloamin'," they called the famed shot which gave the Cubs a 6–5 victory and first place. Before Hartnett reached second, an ecstatic crowd awaited him at third base and escorted him down the foul line, led by Pat Pieper, the longtime field announcer.

Hartnett's storied homer caved in the Pirates. After that game, Pittsburgh's manager, Pie Traynor, who had retired that year as their Hall of Fame third baseman, walked the several miles from the North Side park to a Loop hotel in downtown Chicago, accompanied by coach Jewel Ens and a Pittsburgh sportswriter. "If," said the seething Traynor, as they reached the hotel, "if either of you had said a damned word, I'd have punched you in the nose."

The Cubs bloodied the Pirates' nose the next day behind Lee, their big game winner, 10–1. Pittsburgh lost again the following day, and Chicago clinched the pennant at St. Louis.

Gabby Hartnett, who had come up the hard way, suffering frostbite when working from sun up to sunset at a wire-and-mill plant in Worcester, Massachusetts, never won another pennant in a couple more seasons as manager, but old Tomato Face had the memory of that one in the twilight to keep him a happy Hall of Famer.

Jimmy Dykes didn't make the Hall of Fame — or hadn't, anyway — but, we feel he falls in the category of "contributors," player-managers like Bucky Harris, Al Lopez, Leo Durocher and Charlie Grimm, good ballplayers whose combined efforts on the field and in the dugout made them viable candidates. By 1988, Harris and Lopez had made Cooperstown, but not Grimm or Dykes or Durocher.

Dykes would merit a medal if only because he was the man picked by Connie Mack to succeed him as manager at Philadelphia in 1950, after a half-century in which Mr. Mack had managed the A's. Dykes, who played infield for 22 years, was a solid ballplayer, a .280 hitter, best known for his wit, his bass-voiced, bench-jockeying skill, and the ability to get the most out of the least of the talent he managed.

Dykes managed 23 years, nearly 13 with the Chicago White Sox, to whom he was traded in 1933 when the A's hit the financial shorts. The cigar-puffing pixy was always in demand because even though he never finished as high as second, he finished ahead of his own ball clubs.

As a player of dwindling talent, but still able to hit .300 on part-time duty, Dykes played until he was past 42. Meanwhile, with the devilish nature he enjoyed, James J. Dykes persisted in ruining things for the rival Cubs. The Sox and the Cubs played a best-of-seven fall series in those days, and, though finishing no better than third three times with tired old pitching, the Chisox won all six series and 28 games to just 11. This, mind you, in an era in which the Chicago Nationals were constant pennant contenders and twice NL winners.

Finally, however, seeking to impress World War I buddies as they convened in Chicago for the 1939 American Legion convention, Dykes overdid it. By 1939, he had stayed on the bench, using his smarts and that tart tongue to win an occasional game and to needle the foe or the umpires. Now, nearing 43, it would be nice to show off, nice to let the old Army doughfoot know that one of 'em was still spry enough to play big league baseball. So he put himself in the lineup at third base. Yes, sir, the old boys had come out to see ol' Jim.

Oops, first he reached down for a grounder and, as Shirley Povich of the *Washington Post* would write, he felt nothing. A ball had gone through untouched. Next, he kicked a ground ball. Finally, a sharp grounder glanced off his legs, felling him. As if by pre-arranged signal, indicating that joker James had created his own funny men, members of the White Sox rushed out with a stretcher, obviously borrowed from Comiskey Park's first aid room, and carried off the old gladiator.

James J. (For Joy) Dykes, as *Chicago Daily News* sports editor John P. Carmichael had rechristened him, was too embarrassed to sit up or maybe smart enough to go along with a gag. The grand clamor of the player-manager of the Depression '30s had ended—sadly.

12
Bellcows
of the
Bullpen

Once upon a time you wouldn't spell relief R-O-L-A-I-D-S—you're entirely welcome for the free commercial, Mr. Chairman—but then the antacid company wouldn't have wanted to be connected, even remotely, with baseball's equivalent of the low man on the totem pole.

Baseball has come a long way with the so-called short men, figuratively, since Henry (Father) Chadwick, the press box pioneer, questioned in print the courage of pitchers because some couldn't finish what they started. To the ex-British cricket player . . . well, it just wasn't cricket—a bit of white feather, don'tchaknow—to beg off or be bombed off or out before the 27th out.

Now, the men who take over, particularly the short-shrift guys who finish up, are often more valuable to any ball club than the top starter or starters. If it's true in life that men mumble and money talks, it's equally certain in baseball that the relief pitcher puts it in the bank— the ball game and the winner's share. See Bruce Sutter, reportedly signed by Atlanta for $43,000,000 over a 30-year period and collected as damaged goods!

And, as mentioned, Rolaids even awards cash prizes and extra publicity for the top relief pitcher in each major league annually, a commercial that obviously hasn't hurt the pharmaceutical supply company and, obviously, has eased the heartburn of a manager blessed with, say, a Rollie Fingers, a Bruce Sutter, a Goose Gossage, a Dan Quisenberry, or. . . .

The list of prominent relievers gets longer because, now, even in the minor leagues they're schooling pitchers to train resilient arms to come back quickly so that a career can be made as a game-saving specialist.

In an interview Carl Hubbell, the lean, elbow-twisted ace of a screwball that struck out five straight superstars in the 1934 All-Star game as one of his highlights, once expounded on the difference between the status of the starter, then and now.

Said Hubbell, who directed the Giants' farm system at New York and San Francisco after winning 253 games, including 24 straight one two-season stretch: "I can remember when the reliever was either the oldest or worst pitcher on the staff and certainly the lowest paid. He was the fellow who wasn't good enough to start games. Now, the relief man is frequently the best and highest paid pitcher. If a club hasn't got a good relief pitcher today, it better hurry out and try to find one, or it won't win."

That interview wasn't taken just after Hubbell walked out to the mound at Candlestick Park at the 1984 All-Star as a half-century symbol of his famed strikeout sequence over Babe Ruth, Lou Gehrig, Jimmy Foxx, Al Simmons, and Joe Cronin. Nor was it after any of current relief aces except Fingers was born—and Rollie barely was past counting on his fingers as a kid learning his ABCs—when Hubbell's commentary helped sell a magazine story.

It was back in 1953, still the prime of the national weekly, the *Saturday Evening Post,* and it was a piece prepared by one of this book's authors. The title is as likely any season now as it was then: "Will Relief Pitchers Win the Flags Again?"

That's how far back the "firemen" or "knights of the bullpen," as the press box poets began to call them, began to receive the published recognition that had been dashed by Chadwick and others when obviously the game was played differently. Chadwick breathed his stiff upper-lipped last in 1908 at age 84.

The newspaper novice or diapered baseball buff might have felt previously as if relief pitching didn't earn a capital "R" for Rolaid until muscular Mike Marshall. You know, the well-traveled, outspoken Michigan State doctor of matter over mind who did contribute incredibly toward bringing his former occupation into prominence by appearing in a record 106 games in 1974 for Los Angeles.

Fact is, though, only three years after critic Chadwick's last published displeasure about those sniveling cowards who couldn't finish round "9," the New York Giants' John McGraw gave relief pitching its first small step toward respectability. Between 1908–13, he employed Otis Crandall often in relief, frequently because Crandall could pinch-hit and take over the baton, saving a roster move.

Crandall, appearing in up to 41 games, most of them in relief, was so good in World Series play that a hungry young New York writer from the Rockies with a bright future called him "the doctor of sick ball games." The nickname for Crandall stuck—"Doc"—but the writer is better remembered for colorful short stories that became movies: Damon Runyon!

Ever since Crandall, the game-saver has taken stepping stones of specialization, but they were as small and as mincing as Babe Ruth's footsteps when the Babe trotted out a home run. Too often over the years as the number of complete games began to shrink with a ball juiced up first with a cork center in 1910, then whitened, sanitized, and rubberized in the '20s, relievers began to deserve more credit than they received.

Oh, occasionally one would catch the fancy, such as at Pittsburgh in 1921 and '22 when the Pirates had an honest-to-Indian red man named Moses (Chief) Yellowhorse. Forbes Field fans loved to chant, "We want Yellowhorse!"

The professorial author also can remember an uncle chuckling in recollection of an even more ridiculous situation in St. Louis, where the Browns often left a brown taste in the mouth. When the game was gone, which it was so often, a lonely figure would warm up in the left-field bullpen at Sportsman's Park, and the folks knew it was time to head for the streetcars. They would imitate the voice of the field announcer intoning into his microphone: "(Bill) Burwell now pitching . . . Bur-well now pitching."

At Washington, finally, a reliever got a large measure of respect, in part because he was himself a giant. Fred (Firpo) Marberry, nicknamed for the big Argentine heavyweight (Luis Firpo) who briefly draped Jack Dempsey's keister into ringside reporters' typewriters, starred for Washington from 1923 through '32. Yeah, even when the Senators were first in the American League, too. Imagine, a pitcher getting into 64 ball games even if he started some!

Bucky Harris, a hard-nosed second baseman and a wunderkind manager at Washington respected over the years for his smarts, made capital use also of another reliever named Allan Russell. A decade later when Washington won its last pennant (1933) under another aggressive field foreman, Joe Cronin, an unrelated Russell—Jack—starred for the Senators. The Philadelphia Phillies' spring stadium at Clearwater, Florida, is named for the 15-year pitcher—Jack Russell.

By then, relief got its maximum (limited) mileage out of the efforts of a big country righthander with the New York Yankees' 1927 Murderers' Row. Wilcy Moore, a 30-year-old rookie, was both good and lucky that year, really the only successful one of six he played in the majors. He was 19–7 even though he started only 12 times in 50 games. He had a 2.28 earned-run average and even started and won a World Series game against Pittsburgh.

Cy Moore, a flash in the firmament, was almost as proud then as when he won a bet from Babe Ruth. The Babe, en route to his 60 homers, thought the big Oklahoma farmer was about as horrible a hitter as he ever saw. Ruth bet Moore $500 he wouldn't get five hits all year. Cy got five — exactly — and bought two mules for his farm. Named one "Babe" and the other "Ruth."

Before World War II, relief pitching, philosophically, got its biggest boost from an imaginative manager and a toe-plated humorist. The Cardinals' 1939 manager, Ray Blades, a thinking-man's disciple of old boss Branch Rickey, upgraded Rogers Hornsby's blunt theory of win-today's-game-because-it-might-rain-tomorrow. Razor-sharp Blades leaned heavily on two pitchers obtained from the Chicago Cubs for Dizzy Dean, along with a king's Depression ransom of $185,000 and an outfielder, Tuck Stainback, to carry the loot. They were lefthander Clyde (Hard Rock) Shoun and a willowy, wan righthander, Curt Davis.

Coonskin Davis, starting *and* relieving *and* hitting .387, sidearmed his way to a 22–16 record and his club to a close-call second to Cincinnati. Cincy's Gabe Paul, then a young traveling secretary on the way to a long, well-traveled career as a shrewd general manager, made an observation. He still stands by it: "If you want to earmark a bullpen dependence, you've got to start with Ray Blades in 1939."

Although trigger-quick St. Louis owner Sam Breadon would fire Blades a year later, certain the ex-outfielder had fouled up his pitching, Blades continued to win respect. When Marty Marion became a manager 11 years later, he wanted Rickey's product (Blades) for his skill at inventing and giving baseball signs. Thirty years afterward, shortly before Blades' death, National League manager Dave Bristol wanted to be introduced to him at a baseball reunion in St. Louis.

"I've heard so much from Gene Mauch about him as a manager and strategist," said Bristol. Mauch often is regarded as just about the finest manager *never* to win a pennant.

So Blades merely was ahead of his time when his pitching breakthrough failed temporarily in a second experiment (1940), but just about the time the specialist idea was fanned with the momentum of Lefty Gomez's good humor.

As El Goofy, Happy Hidalgo of Yankee Stadium, the gifted lefthander at his best in blue-chip games, graciously highlighted his stand-in, jut-jawed Johnny (Grandma) Murphy, a husky Fordham righthander who so often gave Lefty even a bigger hand than the fans did.

When asked about his prospects in a season or a game, Gomez would answer, "Ask Murphy." And explaining his success that led to the Hall of Fame, the longtime funny man for Wilson Sporting Goods would suggest: "Clean living, a fast outfield—and Johnny Murphy."

In 1943, Mel Ott, managing the New York Giants, touched imagination in wartime baseball by using a right-handed reliever 70 times. The man's name was Ace Adams, indicating either his parents thought they had given birth to a slick card player or, clairvoyantly, a big league ballplayer.

Like many relievers, past and present, Adams couldn't hold up to the wear and tear, but by now, meaning the end of World War II, the personal pre-eminence of the reliever was beginning to take form in a shape better than that of pot-bellied, knock-kneed Hugh Casey. Casey was the round-faced darling of the Brooklyn Dodgers, the master of intimidation for the "stick-it-in-their-ear" managerial methods of Leo Durocher. For a couple of seasons "Huge," pronounced advisedly, flourished. Across the Brooklyn Bridge at the Stadium so did a handsome, flame-throwing Yankee lefthander, Joe Page. They completely dominated the 1947 World Series, a sloppy, yet exciting seven-game set. Casey worked in six games, Page in four. The bulky Brooklyn guy won two games, and the brisk business-like Yankee one.

The late-inning guys were standing tall now, and two years later came a breakthrough that Paul Richards, the lean tactical catcher who was a pitching whiz as a manager at Baltimore and with the Chicago White Sox, listed as among the top 10 baseball highlight wonders. A relief pitcher won a baseball Most Valuable Player Award for the first time.

Philadelphia's Whiz Kids were one-year wonders in 1950 as they brought the oft-phutile Phillies their first pennant in 35 years, largely because of a spectacled, professorial relief pitcher named Jim Konstanty. Konstanty had picked up a "palm" ball from a New York State undertaker, of all people, and, dipping his left knee deceptively in his delivery to keep hitters off stride, Konstanty simply buried the foe.

Working a record 74 games, Konstanty was in more perils than Pauline, yet was 16–7 in relief and was credited with 22 "saves," a category that actually was not listed until originated by *The Sporting News* in 1960 and then researched, past tense, by MacMillan's *Baseball Encyclopedia*.

If others previously dented the caste system against the relief pitcher as a secondary pitcher, if not a mop-up man, Konstanty broke it. Subsequently, Mike Marshall and Bruce Sutter won Cy Young Awards as pitchers of the year in a relief role. Quisenberry probably deserved the top role in 1983 because Kansas City would have finished in the subcellar without the most effective submarine-delivering pitcher and one who best symbolizes now the good humor that comes out of the bullpen.

With the kind of box car salaries now paid Sutter, Gossage, Fingers, an incapacitated Al Hrabosky, and others who crank 'er up when the going gets late and tough, it's really not necessary to salve wounds by listing an honor roll of relief. Still, so many of the good ones toiled well for a subway token by comparison with present prices and standards of appreciation.

So with justice to all and malice to none, here are just *some* of the maharajahs of the mound who were probably never fully paid or appreciated:

Clint Brown . . . Joe Heving . . . Ted Wilks . . . Nelson Potter . . . Clem Labine . . . Lindy McDaniel . . . Dick Radatz . . . Ray Narleski . . . Allie Reynolds . . . Larry Sherry . . . Ron Perranoski . . . Elroy Face . . . Ken Sanders . . . Don Mossi . . . Moe Drabowsky . . . Luis Arroyo . . . Phil Regan . . . Jim Brewer and—.

Why, at Cincinnati alone, saddled by tender-armed pitchers like Gary Nolan and Don Gullett, Sparky Anderson made starting pitching a five-or-six inning venture with consecutive World Championship ball clubs in the 1970s, fortifying a so-so front line with a medley relay of Clay Carroll, Rawly Eastwick, Wil McEnaney and Pedro Borbon. Last in complete games, itself a baseball dodo, the Reds often were first in the standings. Even though they had a powerful regular lineup, you don't win without pitching, especially relief pitching.

The game-savers achieved their first membership in the Hall of Fame (Hoyt Wilhelm), undoubedly breaking the barrier for the future just as Konstanty did with his MVP recognition and, especially, the origin of the "save."

A sweeping bow of gratitude for rewarding relievers belongs to Jerome Holtzman, longtime Chicago baseball writer, first with the *Sun-Times*, then the *Tribune*. Back in 1960, aware that there was no yardstick of measurement for bullpen excellence, Holtzman prevailed for cooperation from publisher J. G. Taylor Spink of *The Sporting News*. Spink recognized a good idea when his sharp editorial nose sniffed one. He endorsed and publicized the idea. So Holtzman and Lou Boudreau, Hall of Fame shortstop broadcasting Chicago Cubs' baseball, set down the ground rules.

Originally, rules were almost too rigid. A pitcher had to face the tying or winning run to receive credit. When others stuck their thumbs in their typewriters, trying to help, they made it too simple, even awarding a save for a final pitching appearance if the last pitcher did not receive the victory. So, accidentally or deliberately, saves were credited to a man appearing in the final inning of a game in which his side had a sizable lead. For instance, John Hiller at Detroit.

More recently, a result of official recognition as a pitching statistic, the save is reasonably dead-center as neither too restrictive nor too liberal. It's awarded for (1) appearing for three innings as the final pitcher, (2) for facing the potential tying or winning run as batter or next-up at any time, and (3) pitching a scoreless ninth (or last) inning with no more than a three-run lead. Under these guidelines, the Phillies' Steve Bedrosian earned a record 13 straight saves in 1987.

Why the present system? The question was asked James L. Toomey, former baseball writer and since 1949 with the Cardinals as publicity director and assistant general manager. Toomey said that requiring three innings' effort, no matter how large a team's lead, would discourage a manager from giving a pet reliever a cheap save because three innings would cut into the pitcher's future use. The significance of a save occurs when the tying or winning run is in the on-deck circle. But what about the one-inning requirement with a lead of three or fewer runs?

"Because," explained Toomey, "it's really the equivalent of getting, say, one out with a lead of two or fewer runs when the tying or winning run is on deck, and, at the same time, it doesn't count if a lead is considered large or decisive (three or more runs)."

Toomey had an idea that so far has been rejected by the rules' committee. He would balance a save with a "squander," explaining, "A squander would be a demerit for a reliever coming in, personally allowing the tying run charged to him, and then not winning or losing the game."

We seconded the motion. So did Rolaids. In 1988, the antacid people deducted for a lead lost, but the rules committee told Toomey there were enough negatives in statistics.

Amused, Toomey observed, smiling, "Statistics are full of negatives. Like the official time at bat in which the hitter doesn't get a hit, and even the good ones don't most of the time, say, seven out of 10."

The Philadelphia Phillies and Baltimore Orioles go a step farther by using what they call a "hold," an effort to evaluate and honor the long man or, as he's also called, the middle-inning reliever.

The Phils give a middle-inning reliever or two a hold if he (1) enters a game in a save situation—no more than two runs behind—finishes the inning without a run scoring, and subsequently is removed; (2) takes over in a save situation and retires all the batters he faces, even if not finishing the inning, or (3) takes over with a three-run lead or deficit and pitches a full inning or more without allowing a run.

What the middle men need even more than a recognized formula, the Phils' or Orioles' or any other, is more merry men like Moe Drabowsky, an innocent-looking, leg-puller, born in Poland, who was a masterful prankster.

Drabowsky, really only a durable journeyman through 17 years, was at his best in a middle-inning role that became a game-winning role in the 1966 World Series. Called on by Baltimore manager Hank Bauer to rescue Dave McNally in a third-inning situation at Los Angeles, Drabowsky pitched six-plus innings of one-hit ball and struck out 11 of the 23 batters he faced. That golden moment Moe was in the spotlight led to a four-game sweep.

Ordinarily, Drabowsky was a better prankster. Detecting that he could phone the other club's bullpen through a ball park switchboard, the clever mimic would match the other manager's voice and order the foe's best reliever to warm up at the oddest times—like too early when the best starter was pitching perfectly.

Whether Drabowsky was upsetting Atlanta's symbol, Chief Nockahoma, by throwing a stink bomb in the cigar-store Indian's scoreboard-area tepee or whether Ed Roebuck was interrupting 80 consecutive games of relief without defeat by tossing cherry bombs, the bullpens are indeed a place apart.

So far that one day when Joe Cronin was managing the Boston Red Sox, a game had to be held up because the reliever he had called, Jack Wilson, was listening to scholar-athlete Moe Berg finish a tale of historical impact almost as dramatic as bullpen catcher Berg's spying in World War II. Wilson didn't want to leave without hearing the punch line.

As far back as John McGraw's day as manager of the Giants, McGraw finally tired of the alcoholic escapades of Arthur (Bugs) Raymond. To bargain for a shot of whiskey from a bar across the street from the Polo Grounds, Raymond gave up the new ball he was supposed to use to warm up.

Another McGraw, more recent and equally colorful, Tug, a screwball who threw a screwball, remembered that when he was a hero at Shea Stadium before taking his "I Believe" to Philly, they would order up from a deli across the street and have the food service sneak in barbecued ribs in the middle of the game. Great sustenance for a reliever.

Or as they told of Gomez in an early day when the famed Yankee starter was trying to make it in relief, Lefty was munching on a hot dog when he was ordered suddenly to warm up. The Yanks were playing the Philadelphia A's, then blockbusters of the American League. Gomez wondered who was coming up?

"Cochrane, Foxx, and Simmons," he was told, a litany of slugging power. Gomez sighed, nodded, and pointed to his half-eaten sandwich. "Don't touch that," he said, "I'll be right back."

Characters all and good pitchers, such as Sparky Lyle, Dave La-Roche, and even the quiet ones like well-traveled Stu Miller, who got into the limelight by being gusted off the mound into a balk by a Candlestick Park stiff gust in the 1961 All-Star game. Miller's head-jerking motion, which made him look as if he had St. Vitus Dance, was as deceptive as his change-ups . . . slow . . . slower . . . and slowest.

To last, it helps to have a pet pitch other than a fastball as humming as Gossage's or Radatz's or Ryne Duren's. Duren, a former wild-armed, near-sighted Yankee reliever, drunk or sober, kept the hitters loose. Warming up, he squinted like Mr. Magoo. He would fire an intimidating pitch wildly off the backstop. Hitters batted as gingerly then as when they tried to dig in at the plate against Dizzy Dean. Dean would drawl in his twang of the Southwest, "That's right, pod-nuh, dig a nice big hole up there so they can bury you."

The pranks they play in bullpens, some enclosed from bench view, are so numerous that it's only a white lie that anybody ever did anything in the bullpen except talk romance or read the *Wall Street Journal*. But a life in the bullpen did help hone the humor of two catchers who went on to fame and fortune behind microphones not behind the plate—Joe Garagiola and Bob Uecker.

Ueck enlivened more than one dugout or pen. He saved his best for action one night when catching for the champion Cardinals in 1964. With the score tied in the 10th, three on for the Giants, one out, the infield played halfway. When a batter grounded sharply to Julian Javier at second base, Javier juggled the ball just long enough to fear he couldn't get a double play. Hoolie threw a strike to the plate, figuring a force-out, but the throw, belt high, almost ruptured the umpire. Uecker had left the plate to rush down to first base to back up a double play threat!

After the winning run scored, a stunned reporter ran into the Giants' superscout, Tom (Clancy) Sheehan and suggested that, boy and man, he had spent 40 years in a ball park and hadn't seen a game lost similarly. Sheehan understood and was almost as funny as Uecker was on that play or as the broadcaster is on the air.

"Boy and man," inquired Sheehan, "how many catchers you ever seen whose last names begin with the letter 'U'?"

Garagiola, a gifted guy even though he wasn't the best boyhood player on his block (Yogi Berra lived across the street), remembered how it was in National League ball parks after the Pirates introduced the full-templed plastic batting helmets in the early 1950s. (Brooklyn first used fiber inserts in their caps in 1940.) "Kids threw so many marbles and pennies off our helmets," quipped Pittsburgh's Garagiola, "we felt as if we were a giant bell ringing."

Yogi's pal Joey could recall the time, too, when he was with the Cardinals and the pitching coach fell asleep in the bullpen. As he leaned against a bullpen gate, players removed the fence chain and looped it through his belt. Then suddenly someone shouted to the sleeping beauty that the manager wanted him. Garagiola laughed. "The startled guy leaped up and then took off for the dugout with about 10 feet of chain fence dragging behind him."

One of Garagiola's batterymates, Gerry Staley, used his sinkerball to help pitch the Chicago White Sox to a pennant in 1959. Trick pitches do provide more bullpen consistency and durability than is often the case in a situation in which relievers' careers either are short-lived or as up and down as a yo-yo.

Tug McGraw, like Mike Ryba, an earlier reliever, lived with his screwball. Elroy Face had his fork ball. Lindy McDaniel featured the same wide-fingered pitch. Rollie Fingers sinks 'em with a sinker, and Kent Tekulve, like Dan Quisenberry, comes submarine in his delivery. Bruce Sutter, long-fingered and, like Face and Murry Dickson, durable because of the overhanded off-season use of the arm in carpentry, specialized in a lopsided fork ball he calls a "split-fingered fastball."

Then there's the knuckleball, the pitch that kept Phil Niekro as a winning 300-game starter into 1987 at age 48. It kept Hoyt Wilhelm pitching so long that he was old enough to qualify for the pension plan when he hung up his finger-tip pitch in 1972.

Wilhelm, the wry-necked, deadpanned Carolinian, gave relief pitching its greatest breakthrough, even more than Jim Konstanty's Most Valuable Player Award and Mike Marshall's and Sutter's Cy Young trophies. In 1985 he was elected to the Hall of Fame in the Baseball Writers' Association of America's annual balloting.

Wilhelm was no kid when the 29-year-old war veteran came up to the Giants in 1952, the season that did the most for the bullpen. We call it the Year of the Relief Pitcher, as depicted by the pennant success of the three National League clubs.

For Brooklyn, another rookie, Joe Black, also no kid at 28, was spectacular in 1952. Starting only two of 57 games, he was 15–4 with a knife-cutting sharp slider, saving 15 games. Joe was so good in relief that manager Charley Dressen, shorthanded, started him three times in the World Series against the Yankees and the reliever pitched well, winning one game and losing two, low-score. If only he hadn't suffered the arm injury, which turned him into a goodwill representative of the Greyhound Company. . . .

Similarly in '52, another rookie, a rawhide righthander named Eddie Yuhas, teamed with veteran sidearmed southpaw Alpha Brazle to give the St. Louis Cardinals a strong third-place season, 88–68. Brazle was 12–5 with 16 saves and Yuhas was 12–2 with six saves. Between them they were in 110 games, only eight of them starts, and each compiled a 2.72 earned-run average. But from the time Yuhas threw his first pitch in spring training in '53, the big kid was sore-armed and through.

So that left Wilhelm, who broke in spectacularly in more ways than one. In his first time at bat in the majors, Hoyt homered. For 21 seasons he batted an assorted 432 times and never hit another home run. H'mm, must have thought he was hitting his dancing knuckleball, the butter for his bread from the beginning.

As the crippled Giants made a gallant bid in '52 to retain the pennant Leo Durocher's Little Miracle of Coogan's Bluff had contributed a year before, Wilhelm was 15–3, appearing in 71 games, all of them in relief, and was credited officially with 11 saves. Because of the requirements then for the earned-run leadership, i.e., an equivalent of one inning every game, 154, Wilhelm's 2.43 ERA was the lowest in the National League.

Over the years, Wilhelm appeared in a record 1070 games, starting only 52, one of them a no-hitter for the Orioles. He won 143 games, as many as 15 only two seasons, but he saved 227. In truth, he was a Pied Piper of pitching for nine clubs—New York, St. Louis, Atlanta, Chicago, and Los Angeles in the National League; Cleveland, Baltimore, Chicago, and California in the American.

Even when still short of the short man officially in the Hall of Fame, relief pitching had come a l-o-n-g way since the long and short of excellence, and forgive us for hailing short-shrifters, Father Chadwick.

The longest, most successful relief performance was Ernie Shore's celebrated 27-man-out performance at Boston in 1917—an asterisked perfect game in relief of an exasperated, ejected pitching bloke named Babe Ruth.

The shortest, most successful relief performance came seven years later by Bill Sherdel, ordinarily a left-handed starter for the Cardinals. Wee Willie came in to face Philadelphia with two men on, none out, and threw one pitch: George Harper hit the bejesus out of it—into a triple play!

13
From Peanuts
to Penthouses

Until baseball players came across buried treasure in 1976, the year an arbiter negated the reserve clause, salaries were measured with the grand poobah of athletic pay, the $80,000 made by Babe Ruth as the Depression began in 1930.

Over the years, economically, as we and obviously many others have realized, there's a tendency to live in the past financially as well as historically, to remember fondly the cost of a haircut, a movie, or a loaf of bread as contrasted with an inflationary present.

But if you use the theory of economic relativity, begging Prof. Einstein's pardon, it's much more practical to compare dollars and cents with the Gross National Product and other means of determining whether a buck is as small as Bambi or as large as a bull moose.

So for the misty-eyed in memory, don't fret. Even guys now hauling down a million dollars or more, able to use the leverage of free agency to win box car salaries, really don't take more to the bank than the Babe could have if Ruth hadn't lived as if tomorrow would never come.

Actually, if the Babe, a wild beer-sipping kid at his father's saloon at only seven, hadn't had a firm second wife and a shrewd business manager, he might have died broke at only 54. But, fact is, he lived well, if not long enough, and was indeed paid a salary even more top-heavy than the Bambino himself.

Fact is, Ruth's salary, as the Depression burst onto the scene with a stock market crash on an infamous Black Tuesday in October 1929, was $80,000. The Babe, then 34, just had played a season in which, though missing 20 games, he had hit 46 home runs and driven in 154, batting .345. But, after all, the buck stopped here, times were getting tougher, and, heck, Babe, as he was told, was already making $5000 more than the President of the United States.

"Yeah," the Babe grunted in a voice that was a subdued roar, "but I had a better year than he did." H'mm, Herbert Hoover *was* having it tough with unemployment and also just about everyone wanting beer.

The point is, paying less than $5000 in income tax then and with the dollar's buying power beginning to swell to manhole-sized capacity in the tough-times' period, Ruth's buying power was probably 10 times more than 55 years later. Then, heavily taxed, inflated, the *average* salary in 1988 was well over $400,000. The estimate came from a Federal Reserve executive, amused about the question. If so, the Babe probably was making close to a million back there when the reserve clause was as restrictive as a woman's old-fashioned corset.

Through the Depression, slowing down with the economy, the Babe did take salary cuts even though he still swung a powerful bat, i.e., 46 homers, 41 and 34 the next three years and with productive RBIs and averages. By the time he slumped in 1933 to just .301, hitting "only" 34 homers with 114 runs-batted-in, Ruth was 38 years old (or 39) and forced to forego his glamorous salary holdouts in exchange for a $35,000 contract, his last with the New York Yankees.

But his pay then was extremely high, relatively, because 1934 was just about the pits in the Dirty Thirties, a period of dust and drought, hunger and highwaymen. For a fact, Ruth still could buy as much as many of the spearcarriers now paid salaries that, dollarwise at least, are higher than the superstars then and previously.

Prior to the time this book was prepared, at a time basketball players and baseball performers in particular were making the most in individual sports, boxers fought seldom, but scored heavily through television receipts and/or cable or closed-circuit network receipts. Yet some economists doubt whether a champion with a $10,000,000 or $15,000,000 purse clears as much as Gene Tunney did in 1927. As heavyweight champion, he paid only $11,000 tax on a purse of $990,000.

As mentioned earlier, the hide-and-go-seek of baseball salaries became moot after arbitrator Peter Seitz first declared Oakland's Jim (Catfish) Hunter and Los Angeles's Andy Messersmith free agents. The reserve clause, adopted by the National League at Buffalo's Palace Hotel in 1879, shriveled and disappeared.

Obviously, as the ball moved into the other court, from management's side to labor's, ballplayers began to achieve $1,000,000-plus contracts that were long-term, by sharp contrast with the skimpier past when a player, bound by contract to one club, was forced usually to accept one season at a time.

The box office bromide was, in effect, that a player was paid next season for what he did the previous year and, if you'll pardon our prejudiced opinion, that seemed to be preferable and more productive. Somehow, intentionally or not, some athletes become fat cats mentally when they can see beyond one October's final paycheck through that next season or two's last tab. Financial anxiety seems to make the adrenalin pump and to serve as a hotfoot of inspiration. But — and this is as big a butt as Fat Fothergill's, a former hard-hitting Detroit outfielder — ballplayers *were* underpaid too often and too long.

Not that, as we'll attempt to show, payment relatively wasn't nearly so niggardly as a present day look at the past would indicate. After all, everything else and everyone else was paid less, too. For instance, back in the period from 1932–34, congressmen were paid $8500, airline pilots averaged $8100, lawyers $4000, doctors $3500, college teachers $3000, etc.

But, if those esteemed fields of endeavor drew small sums by present standards, remember, please, that surveys indicate that even *before* the financial ceiling collapsed in 1929, about 70 percent of the working population was paid $2000 or less a year. Uh-huh, and still managed to dabble in the market with its 10 percent margin and sky-high potential. By mid-1984, more than 50 percent of the work force reportedly earned more than $15,000 a year.

You see, it's so easy from this inflated, comfortable, financial distance to give a horse laugh — or nicker or neigh, anyway — at what ballplayers were paid at different times. For instance, in 1930, several months after the stock market crashed, the market dropped further as cotton dipped and wheat and corn reacted. The population census then was listed at 122,698,190, an increase of 16.1 percent over 1920.

You could get two diamond rings for $16.85, which meant 50 cents down and 50 cents a week, if you had a spare half-buck. A two-pants suit sold for only $25 and a matched set of golf clubs, a frivolous sport for the period, for just $38.95.

So it wasn't too unlikely for a rookie battery of Paul Dean and Bill DeLancey to get only $3000 each from the St. Louis Cardinals by 1934, as a buck's value grew in size as dollars disappeared. But, then, Frank Frisch, player-manager of the Cardinals, described in more detail in Bethany Press's *The Pilot Light and the Gas House Gang,* was getting only $18,500, twice any other Redbird player. Earlier, in better financial days, as a player alone, Frisch had been paid $28,000.

The Gang's workhorse wonder, Dizzy Dean, was paid $7500 for

that season, one in which he won 30 games and lost only seven, and Ol' Diz, who went on a brief sitdown strike trying to get brother Paul a raise, would beef later about how little he had been paid. But a 100 percent increase in 1935 to $15,000 was a handsome hike for the period.

St. Louis's loud, lippy shortstop then, Leo Durocher, who would become a long-lived, volatile, and imaginative manager, tried to set things straight for the elder Dean, then only 23. "Hey, Diz, quit horsing around," complained the Cardinals' captain. "I need that $6000 (Series money). I'm 10 grand in the red."

Probably. Durocher, who lived well and dressed better, had signed in 1934 for only $6500, a contract that would be shrunk by alimony, child support, and debts, as indicated by a flimsy insert of deductions stapled into his contract and initialed "L.E.D." (Leo Ernest Durocher) and "B.R." (general manager Branch Rickey).

If Leo was a good boy and met his obligations, leaving him about $1000, he would be given a $1000 bonus, the contact stipulated. That meant he had a grand to two grand on which to live. No wonder Durocher snarled among the most hungry of the Gas Housers.

One of the dramatics of World Series achievement was lost with larger salaries recently. When a guy could double his salary or increase it largely in Series checks, the impact of finishing first was greater than in 1986. By then, the average player's salary had soared to more than $300,000, but the Series limits were s-o-o high. The Cardinals received $43,279 each for *winning* over Milwaukee in 1982, but $54,821 for *losing* to Kansas City City in '85. Yet the sizable sums meant far less to the athletes than that nearly $6000 did to Durocher and his cut-throat teammates in '34.

Truthfully, only pride, a commodity on which there really is no price, can bring out the best in ballplayers now. A factor demonstrated often enough in the best — and acknowledged by some players — is that multiple-season contracts tend to take away the intensity needed to play every game all-out.

But for the bonanza of present day players' pay, perquisites and pensions, members of the Major League Baseball Players' Association owe their largesse largely to (1) owners' greed, (2) radio-television receipts, (3) responsible conference-room expertise and (4), ultimately, a fond farewell to the old reserve clause.

As noted by Lee Allen, premier historian in *The National League Story,* player restrictions were imposed shortly after Orrick Bishop, a St. Louis sandlotter who became a judge, formalized the first major league with its constitution in 1876.

By Allen's research, Arthur Soden, a Boston roofer who became interested in baseball, formalized the renewal clause in the contract just two years after the NL replaced the old National Association and other disorganized efforts to organize.

At the time the ball clubs merited sympathy, as they would on rare occasion, over the years. In 1877, for instance, William Hulbert's Chicago team's failure to repeat as pennant winners showed need for some kind of checks and balances. Players jumped contracts, including pitching star "Will" White, who hopped to Boston. Only Chicago made money, however, as St. Louis lost $6000, Cincinnati $4000, Hartford (Brooklyn) $2500, Louisville $2000, and Boston $1500.

Of Soden, Allen wrote that along with A. G. Spalding, the improper Bostonian became a political power in league affairs. Allen was at his cotton-pickin' best when he added of Soden, Boston club president for 30 years: "He was an autocrat, and his enemies claimed that he had reduced parsimony to an exact science"—an eloquent way of saying damned cheap—"but he would give the league the executive strength it needed to survive."

Gradually, as baseball began to prosper, sportsmen who had spawned it were replaced by the avaricious, of whom the most noteworthy was New York's Andrew Freedman. Freedman, aligned with Tammany Hall, had made money with real estate and transit deals. He bought the Giants for less than $50,000 and was a bummer for press, public, and players.

Why, for one, the great early day pitcher, Amos Rusie, was so incensed at the salary Freedman offered that he sat out the 1896 season and returned in '97 only because other clubs passed the hat to keep the box office man on the mound.

Baseball hasn't changed much. In 1886, for instance, one newspaper accused members of the Washington team of using opium, adding the sage postscript, as noted by Lee Allen in *100 Years of Baseball*, published by Country Life Press in 1950: "You can not hit the pipe and hit the ball."

So the drug scandals and alcohol abuse of the 1980s merely were an updated version of old, unfortunate habits. Heavy drinking was actually a national habit that led to another unfortunate backlash, Prohibition, the spawning grounds for gangsters. But, largely, baseball's problems early were salaries that were too small, not enough owners who cared, and the reserve clause, which was virtually peonage.

Sure, comparisons can be deceiving. Back in 1869 those redstockinged Cincinnati professional dandies, triumphing from Boston to San Francisco, received what now would seem a pittance. After all, a dollar was as big as a manhole cover following the Civil War. Shortstop George Wright was paid $1400, and brother Harry, the centerfielder, $1200. They were top paid.

But even though the game grew, particularly after formation of the

National League in 1876 with Chicago, Boston, Philadelphia, New York–Brooklyn, Hartford, St. Louis, Cincinnati, and Louisville, salaries merely crept along. Then, as mentioned, Soden, the Boston roofer, came along with the reserve clause that served as a salary ceiling. Even John T. Brush, a much more reasonable man than Freedman who operated first in Indianapolis and then in New York, favored a Class A–to–E salary scale that 15 years later would pay a player only $1500 to $2500.

Only now and then did the athletes have an "inning" as, for instance, when the American Association formed as a major league rival in 1882 for a 10-year period, one dominated considerably by the St. Louis Browns, led then by a bulbous German saloonkeeper, Christ Von der Ahe. Von der Ahe, spending more money than his colleagues and rivals in both leagues, helped manager Charley Comiskey, his first baseman, field a team that won four straight pennants, 1885–88. Hustling baseball to boost business at his nearby saloon, Von der Ahe would tote the loot down Grand Avenue followed by a security man with a foot-long revolver.

Von der Ahe, though he died broke years later, picked up tabs regularly for former players who hit the juice too much, but the most boisterous and colorful character of early day clubowners soon became blinded by dollar signs, too. Especially when Al Spalding at Chicago created a sensation on St. Valentine's Day, 1877, by selling Michael (King) Kelly to Boston for $10,000.

Kelly, who just had led the league in hitting with a .388 average, was a handsome, hard drinking, hard sliding ballplayer, the most spectacular of his time, but, as Spalding and manager Cap Anson agreed, difficult to handle. Kelly, regarded by many as a showoff, yet obviously box office, was to receive only the $2000 limit from Boston, but to keep The King happy, the Beaneaters added $3000 "for use of his picture," as Lee Allen reported. Kelly was so happy that he drank himself to death soon rather than later. He was only 36 in 1894.

From the five-figure price paid for Kelly's contract by Boston, Von der Ahe and other owners got the bright idea that not only could they control the peons, but they also could sell them at a profit. Von der Ahe sold stars with reckless abandon. The misjudgment left him with nothing at his death except a king-sized statue built previously for him at the Bellefontaine Cemetery, St. Louis.

Meanwhile, another St. Louis man named Henry V. Lucas, whose uncle had sponsored the city's first major league ball club in 1876, grew up as an idol worshipper. As a result, he tried in 1883 to operate a third major league, the Union Association, one in which the players would get a better financial break. Haughtily, the National League and even the American Association, previously derided because of beer-and-whiskey sponsors, two-bit seats, and playing ball on Sunday, railed at Lucas and his associates. They called him "St. Lucas" and the Union the "Onions."

As author Allen noted, suddenly major league baseball in 1884 included 34 clubs, obviously too many then when the game wasn't truly national and few cities sufficiently sizable. By contrast, baseball existed with 16 major league teams from 1901 for 50 years. By 1988, the number was 28 clubs with a hint of an ultimate increase to 32.

Briefly, back then, reacting to the new threat, the National League dropped Troy, New York, and Worcester, Massachusetts, adding New York City and Philadelphia teams that became, ultimately, the Giants and Phillies. The American Association, begun originally with St. Louis, Cincinnati, Louisville, Baltimore, Philadelphia, and Pittsburgh, expanded to include New York (Metropolitans) and Columbus, Ohio. Ultimately, the AA reached 12 teams, adding Toledo, Indianapolis, Brooklyn, and Washington.

Why? Because of "St. Lucas's Onions," that's why. The noble Lucas, seeking to free the baseball slaves, enlisted Boston, Cincinnati, Chicago, Baltimore, Philadelphia, Washington, and—.

Altoona?

Yes, Altoona, Pennsylvania, which gave up the franchise ghost to Kansas City by the end of May. St. Louis's Maroons, managed by Ted Sullivan, who recruited the best contract-jumpers, romped off with the Union Association pennant, winning 91 games and losing only 16. That was another blow to a league that folded with a financial thud. Only Kansas City and Milwaukee voted to carry on in 1885.

From the American Association and National League, only 27 players had jumped to the Union Association. They were welcomed back by their original clubs, and the AA rolled back to eight clubs. And, as Allen wrote, "The powers that ruled the game became even more imperious than they had been before. . . ."

So the National Professional Brotherhood of Professional Baseball Players, promoted by a Cleveland sports editor named Billy Voltz, a former minor league operator at Chattanooga, Tennessee, began to flex its muscle. Not until Marvin Miller and the Major League Baseball Players' Association brought baseball to its knees in the mid-1970s did the jocks ever come so close to doing what they achieved: That is, take over the asylum.

Originally, dunned $5 a month for a $6000-a-season sick-and-indigent fund, the Brotherhood brought togetherness to the players. When the National League and American Association drew a hard-and-fast $2000 salary limit, the Brotherhood established the Players' League in 1889.

After the 1888 season, executive Al Spalding had taken two all-star

teams for a trip that reached Australia, with far-flung stops from Cey-
lon to Egypt. Among them was a brilliant man, John Montgomery
Ward, a perfect-game pitcher, brilliant shortstop, and a graduate lawyer. Like John K. Tener, a pitcher of the 1880s who became governor
of Pennsylvania and then president of the National League, Ward
added class to the players' ranks and to the game.

When Ward and other players returned from Spalding's global
tour, they were honored at New York's famed Delmonico restaurant
at a ceremony attended by Theodore Roosevelt and Mark Twain. It was
then they learned of the financial squeeze.

Ward spoke earnestly and honestly for the players: ". . . To get
men to invest capital in baseball, it is necessary to have a reserve rule.
The reserve rule, on a whole, is a bad one, but it can not be rectified
save by injuring the interests of the men who invest their money, and
that is not the object of the Brotherhood."

But justice was, indeed, justice and a few extra bucks, which, in
frustration, Ward and others sought when they formed the Players'
League in 1890, competing with the National League at a time the
American Association was experiencing a death rattle.

If the players knew how close they came to caving in the NL, too,
the history of baseball might have been changed considerably. Assisted by sportsmen in towns where they were heroes, the athletes
fielded teams that attracted such reserve-clause contract-jumpers as
Connie Mack, John K. Tener, King Kelly, Roger Connor, Pete Browning, Orator Jim O'Rourke, Buck Ewing, George Van Haltren, Jake
Beckley, Hugh Duffy, Dave Orr, Jim (Pud) Galvin, and Old Hoss Rad-
bourne. Fact is, just about every big name except Cap Anson. Pop
didn't move probably because he had stock in the Chicago White
Stockings.

At a time a famous attorney and agnostic, Robert G. Ingersoll,
flatly told the Brotherhood that the reserve clause wasn't worth the
paper of lawsuits filed in behalf of the National League and American
Association—judges and juries agreed, too—the Players League apparently won a newspaper decision in the three-league attendance
war.

The AA's gate was so bad that Lee Allen didn't even bother to record it, and actual figures were as closely guarded as Fort Knox, but
an observer described as "unbiased," Clarence Dow, listed the Players
League at 980,887 to 813,678 for the NL. High was Philadelphia
among the Nationals to only 16,064—uh, huh, only 16,064—for Pittsburgh. The Brotherhood's range was 197,346 for Boston to 58,430 for
Cleveland. Obviously, everybody lost his high-collared shirt—and his
BVDs.

Strangely, though, the Brotherhood—the players—don't realize how close they came to winning the war, which, in effect, could have changed baseball history, past and present, perhaps geographically and certainly financially. Athletes undoubtedly would have come up with a larger piece of the pie before free agency permitted them, if you'll forgive the mixed pastry metaphor, to take the cake.

The National League, which had lost few players to the American Association, suffered markedly with loss of talent and distillation of crowds. The NL, in effect, was ready to sue for peace, one which obviously would have been more favorable to the athletes. But the Brotherhood had felt the pinch, too, and the players moved first for peace. Alertly, with the poise that had carried him far in baseball and the sporting goods games, Al Spalding disguised his relief. He insisted on unconditional surrender.

So the players returned to their NL clubs and the American Association bellied up a year later, prompting the National League to reinstate salary limits and to expand to an unwieldy 12 teams. The NL in 1892 included Baltimore, Boston, Brooklyn, Chicago, Cincinnati, Cleveland, Louisville, New York, Philadelphia, Pittsburgh, St. Louis, and Washington.

Interestingly, as noted in Allen's *100 Years of Baseball,* the nightmare of the cumbersome eight-year period of 12 teams was dominated by Boston, for which little Hugh Duffy hit .438 when the pitching distance was increased and another physical piker, Bobby Lowe, hit four homers in a game. And when the Bostons weren't best, it was Ned Hanlon's Baltimore Orioles, the hit-and-run "hooligans" whose smart, rough play forced a rewrite of the rule book. The Orioles made most use of the hit-and-run play, incidentally, but in Allen's research, Frank Selee at Boston was the first to send in motion a runner and then seek to hit through the position vacated by the shortstop or second baseman.

Over that period Boston had a 706–400 won-and-lost record for a .638 percentage to .592 for Baltimore, creating a further drop to Cincinnati's .542. Factually, eight of the 12 teams did play over .500, but Chicago was poor (.499), Louisville bad (.380), Washington worse (.370) and St. Louis—.

Well, St. Louis was so bad, playing only .361 ball with just 399 victories and 706 defeats, that when Frank DeHaas Robison and brother Stanley, who owned a traction company that operated in Fort Wayne, Indiana, bought the moribund Browns after the 1898 season, they made a bold move. Miffed because their Cleveland club hadn't drawn despite a decent won-and-lost record (.518), they swapped the entire Cleveland roster for the St. Louis players!

Syndicate ownership wouldn't be tolerated now, but the twin-team sponsorship in one form or another was reasonably frequent in the last century. The Robisons merely overdid it when they sent the Spiders, as Cleveland then was called, to St. Louis. Included were a great pitcher, Cy Young, and a .400 hitter, Jesse Burkett, and other good talent.

Cleveland got the dregs, as drab as the nickname color of the Browns, as the St. Louis club had been known in both the National League and the American Association. The Browns were so bad in Cleveland uniforms, *too,* that they quickly were ostracized by properly angry Forest City fans and took many home games on the road to neutral cities.

The flanneled nomads were so bad that they were called, derisively, the "Exiles." The Exiles wound up with the worst major league record ever, only 20 victories compared with 134 defeats.

All this, mind you, was comic relief for the clash ahead in which the National League got its comeuppance. Managing Cincinnati then, having left Chris Von der Ahe angrily when the St. Louis operator sold off his stars, Charley Comiskey had tried to help the Brotherhood. The man criticized for coolie wages later, when eight of his Chicago White Sox threw the 1919 World Series, had earned a handsome sum for the time, $9000.

Comiskey was impressed at Cincinnati by a brash young sportswriter named Byron Bancroft Johnson, son of a minister and a graduate of Marietta College. Commy was with Ban all the way as they plotted first the Western League as a coverup for their grand plans— the American League.

Comiskey even cut away from his major league job to acquire the Sioux City, Iowa, franchise in 1895 and to move it to St. Paul, further strengthening the Western League and enhancing his chances as a major league operator. Johnson and Comiskey were helped by Alfred H. Spink, representing the *St. Louis Post-Dispatch.* Al Spink and brother Charles had founded *The Sporting News,* a sports-and-theatrical publication which prospered under C. C. Spink and especially his dynamic son, J. G. Taylor Spink.

The Spinks were strong allies behind Johnson, even to the point that Taylor named his son and successor, C. C. Johnson Spink, in tribute to the bold warrior who brought the National to its knees. Ban Johnson became so competitive that in addition to supporting umpires better than ever before, he uniquely (1) asked the chief ump to explain by wire the reason any American League game lasted more than two hours and (2) sent a telegram of congratulations himself to any American League manager who won even an exhibition game over a NL team.

This, of course, followed a cutback to eight teams by which the National League dropped Cleveland, Louisville, Washington, and Baltimore in 1900, opening up potential franchises and, more importantly, some talent that could be obtained reasonably. Reasonably, that is, by comparison with the cost of pork chops and a streetcar token at the turn of the century.

Johnson immediately scooped up dangling franchises to go with a former one-time National League City, Detroit, and a two-team confrontation with New York, Philadelphia, Boston, and Chicago, where he went along with the aspirations of his former conspirator from a Cincinnati barroom, Charley Comiskey. Commy, now a full-fledged executive, became the "Old Roman." The Irishman turned over the manager's job to a wiry, bushy-browed little pitcher who had a date with destiny in Washington — Clark Griffith.

Griff won the first American League pennant for Comiskey and Chicago in 1901. The Milwaukee franchise was transferred in 1902 to St. Louis, creating another two-team town and a status quo in franchises that would last for a half-century. And in the first so-called "modern" World Series, the Boston Red Sox upset the Pittsburgh Pirates in five games of a best-of-nine set in 1903.

How could a new major league achieve parity so quickly? In part, of course, because of the insidious NL $2400 salary limit which caused enough players to jump contracts and because some players were frozen out when the NL cut back franchises.

As researched by Allen, 111 of the 182 players who performed for the AL in 1901 had performed previously in the National. Included were such prominent names of the time as John Anderson, Jimmy Barrett, Roger Bresnahan, Steve Brodie, Jimmy Collins, Lou Criger, Lave Cross, Harry Davis, Turkey Mike Donlin, Jiggs Donohue, Hugh Duffy, Kid Elberfeld, Bones Ely, Clark Griffith, Bill Hoffer, Dummy Hoy, Frank Isbell, Fielder Jones, Ted Lewis, Jimmy McAteer, Joe McGinnity, John McGraw, Sam Mertes, Doc Nance, Fred Parent, Wilbert Robinson, Fred (Crazy) Schmidt, Ozzie Schreckengost, Cy Seymour, Chick Stahl, and its best pitcher, Cy Young, and best hitter, Napoleon Lajoie.

Cy Young fled St. Louis, twice a 20-game winner, glad to get out of the heat. Lajoie, if not the best hitter, the best all-around player prior to Ty Cobb, was hurt emotionally because his Philadelphia Phillies' clubowner, Colonel John I. Rogers, wasn't paying him as much under the table as he was slugger Ed Delehanty.

Years later, the stoic Lajoie broke his silence and explained why and how he had jumped leagues. He had seen a $300 check for extra money paid Delehanty. So, silently, he had accepted the $200 additional given him by Rogers — silent and hurt.

222 _____ BASEBALL from a *Different Angle*

When the American League was founded and Connie Mack offered him $6000 each in a four-year contract, Lajoie found Colonel Rogers now willing to pay him $12,500 each for a two-year period. "If," Lajoie said, "you'll pay me the $400 you owe me for the last two years, we can talk contract."

The Colonel insisted he didn't owe the big Frenchman anything. Lajoie, properly pronounced LaZhwa, but called La-joyee by many and settling for Laj-a-way, walked away and joined the rival Athletics. Immediately, he had his greatest season. Helped no doubt by some minor league pitchers brought up by the new league and aided further because the AL didn't adopt for two more years a new NL foul-strike rule — previously no foul ball was a strike — Nap had his best year. He hit .422.

Opening day, 1902, as Lajoie singled off Baltimore's Joe McGinnity — before Baltimore went into major league hibernation until 1954 — a telegram notified him that the rival Phillies had obtained an injunction restraining him from playing for the Athletics. He could play on the road, but not in Philly. So, reluctantly, but for the good of the American League's cause, Mack sold the great second baseman to Cleveland. Whenever Cleveland played in Philadelphia, "Larry" bypassed the City of Brotherly Love for the boardwalk at Atlantic City.

Thereafter, with the exception of the Federal League effort to become a third major league in 1914–15 and the immediate post–World War II unrest that led to contract-jumping to Mexico, the clubowners had a solid upper hand. So the stories that immediately follow are, only relatively, somewhat like the situation that became prevalent when the renewal clause was overturned.

For instance, when colorful barrel-chested, bow-legged Honus Wagner hit .381 in 1900 for Pittsburgh, Ban Johnson and the American League came calling with an offer that included the most money the former coal miner ever had seen. Paid then, presumably, $2400, unless owner Barney Dreyfuss slipped him some cash on the side, Wagner looked at 20 bills of $1000 laid before him by Clark Griffith, representing the New York Highlanders.

The high-principled Dutchman shook his head. He didn't reach $10,000 until he threatened to quit seven seasons later. Thereafter, until he retired in 1917 at 43 with a lifetime .329 average, he would sit down with Dreyfuss. When asked what he wanted, Honus would say: "Same as last year."

Years later when a sporting goods business operated by Wagner and subsequent Pittsburgh superstar Pie Traynor collapsed with the Depression, Wagner was hired as a Pirates' coach and remained in uniform until he was 75.

In 1903, the National League recognized the worst—the AL was here to stay—so they signed an agreement that eliminated competitive bidding except for unsigned players. Box car bonuses went out the window, essentially, after a reverse-order draft like pro football's was established in 1965.

A gap existed in the World Series when John T. Brush, Indianapolis clothing man, refused to let his New York Giants acknowledge an appeal from the Boston Red Sox for a renewal of the Series begun the previous year with Pittsburgh. Brush, run out of baseball when Indianapolis went down with the American Association, got back into the game first at Cincinnati, then by buying the Giants from Andrew Freedman. Although stiff-arming the AL by refusing to play the Series in '04, Brush set up ground rules that became future standards for the post-season attraction.

Sure, the Giants wanted to play the Red Sox in 1904. Maybe even manager John McGraw, but McGraw and Brush still were trying to brush off the American as "minor league." For the players, though, chances went out the window to make perhaps $1500 each out of the Series.

The drama of World Series money long has been lost. Series victors through most years from 1919 until 1953 received $5000 or $6000. During the Depression years, especially, that could mean twice as much as, say, Paul Dean and Bill DeLancey each made as a rookie star battery with St. Louis's 1934 Gas House Gang.

By the time World Series shares began to inch up—$8000 in 1953, $11,000 in '54, $20,000 in '72, and $26,000 before free agency opened sesame in 1976—Series money still was meaningful. After all, as noted at the outset of this chapter, we take the view that changing financial times have to be regarded as significant.

For instance, it was one thing to be paid only $3000 in 1934, but, as disclosed by Ford Frick, then National League president, a contrast with 31 American Leaguers and 11 National Leaguers making less than $5000 in 1946. A period of wartime inflation and higher taxes had shrunk the value of a dollar. Trouble was, baseball pay lagged.

So it was a sacrifice of long-range benefit in 1946, a year when because both the Cardinals and Red Sox had small ball parks, the Series winner's share dipped to $3742.34 and the loser's to $2140.89. The St. Louis and Boston players passed up the $100,000 radio rights. Television did not enter into the picture until 1947, and, naturally, the spiraling TV receipts have been figured into the plush present Series payoff.

The waiver of Series radio money in '46 contributed to the smallest winner's share since 1918, a war-shortened season, and the smallest since the same year for the losers, too. The Cardinals and Red Sox were kicking off the players' contribution to the pension plan, which will be discussed later.

Over the years, as suggested, only rarely did a ballplayer faced with the ball-and-chain of the reserve clause ever score a financial victory.

Back in '14, a year after it had functioned as a minor league team, the Federal League burst forth with more prominent ownership and "third major league" notions. Just after the majors themselves had completed a wave of new parks, the Feds threw up eight structures. One of the owners, Charles Weeghman, Chicago cafeteria king, built the basis of what is now historic Wrigley Field. Other prominent owners included oil baron Harry Sinclair, Robert B. Ward of a famous baking company, and Phil Ball, ice-and-fuel operator.

The eight-club Feds operated in '14 in St. Louis, Chicago, Pittsburgh, and Brooklyn — St. Louis and Chicago had three big league teams at the time, and the New York area four — and also in top minor league towns, i.e., Baltimore, Buffalo, Kansas City, and Indianapolis.

The Federal League president, James A. Gilmore, labeled as illegal and unconstitutional the reserve and 10-day release clauses. Joe Tinker, former Cubs' star, was named manager of the Chicago Whales.

Attracted by bigger pay were such names as Mordecai (Three Finger) Brown, Eddie Plank, Chief Bender, Hal Chase, Otto Knabe, Danny Murphy, Mickey Doolan, Tom Seaton, Ed Konetchy, Cy Falkenberg, Jim Delehanty, George Mullin, and Howard Camnitz. A new player, Benny Kauff, was called the "Ty Cobb of the Federal League," but he ran afoul of big league pitching and also of Judge Landis later.

A box office attraction the Feds dearly wanted was Walter Johnson, Washington's Big Train and maybe the greatest pitcher ever. In 1913 Johnson was phenomenal, following a 32-game season with an astonishing 36–7 year in which he had five one-hitters, 56 consecutive scoreless innings and a 1.14 earned-run average.

Playing for Washington and for Griffith, who really didn't have the kitty, Sir Walter was hard-pressed. He wanted more than the $12,000 the Senators paid him. The Chicago Whales offered $16,000 and a $10,000 bonus for signing. Griff didn't have the scratch, and not even Ban Johnson would contribute league funds.

Wisely, Griffith went to Chicago to see Charley Comiskey. Why, Griff, should Commy help? "Because," said Griffith, "if Johnson signs with Tinker's club (the Whales), how would you like to see him pitching on the North Side next summer and drawing all your fans from the South Side?"

So Comiskey gave Griffith $10,000. Griff gave it to Johnson. The nice guy promptly used it to pay off a debt incurred by a brother in a new garage business with a worthless partner.

Indianapolis won the first pennant, Tinker's Whales won the second, and then the Federals filed suit under the Sherman Anti-Trust Act, charging all National and American League teams with an illegal instrument, the National Agreement. Approval of the suit could have been even worse than Sinclair's threat to move his Newark franchise to New York. For years the conclusion has been that as a fan as well as a jurist, tough-cookie Judge K. M. Landis didn't want to umpire the case.

Happily, he didn't have to. A compromise was reached shortly after the 1915 World Series. Even the most adamant antagonist, Ban Johnson, was forced to accept $385,000 worth of Federal League player contracts. (Forty-eight of 200 had contracts through 1916, 36 through 1917.)

Under terms of the treaty, the Wards were to receive $20,000 a year for 20 years to butter their bread. Sinclair, not yet caught in the Teapot Dome scandal, was promised $10,000 for each of 10 years. Pittsburgh got $10,000 for each of five years. Organized baseball also acquired the Federal League's ballparks in Newark and Brooklyn, two of eight hastily thrown up by the shortlived "major" league.

As Allen noted, "By dropping all claims to disputed players, the National and American moguls were spared the embarrassment of proving in court their contracts were sacrosanct, and the Fed players were thrown on the open market."

The Giants paid $35,000 for the poor man's Cobb, meaning Kauff, and the Yankees paid $22,500 for infielder Lee Magee. In addition, as part of the compromise, Weeghman was permitted to buy the Chicago Cubs. And Phil Ball, a curt St. Louis curmudgeon but a true sportsman, took over the Browns and Sportsman's Park.

The folding of the Feds had financial ramifications for players, teams, and even baseball history. Take, for example, Tris Speaker, one of the best ever as an outfielder and a batter. The prematurely Gray Eagle was a superstar whose salary had hiked up to $18,000 with the Boston Red Sox during the war with the Federals. When the Feds faded, even though he was the standout player of the 1912 and 1915 World Champions, Speaker was asked to take a 50 percent cut.

Speaker, expecting a raise, was shocked. Yet, aware that the owners held the upper hand, he refused a cut to less than $15,000. As middle man, manager Bill Carrigan, who would prove himself a sound banker later, arranged with Speaker and clubowner Joe Lannin for "Spoke" to work out with the Red Sox at Hot Springs, Arkansas. En route home in exhibition games, Speaker would play for a fixed fee. Carrigan hoped management and labor would get together.

They did, finally. At Brooklyn, two days before the season opened, Speaker hit a game-winning homer off lefthander Rube Marquard. Lannin was waiting for the outfielder in the runway and put his arm around him. "You win, Spoke," he said. "We'll sign when we get to Boston tomorrow."

Relieved, Speaker was packing in his hotel room hours later when he received a phone call from the lobby. Cleveland's general manager, Bob McRoy, was calling. Curious, Speaker invited him to the room. After generalities, McRoy asked, "How would you like to play for Cleveland, Tris?" Tris wouldn't. "You not only got a bad ball club," he said, "but you've got a bad baseball town."

McRoy hesitated. "I wish you didn't feel that way," he said. "We just made a deal for you."

Speaker protested, stubbornly insisting he wouldn't report to the Indians, remembering unhappily that when he'd wanted to go into baseball, he had to coax his mother for parental consent. The dear lady at Hubbard, Texas, Jennie Speaker, didn't want her boy to be bought or sold "like a longhorn steer."

Unfortunately, the deal already had been announced: Pitcher Sam Jones, infielder Fred Thomas, and $50,000 for Speaker. Spoke insisted he'd go to Cleveland only if he received $10,000 of the purchase money.

Reluctantly, only when Speaker threatened to hop a train for Hubbard, did Lannin agree to the $10,000 slice, a remarkable concession for the time. Speaker paid off immediately, winning the American League batting championship with a .386 average. Four years later he player-managed Cleveland to a pennant. He wound up living on the banks of Lake Erie even though he was in his native Texas when he died on a hunting trip. A good business man, he had reached $50,000 salary heights as medicine man of the Tribe.

The Federal League foldup contributed to the foldup, too, of one of baseball's most formidable teams, Connie Mack's Philadelphia Athletics. The A's were the top team in baseball the first 14 years of this century. It also had a side effect on the 1919 Black Sox scandal, from which eight members of the Chicago White Sox were barred from baseball for having thrown the World Series because of salary discontent.

Trying to compete with the Feds, whose inroads caused a temporary salary spiral, Mack found that interest in the A's had paled at the box office because of six pennants over a 12-year period, including four of the last five. When the proud Athletics were swept in four straight by the lightly regarded Boston Braves in the 1914 World Series, Mack and associates were financially strapped. Also, two of the famous manager's top players jumped to the Federal League for '15.

Baseball's then winningest left-handed pitcher, Eddie Plank, went to the St. Louis Feds after posting a 321–192 (.630) American League record, including 15–7 in 1914. Similarly, Albert (Chief) Bender, Mr. Mack's money-game righthander, 17–3 in '14 as part of a 210–128 career (.621), went to the "third major league" club at Baltimore.

Perhaps hurt as well as unhappy over the Series embarrassment and the A's rocky financial situation, Mack was determined to sell talent and to rebuild. As Ban Johnson, an admirer of Mack, told the *St. Louis Post-Dispatch* in a first-person sum-up series of his career, Connie also misjudged the foe. Until then, traveling on off-days, the skinny ex-catcher had been a one-man scouting genius, but, Johnson recalled, other clubs began to scout more aggressively.

So if the venerable man who would serve a half-century as A's owner-manager thought he could tear down and rebuild rapidly, he was wrong. The Athletics finished in last place seven successive seasons. Not until Mack and associates began to buy top talent, notably a battery of Lefty Grove from Baltimore and catcher Mickey Cochrane from Portland, were they able to make a comeback. Three successive pennants and two World Championships resulted, 1929–31, before Depression and poor attendance once again prompted Mr. Mack to sell stars.

The superstar who was missed most in the breakup and breakdown of the Philadelphia Americans in 1915 was Eddie Collins, the sharp hitting, slick fielding, base stealing second baseman. Cocky Collins, a graduate of Columbia University, was one of the few players who, like Tris Speaker, profited from a player sale.

When Johnson learned that Mack proposed to sell Collins, arguably the greatest second baseman ever, the American League founder wanted New York to have him. (Wisely, because the AL was trying to break John McGraw's National League monopoly in the Big Apple.) To Johnson's dismay, new owners of the Yankees, née Highlanders, felt no ballplayer was worth the cost of $50,000. Later, of course, in the purchase of Babe Ruth and the rape of other Red Sox talent, Colonel Jacob Ruppert spent money like an early day George Steinbrenner.

Collins, married to a Philadelphian and crushed by the sale, wanted mostly to stay in Philly, but, second, to go to Boston. Johnson, aware that Lannin's club was good enough to win a pennant, which it did in 1915 with Ruth, Speaker, etc., opted instead for Chicago. After all, there was the Federal League and Joe Tinker managing the Whales.

Although Comiskey would emerge later as a miser in the Black Sox matter, Commy knew talent and a potentially tough situation. To go to Chicago, Johnson already had promised Collins $5000 out of league funds. Now, Cocky demanded—and got—a five-year contract from Comiskey for $15,000 a year. Uh-huh, and a $10,000 bonus to sign and, oh, yes, Mr. Johnson, what about that $5000 from the league?

But that was only if he merely would consider the White Sox and—. Collins was adamant. So Johnson, as he told John E. Wray and J. Roy Stockton of the *Post-Dispatch,* signed his "personal check" to the second base slicker for $5000 more.

Collins immediately turned his talents to help the White Sox on a stepping stone to a pennant and World Championship. They were third in 1915, second in '16, and won it all in '17, a year Eddie hit .409 in a six-game Series victory over the New York Giants. A smart, heady player, Cocky was at his best in the spotlight.

In the sixth (and final) game of the Series, Collins was on third base, Jackson on first. Hap Felsch hit the ball back to the pitcher. Aware that he'd have to feint a break for the plate, at least, to avoid a pitcher-to-shortstop-to-first-baseman double play, the fleet Collins faked for home, then, as pitcher Rube Benton threw to the plate, Eddie retreated toward third.

The quicksilver runner with the sleepy-looking brown eyes suddenly sparkled. He noticed the catcher Bill Rariden, after throwing to third baseman Heinie Zimmerman, had followed the ball up the line. Neither first baseman Walter Holke nor Benton, the pitcher, had backed up the catcher. Suddenly, halting his retreat, Collins reversed stride and burst for the plate, past Rariden. Zimmerman chased Collins all the way across the plate with the leading run in a 4–2 victory. Afterward, the unthinking tried to fit the dunce cap on Heinie.

Zim wouldn't have it. The Keystone Kop chase wasn't his fault. Classically, Zimmerman wailed, "Who 'n hell was I supposed to throw the ball to? Klem?" Klem, of course, was the plate umpire—Bill Klem.

Collins, missing much of the 1918 season, in which the Red Sox beat the Chicago Cubs in a hastily arranged World Series, came back in '19, the year of the "trouble," as the Irish might put it.

That $15,000 salary, hefty at that time and more than double Jackson's $6000 and other White Sox pay, was part of the problem. Some of the cruder characters didn't like the confident, educated second baseman, anyway. It didn't help, either, to learn through the scuttlebutt that Cincinnati's Eddie Roush, a star centerfielder and batter, yet no Jackson, was paid $10,000.

Part of the seeds of discontent that flowered unhandsomely in October was failure to understand that many ball clubs had lost money in 1918, a season shortened to Labor Day by a work-or-else order from the government. The war-worried public even stayed away from the World Series.

So salaries generally were tight in 1919 at a time of outrageous inflation, notably lack of rent controls as Johnny Doughfoot came marching home. (After World War II, GI Joe got a break as Uncle Sam maintained a rent freeze immediately after the war.) So players after WWI felt the pinch in the pocket even more. By the time Comiskey paid off with raises in 1920—Jackson's salary, for example, was increased 50 percent to $9000—the damage was done, i.e., the Black Sox scandal.

The salaries paid all of the White Sox were much higher in 1920, the year the whistle was blown on them in late September when Comiskey no longer could ignore charges and suspicions. So 1920 became a significant season, other than for the elimination of the spitter and other foreign substances and the use of an improved, whiter ball. It was the year Babe Ruth moved from the Red Sox to the New York Yankees, changing hunks of baseball history larger than the figurative and literal size of the Babe himself.

By even dollar standards then, the $150,000 and a loan of $300,000, given by Ruppert and the Yankees to theatrical operator Harry Frazee for Ruth was a bargain for New York. After all, a great pitcher with an 89–46 record and an ERA barely above 2.0 for four-plus pitching seasons, not to mention a 3–0 record and 0.87 in three World Series, the Babe had displayed uncommon batting ability.

In 1918, for instance, although appearing in just 95 games, 20 of them as a pitcher, he tied for the American League in home runs with 11. And in '19, batting .322 in 130 games, 17 of them pitching, the outfielder hit well. More significantly, driving in 112 runs, he set a new major league record with 29 homers.

The purchase price, therefore, was not nearly so staggering as the $250,000 and a player (shortstop Lyn Lary) the Red Sox gave Washington for shortstop-manager Joe Cronin in the Depression depths after the 1934 season. Yet Ruth alone did more for one franchise than any player, before or since.

Immediately, hitting an astonishing 54 homers for the Yankees then, playing at the rival Giants' Polo Grounds, the Babe and the Judge, meaning scowling jurist K. M. Landis as baseball's first commissioner, sugar-coated for the public the sour taste of the Black Sox scandal. The Babe drove in 176 runs in 142 games, batting .376.

A year later, he upped his average to .378, his RBIs to 170 and his record homer total to 59. The Yankees won their first pennant and lost the World Series to their New York rivals, the Giants. But they already had become the first big league team to draw 1,000,000 at home—

and on the road, too — and, as a result, were pressed to get out of the Polo Grounds by a jealous foe, John McGraw. The Yankees used their profits to build Yankee Stadium.

The oddly shaped ball park, opened in 1923 in The Bronx, became almost a national shrine. Ruth's first year there, he hit .393, drove in 130 runs and hit 41 homers, a low total for the "Sultan of Swat," as the press box poets dubbed him. The Yankees won their first World Championship and dominated the major leagues for the next 30 years.

Ruth was not alone, of course, because immediately behind him in the batting order, beginning daily in 1925 until his dramatic death after amyotrophic lateral sclerosis sidelined him in 1939, was a powerful hometown first baseman, Lou Gehrig. Larrupin' Lou was a home run hitter, too, and a most productive RBI man who played 2130 consecutive games, a streak that became as ironic as his nickname — "Iron Horse" — when he left the lineup one day and never returned.

To maintain the continuity of Yankee success, a year after Ruth retired and shortly before Gehrig's fatal disease, the Yankees "lucked" into their next superstar, Joe DiMaggio, a standout with the San Francisco Seals of the Pacific Coast League. DiMaggio had an injured knee, one from which the Chicago Cubs balked at a $25,000 price even though given a look-see opportunity.

The Yankees took the chance and wound up in 1936 with a great batting and defensive outfielder. Just as DiMaggio decided to quit prematurely in 1951 because of persistent heel problems aggravated by a back condition, a pittance bonus to a kid from Commerce, Oklahoma, paid off in arrival of another A-1 talent, Mickey Mantle. The continuity of talent brought steady success.

But it all began because Frazee sold Babe Ruth to the Yankees in 1920 and also sent to the Stadium pitchers Carl Mays, Herb Pennock, Waite Hoyt, shortstop Everett Scott and third baseman Joe Dugan. These men — en toto! — produced the springboard to success with five pennants and three World Championships in eight years. With cash-sale impetus and one of the first and best farm systems, the Yanks won 31 pennants and 21 World Championships over a 43-year period through 1964.

Subsequently, with a more recent willingness to spend heavily by George Steinbrenner in the free-agent market, the Yankees have won four more pennants and two championships, but, obviously, Bowie Kuhn, voted out in 1984 after 15 productive seasons as commissioner, established a stand to avoid a situation similar to Boston's after World War I. Kuhn overruled Charles O. Finley's sale of top Oakland players who had contributed to three straight championships, 1972–74.

(Oakland is the transplanted Philadelphia Athletics' franchise, by way of Kansas City. When Connie Mack couldn't afford a second round of champions, forced by lack of funding and the Depression to break up his 1929–30–31 pennant-winners, Mack sold leftfielder Al Simmons, centerfielder Mule Haas, and third baseman Jimmy Dykes to Chicago. Catcher Mickey Cochrane became player-manager immediately at Detroit. Highlighted players sold to Boston were pitcher Lefty Grove and first baseman Jimmy Foxx.)

Finley, taking advantage of first-round choices in the revised baseball draft and a willingness to pay bonuses for talent exposed by good scouting, soured suddenly on his players. After losing pitching star Jim (Catfish) Hunter to free agency in an unexpected decision by arbitrator Peter Seitz—Hunter felt that Finley had not lived up to deferred agreement in a contract—the Oakland owner angrily sought to unload his superior athletes.

However, when Finley tried in June 1976, to sell three top players for $3,500,000, Kuhn voided the deal. The commissioner insisted that sale of relief ace Rollie Fingers and outfielder Joe Rudi to Boston for $1,000,000 each and pitching star Vida Blue to the Yankees was "not in the best interests of baseball." Court cases uphold the commissioner's authority and also his judgment in turning down sale of Blue to Cincinnati in the fall of '76 for minor league first baseman Dave Revering and $1,750,000 in cash.

Seeking to retain reasonable player balance within the leagues and to avoid traumatic disruption of franchises weakened overnight, Kuhn urged more players and less money in deals. He set an arbitrary $400,000 guideline as a cash maximum in a player transaction.

Summing up his findings in the case of Blue, ultimately dealt to Kansas City, Kuhn focused a viewpoint with which we agree, particularly having seen the old St. Louis Browns stay alive only by selling outstanding players, thereby lessening the club's victory chances.

Said Kuhn in January 1978, "The proposed assignment would send Vida Blue, an established star pitcher, from Oakland to Cincinnati. Cincinnati is one of the strongest clubs in its division of the National League. In the last six years the National League West championship has been won only by the Dodgers and the Reds—two times by the Dodgers and four times by the Reds. In two of the last three years, the Reds have won the world championship. . . . The proposed assignment would also worsen the competitive position of the Oakland club by making this (already) weak team even weaker. . . ."

For years, the rich did get richer and the poor poorer among ball clubs, especially before Branch Rickey came up with the grow-your-own farm system. Previously, the St. Louis Cardinals, a team of little talent and less money, floundered annually.

A problem was that even if a person scouted well, as Rickey did himself and through the eyes of early talent hunter Charley Barrett, a young player signed and shipped to a minor-league club for development would be sold often enough then to another big league team, a higher bidder. Minor league franchises, independently operated, relied largely on sale of players to survive. Few showed loyalty to the club which first assigned a young player to the minor league team.

So Rickey prevailed on owner Sam Breadon, an automobile dealer who had been caught up in a swell of civic pride, to plow into B. R.'s farm system brainchild the money ($350,000) that was realized from sale of the Cardinals' old ball park, Robison Field, for location of a St. Louis public high school. Breadon, a Scotch-sipping, barber-shop-singing Democrat, formed a winning Odd Couple with Rickey, a tee-totaling, psalm-singing, evangelistic Republican.

The results were dramatic. In 1920 the Cardinals bought a piece of the Houston Texas League franchise, then purchased the Fort Smith, Arkansas, franchise in the Western League. By 1926, largely a result of home-grown talent, the Cardinals had won their first pennant.

Through the next 20 years St. Louis won nine pennants and six World Championships, no longer having to bid for players against National League rivals New York, Chicago, and Pittsburgh. Followed earliest by the alert Yankees of the American League, the Redbirds spread their wings. By World War II, they were affiliated with 30 farm teams, owning outright half of them, including the most significant—Rochester, New York; Columbus, Ohio; Houston, Texas; and Sacramento, California.

The capsheaf of conquest came in 1942 when the Cardinals won at least one half or both halves of every significant pennant race in the minors. In addition, rallying, the St. Louis Swifties, as New York cartoonist Willard Mullin had nicknamed a young, rapid-running team, won 106 of 154 games. They finished two games ahead of Brooklyn.

One of the St. Louis "farm hands" waiting patiently then was Robert (Bud) Blattner, who at 16 had been a world's doubles table tennis champion. Blattner, a great basketball player, tennis player, and utility infielder for the majors, became a topflight broadcaster. He summed up the baseball situation years later. Smiling, Buddy said: "I honestly believe you could have taken our top talent in the minors—Sacramento, Rochester, Columbus, and Houston—and finished third (1942) in the National League behind the Cardinals and Dodgers."

St. Louis's decline resulted largely when Breadon, who had achieved 78 percent ownership, dismissed Rickey. Rickey went to Brooklyn and quickly gave the black player his first legitimate big league chance in 1947 (Jackie Robinson). The Dodgers, also quickly tapping another

Hall of Famer, catcher Roy Campanella, and a standout pitcher, Don Newcombe, replaced the Cardinals as National League leaders.

Breadon, before selling the ball club after the 1947 season, sold what he regarded as a surplus of talent. For instance, the Boston Braves, a rag-tag team since an unexpected pennant in 1914, won under new ownership in '48 with so many former St. Louis players that they were called the "Cape Cod Cardinals."

The farm system concept, often derided as "chain-gang baseball," an oblique reference to some southern states' penal colonies, was not liked by many, including baseball's first commissioner, Judge Landis, a bone in Branch Rickey's throat, and vice-versa.

Unlike Kuhn later, Landis hadn't acted with the Yankees' cash-on-the-barrel climb in the early 1920s, though he did insist on creation of a part stopgap, urging installation of a rule that would prohibit exchange of players after a mid-June trading deadline except for waiver-price exchanges. The Judge acted after the St. Louis Browns protested New York's late-season purchase of Boston third baseman Joe Dugan in 1922. Both contending clubs' weakest position that season was the same — third base.

Waiver-price exchanges did enable a lower club to have priority of purchase in the league from which a player was moved. Over the years, however, clubs would rely on subterfuge or a gentleman's agreement to slip a player out of one major league to the other, as witness the Yankees' sale of right-handed pitcher Hank Borowy to the Chicago Cubs in the summer of 1945. The $100,000 purchase of Borowy, who had a 10–5 record with New York, was a bargain for Chicago. There, he was 11–2, aiding the Cubs to their last pennant until the 1984 half-loaf, i.e., a division title at Wrigley Field.

By then, as described earlier, the Yankees had achieved dominating stature, interrupted only briefly by World War II and by the death of brewer-sportsman Jake Ruppert. Successor Larry MacPhail, undoubtedly raising money for the three-man inexpensive takeover of the Yankees from Ruppert's tax-troubled estate, contravened the old damyankee custom by selling not buying.

Actually, acquisition of Babe Ruth had done almost as much for opposing ballplayers — and his teammates — as for the sizable symbol. When the Bambino — a favorite nickname hung on him by Italian admirers — hit so many home runs, New York and elsewhere, he helped the box offices of all ball clubs. His soaring salaries aided other players, as pitching star and former drinking partner Waite Hoyt recalled amusingly. Said Hoyt, later a baseball-broadcasting institution at Cincinnati: "I told my kids at bedtime, 'Thank God, thank Mommy, thank Daddy — and thank Babe Ruth!'"

In the good times of the Roaring Twenties, salaries climbed generally, though there could be occasional disturbing exceptions, such as at St. Louis when Rogers Hornsby, after having player-managed the Cardinals to their first pennant in 1926, sought a three-year contract at $50,000, a whopping amount then. Owner Breadon not only had an abiding aversion ever to becoming poor again, but he hadn't liked the blunt backtalk of the tough Texan. Aware of Hornsby's pride, Breadon stubbornly offered only a one-year contract at $50,000.

Hornsby prickled his cactus pride, refusing to sign. The feeling between the two men had been colder than one of Breadon's Pierce-Arrow auto agency engines on Christmas Day. The former New York bank clerk and St. Louis grease monkey was a proud man. Hornsby had startled his boss down the stretch in September. Unable to cancel an exhibition game The Rajah wanted aborted in New Haven, Connecticut, to rest his weary troops, Breadon made the tactical mistake of telling the Texan after a losing game.

Hornsby's vulgar answer to the boss was best described with a great writer's skill when J. Roy Stockton of the *St. Louis Post-Dispatch* mentioned that the manager "recommended an utterly impossible disposition of the game." The clubowner left in an unforgiving huff.

So Hornsby was dealt to the New York Giants in December 1926, an incredible deal considering a five-year *average* of more than .400 through 1925 and a pennant-winning and championship season in '26. Irate St. Louis fans festooned Breadon's home and auto agency with black crepe paper, and the city Chamber of Commerce even denounced him in a written resolution.

Worse, hard-nosed Hornsby wanted $120,000 for the 1000 shares of stock he had acquired for $45,000 from an angry Branch Rickey when he succeeded Rickey as field manager, Memorial Day, 1925. Breadon, who had endorsed a note for Hornsby at the time, offered only $80,000 for the stock. An impasse existed. That is, until Judge Landis got into the act.

The commissioner wasn't about to let a guy play second base for one club when he owned stock in another. So, ultimately, he called together National League clubowners and got each to ante up $5000 to meet the difference between Hornsby's asking price and Breadon's offer.

With the Giants, Hornsby became a $40,000-a-year second baseman and captain under John McGraw, but, even though he batted .361 in 155 games, hitting 26 homers and driving in 125 runs, he lasted just one season at the Polo Grounds.

Another future Hall of Famer, Frank Frisch, obtained along with a rinky-dink right-handed pitching veteran named Jimmy Ring, took himself and Breadon off the spot marked "X." The Fordham Flash had his flashiest, most spectacular season in 1927. The cat-like base stealer batted .337 in 153 games despite late-season injuries. He hit 10 homers, drove in 78 runs, and stole 48 bases, a high total at the time. His far-cruising fielding set a record that still stands for most chances by a second baseman, 1037.

Frisch, player and then manager with the Cardinals through 1938, reflected the salary situation of the times. The Flash's player pay reached $28,000, a solid sum for the good times of the era, but he was down to $18,500 as player-manager by the time his Gas House Gang, as tough as the financial times, won the World Championship in 1934.

Although he no longer was as outstanding as a player, still he was field foreman, too, doing the work of two, in effect, for one salary. But, again, because pay was shriveled in the period of high unemployment, any attempt now to sneer at salaries then is a misjudgment.

Actually, if the approximate 10–to–1 difference between 1934 and 1984 in the buying power of a dollar when it was king-sized to peewee pay, from virtually no taxation to as high as 50 percent, the $72,000 minimum rookie pay guarantee in '88 is little larger than the $3000 paid, as mentioned, to St. Louis's freshman battery of Paul Dean and Bill DeLancey in '34.

The difference now, obviously, is a result of arbitration, permitted after the third season, and the ability of big leaguers to play out their options after five seasons with one club or 10 years in the majors. Those one-sided aspects of free agency resulted in dramatic pay increases beginning in the mid-1970s and spiraling like a rocket out of orbit.

As detailed by Murray Chass, enterprising baseball writer of *The New York Times,* the salary assault, begun as clubs sought to avoid losing players they no longer could shackle with the reserve clause, reached promising heights in 1977 for the daffy financial future.

After 24 players played out their options the first year, 89 went the same route in '77, causing a steep pay hike, individually and collectively. Back in 1969, after two successive pennants, St. Louis had achieved the first $1,000,000 payroll. Rightfielder Roger Maris, obtained from the Yankees, drew down $75,000 or three more than the total top nine paid Frisch's merry men of the Gas House Gang in '34.

By 1977, the Philadelphia Phillies had the top team payroll of $3,497,900, an average of $139,916. By contrast, St. Louis, which had peaked first past $1,000,000, was $1,782,675 — 12th! By 1985, at a payroll near $6,000,000, St. Louis had dipped to No. 19!

By further contrast, in '86, the average big leaguer's salary was $350,000. A far cry, indeed, from 1938 when Enos Slaughter broke in with the Cardinals at $2400, a sum kicked up to the equivalent of $3600 a season in June when nosey newspapermen came to the 21-year-old kid's rescue. Yet as late or, more accurately, as recently as 1946, when World War II had inched up the standard of living a bit, Brooklyn's rifle-armed rookie rightfielder, Carl Furillo, said he was paid only $3750.

Although ticket prices had soared and, most definitely, national and local television rights — radio, too — veteran baseball men calculated that if the reserve clause had not been cancelled, *TOP-SALARY* players would have gone into 1986 with pay little more than the $300,000 *AVERAGE*. Before free agency in '76, only Richie Allen and Hank Aaron were barely over $200,000. If so, the $1,000,000–to–$2,000,000 blockbuster pay, including long-term contracts that seemed to lead to some indolence, more time in sick bay, and conserved effort, would still be in the future — if at all.

Back in 1934, Babe Ruth's last season with the Yankees, when the Babe dipped to $35,000, sports editor Alan J. Gould of the *Associated Press* listed approximate salaries behind the Babe's:

Bill Terry, Giants, $30,000; Al Simmons, White Sox, $27,500; Lou Gehrig, Yankees, $23,000; Chuck Klein, Cubs, $22,000; Mickey Cochrane, Tigers, $20,000; Joe Cronin, Senators, $20,000; Jimmy Foxx, Athletics, $20,000; and Frank Frisch, Cardinals, $20,000. (As mentioned, Frisch actually was paid $18,500. Foxx also said he never got 20 grand.)

Players struggled then for the equivalent of a big buck, even the great ones. For instance, in 1937 when Joe DiMaggio hit .346 his second full season with the Yankees, driving in 167 runs with a league-leading 46 homers, Joe Dee wanted a pay raise to $45,000. The Bronx Bombers' general manager, burly, bushy-browed Ed Barrow, who had glared down DiMaggio to $15,000 when the graceful outfielder asked for $25,000 after his rookie season, did a slow burn.

"Young man," said Barrow, "do you know how long Lou Gehrig has been with this club? Well, I'll tell you — 13 years — and do you know how much he gets? $41,000. What have you got to say to that?"

DiMaggio, a shy guy who became a smooth senior citizen, was not exactly tongue-tied. "I'd say, Mr. Barrow," said DiMag, putting it quite well, "that Gehrig is badly underpaid and. . . ."

Barrow almost blew the great athlete out of his office, and, after a holdout, DiMaggio got no more than what the club wanted to pay, 25 grand. Fact is, by the time he hit his historic 56 straight games in 1941, Barrow suggested a paycut of "only" $2500 — the war, y'know, my boy — but DiMag muscled a hike to $43,750 before putting on military khaki a year later.

Whether DiMaggio actually became the first $100,000 player is a question. Fact is, Joe Dee might never have received that much because his best years were before World War II, prior to the heel spur and bad back that forced this proud superstar to hang it up when he wasn't even 37 (1951).

Highest paid right after World War II, when GI Joe and his Jane had fun and made families, probably was Bob Feller, pitching for Bill Veeck, to whom every night was New Year's Eve, at Cleveland and elsewhere. Feller incorporated himself. "Ro-Fel Inc.," Rapid Robert called himself. He was a confident, cocky, capable pitcher who was paid $80,000 a year by Veeck after a 26–15 season, 2.18 and record 348 strikeouts his first full year back from service, 1946. Watching Feller organize white-and-black teams for post-season tours and show business acumen far removed from that farm country at Van Meter, Iowa, it's hard to realize that he ever would encounter difficult financial times, but he did.

Probably the first $100,000 player, though none then could approach Babe Ruth's $80,000 salary at the outset of the Depression, was Ted Williams, who lost three seasons to military service in World War II and almost two more as a jet pilot for the Marines in the Korean conflict. Williams, a .344 career hitter, apparently was up to $125,000 from his ever-loving boss and friend, Tom Yawkey, the free-spending sportsman who tried to turn the Red Sox into the Gold Sox after he bought them in the bowels of the bad times.

At 39 years old in 1957, Teddy Ballgame, as Williams called himself, batted .388 in 132 ball games, meaning he was nearly a .400 hitter near the end of his career as he had been at the virtual beginning (1941). Williams once reportedly turned down $300,000 for a three-year contract offered by the brothers Pasquel to jump to the Mexican League.

The man who became the first full-fledged $100,000 played in the National League, Stan Musial, also put his loyalty and honor ahead of the dollar sign in 1946. At the time, skipping to the third season of a three-year contract after one in the Navy, Musial was making $13,500. Over the years, Sam Breadon got nervous-in-the-service when a player approximated $15,000.

Representing brother Jorge, Bernardo Pasquel dumped $75,000 in cash on a bed in St. Louis's Fairgrounds Hotel, close by Sportsman's Park, and offered a five-year contract for $125,000 to the son of a poor Polish immigrant. Musial turned it down. Moving to first base in mid-season to fill a weakness, Musial batted .365, winning the second of his three Most Valuable Player Awards, as the Cardinals nipped the Brooklyn Dodgers for the pennant and upset Williams and the Boston Red Sox in the World Series.

By August, Cardinals' manager Eddie Dyer convinced clubowner

Sam Breadon to give Musial a $5000 bonus. When the Cardinals drew more than 1,000,000 for the first time in 1946, Musial sought a healthy salary hike to $37,000. He hand-wrestled Breadon to $31,000, en route to the historic first National League six-figure salary a decade later.

With a signing bonus, veteran slugger Hank Greenberg, released by Detroit, reportedly received $100,000 in his one season at Pittsburgh, where he helped young Ralph Kiner turn a left-field corner called "Greenberg Gardens" into "Kiner's Korner." But it was Kiner, twice author of more than 50 homers a season, whose salary high Musial sought to break after a seventh batting title in 1957.

So Stan the Man and general manager Bing Devine agreed on $91,000, at which point one of this book's authors, needled more than once by Gussie Busch for spending the brewery's money as if it were his own, phoned Devine. After all, Musial was 37 and wouldn't the "old man" (Busch) like to have the distinction of paying the first $100,000 salary in the National League?

Before you could say August Adolphus Busch Jr., the gravel-voiced, baronial sportsman got Musial on the phone and rasped, "Forget that $91,000, Stan, we're going to make it 100."

Times then, certainly, were different and more paternalistic than earlier or later. (Williams *insisted* on a salary cut after a bad season, 1959.) Even more than immediately after World War I, the climate following WWII was for better pay and, in addition, the Pasquels' threat to major league baseball contracts led to salary hikes—and the pension plan.

By May 1946, a Boston lawyer named Robert Murphy came within a close clubhouse vote at Pittsburgh of making his idea for an American Baseball Guild more than just small talk. Pirate players almost failed to play before a full house at Forbes Field. At the last minute, right-handed veteran Truett (Rip) Sewell slapped a ball defiantly into his glove and said, "I'm going out to the mound and I hope eight others will take the field with me."

Pressured into improving working conditions, the clubs urged each team to submit suggestions, omitting, of course, the reserve clause, which, if only naïvely, many players thought was integral to baseball's existence, too.

One by one, clubs voted to ask for (1) more meal money, (2) a $5000 minimum salary, (3) buses from trains to hotels and ball parks rather than hit-or-miss taxi cabs, (4) club responsibility for handling players' personal luggage, and—.

Nice little improvements, easily met, but with the help of the Cardinals' longtime trainer, colorful Harrison J. (Doc) Weaver, an osteopath who was the Redbirds' muscle-and-morale man from 1927 until his death in '55, St. Louis shortstop Marty Marion conceived the capital idea—a pension plan.

Marion's concept, spelled out in the *St. Louis Post-Dispatch* and then given good coverage nationally by the *Associated Press*, called for (1) matching financial contributions by players and ball clubs; (2) profits from the annual All-Star game; (3) radio receipts from the All-Star game and World Series, and if necessary, a midsummer series of exhibitions between natural rivals, i.e., Yankees and Giants, Cardinals and Browns, Phillies and Athletics, Red Sox and Braves, etc. The goal: A $100 a month pension at age 50 for 10-year men.

Immediately, players elsewhere saw the benefit in the plan. Club officials Larry MacPhail, Tom Yawkey, Phil Wrigley, and Sam Breadon applauded the effort. Player representatives were established for each club, setting up the current Major League Ball Players' Association, and the New York Yankees' Johnny Murphy and Brooklyn's Fred (Dixie) Walker became the first league player reps.

With players contributing $2 a day originally, the clubs' matching it and, as suggested, receipts earmarked for the pension, the touch-and-go necessary was for the World Series opponents to agree foregoing the $150,000 radio receipts. The parks were small (St. Louis's Sportsman's Park and Boston's Fenway Park), so receipts would be low. They were, the smallest shares since 1918.

The Cardinals agreed. With unanimity required, a couple of older baseball citizens of the Red Sox balked, jeopardizing the plan. But, probably accounting for one of the many reasons Yawkey is the sole modern day clubowner in the Hall of Fame, the sportsman shamed the Sox into going along. Yawkey said he'd pick up for any who didn't contribute.

So effective for players, coaches, and trainers on major league rosters in September 1946, pension credits were assembled. Back service, i.e., years of big league experience previous to '46, spiraled the expenses. As a result, too hastily his critics thought, baseball's second commissioner, A. B. (Happy) Chandler, sold a new windfall, television rights. Happy meant well, they said, but—.

Meanwhile, the Philadelphia Phillies, unaccustomed since 1915 to running up a championship flag, almost kicked over the financial traces by threatening to decline to give up the modest early TV World Series shares (1950) for the pension. But the pension prevailed, aided by third commissioner Ford C. Frick and his assistant, another former sportswriter, Charley Segar. The pension, wobbling on rubber legs, got over its sick spell and grew into a powerful giant.

Initially, when the players were hoping for that 100-bucks-a-month-for-10-year-men, the pension virtually exploded. Not only were managers included, but under pressure by the ballplayers' association, years of vested service were lowered. First, five-year players were eligible to receive pensions at a reduced rate at age 50, with automatic payment at age 65. Next, four years were the minimum years required for eligibility. Third, as payments increased from the soaring television fund, 45 became the minimum age for eligibility.

Through the growth of TV contributions to the fund and prospering investments, plus efforts made by executive director Marvin Miller of the players' association, the pension plan soared to a staggering government ceiling in 1987 — $93,000 for an active participant of 10 years at age 65.

An incredible change from the $2400-a-year pay ceiling at the turn of the century and one of the cruelest clauses in the old-fashioned contract, the 10-day release notification. A player would be paid off for only 10 days when he was released. Now, if a man is on a major league roster opening day and out the next day, he receives a full year's pay.

Shortly before ballplayers delayed the opening of the 1972 season with a nine-day strike, which seemed frivolous, ill-conceived, and fruitless subsequently, St. Louis catcher Ted Simmons took a forward step for the ballplayers. Annoyed at a contract raise, stalled in negotiations with club president August A. Busch Jr., Simmons did not sign his contract. Under the reserve clause, the Cardinals renewed his contract "for one year" at a 10 percent pay hike when, previously, ball clubs could invoke a maximum cut of 20 percent. That, in itself, was a concession gained over earlier, much more sizable automatic deductions.

Keeping his mouth shut and his head high, Simmons became the first player to perform without a signed contract. (Back in 1930, the New York Giants' Edd Roush, an outfielder, held out the entire season.) By mid-season, with Simmons hitting and playing well, the Cardinals effected a salary compromise by persuading the catcher to sign a two-year contract.

By then, the civil liberties' movement was taking figurative swipes at the ball and the ball game. The signs of the times: Aggressive players' representative Miller and an arbitrator named Peter Seitz.

The renewal sentence "for one year" began to be understood for what it said, not what it meant. One season, not a lifetime. In 1975 pitcher Andy Messersmith of the Los Angeles Dodgers did not sign at all. Nor did Baltimore lefthander Dave McNally. Arbitrator Seitz interpreted literally the provisions of 10–A in the players' contract — the right of renewal for "one year."

Seitz said Messersmith had served that one year. A federal court upheld him. Therefore, a free agent, Messersmith sold his services for a profit to Ted Turner and the Atlanta Braves. Angrily, baseball dismissed Seitz, a 70-year-old arbitrator for 40 years. Said Seitz, "I'm not a new Abraham Lincoln freeing the slaves. I wasn't striking a blow at the reserve clause. This decision does not destroy baseball. My own feeling is that the problems of the reserve ought to be worked out by the parties in collective bargaining. . . . "

Uh-huh, but not satisfactorily—at least for the clubowners.

When no compromise could be reached, management locked out players in 1976, declining to open gates for spring training. Interested players trained on their own and at their own expense. Many thought Commissioner Bowie Kuhn ordered camps open in mid-March at a time management felt players would capitulate to a more meaningful compromise.

For one, Richard A. Meyer, a member of baseball's executive council and president of Anheuser-Busch, had urged an effort to effect a compromise with the renewal clause before it could be beaten. In '76, relying on many years' experience in negotiating with labor, he urged against approving binding arbitration.

The compromise after long haggling produced provisions by which (1) players could not seek mediation until two years in the majors; (2) players could request to be traded after five seasons; (3) an untraded player could become a free agent after his sixth major league season; or (4) a traded player could decline trading to certain teams after five years with one club or a total of 10 in the majors.

The killer provided for binding arbitration after a player's second season. The arbitrator could not mediate. He could not interpret or effect a one-penny compromise.

If, for instance, a young relief ace named Bruce Sutter, earning $75,000 from the Chicago Cubs, asked for a whopping increase to $700,000 and the Cubs countered with a handsome hike to $350,000, the arbitrator couldn't even split the drastic difference. Sutter got his big boost and, as a result, was dealt to St. Louis, then zoomed to an astronomical $43,000,000 for a 30-year tie-up with Atlanta.

The race to the monetary moon was off. The players' nine-day strike in 1972 really served nothing except to deprive Boston of a chance at an American League Eastern Division title won by Detroit, which played and won one more game in the fragmented schedule. Nine years later, out for two months from near mid-June to August 10, the players effected a slight compromise by which top talent opting for free agency would require the other club to receive a lesser replacement.

That costly strike overall was felt especially by Cincinnati and St. Louis in the National League. Taking advantage of club rankings at the time of the strike, Kuhn and the executive council split the season. Thickly populated areas with TV potential—the New York Yankees,

Oakland (San Francisco) A's, Los Angeles Dodgers, and Philadelphia Phillies—were assured of a playoff before the playoffs. As a result, Cincinnati and St. Louis, though leading overall for the bobtailed season, did not qualify because neither the Reds nor Redbirds finished first in either half of the gerrymandered season.

From regional to national, day to night, trains to planes, grass to carpets, from 16 cities wedded to franchises for a half-century to 28 over the more recent 25 years, baseball has changed, drastically and dramatically. Never more so, even with a sweeping bow to the Sultan of Swat, Babe Ruth, than in compensation paid to players—before and after their playing careers.

Doubtless, as baseball rounded third base figuratively in this century, the poorest peons in polyester now likely would become as wealthy as the richest of the old flannel set. Typically of the man who couldn't stand to finish second in anything, including use of a bush league bath tub, it was not the Babe himself, but his predecessor as the game's most influential player, Ty Cobb.

Cobb didn't live long enough to see free agency give him what he obviously would have liked most—the chance to tell clubowner Frank Navin at Detroit to stuff his Tigers—but the spirited Georgian went a lot farther even from his $1800 salary after his second major league season (1906) to the $70,000 he received at Philadelphia his last season (1928).

En route to superstardom, a legend at bat and on the bases, Ty Cobb became friends with the young president of a "different" soft drink in Atlanta and also was persuaded to join the purchasers of an automobile company built in Detroit by a Swiss race driver named Louis Chevrolet.

Tyrus Raymond Cobb put his money where teammates couldn't or wouldn't and, as a result, became what players couldn't dream of becoming until recent times. He bought and bought—and held and held—Coca-Cola and General Motors.

14
What Cy Saw

When we or others suggest that baseball really hadn't changed in the 20th century, coming across as T-R-A-D-I-T-I-O-N, enunciated by Russian Jewish immigrant Tevye in *Fiddler on the Roof,* we or they are talking broadly—too broadly.

Sure, settling on the final pitching distance in 1893 and then altering the core and quality of the ball and the size of ball parks stabilized the game. The size and shape of the bat, too, and the improvement in gloves.

But the point is that, as Tevye would chant whether sung by Zero Mostel or Herschel Bernardi on Broadway or by Israel's Topol in the movie, tradition has been shattered in many other ways. As a radio commercial for ice cream put it, in "subtle little differences."

For instance, if you're old enough to have played with the big boys or the little ones before the middle 1950s, you've witnessed many differences at both the major and minor league levels and especially in the peewee and prep level. Now, no kid risks ruin to a good glove, much more expensive than before 1954, because he simulates big leaguers by skimming his mitt beyond his playing position between innings.

Yet, until baseball barred any equipment from the field except for the bases, plate, and pitching mound, it was traditional to leave the playing glove on the field. In reflection, that was silly, potentially dangerous, yet there are no historic instances — in our review — to indicate a significant game having been won or lost because a fielder tripped over his rival's glove backing up for an infield fly or coming in for a short, looping outfield pop. None, again significantly, for a batted ball having struck, say, the second baseman's glove or sun glasses, often tucked inside the mitt, and skittered askew.

The tradition was foolish. More than one big leaguer had sun glasses destroyed "accidentally" by an angry foe stepping on the glove coming in or going out between innings. But the impact was worse among kids who slung gloves on hard, sunbaked, skinned fields, damaging the leather just so they could be like big leaguers.

The subtle little differences which changed tradition were planned early as a chapter in this book. So it was amusing and a reassurance of our plans when seeing a re-run of Jackie Robinson, playing himself in a movie made of his career in the early '50s, flipped his glove behind him after making a stop and an inning-ending throw to first base. Young viewers wondered why.

The rules' change in 1954 caused the old horizontal bat rack to disappear. Traditionally, bats fronted the dugout, ash by ash. Batters studying the supply did create an atmosphere of anticipation and tension, especially if it was a power hitter coming up in a dramatic situation or a pinch hitter emerging from the dugout to look over the lumber, as the crowd hooted or hollered, depending on whether he was friend or foe. But the move to vertical bat racks attached to one side of the dugout made such good sense. Why have catchers risk life or limb, which they did so often, when they charged over to a dugout chasing a pop foul? The old string of bats was like a banana peel, or worse, a booby trap for the spiked catcher or infielder trying to look for the ball more than where he was going.

The practicality of the 1954 rules' change against cluttering the playing field is so obvious that you wonder why it wasn't done earlier. Many an old-fashioned Mom or Dad — we used to call him Pop more in days gone by — must wonder now, too.

Tradition at times comes the hard way. Just as baserunners now are schooled from Day One to move up and touch the next base automatically, to avoid a Merkle mishap of 1908, catchers are coached early, when glancing up to locate a pop fly or foul, to fling away their masks with force and at a distance. They seek to avoid a duplication of misfortune experienced by the New York Giants' Hank Gowdy. "Golden-Rod," as they called Gowdy, tangled a foot on the mask he'd dropped in the 1924 World Series. The reprieved batter, Earl McNeely, then drove in the Series' winning run for Washington.

Tradition was upset twice more in the mid-'50s by policy more than by rule. At Cincinnati, where Matty Schwab had been a meticulous goundskeeper, manager Luke Sewell suggested that if it was wise to manicure an infield before a game, why not drag out the clods and the cleat marks midway through the contest? General manager Gabe Paul liked the idea of a slight interruption to help the concessions business. The pause that refreshes could be a bit longer.

So Cincinnati, home of the first professional ball club back in 1869 and annually given the distinction, like Washington, of beginning the big league season a day earlier, instituted the fifth-inning infield cleanup, now itself a latter day tradition.

About the same time, also at Crosley Field, where the Reds then played, an episode gave National League president Warren Giles an excuse to follow a policy set by some cities. As a result of too many photographers, New York and Chicago, particularly, in the National League had barred cameramen from the field. Now and then, but rarely, a photographer would get into a runner's way. For instance, one time George McQuinn of the old St. Louis Browns, rounding third base, bowled into a photographer. But, roving at ground level, even though new equipment permitted them to improve pictures from a distance, photographers were able to get closer and better views than from the stands.

One illustration is the famed photo of the St. Louis Browns' midget, perhaps baseball's greatest stunt perpetrated by Bill Veeck as a frosting-*out*-of-the-cake at the American League's 50th anniversary celebration in 1951. Veeck popped 3-foot 8-inch Eddie Gaedel onto the field, wearing No. 1/8 on his back. For posterity, a *St. Louis Post-Dispatch* photographer, Jack January, raced along the first-base line so that he could provide a cozy close-up of the little man wheedling a base on balls as a first-inning pinch hitter against Detroit lefthander Bob Cain.

In more recent years, permission for photographers to work on the field has been limited to an occasional American League town. The National League barred the practice after an episode in which Cincinnati manager Birdie Tebbetts challenged a decision made by umpire Bill Stewart.

Even from the height of the Cincinnati press box, it seemed that Wally Moon, playing center field for the Cardinals, had trapped a low line drive. Stewart, working at second base, jerked thumb up to indicate a catch sign, bringing out a waddling Tebbetts on a trot to protest. *Associated Press* photographer Gene Smith tagged along.

At second base, Tebbetts, a puckish psychology major from Providence College, shrilled at Stewart: "You blew it in the World Series, you blew it in the All-Star game, and you blew it tonight."

Stewart, a fellow New Englander who actually had helped Tebbetts as a kid, reacted as if the Reds' manager had touched a raw nerve, which he had. The nervy bench-jockey field foreman referred to a missed pickoff call Cleveland pulled on Boston catcher Phil Masi in the 1948 World Series. Also, in the 1954 All-Star game at Cleveland, when St. Louis's Red Schoendienst attempted to steal home, Schoendienst was tagged out even though the National League protested that Washington lefthander Dean Stone had balked on the pitch. Each time Stewart was the vulnerable umpire.

Hardly had the short, barrel-chested Stewart chased Tebbetts for his sarcastic smarts at Crosley Field when photographer Smith was on the field phone to the press box, relaying the wisecrack to newspaper colleagues. Writers dying for playing-field commentary couldn't wait to repeat Tebbetts' amusing line. The league was embarrassed for Stewart. So Giles barred photographers from the field. Alas, a loss!

Photographers not only disappeared from the playing field, but so did field announcers, much earlier except for Chicago's Wrigley Field, where Pat Pieper, a restaurant waiter dressed in dark brown, cap to shoes, as if a high-rent limousine chauffeur, held forth into the 1960s. Ultimately, they pushed the aged Pieper back up into the press box, where he delivered his lines with the shrill voice Cub fans had known since Tinker, Evers, and Chance were bearcats.

In flash-bulb photo history, Pieper's beaming phiz still surrounds Gabby Hartnett as the happy, Chicago manager trots home with the pennant-winning "homer in the gloamin'" in the final week of the 1938 season. And it was Hartnett himself who figured in another change in baseball tradition.

Previously whenever a cute chick, grand gaffer, or little kid could persuade a ballplayer to stop and sign from the field, autographing from the diamond was a common occurrence at the box seats. Suddenly, a Chicago newspaper displayed a photo of Hartnett signing for Al Capone's boy as the famed hoodlum sat surrounded by sober bodyguards.

Baseball's first commissioner, Judge Landis, called in Hartnett to censure him for his indiscretion. Gabby had the best word, if not the last one. "If you don't want me to talk to The Big Guy, Judge, *you* tell him," said Hartnett. So Landis barred autographing from the playing field, a policy relaxed only on occasion now.

The disappearance of the megaphone-toting field announcer began as far back as 1929 when the New York Giants installed the first public-address system in a big league park. Actually, the Jints went so far that day as to wire bulky umpiring veteran Cy Rigler with a microphone so that his ball-and-strike calls were audible.

Until then and in most places for some years thereafter, lineups and battery changes were provided by a man walking in foul territory with a giant megaphone, a super-sized version of the kind Rudy Vallee and other crooners used in dance halls and supper clubs.

In St. Louis, for instance, an ample and affable man named Jim Kelley waddled from the right-field pavilion to the bleacher corner in left field. Behind the plate, he would intone the batting order to the high reaches of the press box so that, really, only the writers and nearby customers would benefit from the official lineup. The far reaches had to be satisfied with the sparse battery of the visiting club and the Cardinals' or Browns.' The paid P.A. didn't come in at Sportsman's Park until 1936, partly a result of the press chiding management to get off its old-fangled derriere.

The Fourth Estate was an annoyance to management, too, particularly when broadcast baseball, revived after ownership feared it would destroy the game, permitted radio listeners to know more than paying patrons. For years, hand-operated scoreboards with metal numbers had no room for "hit" or "error" designations. Players didn't like to be "shown up," either. Yet the word was slipped over the ether.

Nursing their nickels and dimes, ball parks went to great lengths to camouflage the identity of players, numberless and with no names on their uniforms. They were identified only by what amounted to a secret code on the scoreboard. Clubs changed players' _scorecard_ numbers every few days so that, unless a person knew each player physically, the only clue was the scoreboard number as the batter stepped up to hit. And by the time the field announcer finished intoning a pinch hitter or relief pitcher in his foul pole to foul pole trek, the batter often was back in the dugout or on base and the pitcher in the dugout or headed for the shower.

This tradition, to be sure, was one of the foulest of the era and the least appealing, even nostalgically. The purpose of changing scorecard-scoreboard numbers every now and then was to foil maverick printers outside the park who "bootlegged" cards to spectators headed into the park, usually two for the price of one. A nickel earned. . . .

Although the _St. Louis Post-Dispatch_ photo files definitely show Jim Bottomley perched as a runner on first base in 1923, wearing a small-sized "5" on his left sleeve, as determined by eagle-eyed historian Cliff Kachline, team players' numbers really didn't come in until 1929. The New York Yankees did it, basically by batting order, which became the early trend.

The last to permit his players to be numbered, perhaps in penurious even more than patriarchal deference to the old you-can't-tell-'em-without-a-scorecard—and you couldn't, either, not most of them—

was kindly Connie Mack of the Philadelphia A's. Mr. Mack didn't give in until the early '30s. So, by marked contrast, the 1931 World Series was played with St. Louis numbered, Philly blank-jersey anonymous.

Not until a generation later, the first of the 1960s, were names displayed on the backs of uniform shirts. Showman promoter Bill Veeck of the Chicago White Sox began the practice, followed closely in the National League by Bing Devine, general manager of the St. Louis Cardinals. Devine was the first G. M. to have the P. A. announcer repeat the batting order throughout the game rather than merely announce hitters the first time around.

Veeck played a prominent part, too, in another element of the scoreboard, now so sophisticated through computer use and animation that the color-photoed, instant-replay, comic-character board will do just about everything to top Walt Disney's fanciful best. Veeck's scoreboard with the Chicago White Sox became as explosive as a spaceship takeoff, as versatile as famed cartoonist Al Capp's "Marryin' Sam" judge whippin' up a $5 weddin.'

In the beginning, scoreboards were rough and rudimentary, small white-on-black instruments on which a kid or older fan simply draped black run-scoring figures, top and bottom, on each half-inning of the game played. Former commissioner Bowie Kuhn was a boyhood scoreboard operator at Washington.

For years, at best, big league ball parks listed only scores of the four games played in that club's league, a result of behind-the-scenes activity. A scoreboard operator or two, climbing ladders in the backdrop, would use information gained off a Western Union stockmarket-type ticker tape to keep the score and pitching changes of out-of-town games. Few boards were large enough to accommodate eight games, the two-league maximum until expansion in 1961.

As an aside, despite the colorful detail provided in up-to-date boards, there was a loss of excitement when changing single-line totals replaced the strung out scoreline of previous times, such as Chicago's Wrigley field retained. In an applauding return to the past, Roy Eisenhardt at Oakland revived the handset, manual scoreboard in 1986.

So many little things changed over the years. First, a batting circle was drawn off either side of home plate, to keep the next hitter in his place, just as the coach's box theoretically does the same to the first-base coach and the so-called hot corner "traffic cop." Most recently, to speed up the game, pitchers have been required to kneel in the on-deck circle when next up, by contrast with the past. That is, then, the leadoff man would move out of the dugout a batter early.

Of course, with introduction of the designated hitter in 1973 by the American League (an innovation copied by all levels from peewee to minor leagues) the pitcher didn't even have to bat. Curiously, the first "tenth man" idea, as it was called then, was proposed in 1929 by John A. Heydler, at the time president of the National League. The NL has been the sole dissenter to bucking tradition. In view of the designated hitter lessening strategy, cutting out controversy of managerial judgment, and taking away a potential edge from a pitcher who is a superior athlete, we tend to lament the good ol' days.

If pitchers basically don't hit now, they trot instead of ambling from the bullpen, thus eliminating a traditional time-consumer of the past. Games aren't so short or fast as at a time when there was a larger strike zone, fewer walks, and less jockeying for position between dawdling batters and pitchers who step off the mound. But games are no longer now than in the 1940s and '50s when managers could make unlimited trips to the mound and also come out to argue the ball-and-strike location with the umpire. The two-trip limit to the mound and no game-interrupting quibble over whether it was or it wasn't a strike were positive improvements.

The changes over time in baseball, basically the same game, are impressive. For example, also, the installation in recent times of the circle to either side of home plate, used by fungo-batting coaches to exercise players with ground balls and fly balls. The U-shaped batting cage, more protective for teammates and others from a viciously slammed foul ball, does earn its cost and keep by preventing more pitches from slicing into the stands. The fungo batting ring, similarly, serves as a compass for the coach so that he won't stray into the line of batting-practice fire. Where teams play on grass instead of artificial turf the ring also lessens areas of worn-out surface.

Actually, ersatz grass probably ranks with night baseball, coast-to-coast big league ball, and the accompanying switch from the railroad to the airplane as the major change in the game, certainly since the pitching distance was changed effective in 1894.

As calculated by Sam Breadon, longtime clubowner of the Cardinals (1920–47), night ball "makes every day Sunday," giving the working stiff a chance to go to the park on week nights. Attendance upheavals would indicate Breadon was as right as men who tinkered with the night ball idea before Independence, Kansas, installed lights in 1929 and Des Moines a year later.

From a maximum of seven night games permitted Cincinnati by Commissioner K. M. Landis in 1935, acting even more cautiously than before permitting convicted felon Edwin (Alabama) Pitts to play professional baseball the same year, night ball burgeoned in all places except Chicago's near North Side. There, the Cubs still were without lights in 1988.

By then, the Cubs, who just had come close to their first pennant since 1945, were a national lightless curiosity. Perhaps a neighborhood nuisance, as suggested, if they went to night ball, as *Chicago Tribune* newspaper ownership and even the commissioner wanted. But, begging Mr. Jurisprudence's pardon, if he doesn't mind the opinion of a college professor and a sportswriter who knows more about tarts than torts, we believe the court talked — and acted — frivolously when upholding a discriminatory law that restrained the Cubs' management from making the moon shine like the sun over Wrigley Field. However, at this writing we are happy to report the prospect of a break in tradition seemed bright allowing a limited number of night games at the Friendly Confines in '88.

More than one baseball pitcher probably would have voted against artificial turf, too, because the ball zips more lively than over grass. Also, since a baserunner can dig in better on the well-knit nylon than on loose turf, a dramatic swing to renewed base stealing has burdened pitchers and the men at the other end of the baseball battery, the catchers. Still, though hitters were helped and would have hiked averages even more if fewer batters struck out than in the past, the offsetting advantage was in ideally improved fielding.

Baseball played indoors was indeed a giant stride and, naturally, a break with tradition from the time-honored raincheck and the weather-bobtailed game. Even at a time only Houston, Minneapolis and Seattle also were playing big league baseball in domed stadiums, we who learned to respect their elders and tradition wished another change could be made. That is, to eliminate the shortened game. If only one pitch has been delivered or if only one still must be made, a big league ball game should be no fewer than 27 outs to the losing side.

Few games might be involved, but they *are* a precious few. To wash out an apparent victory or almost certain defeat, scrub off the books a home run or a likely pitching accomplishment seems as unfair as any schedule-shortening tampering with the pennant race, whether or not the vagaries of weather. And with the box office promotions that became prevalent in most cities, an added attraction any time would be either an unexpected doubleheader or a fractional finish that might be most appealing.

As for the raincheck, it *could* be preserved if any clubowner insisted, keeping the five-inning minimum or any other, and the way the lords of baseball are larding out the salaries, we submit they need all the goodwill they can get to keep underpaid patrons happy. Also, the clubs get all or a percentage of concessions at an incomplete game. Permitting cash customers to keep baseballs batted into the stands proved to be expensive, yes, but a big box office lure.

Tradition has taken a beating, all right, the kind Brooklyn's great young centerfielder, Pete Reiser, took in crashing into outfield walls before Ebbets Field, the Dodgers' home field then, installed the first outfield warning track (1948). The crunched hard-shell surface was designed to help alert outfielders that they were nearing concrete fences. But it was too late for Reiser, regarded by many as potentially an all-time great.

Tradition actually began to crumble early when a gentleman, obviously as weak-backed and yet also stronger-minded than the men who prepared this book, decided that it was much nicer to sit in regular seats than hunched on board planks. William H. Cammeyer of the Brooklyn Mutuals installed special seats in front of and above his team's dressing room, charged two bits more, and called 'em "box seats" 'way back in 1871.

Not until World War II were blacks permitted to sit in St. Louis grandstands, but a black man who grew up just a long fly ball from Sportsman's Park, Elston Howard, introduced the batting "doughnut." For years batters went to the plate swinging two and three bats, lightening the weight of the bat they would use. Howard, passed up by St. Louis because of his color, became a standout catcher and then coach with the New York Yankees. When Ellie designed his on-deck bat weight to help strengthen his wrists and to use when awaiting his turn at bat, the first club to purchase his patent in 1968 was—St. Louis!

Another catcher, the Dodgers' Steve Yeager, introduced another helpful gimmick. Yeager hung the turkey-wattle flapper at the base of his mask to protect his throat from foul balls. Umpires', too. H'mm, why did it take so long?

Why did it take so long, too, for most ball clubs to give cash customers the same service they extended to a radio audience they resented for too long? Newspapermen like the *St. Louis Post-Dispatch*'s John Edward Wray, even though the press competed more actively against radio then than now, chided the Browns and Cardinals more than a half-century ago about giving away free information they withheld from the men and women who paid their way into the park.

As a result, fans often left a park miscalculating totals of the game they had seen. Players, too, could be fooled. In the early '30s at St. Louis, members of the Chicago Cubs thought the Cardinals' first base-reaching play by the leadoff man had been an error. At game's end when the Cubs mobbed the mound, thinking that Guy Bush had pitched a no-hitter, Chicago sportswriters finally caught their attention from the lofty chicken-coop press box. Not a no-hitter, a one-hitter! Angry Chicago players rushed the backstop screen and looked as if they would try to climb it. To the official scorer's relief, they couldn't.

Now, angry players rarely wave towels derisively toward the press box, which became a custom when scoring decisions were either announced or flashed on the scoreboard. League officials take a dim view of the players' visual petulance.

Angry players helped change some of baseball's traditions. Angry players, that is, and progress. For years a mark of achievement for baseball hitters was to bat long enough in spring training and early season so that they would develop calluses at the base of their fingers on each hand, permitting the player to meet the ball without pain. In recent times, players began using light kid gloves, which help some grip the bat better, but most certainly remove the need to grow calluses.

For years, batters stood up there at home plate with nothing between them and a pitched ball except the thin texture of a cap. To our knowledge, no one ever dug up the dirt on when the jock strap was designed, particulary with the cup insert for the athletic supporter, certainly a "must" for most players. Quaintly colorful, hard-nosed Pepper Martin of the Cardinals' old Gas House Gang disdained not only a cup, but also the jock strap itself.

The helmet story, certainly less funny, showed what anger can do. Before a game played at Brooklyn in 1940, shortly after Joe Medwick was traded by the Cardinals, the slugging outfielder and longtime friend of his new manager, Leo Durocher, encountered Cardinal pitcher Bob Bowman in a hotel elevator in New York. One nasty word after another by three parties who could be improperly surly led Bowman to threaten to "stick it in your (Medwick's) ear."

The intimidating suggestion that a pitcher might throw at a batter, used often by Durocher over the years from the safety of the dugout, had a horrible result. Accidentally or not, Bowman skulled Medwick that day with a pitch, hospitalizing him, and depriving the hitter of his ability to hang in at the plate thereafter as devastatingly as before.

Brooklyn's general manager, Larry MacPhail, ever the fighter especially when buoyed by a liquid lunch, lurched onto the Ebbets Field playing surface, seeking to avenge Medwick. A St. Louis–Brooklyn fight was averted—that time!—but the imaginative MacPhail immediately arranged for fiber inner linings for his players' baseball caps. St. Louis quickly followed suit.

But the modern plastic helmet that became standard from peewee ball to the bigs didn't make its appearance until Branch Rickey, who dealt Medwick from St. Louis to Brooklyn, brought in the black player and success to the Dodgers, was ousted by partner Walter F. O'Malley and moved to Pittsburgh. At Forbes Field, where his winning touch was lost in an expensive signing of undersized talent, the brilliant Rickey made his next-to-last positive contribution to baseball. Last was his effort to form a third major league, the Continental, prompting the National League in 1960 to grant a franchise to Houston two years later and to return a team (the Mets) to New York, which had lost the Giants to San Francisco, the Dodgers to L.A.

In what we regard as understandable miff at the Nationals' unilateral action, the American decided immediately to move in 1961. The AL would contest O'Malley at Los Angeles with the Angels, subsequently moved to Anaheim, and also take in Minneapolis-St. Paul. With a low blow to Washington, which might have wished it had been wearing an athletic cup, the Americans moved the Griffith family's Senators to the Twin Cities and put a skeltonized expansion franchise in D.C.

Many laughed at the quicker-than-the-hand fol-de-rol prompted by Rickey's eloquent threat to form the third major league, which the majors hadn't known since the ill-fated Federal League efforts in 1914–15, but soon none laughed any more at the full-sized batting helmets, originally greeted as "miners' caps."

Fact is, by 1971 the official rules were rewritten to require helmets, which by then also had a protective ear flap. Many batters also decided to wear their helmets pinch-running, though the plastic could prove a problem to a second baseman's knees on a pivot play. Defensively, as Dan Krueckeberg noted with a smile, former Cincinnati shortstop Woody Woodward might have wished he'd had on his helmet afield. In a late-season game at Dodger Stadium in '71, a 10-pound sack of flour, dropped or thrown from an airplane, hit the ground 15 feet from Woodward and splattered.

A change in baseball, despite the false courage of the helmet for hitters, was an increased touchiness of batters when pitchers delivered the ball up and in, trying to keep batsmen from leaning too aggressively over the plate. With a protective cup and the helmet combining to limit serious injury, we wonder why so many hitters are so touchy about it that they want to charge the pitchers? Umpires are quick to issue a warning and an automatic $50 fine if they calculate a high-and-tight pitch is thrown with malicious intent. Actually, some umpires believe other umps impose an ejection penalty too hastily.

It is, indeed, a far cry from the heyday of the "intimidation pitch," as Branch Rickey so aptly phrased it. As far back as Cy Young's day at the turn of the century before the foul ball was a strike, Slidin' Billy

Hamilton bragged to Young that he had fouled off 29 consecutive pitches the previous day against Baltimore's Sadie McMahon. Off Cy that day, Hamilton punched three in a row foul, at which point the big Ohio sodbuster strode down off the mound and said, "If you foul off one more, I'll stick the ball in your ear."

If, as a researcher indicated to us, Hamilton had hit safely 27 straight times off the history's winningest pitcher, two guys wonder why it took Cy so long to threaten to low-bridge Slidin' Billy!

Back in the era before Old Tuscawaras, as they called Young as he finished a 22-year career at age 44 in 1911, the year the cork center began to liven the ball, Young had seen s-o-o much. A big leaguer since 1890, he was born in 1867 and was old enough, therefore, to remember when the National League was organized (1876).

He might not have remembered when those nearby Cincinnati Red Stockings came out with the first knee-length bloomers, but he lived long enough to watch the Hollywood Stars play in Bermuda shorts. (Young died at 88 in 1955 so he didn't see the White Sox in shorts.) As a farm kid, Cy could have been practicing the hook slide invented in the 1860s by William S. Gummers at Princeton or trying to prove, as Fred Goldsmith had with stakes stuck in the ground, that Yale's Arthur (Candy) Cummings had been right about his ability to throw a curveball.

Yes, the Young who lived until he was old saw so many of the traditions established that we accept now. For instance, a preprofessional team from Chicago went south in 1870 to prepare for those professional Red Stockings. Same year of the first recorded spring training, baseball had its first holdout. Charley Sweasy, playing second base for the Red Stockings, wanted a hike from $700 to $1000. Charley held his ground and got the grand.

Although the strike zone, the basic ball-and-strike zone, and the pitching distance, as related elsewhere, took decided changes between the time Cy Young started and finished—and he failed to finish only about three of an average 40 starts a year in his career—he saw the great game take form.

As early as the big kid from the country was throwing stones at the squirrels, M. J. Kelly, editing *DeWitt's Baseball Guide,* devised "K" as the symbol for the strikeout (1872). (Really not so complicated if you agree with Mr. "K" that "K" also is the last letter of the word "struck.")

By the time Hartford sold the first season ticket as a charter member of the National League in '76, Brooklyn already was charging an extra two-bits for "box" seats. By 1877, William Henry (Whoop-La) White, pitching for Boston, needed eye glasses. By 1921, when Young was back home tending to his farm, St. Louis second baseman George Toporcer, a Hell's Kitchen boyhood pal of Jimmy Cagney, was the first bespectacled infielder. The Cards' Chick Hafey won the first batting championship wearing glasses (1931), and Clint Courtney of the rival Browns first caught with specs (1952).

Although others were better remembered front office shylocks, of which Boston's Arthur Soden was most prominent, William B. Pettit, president of the Indianapolis team that lasted just one year in the NL (1878), invented the reserve clause. Same year, an Albany, New York, shortstop named Louis Say pulled a dirty trick, too. He became the first to use the hidden ball trick on a Worcester, Massachusetts, player, who doubtless was red-faced.

By the 1880s when Denton True Young was throwing so hard as a kid that they called him "Cy," short for "cyclone," John Lee Richmond of Worcester had pitched the big leagues' first perfect game. Harry Stovey, hard hitting, base stealing Philadelphia star we feel has Hall of Fame credentials, had improvised with his first sliding pads to protect painful leg bruises. Guess the "sissies" were taking over. When left-handed catcher John Clements of the Philadelphia Keystones in the one-year Union Association developed a chest protector in 1885, an obvious godsend for catchers and umpires, the derisive labeled the belly savers "sheepskins."

By the fall and winter of 1888–89, just before Young toed the rubber at Cleveland, Spalding, Anson, and multi-talented John Montgomery Ward, law student, shortstop, pitcher, switch hitter, manager, and league president, took a 20-player team around the world.

They were reciting "Casey at the Bat," subtitled, "A Ballad of the Republic," even before the pitching distance was increased six and a half feet in 1893, Young's third year in the majors. Cy flattened out a bit that year, down from 32–16 to 25–22, but, shucks, he led the league a year later with a 35–10 record. Just a matter of getting the fast one and curveball over.

By the turn of the century when stirrups were added to players' stockings, the game of unknown exact origin was a quarter-century old with professionally organized two-league majors, now that the American muscled in (1901), little Miller Huggins, a shrewd one, brought the delayed steal into the National League with him at Cincinnati. Although the bunted ball for a base hit had become old hat, a new trick came in the nimble reflexes of quick-reacting Wee Willie Keeler. When New York Highlanders' pitcher Jack Chesbro broke for the plate, thinking he had been given the steal sign, Keeler bunted to protect the runner, who scored. Manager Clark Griffith arched his bushy brows and told 'em to keep it up—the squeeze!

The terminology of the game was making its way into the language to become colorful, even if clichés:

"Doubleheader" was taken from railroad lingo, i.e., two locomotive trains. . . . "Battery" was lifted from the military, the pitcher firing to a target, his catcher. . . . "Around the horn" was logical for a long third-to-second-to-first throw before the Panama Canal cut short the stormy ocean trip around the tip of South America. . . . "Hot corner" was used by an appreciative Cincinnati sportswriter after William Warren (Hick) Carpenter sucked up so many line drives at third base (1888). . . . "Texas Leaguer" became national rather than regional after it was applied to seven bloop hits by John H. Pickering at Houston in 1906. . . . "Bullpen" was, as authority Lee Allen researched it, a take-your-choice view of late-arriving fans roped off in outfield-area foul territory for half price or, as most ball parks then featured in fence-adorned advertising, the perennial Bull Durham tobacco sign.

Other expressions had generic background. Because John McGraw remembered Sioux City, Iowa, where a weary old horse named Charley took so long to drag the infield, a gimpy player had a "Charley horse." Or do you like the earlier version researched by Lee Allen? The one about Chicago infielder Joe Quest using the term to tease any limping teammate, a recognition of his father's old nag, Charley.

The "lucky seventh" was a term off the typewriter of the *Cincinnati Enquirer*'s O.P. Caylor, a tribute to shortstop Henry Kessler, who so often hit safely in the inning. . . . "At bat, on deck, in the hold," when used properly, a nautical expression to denote 1-2-3 batting rotation any inning since 1872 at Belfast, Maine.

Team nicknames were taking shape or changing. For example, the Detroits became the "Tigers" in the metropolitan Michigan press after manager George Stallings orange-striped the team's dark stockings. The New York Americans originally were the "Highlanders," but the Irish raised a fuss about the Scottish nickname, so management wisely decided on a U.S.A. label, the "Yankees."

Early, teams were influenced by the success of Cincinnati's original Red Stockings. Chicago originally was the White Stockings, used with Cap Anson's National Leaguers. Later, when Chicago had a young, inexperienced club, a writer referred to them repeatedly as the "Cubs." Boston, ultimately, zeroed in closely with a Red Sox version of the Red Stockings. When Chicago joined the American League, a charter member as the White Stockings had been in the NL, Charley Comiskey wisely decided to pick up a traditional nickname.

When the same Comiskey was player-manager at St. Louis's American Association champions in 1885–88, the "Browns" was a nickname that hung over even after the National replaced the Association as the town's major league team. When the AL came to town its second season, 1902, the old nickname was revived.

Meanwhile, a result of the Robison brothers, Frank and Stanley, having changed from brown trim to red when they switched franchises with their Cleveland club in 1899, reference was made to the color as "a lovely shade of cardinal." So the club was nicknamed the "Cardinals" by a rabbit-eared reporter, Willie McHale. The hue became the bird of the same name some years later when Branch Rickey went to a luncheon at which the dear lady doing head-table decorations had turned the color into a bird—a red bird perched on a bat.

A proud owner's adulation of his New York Nationals turned his "giants" into a capital-letter salute just about the time John McGraw made them as formidable as the name sounded. The Brooklyn rivals, early the "Superbas" because of a vaudeville show run by a man with the same surname as manager Ned Hanlon, later were called the "Robins," a tribute to Wilbert Robinson, manager from 1918-31. Always, though, they had been the "Trolley Dodgers," a reference to zigzagging between the many streetcar lines that brought the Flatbush faithful to their games. Ultimately, the first part was dropped. So the "Dodgers" prevailed, then and in Los Angeles.

McGraw's other early day rival, Connie Mack at Philadelphia, inherited "Athletics," a longtime local nickname. At one juncture, too, with a trumpeting symbol on the shirt front, Mr. Mack's men were labeled with a secondary synonym—"White Elephants." The neighboring Phillies, lengthened to "phutile Phillies" at their worst and "Phils" at the shortest, were briefly called the "Bluejays."

Similarly, as a Depression-era gimmick, the Boston Braves became the "Bees," but the nickname was shortlived. The "Braves" stuck as the ball club migrated to Milwaukee and then trekked to Atlanta. Pittsburgh, impugned after filching a Philly player, began to like a nasty nickname—"Pirates."

For obvious reasons because of championship status in the Naughty Nineties and the great success of their International League ball club through the early 1920s, Baltimore resurrected a proud name when the Browns were bought from St. Louis in 1954. Baltimore once again became the "Orioles." To be "an old Oriole" is still a Maryland equivalent of Britain's stiff upper lip.

For, lo, those many years when Washington had a big league ball club—and it would be nice to see the capital in the majors again—the ball club was known nationally as the "Senators," but in D.C. they were the "Nationals" or, often, the "Nats," presumably not to confuse newspaper readers with political titles. To use Nationals for an American League team was confusing, all right, but United States senators might have found their positions associated so often with defeat a bigger problem.

Cleveland was the "Naps" when Napoleon (Larry) Lajoie mentioned them, but, long since, they've been the "Indians," a reference to Lake Erie tribal inheritance. The Athletics followed the bouncing ball to Kansas City and then to Oakland, used generously as the "A's." Kansas City returned royally to the majors as the "Royals." "Texas Rangers" was a 7–come–11 natural for the team at Arlington. So, too, was the "Padres," a long-standing nickname in the mission country of southern California and San Diego. "Angels" at Anaheim was a carry-over also from similar association in the Pacific Coast League and the club's early AL years in L.A.

For patently painful reasons, second-chance Seattle didn't want to go back as the "Pilots." Ergo, the "Mariners." And when the Colt .45 company wanted the new Houston ball club to subdue its commercialization, management moved from the poetic past to the romantic present as the "Astros."

When the National League moved back into New York, the Big Apple sentimentally drafted the nickname of its first big league ball club—the Metropolitans—shortened to the "Mets," the comparison with the famed opera company notwithstanding. Cleverly, too, amalgamating the color pennants of the triple-tiered past, ownership combined the blue pinstripe of the Yankees with the blue of the Dodgers and the orange of the Giants.

Montreal, adopting a tri-color cap that at first blush looked like a painter's cap or—all right, then, a jockey's—and took a nickname of the 1967 World's Fair, i.e., the "Expos." Maybe conflict with "Royals" at Kansas City kept Montreal from using its longtime International League title. Similarly, Toronto must have wanted to avoid further confusion with the Ontario metropolis's hockey club by dropping Maple Leafs. Why "Blue Jays"? (What's French for "we don't know"?)

Cy Young didn't live long enough to see Canada represented in the major leagues, but he saw plenty. He played long enough to see and play in the first steel-and-concrete stadiums—Philadelphia's and the Chicago White Sox's if not Pittsburgh's—and if the schedule had permitted, Cy could have been there the first time a president threw out the first ball. William Howard Taft, the old Yale player, did it in 1910.

Actually, as suggested, President Andrew Johnson pulled into the Washington park to catch the late innings of a game as far back as 1867, the year Cy was born. But William Henry Harrison of Young's home state, Ohio, was the first president to attend a game formally in 1893. Once Clark Griffith took a gold pass to Taft in 1910 and asked the president to do him and baseball the honor, the Chief Executive seldom has missed: Throwing out the season's first ball. After all, baseball is like hot dogs, apple pie, and Chevrolet.

One of the more amazing openers, other than Walter Johnson's habit of throwing aspirin tablets past the hitters for Washington, came in 1936, a year when Louis Norman (Buck) Newsom pitched the opener for the Senators . . . er, Nats. Franklin D. Roosevelt sat in the presidential box that day. Buck Newsom was called "Bobo" more often because to the big, swaggering righthander, everyone else was "Bobo."

Early in the game in 1936, as third baseman Ossie Bluege swooped in to field a bunt and to fire to first, Bobo forgot to duck. Bluege's powerful throw to the head staggered Newsom, who, though obviously hurt, bade the game continue. Afterward, pitching all of the game and winning, Newsom was told he had suffered a slight fracture. Bobo shrugged his shoulders and drawled: "Ah knew it, but y'all didn't expect Bobo to quit with Bobo Roosevelt in the stands, did ya?"

Informality, of course, which Babe Ruth had demonstrated even better when asked at one opener to say a word to Calvin Coolidge, a starchy man who would have preferred a fisherman's stream to a seat in the ball park any time. The Babe whipped out a red bandana, wiped his forehead and said to frozen-faced Silent Cal, "Hot as heck, ain't it, Prez?"

The dugouts behind which presidents and other high-rent district customers sat were established in the new 1909–10 parks as Young headed for retirement. Baseball made its first trip to Japan in 1913. McGraw's Giants and Comiskey's White Sox played in Tokyo, Yokohama, Kobe, and Nagasaki. The game captivated the country.

The "Star-Spangled Banner," not officially the National Anthem until 1931, was played opening day in 1916 at President Wilson's request. Establishment of the first public-address system at Yankee Stadium in 1929 provided the opportunity to play it without a live band. The anthem became a daily pre-game ritual with the outbreak of World War II (1942).

With the P.A. faster, more efficient, and clearer than the old waddling megaphone man, making it easier to determine the right answer to Abbott and Costello's comic sketch, "Who's on first?," uniform numbers added the best P.R. touch. The Yankees were first in 1929, but were they? Shucks, Cincinnati experimented with player numbers as far back as 1883.

Amazingly, the cradle of professional ball, close by Cy Young's diggings as a baby after the Civil War and as one who lived beyond Korea, Cincinnati has had an indelible place in baseball history! First to play professionally (1869), first to sell beer (1880), first (we guess) ladies' day (1889) (challenged by Buffalo in 1882), first with numbers (1883), first with night-game play (1935), first to fly as a team (1934), and first (and only) to give up a time-honored nickname briefly. When the Red Stockings were shortened to Reds and the Communist scare found a Joe McCarthy in Washington ruining a good (identical) baseball man's name, Cincinnati briefly was persuaded by pressure in the 1950s to change to Redlegs.

But, happily, a rose by any other name is Pete. A Red is not always a Red. Cy Young lived long enough to see the black man (Jackie Robinson) come back into the big leagues to play and to umpire (Emmett Ashford). He missed the first black coach (Buck O'Neill) and the first black manager (Frank Robinson). It's just too bad he didn't live to see Pete Rose or the new uniforms, including the latest slip-over jerseys they wore before the games in 1986 rather than soil uniform shirts in practice.

The guy who began when they played barehanded might not have believed the changes, most certainly the $2,000,000 salaries when he was forced to jump from the National to the American League because there was a $2400-a-player limit as the century began. Certainly, Cy, who saw just about everything, wouldn't believe the diabolical drag of drugs in the 1980s rather than the efficacy of the drag bunt.

But, like Stan Musial, who said so in his Hall of Fame induction, baseball *was* a great game, *is* a great game, and *will* be a great game. Even if, as we suggest, it obviously is from a different angle, baseball's constant charm is a hot hitter, a hot pitcher, a hot race, and — always — the Hot Stove League.

Always, there will be controversial comparisons, the kind Denton True (Cy) Young made in his own particular sunset when he tabbed Wee Willie Keeler over Ty Cobb as the toughest he faced.

"Tougher for me to get out," said Cy Young, who might have been Christy Mathewson talking about nemesis Joe Tinker or a Warren Spahn about Stan Musial or a Bob Feller about Joe DiMaggio or a Bob Gibson about Billy Williams or just about anybody trying to fool the other Williams, Teddy Ballgame. Or a little seldom-remembered lefthander named Hubert (Shucks) Pruitt putting himself through medical school because he had Babe Ruth's number.

Said the Young of old about Wee Willie, the hit-'em-where-they-ain't wonder, "You couldn't fool him with a curve. So I always tried to keep the ball low to Keeler and to work with him on my 'change of pace'—fast, faster and fastest!"

Index

About the Authors

Bob Broeg was born and raised in south St. Louis and is a 1941 graduate of the University of Missouri School of Journalism. His wit and wisdom have graced the sports pages of the *St. Louis Post-Dispatch* since 1945, as well as major sports publications such as *The Sporting News. Baseball from a Different Angle* is his thirteenth book.

Broeg covered the St. Louis Cardinals—his passion, along with the University of Missouri Tigers—from 1945-1958. He served as the sports editor of the *Post-Dispatch* from 1958 until 1985, when he became that newspaper's contributing sports editor.

The Rockne Club of America presented Broeg with its Sportswriter of the Year Award in 1964 and in 1971 he was the recipient of the Journalism Medal from the University of Missouri, the first sportswriter to be so honored.

One of the true giants of the sportswriting profession, Broeg's impressive credentials were recognized in 1980, when he received the Baseball Writers Association's most prestigious award at the Baseball Hall of Fame in Cooperstown, New York. He serves on the Board of Directors of the Baseball Hall of Fame and is also a member of the Hall of Fame's Veterans' Committee.

Bob and his wife Lynette reside in St. Louis.

A native of St. Louis, William J. Miller, Jr. received his Ph.D. from the University of California at Berkeley, and since 1960 has been a member of the faculty of Saint Louis University. He is currently an associate professor of history there, with his areas of specialization being European Diplomatic History and the Far East. He was the editor of the "World of Asia" book series in 1977.

Some of Miller's relatives played professional baseball, most notably his father's grand uncle, Jake Beckley, who is a member of the Baseball Hall of Fame. Miller's scholarly pursuits include baseball research and he has brought that interest and talent to *Baseball from a Different Angle*.

Bill and his wife Irene reside in St. Louis.